Applied Demography Series

Volume 4

Series Editor
David A. Swanson

The field of applied demography is largely driven by the quest for the knowledge required by clients, both in public and private sectors, to make good decisions within time and costs constraints. The book series, Applied Demography, provides a forum for illustrating and discussing the use of demographic methods, concepts, and perspectives in a wide range of settings – business, government, education, law, and public policy–as well as the influence of these settings on demographic methods, concepts, and perspectives. The books within the series can be used as resources for practitioners and as materials serving as case studies for pedagogical uses.

More information about this series at http://www.springer.com/series/8838

M. Nazrul Hoque • Lloyd B. Potter
Editors

Emerging Techniques in Applied Demography

Springer

Editors
M. Nazrul Hoque
Hobby Center for Public Policy
University of Houston
Houston
Texas
USA

Lloyd B. Potter
Department of Demography
Institute for Demographic
and Socioeconomic Research
University of Texas at San Antonio
San Antonio
Texas
USA

ISSN 2352-376X ISSN 2352-3778 (electronic)
ISBN 978-94-017-8989-9 ISBN 978-94-017-8990-5 (eBook)
DOI 10.1007/978-94-017-8990-5
Springer Dordrecht Heidelberg New York London

Library of Congress Control Number: 2014941688

Printed on acid-free paper

Springer is part of Springer Science+Business Media (www.springer.com)

Foreword

Applied demography has comfortably settled into a relatively mature and secure niche at the disciplinary intersection of demography, planning, geography, public health, marketing, and several other fields where the concepts, tools, and data of demography find practical application. The idea is hardly new, of course. The application of demographic thinking to contemporary concerns can be traced from the Black Death and the Bills of Mortality, on the other side of the Atlantic, to unemployment in the Depression, the Great Migration, urban consolidation/suburbanization, an outpouring of migration and population redistribution studies, and the early methodological developments in small-area population research in America.

The origin of applied demography in the United States is difficult to mark with precision. Much has been written on the topic, including key articles and chapters by authors appearing in this volume. What clearly is part of the established record, however, is that by the 1950s the foundations of applied demography were being erected at the U.S. Census Bureau, in a variety of state agencies, and at several universities. A Census Bureau survey in 1955 identified 39 state agencies (mostly in departments of health – agencies that needed denominators for the construction of vital rates) involved in the production of population estimates. In addition, nine universities were found to be doing research related to population estimates (with this number heavily dominated by bureaus of business research). A decade later, 45 states had official agencies producing population estimates or projections, with the largest growth between 1955 and 1965 represented by the increasing delegation of such activities to state planning and development agencies. These decentralized and fragmented activities sometimes led to confusion on the part of data users, and in 1967 the Census Bureau, working with state governments, established the Federal-State Cooperative Program for Local Population Estimates (FSCPE). While originally established as a partnership program to assist the Census Bureau in developing annual population estimates for counties, another chief objective of the FSCPE was to bring a more coordinated approach to the making of population estimates by having a single agency in each state (designated by the respective governors) working cooperatively with the Bureau for the production of estimates.

By the early 1970s a major acceleration in the growth of applied demography was underway, and venues were needed to bring professional applied demographers together. The meetings of the Southern Regional Demographic Group (now the Southern Demographic Association, SDA) quickly became the most popular such venue. By the mid-1970s, many members of the Population Association of America (PAA) were beginning proudly to self-identify as applied demographers. Initially these were demographers working in state and local settings, but soon a small core of business demographers had become allied with the group. The PAA Board granted organizational legitimacy to the group by creating in 1978 a Committee on State and Local Demography (eventually the Committee on Applied Demography), and annual meetings of the PAA began formally to serve as an outlet for reporting a variety of problem-oriented demographic research.

Then, in 1986, David Swanson initiated a meeting of applied demographers at Bowling Green State University, thus beginning a wonderful tradition and legacy of biennial gatherings for demographic practitioners. This proceedings volume, edited by Nazrul Hoque and Lloyd Potter, pulls together in one place several of the papers presented at the 2012 Applied Demography Conference held in San Antonio. While there have been some interruptions in the biennial schedule, these important gatherings continue, with the Institute for Demographic and Socioeconomic Research at The University of Texas at San Antonio having served as organizer and host since 2007. As new developments in data acquisition and reporting evolve, as innovative demographic methodologies are introduced, as the computing and software worlds continue to open new opportunities, and as those who need demographic assistance present fresh analytic challenges, applied demographers will continue to need conferences and venues at which to gather and share their work. Our community is indebted to those who have kept this tradition alive and growing.

November 2013 Paul Voss

Acknowledgements

This book is based on the papers presented at the 3rd Applied Demography Conference that was held in San Antonio, Texas, January 8 through 10, 2012. Many people have contributed to the development of this book and we are indebted to all of them. We would like to thank all the staff members of the Institute for Demographic and Socioeconomic Research for organizing the Conference and the Institute for sponsoring the Conference and also for providing financial support for the book.

We thank the authors of the individual chapters for submitting their work for publication in *Emerging Techniques in Applied Demography*. All the chapters are peer reviewed, and we would also like thank the reviewers for their timely reviews and comments for the authors in regard to the chapters in this volume. Our appreciation is also extended to the authors for their timely response to our requests for revisions.

We sincerely appreciate the support of McKibben Demographics for sponsoring the welcome reception for the conference. We also appreciate the contributions of Patricia Bramwell, Lisa Espinoza, Beverly Pecotte, Jeffrey Jordan, Alfredo Zavala, and Eric Quiroz, all with the Institute for Demographic and Socioeconomic Research, who helped with the conference and also with the book. We very much appreciate the superior editorial work of Karen White. Without her help this book would not have been completed.

We would like to thank Evelien Bakker, the senior editor of the Springer publications, and Bernadette Deelen-Mans, the editor of the Springer publications, and her staff, as well as the staff at the production office.

We thank Paul Voss for contributing the foreword for the book. Acknowledged as one of the pioneer applied demographers, he is one of the most respected experts in the field of population estimates and projections in the United States. We are thankful for his insightful words.

Finally, Nazrul Hoque would like to thank his wife, Noor Jahan, for her unending support and encouragement as he worked on this volume. It is our sincere hope that this volume would be helpful for future research in the field of applied demography.

Contents

Contributors

Adélamar Alcántara Geospatial and Population Studies, University of New Mexico, Albuquerque, NM, USA

Sutee Anantsuksomsri Program on Applied Demographics, Cornell University, Ithaca, NY, USA

Julien Bérard-Chagnon Statistics Canada, Ottawa, Ontario, Canada

Jack Baker Geospatial and Population Studies, University of New Mexico, Albuquerque, NM, USA

Kwame Boadu Office of Statistics and Information, Government of Alberta, Edmonton, AB, Canada

Cristina Bradatan Texas Tech University, Lubbock, TX, USA

Qian Cai Demographics & Workforce Group, Weldon Cooper Center for Public Service, University of Virginia, Charlottesville, VA, USA

Yu-Ting Chang Department of Sociology, Texas A&M University, College Station, TX, USA

Jeralynn S. Cossman Department of Sociology, Mississippi State University, Mississippi State, MS, USA

Ronald E. Cossman Social Science Research Center, Mississippi State University, Mississippi State, MS, USA

Nathan Crouse Geospatial and Population Studies, University of New Mexico, Albuquerque, NM, USA

Kristen Eaton Temple University, Philadelphia, PA, USA

Joe Francis Program on Applied Demographics, Cornell University, Ithaca, NY, USA

Jeanne Gobalet Lapkoff & Gobalet Demographic Research, Inc., Saratoga, CA, USA

Howard Hogan U.S. Census Bureau, Washington, D.C., USA

M. Nazrul Hoque Hobby Center for Public Policy, University of Houston, Houston, TX, USA

Md. Rafiqul Islam Department of Population Science and Human Resource Development, University of Rajshahi, Rajshahi, Bangladesh

Towfiqua Mahfuza Islam Department of Health Care Management and Planning, Tokyo Medical and Dental University, Tokyo, Japan

Kazuo Kawahara Department of Health Care Management and Planning, Tokyo Medical and Dental University, Tokyo, Japan

Elena Kotyrlo Ageing and Living Conditions Center, Demographic Data Base, Umeå University, Umeå, Sweden

Laszlo J. Kulcsar Kansas State University, Manhattan, KS, USA

Shelley Lapkoff Lapkoff & Gobalet Demographic Research, Inc., Berkeley, CA, USA

Stephen R. Leeder Menzies Centre for Health Policy, Sydney School of Public Health, The University of Sydney, Sydney, Australia

Richard Lycan Portland State University, Portland, Oregon, USA

Philip B. Mason Department of Sociology, University of South Carolina, Aiken, SC, USA

Stephanie L. McFall Institute for Social and Economic Research, University of Essex, Colchester, UK

Mary H. Mulry U.S. Census Bureau, Washington, D.C., USA

Nomalanga Nefertari Geospatial and Population Studies, University of New Mexico, Albuquerque, NM, USA

William P. O' Hare The Annie E. Casey Foundation, Baltimore, MD, USA

Dudley L. Poston Department of Sociology, Texas A&M University, College Station, TX, USA

Lloyd B. Potter Department of Demography and Institute for Demographic and Socioeconomic Research, The University of Texas at San Antonio, San Antonio, TX, USA

Stefan Rayer Bureau of Economic and Business Research, University of Florida, Gainesville, FL, USA

Xiaomin Ruan Geospatial and Population Studies, University of New Mexico, Albuquerque, NM, USA

Daren Ruiz Bureau of Business and Economic Research, University of New Mexico, Albuquerque, NM, USA

Charles Rynerson Portland State University, Portland, Oregon, USA

Donna Shai Villanova University, Villanova, PA, USA

David W. Smith Colchester, UK

Stanley K. Smith Bureau of Economic and Business Research, University of Florida, Gainesville, FL, USA

Makiko Sugawa Department of Health Care Management and Planning, Tokyo Medical and Dental University, Tokyo, Japan

David A. Swanson Department of Sociology and Center for Sustainable Suburban Development, University of California Riverside, Riverside, CA, USA

Md. Ismail Tareque Department of Population Science and Human Resource Development, University of Rajshahi, Rajshahi, Bangladesh

Jeff Tayman Department of Economics, University of San Diego, San Diego, CA, USA

Rebecca Tippett Demographics & Workforce Group, Weldon Cooper Center for Public Service, University of Virginia, Charlottesville, VA, USA

Nij Tontisirin Program on Applied Demographics, Cornell University, Ithaca, NY, USA

Srini Vasan Department of Mathematics/Statistics, University of New Mexico, Albuquerque, NM, USA

Jan Vink Program on Applied Demographics, Cornell University, Ithaca, NY, USA

Tom Wilson Queensland Centre for Population Research, School of Geography, Planning and Environmental Management, The University of Queensland, Brisbane, QLD, Australia

Alison Yacyshyn Alberta School of Business, University of Alberta, Edmonton, AB, Canada

Farhat Yusuf Menzies Centre for Health Policy, Sydney School of Public Health, The University of Sydney, Sydney, Australia

Department of Marketing and Management, Macquarie University, Sydney, Australia

Viktor Zhong Program on Applied Demographics, Cornell University, Ithaca, NY, USA

Chapter 1
Introduction

M. Nazrul Hoque and Lloyd B. Potter

Introduction

Applied Demography in the twenty-first century is evolving rapidly and becoming increasingly diverse as its practitioners become involved in emerging issues (Murdock and Swanson 2008). By all the standard measures of scientific progress, the field of applied demography is thriving. In recent years new undergraduate and graduate programs are also opening (for example, at The University of Texas at San Antonio). Scholars from various disciplines including, demography, sociology, economics, political science, geography, and public health are bringing their research and analytical framework to examine a wide variety of public and private issues under the umbrella of Applied Demography.

In January 2012, the 3rd Applied Demography Conference was held at The University of Texas at San Antonio. There were more than 150 participants from various disciplines. More than 100 papers were presented at the Conference by applied researchers from the United States, Canada, Australia, Japan, Europe, and Africa. These papers covered a wide variety of issues important to public and private sectors and provided an overview of many of the concepts, methodologies, and applications of applied demography in present day society.

Upon the conclusion of the 2012 conference, the event organizers invited all participants to submit their manuscript for possible publication. The submissions resulting from the invitation were then sent out for peer review, and reviewer's comments were provided to the authors to revise their manuscript. Revised manuscripts

M. N. Hoque (✉)
Hobby Center for Public Policy, University of Houston, Houston, TX, USA
e-mail: mnhoque@uh.edu

L. B. Potter
Department of Demography and Institute for Demographic and Socioeconomic Research,
The University of Texas at San Antonio, San Antonio, TX 78207, USA
e-mail: Lloyd.Potter@utsa.edu

M. N. Hoque, L. B. Potter (eds.), *Emerging Techniques in Applied Demography*,
Applied Demography Series 4, DOI 10.1007/978-94-017-8990-5_1,

were received and reviewed by the editors, and those found acceptable are included in *Emerging Techniques in Applied Demography*.

This volume is intended for a wide range of potential users, including students in the field of demography, applied demography, sociology, economics, geography, and political science as well as health practitioners and policy makers. It should be of particular interest to professionals in business and government who are involved in activities related to census data, aging, and other health related activities addressed by the authors in their works. In addition, the book should be appropriate as an accompanying text for courses in statistics, marketing, business management, and demography.

Emerging Techniques in Applied Demography will be an important addition to the existing literature of research articles and important books (such as *Applied Demography* by Siegel (2002), *State and Local Population Projections* by Smith et al. (2001), and *Applied Demography: An Introduction to Basic Concepts, Methods, and Data* by Murdock and Ellis, (1991)). It will also continue on the Applied Demography Series started in 2007. Previous editions generated from the Applied Demography Conference include a two edited volume set of the Applied Demography Series. Applied Demography in the 21st Century edited by Murdock and Swanson and Opportunities and Challenges for Applied Demography in the 21st Century edited by Hoque and Swanson, and to some extent Applied Demography and Public Health edited by Nazrul Hoque, Mary McGehee, and Benjamin Bradshaw (2013). The Applied Demography series is published by Springer.

Overview of the Sections and Chapters

This volume is organized into five sections that group chapters related by topics and/or research methods. Section I provides evaluations of population projections, assesses 2010 Census Counts, and proposes new techniques for projecting populations (Chaps. 2–5). Chapters in Section II evaluate population estimates produced by new and current techniques in comparison to 2010 Census Counts (Chaps. 6–10). Section III includes studies related to the labor market, household expenditures, poverty, and displacement of mobile home populations; specific papers also examine topics related to education, medical care, health, and immigration (Chaps. 11–15). Chapters in Section IV focus on GIS, redistricting issues, and cohort analysis (Chaps. 16–18). Finally, Section V (Chaps. 19–23) examines health disparities, such as access to health care in the United States and factors influencing health status and elderly abuse in Bangladesh.

Section I

There are four chapters in Section I that deal with population projections and/or the 2010 Census Counts. In Chap. 2, Stan Smith and Stefan Rayer, examine the accuracy of previously produced population projections. They evaluate the precision and bias of several sets of population projections for Florida and its counties produced by the Bureau of Economic and Business Research (BEBR) at the University of Florida between 1980 and 2005. This study analyzes the effects of the size of population, change in population, and length of projection horizon on forecast errors and investigates two different approaches to measuring the uncertainty inherent in population projections, one based on a range of projections and the other based on empirical prediction intervals. The results presented in this chapter will provide data users valuable insight regarding the forecast accuracy of state and local population projections and improve their ability to use projections for decision-making purposes.

According to Tom Wilson, the preparation of local area population and household projections by age frequently involves many challenges, such as non-trivial input data costs, complex data adjustment and smoothing, boundary changes, complicated or inappropriate software, difficulties in choosing suitable projection assumptions, and tight timeframes. In Chap. 3, he introduces a software named POPART (Population Projections for an Area, Region or Town) to help overcome some of these challenges. POPART is an Excel-based bi-regional cohort-component population projection model coupled with a household model. It contains a number of features that assist in the preparation of projections, including a short training period, limited input data requirements, simplified assumption-setting via summary indicators (total fertility rate, life expectancy at birth, and net migration totals), and an emphasis on graphics to aid the presentation and validation of outputs. He uses this software to produce population and household projections for the local government area of Noosa in Queensland.

Despite the fact that there is a persistent and significant improvement in overall census counts, there remains net undercount of children in the U.S. Decennial Censuses and this problem has received little attention in the demographic literature. In Chap. 4, William O'Hare provides detailed documentation of the net undercount of children in the 2010 Decennial Census based on demographic analysis. According to Dr. O'Hare, in the 2010 census, there was a net overcount for adults (population age 18+) of 0.7 % or 1.7 million people compared to a net undercount for children (population age 0–17) of 1.7 % or about 1.3 million children. With a net undercount rate of 4.6 %, children (age 0–4) have the highest net undercount rate of any age group. Moreover, Black and Hispanic children (age 0–4) have higher than average net undercount rates, and these two groups account for about two-thirds of the net undercount of nearly 1 million children under age 5. Persons aged 14–17 experienced a net overcount in the 2010 Census. The net overcount of people aged 14–17 is completely accounted for by the high net overcount of Blacks and Hispanics in this age group.

Rafiqul Islam and Nazrul Hoque used an exponential growth rate method to project the population by age and sex from 2002 to 2031 (Chap. 5). The population of Bangladesh is projected to increase from 123.9 million in 2001 to 193.7 million in 2031, an increase of 56.39 % during the projection period. These projected populations might be useful in further research as well as in planning associated with socioeconomic, demographic, and health related issues in Bangladesh.

Section II

In non-census years, population estimates are the most important source of demographic data regarding the size, distribution, and composition of population by place of residence. Population estimates are widely used by federal, state, and local governments and by the business community for revenue allocating and sharing and for planning purposes. Several methods have been developed to estimate population. However, population estimates are difficult to complete with accuracy for small areas due to various reasons. Therefore, it is essential to evaluate population estimates produced by different methods against actual census counts in census years (Hoque 2012). Four chapters (Chap. 6–9) in this section evaluate the current methods used by demographers to produce population estimates and examine how these methods can be improved, while one chapter (Chap. 10) proposes a new technique to estimate households and population.

The administrative method is one of the methods used by Census Bureau to produce county level estimates for the entire country. In Chap. 6, Jack Baker, Adelamar Alcantara, Xiaomin Ruan, Daren Ruiz, and Nathan Crouse used the administrative method to produce sub-county population estimates for New Mexico and compared the results to 2010 Census Counts. In Chap. 7, Qian Cai and Rebecca Tippett evaluate population estimates produced by the housing unit method at the sub-county level for the State of Virginia and compare results with the 2010 Census Counts to provide a thorough and careful analysis of housing unit methods for population estimates.

The most common regression-based approach to estimate population of a given area is the ratio-correlation method. In Chap. 8, David Swanson and Jeff Tayman provide a comprehensive evaluation of this method of population estimation, discuss some of its weaknesses, and explore how they can be leveraged into producing more accurate population estimates. In Chap. 9, Howard Hogan and Mary Mulry provide a systematic overview of all the evaluation techniques and present a method to facilitate comparisons across measures when assessing a set of population estimates or studying a proposed estimation methodology. In Chap. 10, Julien Bérard-Chagnon proposes new techniques to estimate families and households using Canadian tax return data. The new method is based on the T1 Family File (T1FF), a file built from various tax sources. According to the author, the T1FF file is available annually and provides very good coverage, making it possible to measure demographic dynamics between censuses instead of relying on the extrapolation of trends. Comparisons with their 2006 Census figures, adjusted for net undercount, indicate that estimates using the new method are more accurate than the estimates from previously used component methods.

Section III

In Chap. 11, Cristina Bradatan and Laszlo Kulcsar examine the effects of education level on the labor force participation and income of European immigrants in the United States. Using secondary data from the Current Population Survey (CPS) and New Immigrants Survey, Drs. Bradatan and Kulcsar compare the labor market outcomes of the native White American and immigrant European population before the 2008 economic crisis, focusing on the differences that education makes in the lives of these immigrants. Fertility is an important determinant of long-term population growth and labor market conditions. In Chap. 12, Elena Kotyrlo examines the effects of time and space dynamics on fertility in Sweden. The influence of time dynamics in postponing or accelerating childbearing is assessed by considering two different effects of earnings. First, the effect within one generation is considered by comparing a family's current earnings with their earnings in the recent past and expected earnings in the future. The second effect, referred to previously as the Easterlin hypothesis, is examined through the generations by comparing a household's earnings for a younger generation with earnings of the parental generation. The hypotheses are tested for the period 1981–2008 using municipality level data for 276 municipalities in Sweden. Although, Australia has a national health scheme (Medicare), many patients still incur out-of-pocket (OOP) expenditures on payments/co-payments towards health practitioners' fees, medicines, hospital charges, and the (optional) private health insurance. In Chap. 13, Farhat Yusuf and Stephen Leeder examine the annual OOP expenditure on healthcare as reported by Australian households. Data from the Household Expenditure Survey, based on a probability sample of 9,774 households, were used for this study. The survey was conducted by the Australian Bureau of Statistics during the 1-year period 2009–2010. In Chap. 14, Donna Shai and Kriston Eaton examine the impact of rapid urbanization on the residents of mobile home parks. According to Drs. Shai and Eaton, when a mobile home park is displaced, a community may disappear. The implications and some possible solutions are also discussed. Their study is based on the census and ACS data from Anchorage, Alaska, but it can be applied to some other cities in the United States or anywhere in the world. In Chap. 15, Srini Vasan, Adélamar Alcántara, Nomalanga Nefertari, Xiaomin Ruan, and Jack Baker explore the relationship between spatially concentrated poverty and educational attainment in New Mexico. Using data from the Albuquerque Public Schools district and spatial regression techniques, they examine the impact of neighborhood clustering effects on school performance.

Section IV

There are four chapters in this section. First, two chapters explain the applications of GIS data in demographic analyses. As you may know, the American Community Survey (ACS) is the replacement of the census "Long Form" and the only source of detailed socioeconomic and demographic data for small areas, such as place and tract levels. In Chap. 16, Joe Francis, Nij Tontisirin, Sutee Anantsuksomsri, Jan Vink, and Viktor Zhong examine the accuracy of ACS using a GIS mapping system. Chapter 17 provides an example of how GIS and other techniques can be used by applied demographers to explain a turnaround in public school enrollment. In the Portland Public Schools district, enrollment began to decline in the mid 1990s, but in the mid 2000s, some of the schools began to show increases in enrollment. Richard Lycan and Charles Rynerson used birth and tax-lot data to explain an enrollment turnaround. According to their findings it is the older moms, not migration, that play an important role in increasing enrollment. Applied demographers are often summoned to testify before public officials about the quality of data. In Chap. 18, Jeanne Gobalet and Shelley Lakoff describe the importance of applied demographic techniques in analyzing data to identify the best method to elect board or council members at the district level.

Individuals' perceptions of belonging to a group is an important area for applied demographic analysis. In Chap. 19, Alison Yacyshyn and Kwame Boadu analyze collected data for different age cohorts in Alberta, Canada. The majority of the respondents perceive that it is the baby boomers and Generation Y cohorts who receive the most media attention in contemporary society. The majority of individuals also agree that it is appropriate for governments to shape policy based on the size of age cohorts in the population. Their analysis suggests that addressing demographic characteristics and cohort-based analysis is essential in both marketing and governmental policy strategies.

Section V

Access to health care is a topic of policy and human interest in the United States. Stephanie McFall and David Smith analyze the 2007 Texas Behavioural Risk Factor Surveillance System to examine three measures of access: health insurance, usual source of care, and being unable to obtain care because of cost (Chap. 20). The authors compare the 32 Border counties to the remaining of 222 counties in Texas. According to the authors, the Border Region has a higher proportion of Hispanics, fewer resources to obtain health care, less insurance and income, and poorer self-rated health than the rest of Texas. Border residents were less likely to have health insurance or a regular source of care. In Chap. 21, Ismail Tareque, Nazrul Hoque, Towfiqa Islam, Kazuo Kawahara, and Makiko Sugawa examine the differentials in rural-urban living arrangements, health status, and elderly abuse in the Rajshahi district of Bangladesh. Their findings suggest that the urban elderly are more educated, have more income, live in a household with better sanitation facilities, and lead better life styles compared with rural elderly. Rural elderly reported more neglect and abuse compared with urban elderly. This research could greatly assist policy makers and planners to develop suitable programs addressing the need and welfare of the elderly population, not only in Rajshahi district but also in Bangladesh in general.

In Chap. 22, Dudley Poston and Yu-Ting Chang examine multiple dimensions of sexuality, namely sexual behavior in one's lifetime, sexual self-identification, and sexual preference, by analyzing the 2006–2008 National Survey of Family Growth data. The authors examine the consistency in the dimensions for heterosexual, homosexual, and bisexual persons. According to their findings, certain percentages of the U.S. adult population may be classified as heterosexual, homosexual, or bisexual. In Chap. 23, Ronald Cossman, Jeralynn Cossman, and Phillip Mason examine the demographic attributes of nursing students and the impact of family members on decisions to become a nursing student. They analyze web based survey data of 1,008 nursing students. Thirty-eight percent of the respondents said that a family member or close friend influenced them to enter the health care profession.

Conclusion

The chapters of this book provide insight into emerging applied demography issues and techniques. Contributors to this book are among the leading applied demographers. They are actively engaged in developing and refining methods and techniques to address issues and problems in developing, assessing, analyzing, and reporting data on a range of demographic topics. The result of their work, presented in these chapters, illustrates the policy- relevant nature of applied demography. This publication also stresses the importance of continuing to share advances in the development and application of the methods and materials of applied demography.

References

Hoque, N., & Swanson, D. A. (Eds.). (2012). *Opportunities and Challenges for Applied Demography in the 21st Century.* Netherlands: Springer.

Hoque, N. (2012). Canadian studies in population. *Official Journal of the Canadian Population Society. 39*(1–2), 91–108 (Spring/Summer).

Hoque, N., McGehee, M., & B. Bradshaw (Eds.). (2013). *Applied Demography and Public Health.* Netherlands: Springer.

Murdock, S. H., & Ellis, D. (1991). *Applied demography: An introduction to basic concepts, methods and data.* Boulder: Westview Press.

Murdock, S. H., & Swanson, D. H. (Eds.). (2008) *Applied demography in the 21st century.* Netherlands: Springer.

Siegel, J. (2002). *Applied demography: Application to business, government, law and public policy.* San Diego: Academic Press.

Smith, S. K., Tayman, J., & Swanson, D. (2001). *State and local population projections: Methodology and analysis.* New York: Kluwer Academic/Plenum Publishers.

Part I
Evaluation of Population Projections and 2010 Census Counts

Chapter 2
An Evaluation of Population Forecast Errors for Florida and its Counties, 1980–2010

Stanley K. Smith and Stefan Rayer

Introduction

Many decisions in both the public and private sectors are based on expectations of future population change. Planning for schools, hospitals, shopping centers, housing developments, electric power plants, and many other projects is strongly influenced by expected population growth or decline. The distribution of government funds and the granting of various types of licenses and permits may be affected as well. It is not surprising that population projections and forecasts are of so much interest to so many people.

A population projection can be defined as the numerical outcome of a specific set of assumptions regarding future population trends. It is non-judgmental in the sense that it makes no predictions regarding the likelihood that those assumptions will prove to be true. A population forecast, on the other hand, is the projection considered most likely to provide an accurate prediction of future population change. It is explicitly judgmental. Given this distinction, all forecasts are projections but not all projections are forecasts. In most instances, however, projections are interpreted as forecasts regardless of the intentions of those who make them. Consequently, it is essential to evaluate the forecast accuracy of previously produced population projections, especially those used for official purposes.

The Bureau of Economic and Business Research (BEBR) at the University of Florida has been making population projections for Florida and its counties on an annual basis since the early 1970s. Since 1977, in addition to the preferred medium series, BEBR projections have included a low and high series to account for forecast uncertainty. These projections are used for planning and budgeting purposes by government agencies, businesses, and other data users throughout the state. In this study, we investigate the accuracy of several sets of state and county population projections published between 1980 and 2005. We analyze the effects of population size, growth rate, and length of projection horizon on the forecast accuracy of the

S. K. Smith (✉) · S. Rayer
Bureau of Economic and Business Research, University of Florida, Gainesville, FL, USA
e-mail: sksmith@ufl.edu

M. N. Hoque, L. B. Potter (eds.), *Emerging Techniques in Applied Demography,*
Applied Demography Series 4, DOI 10.1007/978-94-017-8990-5_2,

medium series of projections and investigate two different approaches to measuring uncertainty, one based on a range of projections and the other based on empirical prediction intervals.

A number of studies have analyzed the accuracy of subnational population projections (Chi 2009; Chi and Voss 2011; Isserman 1977; Rayer 2008; Smith 1987; Tayman 1996), but few have evaluated projections produced at regular intervals over several decades using a consistent methodology. The BEBR projections offer a unique opportunity in this regard. We believe that the results presented here will give data users a great deal of information regarding the forecast accuracy of state and local population projections and that this information will help them apply better judgment when using projections for decision-making purposes.

Methodology

BEBR uses two different approaches in the construction of its population projections. At the state level, the projections are based on a cohort-component methodology in which births, deaths, and migration are projected separately for each age-sex cohort in the population. Three different sets of migration and fertility assumptions are used, providing three series of projections (low, medium, and high). The medium series is considered the most likely to provide accurate forecasts of future populations.

The BEBR county projections are based on a variety of statistical techniques that extrapolate historical population trends into the future. In most years, the medium projections for counties are calculated as the average of several individual projections and controlled to add to the state projection. The low and high projections are based on the distribution of errors from previous sets of projections. Again, the medium series is considered the most likely to provide accurate forecasts of future populations.

A detailed description of the current projection methodology can be found in Smith and Rayer (2012). Although there have been small changes in techniques and assumptions over the years, all the state projections have been based on the cohort-component method and all the county projections have been based on extrapolation techniques. Descriptions and evaluations of a variety of population projection methods can be found in Booth (2006); Siegel (2002); Smith et al. (2001); and Wilson and Rees (2005).

The following terminology is used to describe population projections:

1. **Base year**: the year of the earliest observed population size used to make a projection
2. **Launch year**: the year of the latest observed population size used to make a projection
3. **Target year**: the year for which population size is projected
4. **Base period**: the interval between the base year and launch year
5. **Projection horizon**: the interval between the launch year and target year

Table 2.1 Forecast errors for state projections, launch years 1980–2005

	Launch year							
Horizon (years)	1980	1985	1990	1995	2000	2005	Ave. 1	Ave. 2
5	−2.1	−2.6	0.8	−3.6	−2.3	6.0	2.9	−0.6
10	−5.1	−4.1	−1.6	−6.5	−0.1	–	3.5	−3.5
15	−7.3	−7.6	−4.7	−5.2	–	–	6.2	−6.2
20	−10.8	−11.4	−3.7	–	–	–	8.6	−8.6
25	−11.2	−11.2	–	–	–	–	11.2	−11.2
30	−16.3	–	–	–	–	–	16.3	−16.3

Ave. 1: average ignoring the direction of error
Ave. 2: average accounting for the direction of error

For example, if data from 1990 and 2000 were used to project the population in 2010, then 1990 would be the base year, 2000 would be the launch year, 2010 would be the target year, 1990–2000 would be the base period, and 2000–2010 would be the projection horizon.

In this study, we evaluate forecast accuracy by population size, growth rate, and length of projection horizon for state and county projections with launch years 1980, 1985, 1990, 1995, 2000, and 2005. Using the medium series, we compare projections with census counts or mid-decade estimates for each target year and calculate the resulting percent differences.[1] We refer to these differences as forecast errors, but they may have been caused by enumeration or estimation errors as well as by errors in the projections themselves.

Forecast Accuracy

State Projections

Results for the medium state-level projections are shown in Table 2.1. There was not a perfectly monotonic relationship between forecast errors and length of horizon, but errors generally increased (ignoring the direction of error) as the horizon became longer. Averaged across all launch years, errors were approximately 3 % for 5-year horizons, 4 % for 10-year horizons, 6 % for 15-year horizons, 9 % for 20-year horizons, 11 % for 25-year horizons, and 16 % for 30-year horizons.

How do these errors compare with those found in other studies? Several studies have evaluated forecast accuracy for states, using a variety of time periods and projection techniques (Kale et al. 1981; Smith and Sincich 1988, 1992; White 1954). These studies have reported average errors (ignoring the direction of error) ranging between 5 and 8 % for 10-year horizons and between 10 and 15 % for 20-year hori-

[1] The 1985, 1995, and 2005 population estimates used to calculate errors have been revised to incorporate the results of the 1980, 1990, 2000, and 2010 censuses. The mid-decade estimates upon which the projections were based, however, were the original post-censal estimates.

zons. An evaluation of several sets of cohort-component projections for states made by the U.S. Census Bureau between 1967 and 1997 showed average errors between 2 % and 5 % for 5-year horizons and between 6 and 10 % for 15-year horizons (see Table 2.6 in Rayer 2008). For the most part, then, errors for the Florida projections have been somewhat smaller than those reported in previous studies.

Although errors in the state-level projections increased with the length of the projection horizon for every launch year, the errors themselves varied considerably from one launch year to another. For 5-year horizons, the projection for launch year 1995 had an error of −3.6 % whereas the projection for launch year 2005 had an error of 6.0 %. For 10-year horizons, the projection for launch year 1995 had an error of −6.5 % whereas the projection for launch year 2000 had an error of only −0.1 %. The 20-year projection for launch year 1985 had an error of −11.4 % whereas the 20-year projection for launch year 1990 had an error of −3.7 %. These differences illustrate the variability often found in results for a single place, such as a particular state or county. As shown in the next section, there is much less variability when results are based on averages covering a large number of places.

Most of the errors shown in Table 2.1 had negative signs, indicating that the projections were lower than the populations counted or estimated for the target years. Does this mean that the cohort-component method has an inherent downward bias and that current and future projections based on this method will also tend to be low? No, it doesn't. We note that the 5-year projection for launch year 2005 turned out to be substantially too high. Furthermore, several studies of cohort-component projections for states produced by the U.S. Census Bureau found the projections to be predominantly high for some time periods and projection horizons and predominantly low for others (Rayer 2008; Smith and Sincich 1992). Similar results have been found in studies of projections constructed using other methods (Smith and Sincich 1988). Positive and negative errors tend to offset each other over time and from place to place, suggesting that there is no inherent upward or downward bias in the cohort-component method and most other population projection methods. We believe present and future projections are as likely to be too high as too low.

County Projections

We used several measures to evaluate the forecast accuracy of BEBR's medium county projections. The mean absolute percent error (MAPE) is the average when the direction of the error is ignored. The 67th percentile error (67PE) is the error that is larger than two-thirds of all county errors (ignoring direction of errors). These are measures of precision, or how close the projections were to subsequent census counts or mid-decade estimates, regardless of whether they were too high or too low.

The mean algebraic percent error (MALPE) is the average error when the direction of the error is accounted for; that is, positive and negative errors are allowed to offset each other. This is a measure of bias: a positive MALPE reflects a tendency for projections to be too high and a negative MALPE reflects a tendency for projections to be too low. We use the percentage of errors that were positive (%POS) as

Table 2.2 MAPEs for county projections, launch years 1980–2005

Horizon (years)	Launch year 1980	1985	1990	1995	2000	2005	Average
5	5.0	5.8	4.2	4.7	4.1	5.9	4.9
10	9.8	7.2	8.2	7.6	6.1	–	7.8
15	11.5	10.8	11.7	9.4	–	–	10.9
20	15.5	14.3	14.3	–	–	–	14.7

Table 2.3 67th percentile errors for county projections, launch years 1980–2005

Horizon (years)	Launch year 1980	1985	1990	1995	2000	2005	Average
5	5.2	6.6	5.0	5.5	4.2	7.2	5.6
10	10.6	8.8	9.0	8.5	7.3	–	8.8
15	12.4	12.4	12.7	10.3	–	–	12.0
20	17.4	15.8	16.9	–	–	–	16.7

another measure of bias because a few large errors can disproportionately influence the size and sign of the MALPE.

Tables 2.2–2.5 summarize the precision and bias of county projections with launch years 1980, 1985, 1990, 1995, 2000, and 2005. As shown in Table 2.2, MAPEs averaged approximately 5 % for 5-year horizons, 8 % for 10-year horizons, 11 % for 15-year horizons, and 15 % for 20-year horizons. Although there was some variation from one launch year to another, there was much more stability over time in average errors for counties than for the state as a whole. This stability occurred despite large differences in errors for individual counties. In absolute terms, for example, errors for counties varied from 0.0 to 21.5 % for 10-year horizons and from 0.1 to 59.9 % for 20-year horizons (not shown here).

For each launch year, MAPEs increased approximately linearly with the length of the projection horizon. Similar results have been reported in many previous studies (Rayer 2008; Smith 1987; Smith and Sincich 1992; Tayman 1996; White 1954). There was some indication that errors have become smaller over time, at least for launch years 1980 through 2000. This may have been caused by changes in county size and growth-rate characteristics; we return to this possibility later in this chapter. For launch year 2005, however, the MAPE for a 5-year horizon was larger than in any previous launch year.

Table 2.3 shows the results for the 67th percentile errors. Again, errors increased in an approximately linear manner with the length of the horizon. Differences in errors from one launch year to another declined as the projection horizon became longer. For example, the largest error for 5-year horizons was 71 % larger than the smallest error, compared to 45 % larger for 10-year horizons, 23 % larger for 15-year horizons, and 10 % larger for 20-year horizons.

Table 2.4 MALPEs for county projections, launch years 1980–2005

	Launch year						
Horizon (years)	1980	1985	1990	1995	2000	2005	Average
5	−2.6	−1.5	−1.3	−1.4	−1.9	5.0	−0.6
10	−5.3	−4.2	−4.6	−4.2	−1.0	–	−3.9
15	−9.0	−7.9	−8.2	−3.6	–	–	−7.2
20	−12.9	−11.6	−8.4	–	–	–	−11.0

Table 2.5 Percentage of positive errors for county projections, launch years 1980–2005

	Launch year						
Horizon (years)	1980	1985	1990	1995	2000	2005	Average
5	37.3	35.8	43.3	37.3	35.8	85.1	45.6
10	31.3	26.9	28.4	29.9	55.2	–	34.3
15	20.9	25.4	20.9	37.3	–	–	26.1
20	19.4	20.9	25.4	–	–	–	21.9

Table 2.4 shows the results for MALPEs. All errors through launch year 2000 had negative signs and generally became larger as the horizon became longer. The projections for lauch year 2005, however, had a strong upward bias. These results illustrate the lack of predictability regarding the likelihood that a given set of projections will tend to be too high or too low. Errors for individual counties varied from −42.5 to 21.5% for 10-year horizons and from −59.9 to 36.3% for 20-year horizons (not shown here).

Table 2.5 shows the results for the percentage of positive errors. The 10-year projections for launch year 2000 had a slight majority of positive errors and the 5-year projections for launch year 2005 had a large majority of positive errors. All other sets of projections showed a tendency for the projections to be too low (i. e., less than 50% positive errors). The results shown in Tables 2.4 and 2.5 are consistent with those shown in Table 2.1 for the state as a whole. This is not surprising, of course, because the county projections were adjusted to add to the state projections.

How do the county errors reported here compare with those found in other studies? A study of counties in the United States found MAPEs of 12–15% for 10-year horizons and 25–35% for 20-year horizons (Smith 1987). A similar study covering a different time period found MAPEs of approximately 10% for 10-year horizons and 20% for 20-year horizons (Rayer 2008). A study of townships in Illinois found MAPEs of approximately 12% for 10-year horizons (Isserman 1977). A study of minor civil divisions in Wisconsin found MAPEs of 10–11% for 10-year projections (Chi 2009; Chi and Voss 2011). With respect to precision, then, errors for Florida's county projections have been somewhat smaller than those reported in other studies of sub-state areas.

What about bias? Few studies have addressed this question, but those that have done so have found no predictable biases in most population projection techniques (Smith and Sincich 1988, 1992). For most techniques, some sets of projections turn

Table 2.6 Forecast errors for county projections, by population size and length of horizon

	MAPE				MALPE			
Population size	5 years	10 years	15 years	20 years	5 years	10 years	15 years	20 years
< 15,000	5.6	8.8	12.6	18.3	−1.1	−5.3	−10.4	−17.2
15,000 to 49,999	5.5	8.9	12.5	16.6	−0.6	−4.5	−9.7	−13.8
50,000 to 199,999	4.8	8.0	11.0	14.2	−1.0	−3.6	−5.1	−8.0
> 200,000	4.1	5.5	7.2	9.7	0.1	−2.5	−4.1	−5.7
	67 PE				% POS			
< 15,000	6.8	9.9	15.5	22.4	42.9	27.4	23.5	7.5
15,000 to 49,999	5.9	9.1	12.4	16.9	51.8	36.6	19.7	16.1
50,000 to 199,999	5.8	10.2	13.0	17.9	42.1	35.1	32.9	32.8
> 200,000	4.9	6.7	7.6	12.4	45.3	36.1	27.4	27.3

out to have an upward bias and others to have a downward bias, but there is no way to know in advance which tendency will characterize any given set of projections. We believe the medium county projections published by BEBR have equal probabilities of being too high or too low, and that the same would be true if similar techniques were applied in other geographic areas.

What impact do differences in population size and growth rate have on forecast accuracy? To answer this question, we aggregated errors across all launch years, giving results for six sets of 5-year projections, five sets of 10-year projections, four sets of 15-year projections, and three sets of 20-year projections. For each county, population size was measured in the launch year and growth rate was measured over the ten years immediately preceding the launch year.

As shown in Table 2.6, precision generally increased as population size increased. Similar results have been reported in many other studies (Isserman 1977; Rayer 2008; Smith 1987; Tayman 1996; White 1954). Furthermore, the impact of differences in population size on MAPEs and 67th percentile errors appeared to increase with the length of the horizon. For 5-year horizons, for example, errors for the smallest counties were 35–40 % larger than errors for the largest counties, but for 20-year horizons they were almost twice as large.

Measures of bias displayed no clear relationship with population size. The percentage of positive errors sometimes increased with population size and sometimes declined. Although MALPEs generally declined with increases in population size, this was due to the relationship between population size and the size of the error, independent of its direction. We believe that when differences in growth rates are accounted for, differences in population size have no systematic impact on the tendency for projections to be too high or too low. Several other studies have drawn similar conclusions (Murdock et al. 1984; Rayer 2008; Smith and Sincich 1988).

Table 2.7 Forecast errors for county projections, by growth rate and length of horizon

	MAPE				MALPE			
Growth rate	5 years	10 years	15 years	20 years	5 years	10 years	15 years	20 years
<10%	6.6	8.8	12.5	15.3	1.1	−4.4	−9.4	−13.3
10–25%	4.2	6.1	9.3	12.3	0.7	−2.2	−3.4	−6.9
25–50%	4.4	7.5	10.2	13.7	−1.1	−3.5	−7.3	−9.9
>50%	6.4	9.9	12.8	17.2	−2.5	−6.3	−9.4	−14.0
	67 PE				% POS			
<10%	7.5	9.0	13.3	17.6	56.4	30.0	16.0	9.5
10–25%	4.5	7.5	10.5	13.3	50.8	38.6	32.8	27.0
25–50%	5.3	9.4	12.0	16.7	44.2	33.6	25.6	27.2
>50%	6.0	10.9	14.2	20.8	36.3	32.9	25.0	16.1

Table 2.7 shows the results for population growth rates over the ten years immediately preceding the launch year. Measures of precision displayed a u-shaped relationship between errors and growth rates. For both MAPEs and 67th percentile errors, errors were smallest for counties with 10–25% growth rates and became larger as growth rates deviated in either direction from this moderate growth level. Similar results have been reported in several previous studies (Isserman 1977; Rayer 2008; Smith 1987; Tayman 1996).

Measures of bias showed no clear relationship with differences in growth rates. The percentage of positive errors sometimes increased as the growth rate increased and sometimes declined. This result differs from that reported in several studies, which found a tendency for places with slowly growing or declining populations over the base period to be under-projected and places with rapidly growing populations to be over-projected (Rayer 2008; Smith 1987; Smith and Sincich 1988; Tayman 1996). We are not sure why the results found in the present study differ from those reported previously. This may have been caused by the relatively small sample size, the lack of diversity in growth rates (few Florida counties have lost population and many have grown rapidly), or the aggregation of results over several different launch years.

BEBR's county projections are based on simple techniques that extrapolate historical trends into the future. Could forecast accuracy be improved by using more complex techniques that account for changes in the components of population growth (births, deaths, and migration) or factors such as changing economic conditions, density constraints, or zoning restrictions? The evidence strongly suggests that more complex techniques *cannot* produce more accurate forecasts of total population than can be achieved using simple extrapolation techniques (Chi 2009; Chi and Voss 2011; Murdock et al. 1984; Rayer 2008; Smith and Sincich 1992; White 1954). Similar results have been reported in other fields as well (Armstrong 1985; Makridakis et al. 2009; Pant and Starbuck 1990).

We do not believe that applying more complex techniques would lead to any systematic improvement in the forecast accuracy of BEBR's county population projections—or of other subnational projections, for that matter. Regardless of the specific context, there is an irreducible level of uncertainty with respect to future population growth that cannot be overcome, no matter how sophisticated or complex the projection model. It appears that the relatively small amount of information contained in simple extrapolation techniques provides as much guidance to this uncertain future as the much larger amount of information contained in more complex techniques. In the next section, we describe BEBR's approach to dealing with this uncertainty.

Accounting for Uncertainty

The preceding analysis focused on the medium projections. These are the projections most commonly used as forecasts of the future population. However, as the analysis has shown, forecasts virtually never provide perfect predictions of future population growth. Rather, some forecasts turn out to be very accurate while others turn out to be highly inaccurate. How can this uncertainty be dealt with?

The traditional approach to dealing with uncertainty is to construct a range of projections based on different models and/or assumptions. This approach has a long history and has been an integral part of the U.S. Census Bureau's state and national projections for many years (Campbell 1996; U.S. Census Bureau 1957, 2005). It is widely used by state and local demographers as well and is the approach BEBR uses to construct a low and high series for its state population projections (Smith and Rayer 2012).

An alternative approach for dealing with uncertainty uses statistical measures to construct prediction intervals. These measures can be based on stochastic models of population growth (Hyndman and Booth 2008; Lee and Tuljapurkar 1994) or on analyses of errors from past projections (Keyfitz 1981; Rayer et al. 2009). BEBR uses errors from past projections to construct a low and high series for its county population projections.

State Projections

BEBR produces three series of state population projections by applying alternative sets of assumptions regarding mortality, fertility, and migration rates. These assumptions are based on historical trends and expectations regarding future changes. The medium series is based on the trends thought most likely to occur. The low and high series are based on potential changes in those trends; they provide realistic alternative scenarios but do not represent absolute limits to future population growth.

How did the low and high projections of Florida's population compare with the growth actually occurring over the projection horizon? For launch year 1980, the high projection was above the actual population in 1985 but below it in 1990 and all subsequent target years (data not shown). For launch year 2005, the low projection for the state was above the actual population in 2010. For all other launch and target years, the low and high projections encompassed the actual populations occurring over time. That is, actual population growth fell between the low and high series in four of the six sets of state projections analyzed in this study. It appears that the low and high projections produced a range wide enough to provide a reasonable indication of uncertainty but narrow enough to provide useful scenarios for planning purposes.

A range has several benefits as a measure of uncertainty. It is simple to explain, makes it easy to trace out the effects of differences in assumptions, and gives data users several options from which to choose. However, a range provides no information regarding the likelihood that the future population will actually fall between the low and high projections. Even with a range, data users are left without a clear idea of the uncertainty surrounding a population forecast. The second approach provides explicit measures of this uncertainty.

County Projections

Since the mid-1980s, BEBR's low and high county projections have been based on an analysis of population forecast errors for a sample of 2,971 counties in the United States (Smith 1987). These errors were drawn from projections covering several combinations of launch year and projection horizon between 1950 and 1980. Using this data set, BEBR calculated the 67th largest absolute percent error for counties in several population size and/or growth rate categories and used those errors to construct low and high projections for each county. These projections can be interpreted as empirical prediction intervals showing the range in which two-thirds of future county populations would fall if the future distribution of county forecast errors in Florida were similar to the past distribution in the United States.

Using the low and high projections for launch years since 1985, we tabulated the number of counties in which the actual populations in subsequent years fell within the projected range. The results are shown in Table 2.8. If the prediction intervals were reasonably accurate, approximately 45 of Florida's 67 counties would have populations falling between the low and high projections.

Except for the 5-year horizon for launch year 1985, too many county populations fell within the projected range. That is, the intervals overstated the degree of uncertainty. The tendency to overstate uncertainty grew with the length of projection horizon and was greater for more recent launch years than earlier launch years.

What happened? Why did the prediction intervals generally contain more than two-thirds of the county populations? There are several possible explanations. The distribution of errors for counties in Florida may differ in some unmeasured way from the distribution of errors for counties in other states. The increase in the number of large counties and the decline in the number of small counties in Florida—combined with an overall slowdown in population growth rates—may have reduced uncertainty over the last few decades. Perhaps the 1950–1980 time period used to estimate the prediction intervals was too far removed from the 1980–2010 time period covered by the projections, reducing its usefulness as a measure of uncer-

Table 2.8 Number of counties with populations falling below the low projection, above the high projection, and within the projected range (based on US data)

	Length of horizon			
Launch year	5 years	10 years	15 years	20 years
1985				
Below low	11	2	0	0
In range	41	53	55	53
Above high	15	12	12	14
1990				
Below low	1	1	1	1
In range	56	59	58	61
Above high	10	7	8	5
1995				
Below low	3	1	1	–
In range	59	62	63	–
Above high	5	4	3	–
2000				
Below low	1	0	–	–
In range	63	65	–	–
Above high	3	2	–	–
2005				
Below low	6	–	–	–
In range	61	–	–	–
Above high	0	–	–	–
Average				
Below low	4	1	1	1
In range	56	60	58	57
Above high	7	6	8	9

tainty (especially for recent launch years). Whatever the explanation, the prediction intervals proved to be substantially too wide.

As an alternative, we constructed a set of prediction intervals based solely on data for Florida counties. Using the distribution of errors for projections with launch years 1980, 1985, and 1990, we calculated two-thirds prediction intervals for 5-, 10-, and 15-year horizons through target year 1995. We applied these intervals to projections with launch years 1995, 2000, and 2005 and counted the number of counties whose populations fell within the intervals in target years 2000, 2005, and 2010. The results are shown in Table 2.9.

The results were substantially better than those shown in Table 2.8. Averaged across all launch years, 43 counties fell within the predicted range for 5-year horizons and 49 counties for 10-year horizons; the single 15-year horizon also had 49 counties falling within the predicted range. These numbers were reasonably close to the 45 implied by the prediction intervals. For launch years 1995 and 2000, more counties were above the high projection than below the low projection for all lengths of horizon, reflecting the generally high rates of population growth found in most Florida counties during this period. For launch year 2005, more were below

Table 2.9 Number of counties with populations falling below the low projection, above the high projection, and within the projected range (based on Florida data)

	Length of horizon		
Launch year	5 years	10 years	15 years
1995			
Below low	7	2	3
In range	45	47	49
Above high	15	18	15
2000			
Below low	4	5	–
In range	49	51	–
Above high	14	11	–
2005			
Below low	30	–	–
In range	35	–	–
Above high	2	–	–
Average			
Below low	14	4	3
In range	43	49	49
Above high	10	14	15

the low projection than above the high projection, reflecting the slowdown in population growth occurring between 2005 and 2010.

Empirical prediction intervals cannot provide perfect forecasts of the future distribution of errors, but they offer a useful way to measure uncertainty and give data users an empirically based indication of the range in which future populations are likely to fall. As shown by a comparison of Tables 2.8 and 2.9, however, the specific data set used to construct the intervals can have a substantial impact on their predictive performance. Additional research on the measurement of uncertainty—and on techniques for incorporating that uncertainty into the production of population forecasts—is clearly needed.

Conclusion

Florida is a dynamic, diverse, rapidly changing state that has experienced dramatic population booms and busts over the years, but BEBR's population projections have turned out to be reasonably accurate in many instances. Over the time period covered by this study, state-level forecast errors averaged 3 % for 5-year horizons, 4 % for 10-year horizons, 6 % for 15-year horizons, and 9 % for 20-year horizons (ignoring the direction of errors). County-level forecast errors averaged 5, 8, 11, and 15 % for those horizons, respectively. Based on comparisons with previous studies, this is a good record of forecast accuracy.

Can we expect the same level of accuracy for current and future projections? For the state as a whole, we cannot be sure. As an individual place, it is subject to a substantial amount of potential variability, both in terms of the size and the direction of future forecast errors. Previous errors have varied considerably from one launch year to another, but it is likely that future errors for any given length of projection horizon will fall somewhere in the range shown in Table 2.1.

We can be more confident in the results for counties, but only when those results are aggregated. Average errors are much more predictable than errors for individual places. With respect to precision, we believe MAPEs and 67th percentile errors for current and future county projections are likely to be similar to those shown in Tables 2.2 and 2.3. With respect to bias, however, we cannot make any predictions. There is simply no way to know in advance whether a given set of projections will turn out to be predominantly too high or too low.

Results for individual counties, of course, are much less predictable than results based on averages. Given this uncertainty, data users should consider several possible alternatives rather than a single scenario when using county projections for decision-making purposes. Population projections provide valuable tools, but they must be accompanied by a careful analysis of historical trends and potential alternative scenarios when planning for the future.

To what extent can the results presented here be generalized? That is, can they give data users a reasonable indication of the likely degree of accuracy of projections prepared for other places and time periods? We believe they can, at least to some extent. Based on this and other studies, we believe average errors for state projections will often be 2–3 % for 5-year horizons, 4–6 % for 10-year horizons, 6–9 % for 15-year horizons, and 8–12 % for 20-year horizons (disregarding direction of error). MAPEs for county projections will often be 4–5, 8–10, 12–15, and 16–20 % for those horizons, respectively. For both states and counties, errors are likely to be larger than these averages for small, rapidly growing (or declining) places and smaller than these averages for large, slowly growing places.

We believe the results presented here will help data users make more fully informed (and presumably better) decisions as they plan for the future. We hope more studies of forecast accuracy will be done, drawn from other places and time periods. Although the past is an uncertain guide to the future, it is the best guide we have. The more we know about the forecast accuracy of previous population projections, the greater will be our ability to assess the likely accuracy of current and future projections and use that information for decision-making purposes.

References

Armstrong, J. S. (1985). *Long-range forecasting: From crystal ball to computer*. New York: Wiley.

Booth, H. (2006). Demographic forecasting: 1980 to 2005 in review. *International Journal of Forecasting, 22,* 547–581.

Campbell, P. R. (1996). *Population projections for states by age, sex, race, and Hispanic origin: 1995 to 2050*. Washington, DC: U.S. Bureau of the Census.

Chi, G. (2009). Can knowledge improve population forecasts at subcounty levels? *Demography, 46,* 405–427.

Chi, G., & Voss, P. R. (2011). Small-area population forecasting: Borrowing strength across space and time. *Population, Space and Place, 17,* 505–520.
Hyndman, R. J., & Booth, H. (2008). Stochastic population forecasts using functional data models for mortality, fertility and migration. *International Journal of Forecasting, 24,* 323–342.
Isserman, A. (1977). The accuracy of population projections for subcounty areas. *Journal of the American Institute of Planners, 43,* 247–259.
Kale, B., Voss, P. R., Palit, C., & Krebs, H. (1981). "On the question of errors in population projections", paper presented at the annual meeting of the Population Association of America, Washington, DC.
Keyfitz, N. (1981). The limits of population forecasting. *Population and Development Review, 7,* 579–593.
Lee, R., & Tuljapurkar, S. (1994). Stochastic population forecasts for the United States: Beyond high, medium, and low. *Journal of the American Statistical Association, 89,* 1175–1189.
Makridakis, S., Hogarth, R. M., & Gaba, A. (2009). Forecasting and uncertainty in the economic and business world. *International Journal of Forecasting, 25,* 794–812.
Murdock, S. H., Leistritz, F. L., Hamm, R. R., Hwang, S. S., & Parpia, B. (1984). An assessment of the accuracy of a regional economic-demographic projection model. *Demography, 21,* 383–404.
Pant, P. N., & Starbuck, W. H. (1990). Innocents in the forest: Forecasting and research methods. *Journal of Management, 16,* 433–460.
Rayer, S. (2008). Population forecast errors: A primer for planners. *Journal of Planning Education and Research, 27,* 417–430.
Rayer, S., Smith, S. K., & Tayman, J. (2009). Empirical prediction intervals for county population forecasts. *Population Research and Policy Review, 28,* 773–793.
Siegel, J. S. (2002). *Applied demography.* San Diego: Academic Press.
Smith, S. K. (1987). Tests of forecast accuracy and bias for county population projections. *Journal of the American Statistical Association, 82,* 991–1003.
Smith, S. K., & Rayer, S. (2012). "Projections of Florida population by county, 2011–2040," *Florida Population Studies* Bulletin 162, Bureau of Economic and Business Research, University of Florida.
Smith, S. K., & Sincich, T. (1988). Stability over time in the distribution of population forecast errors. *Demography, 25,* 461–474.
Smith, S. K., & Sincich, T. (1992). Evaluating the forecast accuracy and bias of alternative population projections for states. *International Journal of Forecasting, 8,* 495–508.
Smith, S. K., Tayman, J., & Swanson, D. A. (2001). *State and local population projections: Methodology and analysis.* New York: Kluwer Academic/Plenum Publishers.
Tayman, J. (1996). The accuracy of small-area population forecasts based on a spatial interaction land-use modeling system. *Journal of the American Planning Association, 62,* 85–98.
U.S. Census Bureau. (1957). Illustrative projections of the population, by state, 1960, 1965, and 1970. *Current Population Reports*, P-25, No. 160. Washington, DC.
U.S. Census Bureau. (2005). Interim population projections for states by age and sex: 2004 to 2030. Suitland MD: Population Projections Branch, Population Division.
White, H. (1954). Empirical study of the accuracy of selected methods of projecting state population. *Journal of the American Statistical Association, 49,* 480–498.
Wilson, T., & Rees, P. (2005). Recent developments in population projection methodology: A review. *Population, Space and Place, 11,* 337–360.

Chapter 3
Simplifying Local Area Population and Household Projections with POPART

Tom Wilson

Introduction

As applied demographers can attest, the preparation of local area population and household projections by age and sex can prove quite a complicated task—often rather more complicated than the neat projection examples in introductory textbooks suggest. Challenges typically faced include: base period data that are incomplete, inconsistent, or suspicious; time series of data cut short by geographical or definitional changes; severe noise in age profiles of fertility, mortality, and migration rates; non-trivial costs and long waiting times for purchased data; tight timeframes; complicated or inappropriate projection software or no software at all; limited guidance from the literature on setting projection assumptions; high user expectations; and reduced resources in the present age of austerity.

This chapter introduces the POPART (*Po*pulation *P*rojections for an *A*rea, *R*egion or *T*own) software, which was developed to reduce the severity of some of these challenges. It produces population projections by sex and 5-year age group and household projections for a single region. The software was created so that it could be operated relatively easily and quickly, with the typical intended users being local and state government demographers and advanced undergraduate and graduate students of demography. In attempting to overcome some of the challenges mentioned above, the system was designed to:

1. keep data input requirements as low as possible (without sacrificing population accounting consistency),
2. enable assumptions to be set and changed quickly,
3. incorporate a user-friendly interface with features such as pull-down menus and buttons,
4. produce publication-ready graphs and tables, and
5. be usable after limited training.

T. Wilson (✉)
Queensland Centre for Population Research, School of Geography, Planning and Environmental Management, The University of Queensland, Brisbane, QLD, Australia
e-mail: tom.wilson@uq.edu.au

M. N. Hoque, L. B. Potter (eds.), *Emerging Techniques in Applied Demography*, Applied Demography Series 4, DOI 10.1007/978-94-017-8990-5_3,

The software is illustrated through an application to the council area of Noosa in Australia. Home to around 50,000 residents in 2011, the area is located on the east coast of Queensland about 130 km north of the state capital of Brisbane. It enjoys a subtropical climate of hot summers and mild winters and an attractive natural environment including a sheltered beach, and it is a popular tourist destination. The area grew rapidly in population in the 1980s and 1990s, particularly through net internal migration gains. In common with many scenic coastal areas in Australia, Noosa's population age structure is shaped to a considerable extent by net out-migration of young adults, net in-migration in the middle and older adult ages, and the shift of the baby boom generation (born 1946–1965) through the middle adult years and into the elderly ages. The council of Noosa was officially reinstated on January 1, 2014, after having been merged with two neighbouring councils in 2008. The case study therefore not only illustrates the kind of demographic change to be expected in many coastal communities of Australia, but it also generates a set of demographic projections for a local area without any recent projections because of its amalgamation with neighbouring councils. Following this introduction, the principal features of the software and projection models are described. Data inputs are the focus of the next section. The following section, Model Validation, presents retrospective projections for the case study area from 2001 to 2011, which are compared with the actual population of 2011 to assess the effectiveness of the projection model. POPART is then put to use in producing population and household projections for Noosa for 2011–2031 under two scenarios, one trend-based, the other dwelling-led. A short summary and suggestions for further development of the software form the concluding section.

POPART

The POPART software consists of an Excel/VBA-based system incorporating a bi-regional cohort-component population projection model and a householder rate household model. Populations are broken down by sex and 5-year age group up to ages 85 and over, with projections proceeding in 5-year intervals over a 30-year projection horizon. Household projections are similarly produced every 5 years for 30 years. Household outputs comprise the total number of households and average household size.

Bi-regional cohort-component models, as the name implies, divide a country into two geographical regions. Their key feature is the explicit modelling of directional, rather than net, migration between regions. Although they require more data than single region cohort-component models with net migration, they use correct populations at risk of migration, avoid generating implausible or impossible projections (such as negatives), and by handling migrants between regions rather than non-existent 'net migrants,' they are conceptually better representations of demographic reality. Similarly, overseas migration is handled as directional flows rather than as net numbers or rates. Details on the advantages of bi-regional models may be found in Rogers (1976), Wilson and Bell (2004), and Renske and Strate (2013).

The accounting basis of the population model is that of transition population accounts (Rees 1981; Rees and Willekens 1986) in which migration is handled as transitions. Transition migration data comprise counts of changes of usual residence between two points in time and are the typical form of migration statistics obtained from a census. They are derived from questions on the individual's usual address on census night and the usual address n years ago. Transition data are conceptually and empirically quite different from movement migration data, which consist of counts of moves across specified geographical boundaries (Rees 1985). POPART was designed to use transition data because this is the principal type of internal migration data available in Australia.

In a bi-regional transition accounts model, the projection equation for any cohort and sex may be expressed as (Rees 2002; UN and Speare 1992; Isserman 1993):

$$P^1(t+5) = P^1(t)(1-d^1)(1-e^1)(1-t^{12}) \\ +t^{21}(P^2(t)(1-d^2)(1-e^2))+T^{o1}$$

where P denotes population, 1 the region of interest, 2 the rest of the country, d mortality probabilities, e emigration probabilities, t transition migration probabilities, and T transition migration flows (in this case from *o*verseas to region *1*). In life table notation, mortality probabilities for the cohort ageing from initial age x to x+5 over the 5-year interval may be expressed as:

$$_5d_{x\rightarrow x+5} = \frac{_5L_x - {_5L_{x+5}}}{_5L_x}.$$

Emigration probabilities are defined as transition emigration over a 5-year interval divided by the population of the region surviving to the end of the interval. Unfortunately subnational emigration data are often unavailable so this component of demographic change will often have to be estimated. For any cohort, the emigration probability is calculated as:

$$e = \frac{T^{1o}}{P^1(\mathrm{t}) - D^1}$$

where the denominator is the initial population surviving at the end of the interval, t+5, once mortality has been accounted for. Internal migration probabilities are calculated as transition migration over a 5-year interval divided by the initial population surviving within the country at the end of the interval (Rees et al. 2000). For example, the migration probability from region 1 to region 2 for any cohort may be found as:

$$t^{12} = \frac{T^{12}}{P^1(t) - D^1 - E^1}.$$

An important feature of the POPART software is the way in which migration projection assumptions are simplified. Headline assumptions are formulated in terms of total net internal migration (NIM) and total net overseas migration (NOM) per annum. These are placed in the shaded cells towards the top-right of Fig. 3.1. They are net migration totals expressed in the more familiar movement accounts perspective and are linked to transition migration terms in the model using a little-known relationship identified by Rees (1977). POPART projects internal migration in two stages. First, base period migration probabilities are multiplied by relevant populations at risk to give preliminary sets of inward and outward migration flows. Second, these flows are then scaled using the plus-minus method to match user-defined net migration totals. This feature of the model makes use of the fact that whilst *levels* of migration tend to fluctuate over time, *age profiles* exhibit much greater temporal stability. Constraining to a specified net internal migration total thus permits migration assumptions to be changed easily. Only the net migration totals require adjustment; the base period age-specific migration probabilities can remain unchanged. The same procedure is applied to overseas migration.

POPART also includes an 'on/off' switch for migration, operationalised with the radio buttons next to 'use assumptions below' or 'no migration' in the 'Headline projection assumptions' box in Fig. 3.1. If 'no migration' is selected, user-supplied migration assumptions are overridden and all age-sex migration values are set to zero. Users can then easily produce a 'no migration' projection variant in which the population changes only from fertility, mortality, and population age structure effects. When such a projection is compared to a regular projection incorporating migration, the importance of migration to the local area's population can be determined. (Note that this is quite different from typing in zero NIM and NOM assumptions. In such cases POPART will adjust initial inward and outward migration flows to obtain total net migration values of zero, though net migration will likely take positive and negative values across the age range.)

The approach to setting mortality assumptions was also designed to reduce input data requirements. Users are only required to set assumptions on life expectancy at birth by sex. They are set using the pull-down menus in the 'Headline projection assumptions' box in Fig. 3.1. Pre-loaded in the software are a series of sex-specific ${}_nL_x$ values for Australia covering a wide range of historic and projected mortality levels, effectively forming a mortality plane. The historic portion of these data was obtained from the Human Mortality Database (HMD 2013) whilst the projected section was created using the direct extrapolation method of Ediev (2008). POPART extracts age-sex-specific mortality probabilities that correspond to user-specified life expectancy assumptions from appropriate points on the mortality plane. The simplifying assumption is that all regions follow the national mortality experience, though from different points on the mortality plane and at different speeds of mortality improvement.

Fertility assumption-setting is also simplified by separating out overall levels from age profiles. Headline assumptions are set in the form of Total Fertility Rates (TFRs), with age-specific fertility rates (ASFRs) being scaled to sum to these TFRs. ASFRs may be supplied by the user, or otherwise the preloaded default rates will

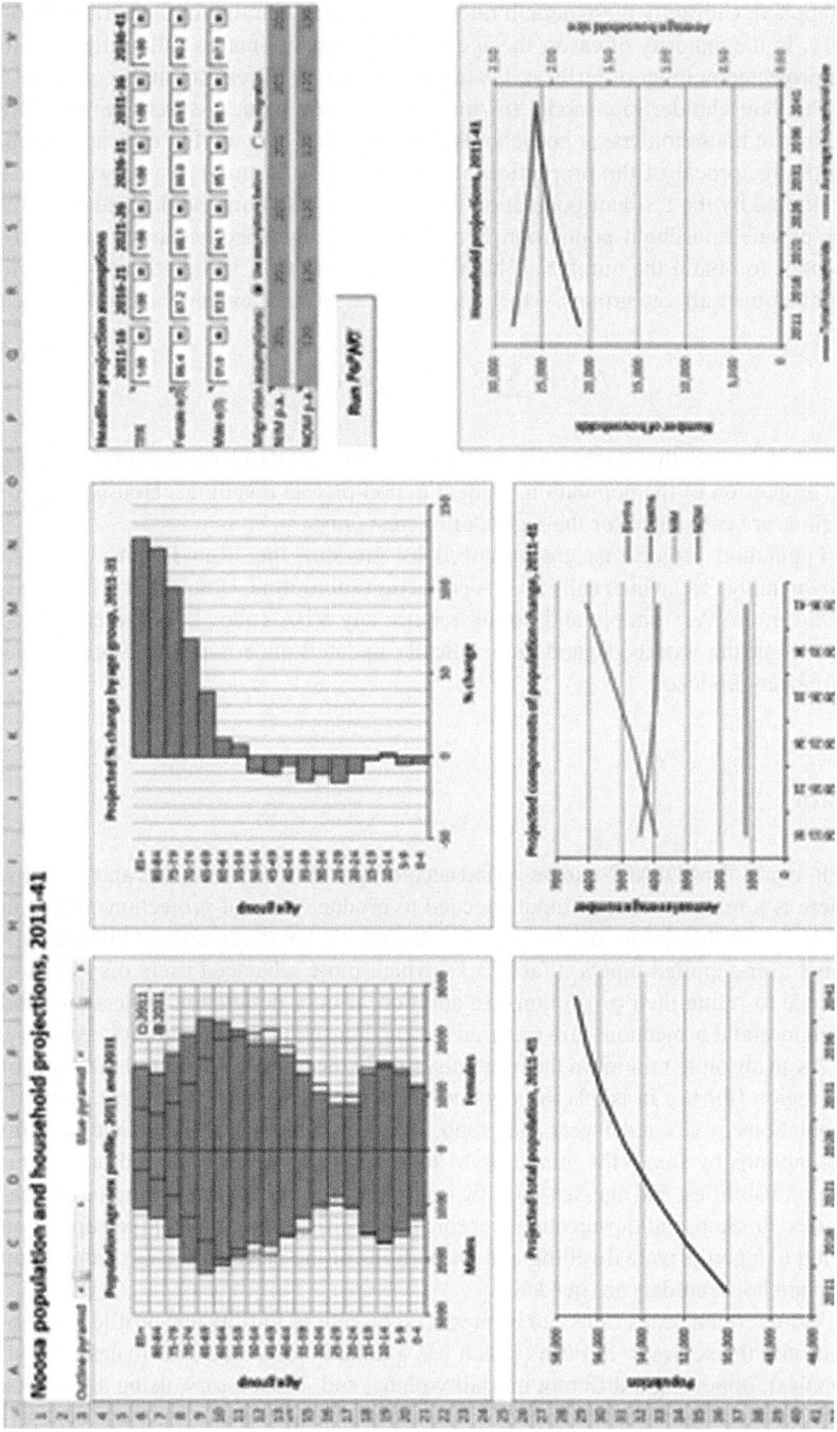

Fig. 3.1 Part of the main screen of the POPART Excel workbook (illustrating the Trend scenario)

be applied. Currently these default rates are those for Australia for the period 2006–2011. In the majority of cases, the age profile of fertility makes little difference to the projected number of births—it is the assumed *level* of fertility that is crucial.

The householder rate model (or the headship rate model) is very simple. The number of householders, or households, is projected as follows. For each age group, (1) the reciprocal of the proportion of the population in non-private dwellings is multiplied by the resident population to give the private household population, (2) this private household population is multiplied by age-specific householder proportions to obtain the number of householders, and then (3) the householders are summed over all age groups. Algebraically these calculations may be summarised as:

$$H^i(t) = \sum_a h_a^i(t) \left(1 - npd_a^i(t)\right) P_a^i(t)$$

where H denotes the number of households, h the householder proportion, and npd the proportion of the population resident in non-private dwellings. Household projections are calculated for the region of interest only.

Population projections are produced by pressing the 'Run POPART' button shown in Fig. 3.1, which calls a VBA projection subroutine. Household projections, however, are very simple and do not require any VBA code. They are calculated directly in the workbook and automatically updated once population projections have been produced.

Data

Data inputs for POPART can be varied according to user requirements and/or skills. There is a minimum set of inputs needed to produce a set of projections, listed in Table 3.1 as 'Minimum user-supplied data inputs'. There are also additional 'Optional user-supplied inputs' (Table 3.1), which more advanced users may wish to include to refine their projections. In addition, if only population projections, and not household projections, are required then no household data inputs are necessary.

As an absolute minimum the user must supply the jump-off year and the name of the region (for use in labels throughout the Excel workbook), study area jump-off populations by sex and 5-year age group, TFR assumptions, life expectancy at birth assumptions by sex, NIM totals, NOM totals, age-sex-specific in- and out-migration probabilities, and age-sex-specific immigration numbers and emigration probabilities. For household projections recent age-specific proportions of the population living in a non-private dwelling and proportions of the private dwelling population who are householders are needed.

More refined projections can be produced by setting fertility age profile assumptions and the sex ratio at birth (which has a default value of 105.5 males per 100 females), importing a different mortality plane, and, if necessary, using alternative rest of country jump-off populations. The current default option subtracts the user-supplied study area population from 2011 national populations for Australia.

Table 3.1 Input data and assumptions required by POPART

Variable	Minimum user-supplied data inputs	Optional user-supplied inputs (otherwise default values used)
Labels	Name of study area; jump-off year	None
Populations	Jump-off year populations by sex and 5-year age group 0–4 to 80–84 and 85+ for study area.	Jump-off year populations by sex and 5-year age group 0–4 to 80–84 and 85+ for rest of country.
Fertility	TFRs for study area and rest of country	Five-year age group age-specific fertility rates for study area and rest of country; sex ratio at birth
Mortality	Life expectancy at birth by sex for study area	Past and projected life table ${}_nL_x$ values; life expectancy at birth by sex for rest of country
Internal migration	NIM totals for the study area by 5-year interval for the projection horizon; recent in-migration probabilities by sex and 5-year age group (rest of country to study area migration); recent out-migration probabilities by sex and 5-year age group (study area to rest of country migration)	None
Overseas migration	NOM totals by 5-year period for the projection horizon; recent immigration numbers by sex and 5-year age group (rest of country to study area); recentemigration probabilities by sex and 5-year age group (study area to rest of country)	None
Households[a]	Proportions of the population living in a non-private dwelling by 5-year age group for the study area for a recent year; proportions of the private dwelling population who are householders by 5-year age group for the study area for a recent year	None

[a] These data inputs are not necessary if just population projections are required

Model Validation

To demonstrate the validity of the POPART model for this case study, retrospective projections for Noosa from 2001 to 2011 were undertaken. As far as possible data inputs were those available in 2002, the year when the majority of 2001 census data were released and when many 2001-based projections would have been produced. Of course, a successful 'projection' for one area over a 10-year horizon does not guarantee an accurate and useful projection over coming decades. Nonetheless, such an exercise can be regarded as an absolute minimum test of a demographic model, is often useful in persuading clients of the effectiveness of one's models, and is a recommended approach in Armstrong (2001). A reasonable projection up to the present demonstrates that the model can potentially generate good forecasts. 'Reasonable' was defined here as a percentage error within 10 %, a figure regarded as acceptable according to a survey of projection users reported by Tye (1994).

To match the approach of the 2011-based projections, two main scenarios were produced with different migration assumptions. The *Trend* scenario assumed that the total net migration of the most recent intercensal period (1996–2001) would continue into the future. The *Housing* scenario assumed that migration would be driven by dwelling construction as anticipated in the *Broadhectare Study* of 2000 (Queensland Department of Local Government and Planning 2001). The projected number of households was obtained by multiplying the anticipated number of dwellings by the proportion occupied on a usual residence basis. In the current version of POPART, the amount of migration required for dwelling-led projections is not automated but is easily determined from a few trial-and-error runs of the software. This involves a comparison of the number of households derived from the dwelling forecasts and the projected number of households produced by the householder rate model. Both scenarios used age-sex-specific migration probabilities averaged over the 1996 and 2001 censuses.

A third scenario, *Observed Headline*, was also created. This used net migration totals calculated as accounting residuals and reported TFRs for the 2001–2011 period. Ideally it would also have incorporated observed life expectancies at birth but lack of data prevented this. The purpose was to assess the performance of the model using observed headline indicators of fertility, mortality, and migration but assumed age profiles. If this were to produce accurate projections then the simplified assumption-setting for fertility, mortality, and migration age profiles would prove reasonable.

For the Trend and Housing scenarios the Total Fertility Rate was set to 1.73 throughout the 2001–2011 period. This was calculated as the ABS national fertility assumption of the time (ABS 2002) scaled by the ratio of Noosa's TFR to the national TFR over the 1996–2001 period. Similarly, life expectancy at birth assumptions were formulated as the ABS national life expectancy assumptions of the time multiplied by ratios of Noosa's life expectancy to national life expectancy over the 1996–2001 period.

According to ABS Estimated Resident Populations (ERPs), the 2001 population of 43,724 increased to 50,068 by 2011. Errors in projecting this 2011 total are

Table 3.2 Errors in retrospective projections of Noosa's total population, 2001–2011. (Source: Author's projections and ABS ERPs)

	Projection scenario			
	Trend	Housing	Observed headline	Actual
2001 ERP	43,724	43,724	43,724	43,724
2011 projection	54,816	47,625	50,106	50,068
Percentage error	9.5%	−4.9%	0.1%	–

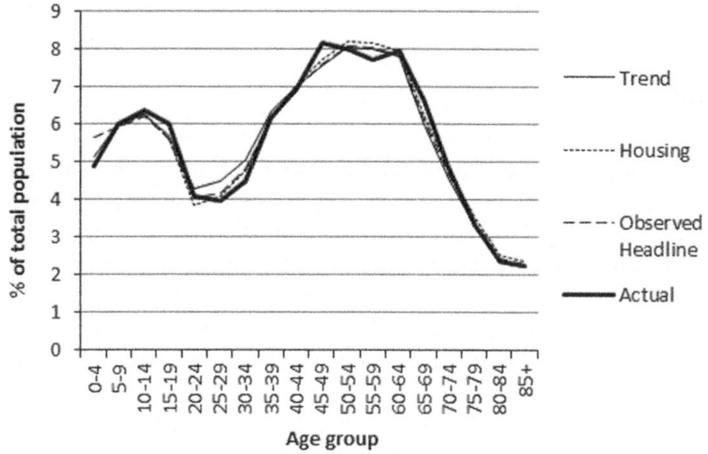

Fig. 3.2 Projected and actual age structure of Noosa's population, 2011. (Source: Author's projections and ABS 2011 ERPs)

shown in Table 3.2 below. Neither Trend nor Housing scenarios did spectacularly well in forecasting total population, though the housing-led approach was better. Nonetheless, these sorts of errors are typical for local area projections over a 10 year horizon. In an ex post analysis of Queensland local government area population forecasts, Wilson and Rowe (2011) found median errors to be 7–8 % (depending on the time periods studied) over 10 year horizons. Reassuringly, the Observed Headline scenario projected the total population well.

Projections of population age structure in the Trend and Housing scenarios were more accurate than their total population figures. Figure 3.2 illustrates the population age structure projected by the three scenarios against the actual 2011 age structure. All are successful forecasts, with the Housing scenario particularly accurate, projecting the 2011 population age structure with an Index of Dissimilarity of just 1.7 % (Robinson 1998). The poor performance of the Observed Headline scenario amongst 0–4 year olds may be due to problems with Queensland birth registrations in the late 2000s.

Application: Population and Household Projections for Noosa

Two scenarios for the future demography of Noosa were prepared for the 2011–2031 period: a *Housing*-led scenario, based on anticipated net dwelling additions, and a *Trend*-based scenario, based on the maintenance of recently observed migration trends. Although POPART produces projections over a 30-year horizon, the focus here is on the two decades to 2031 because this is the extent of a typical council planning horizon.

Assumptions

The Trend scenario assumed the total amount of net migration experienced over the 2006 to 2011 period, an average of 321 per annum, would continue into the future. This was divided into 201 NIM and 120 NOM per annum on the basis of 2011 census migration data. The Housing scenario incorporated varying migration levels dependent on anticipated net dwelling additions in the area along with an assumption of the 2011 census usual occupancy rate of 82 % remaining unchanged. Age- and sex-specific migration probabilities were the average of those calculated from the 2006 and 2011 censuses.

Both scenarios used the same fertility and mortality inputs. A constant Total Fertility Rate of 1.88 was assumed, formulated from a national TFR assumption of 1.90 multiplied by a local/national scaling factor of 0.99 reflecting 2006–2011 experience. Life expectancy at birth was set to rise from 86.4 years for females and 81.8 years for males in 2011–2016 to 88.8 years for females and 85.1 years for males by 2026–2031. These assumptions were derived from national life expectancy at birth projections multiplied by the ratio of local/national life expectancy over the 2006–2011 period. Age-specific householder rates averaged over the 2006 and 2011 censuses were held constant.

Results

Figure 3.3 presents total populations generated by the two scenarios from 2011 to 2031 along with historical population numbers. From a 2011 population total of 50,068, the trend scenario projects an increase to 55,844 by 2031 whilst under the housing scenario growth is higher, resulting in a population of 58,059 by the end of the projection horizon. However, population increase is distributed unevenly across age groups. As Fig. 3.4 shows, over the next two decades there is little expected increase in age groups below age 55: all projected growth is concentrated in the older ages. The population aged 65 and over, for example, is projected to rise from 9,685 in 2011 to 17,242 (Trend scenario) or 17,826 (Housing scenario) by 2031; in

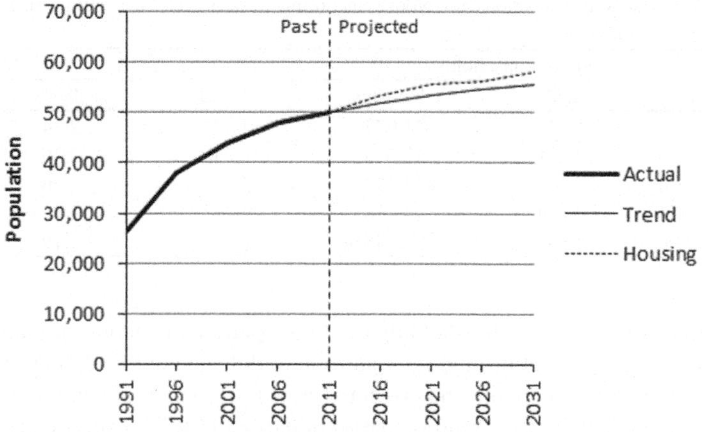

Fig. 3.3 The past and projected population of Noosa according to two scenarios, 1991–2031. (Source: ABS population data and author's projections)

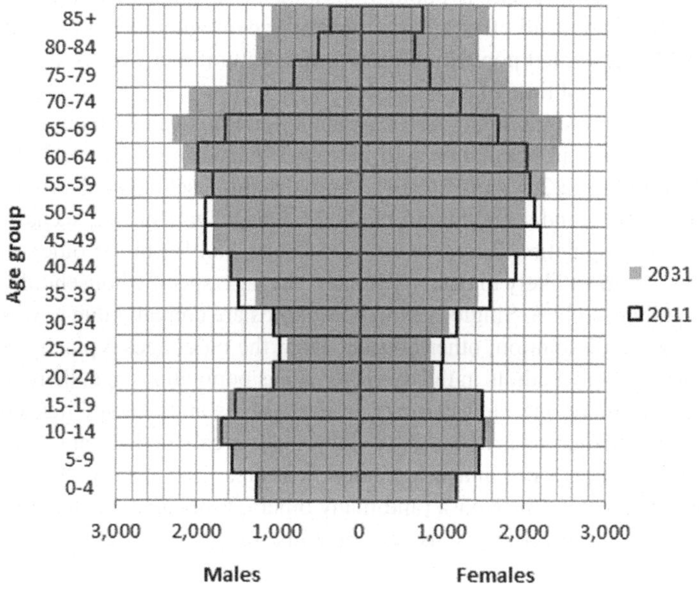

Fig. 3.4 The age-sex profile of Noosa's population in 2011 and in 2031 according to the Housing scenario. (Source: ABS population data and author's projections)

percentage terms this translates to a shift from 19.3 % of the total population in 2011 being aged 65+ to 30.7 % (Housing) or 30.9 % (Trend) by 2031. Such population ageing will be occurring throughout Australia as the baby boom generation moves into the elderly ages, fertility remains below replacement level, and life expectancy continues to rise. However, in high-amenity coastal areas such as Noosa, ageing

Table 3.3 Household projections for Noosa according to two scenarios, 2011–2031. (Source: Author's projections)

	No. of households		Average household size	
Year	Trend	Housing	Trend	Housing
2011	21,077	21,077	2.34	2.34
2016	22,251	22,875	2.29	2.30
2021	23,263	24,192	2.25	2.26
2026	24,119	24,776	2.22	2.22
2031	24,800	25,748	2.19	2.19

will be intensified by the long-standing migration pattern of net out-migration at the young adult ages and net in-migration gains at middle and older adult ages.

Population ageing explains the projected switch from natural increase to natural decrease in the late 2010s (Trend scenario) or early 2020s (Housing scenario). The number of births is projected to decline slightly in line with a small reduction of the childbearing-age population. Deaths, in contrast, are expected to increase significantly. Although age-specific death rates are projected to decline, this is more than offset by large increases in populations at risk in the high-mortality elderly age groups. In Noosa, and all other areas with similar demographic patterns, the capacity for locally generated population growth (i.e. natural increase) is about to come to an end for the first time in its history.

The shifting age structure of Noosa's population is also the principal reason why projected increases in population will be lower than those of household numbers (Table 3.3). Between 2011 and 2031 the number of households will rise by 17.7 % according to the Trend scenario and by 22.2 % under the Housing scenario, whilst the respective population increases are 11.5 % and 16.0 %. In the older adult ages individuals are most likely to be householders, i.e. age-specific householder proportions are at their highest. Single-person households are common due to widowhood and partnership dissolution; other households at the older ages typically consist of couples without other adults in the dwelling. So as populations age, there tend to be proportionally more one- and two-person households and average household size across the population as a whole falls. Table 3.3 reveals both Trend and Housing scenarios projecting a fall in average household size from 2.34 in 2011 to 2.19 in 2031. The implication for Noosa (and many other coastal areas) is that the number of households and dwellings must increase just to prevent total population from falling.

Conclusions

This chapter has introduced POPART, an Excel-based software package for producing population projections by age and sex and household projections for a region or local area. Efforts have been made to minimise data inputs, simplify assumption-setting, and enable projections to be produced quickly and easily. Data inputs have been reduced relative to standard single year of age models by using 5-year age groups and projection intervals and by preloading some data into the Excel workbook. For most Australian applications, all data are immediately available from the ABS website, thus avoiding the expense and delays of ordering customised tables. Assumption-setting has been simplified by separating the *levels* of demographic drivers of change from their *age profiles* and by preloading a mortality plane. The interpretation of projections is assisted through ready-made graphics and tables.

In future versions of the software, it is planned to:

- automate the dwelling-led projections,
- incorporate a range of preloaded model migration age schedules to extend the usability of the model to very small areas where 'raw' migration age profiles suffer from considerable noise,
- add an option to allow the use of movement migration data, and
- add labour force projections.

In the meantime, it is hoped that POPART will prove a useful tool for demographers and students of demography.

Software

The POPART software is available from the author. Please email: tom.wilson@uq.edu.au.

References

ABS (Australian Bureau of Statistics). (2002). *Population projections, Australia, 2002–2101*. Canberra: ABS.

Armstrong, J. S. (2001). Evaluating forecasting methods. In J. S. Armstrong (Ed.), *Principles of forecasting* (pp. 443–472). Boston: Kluwer Academic.

Ediev, D. M. (2008). *Extrapolative projections of mortality: Towards a more consistent method. Part I: The central scenario*. Vienna Institute for Demography Working Paper 3/2008.

HMD (Human Mortality Database). (2013). University of California, Berkeley (USA), and Max Planck Institute for Demographic Research (Germany). www.mortality.org. Accessed 2 July 2013.

Isserman, A. M. (1993). The right people, the right rates: Making population estimates and forecasts with an interregional cohort-component model. *Journal of the American Planning Association, 59*(1), 45–64.

Queensland Department of Local Government and Planning. (2001). *Broadhectare study: Caloundra city, Maroochy shire & Noosa shire* (2000 ed.). Brisbane: Queensland Department of Local Government and Planning.

Rees, P. H. (1977). The measurement of migration, from census data and other sources. *Environment and Planning A, 9*(3), 247–272.

Rees, P. H. (1981). *Accounts based models for multiregional population analysis: Methods, program and users' manual*. Working Paper 295/Computer Manual 13, School of Geography, University of Leeds, UK.

Rees, P. H. (1985). Does it really matter which migration data you use in a population model? In P. E. White & G. A. van der Knapp (Eds.), *Contemporary studies of migration* (pp. 55–78). Norwich: GeoBooks.

Rees, P. (2002). New models for projecting UK populations by ethnic group at national and subnational scales. In J. Haskey (Ed.), *Population projections by ethnic group: A feasibility study* (pp. 27–42). London: The Stationery Office.

Rees, P., & Willekens, F. (1986). Data and accounts. In A. Rogers & F. J. Willekens (Eds.), *Migration and settlement: A multiregional comparative study* (pp. 19–58). Dordrecht: D Reidel.

Rees, P., Bell, M., Duke-Williams, O., & Blake, M. (2000). Problems and solutions in the measurement of migration intensities: Australia and Britain compared. *Population Studies, 3*(2), 207–222.

Renske, H., & Strate, S. (2013). Evaluating alternative migration estimation techniques for population estimates and projections. *Journal of Planning Education and Research*. doi:10.1177/0739456X13484362.

Robinson, G. M. (1998). *Methods and techniques in human geography*. Chichester: Wiley.

Rogers, A. (1976). Shrinking large-scale population projection models by aggregation and decomposition. *Environment and Planning A, 8*, 515–541.

Tye, R. (1994). *Local authority estimates and projections: How are they used and how accurate do they need to be?* Working Paper 9, Estimating with Confidence project. Department of Social Statistics, University of Southampton, UK.

United Nations, & Speare A. (1992). *Preparing migration data for subnational population projections*. New York: United Nations.

Wilson, T., & Bell, M. (2004). Comparative empirical evaluations of internal migration models in subnational population projections. *Journal of Population Research, 21*(2), 127–160.

Wilson, T., & Rowe, F. (2011). The forecast accuracy of local government area population projections: a case study of Queensland. *Australasian Journal of Regional Studies, 17*(2), 204–243.

Chapter 4
The Net Undercount of Children in the 2010 U.S. Decennial Census

William P. O' Hare

Introduction

The net undercount of children has been documented historically in the U.S. Census and it has been observed in the censuses in many other countries around the world. The net undercount of children, particularly young children, has been documented in societies as varied as the United States, China, South Africa, Laos and the former Soviet Union (Goodkind 2011; Anderson and Silver 1985; Anderson 2004). The Canadian censuses of 2001 and 2006 also show a relatively high net undercount for the population age 0–4 (Statistics Canada 2004, 2010).

However, the net undercount of young children in the U.S. decennial census has received little systematic attention from researchers with only a handful of reports and working papers focusing on this issue (O'Hare 1999; West and Robinson 1999; Edmonston 2001; Daponte and Wolfson 2003; Pitkin and Park 2005; Zeller 2006; O'Hare 2009; Hernandez and Denton 2001).

After describing the Demographic Analysis (DA) estimation methodology and identifying a couple of innovations in the 2010 DA program, DA estimates for children are compared to the 2010 decennial census counts to detect net undercounts and overcounts. Results are examined by single-year of age, by sex, and by Black and Hispanic populations for all children (people under age 18) and for those under age 5.

Demographic Analysis Methodology

Assessing the net undercounts in the census is typically based on one of two methods: (1) Demographic Analysis (DA), or (2) Dual System Estimates (DSE). This paper focuses on data from DA, which is based on comparing the census results to

W. P. O' Hare (✉)
The Annie E. Casey Foundation, Baltimore, MD, USA
e-mail: billohare1@gmail.com

M. N. Hoque, L. B. Potter (eds.), *Emerging Techniques in Applied Demography*, Applied Demography Series 4, DOI 10.1007/978-94-017-8990-5_4,

an independent population estimate. When this paper was being written in January 2012, the DSE results for 2010 were not yet available. Since there are already several detailed descriptions of the DA methodology available (Robinson 2010), I will only review the method briefly here.

The DA method has been used to assess the accuracy of decennial census figures for more than a half century and its origins are often traced back to an article by Price (1947). As Price documents, the unexpectedly high number of young men who turned up at the first compulsory selective service registration on October 6, 1940, alerted scholars to the possibility of under-enumeration in the 1940 decennial census.

The relatively high net undercount among young children was uncovered early in the history of DA. In one of the first systematic efforts to use DA to examine decennial census results, Coale (1955) found children under age 5 had a high net undercount rate in the censuses of 1940 and 1950. Siegel and Zelnik (1966) also found a significant net undercount of children under age 5 in the 1950 and 1960 censuses.

The DA method employed for the 2010 Census uses one technique to estimate the population under age 75 and another to estimate the population age 75 and older (West 2012). Since this study focuses on children, I only discuss the method used for people age 0–74 (people under age 1 are classified as age 0).

The 2010 DA estimates for the population age 0–74 are based on the compilation of historical estimates of the components of population change: Births (B), Deaths (D), and Net International Migration on (NIM) immigration. The data and methodology for each of these components is described in a set of background documents prepared for the development and release of the 2010 DA estimates (Bhaskar et al. 2010; Devine et al. 2010; Robinson 2010).

The DA population estimates for age 0–74 are derived from the basic demographic accounting equation (1) applied to each birth cohort:

$$P_{0\text{–}74} = B - D + NIM \tag{1}$$

$P_{0\text{–}74}$ population for each single year of age from 0 to 74
B number of births for each age cohort
D number of deaths for each age cohort since birth
NIM net international migration for each age cohort

For example, the estimate of the population age 17 on the April 1, 2010, census date is based on births from April 1992 through March 1993, reduced by the deaths to that cohort in each year between April 1,1992, and April 1, 2010, and incremented by Net International Migration (NIM) of the cohort over the 17-year period.

Births are by far the largest components of the population estimates in DA, especially for children. Births account for 97 % of DA population estimate for age 0–17 in 2010 and for 99.6 % of the DA population estimate for the population age 0–4 (U.S. Census Bureau 2010, Table 8).

The birth and death data used in the Census Bureau's DA estimates come from the U.S. National Center on Health Statistics (NCHS), and these records are widely viewed as being accurate and complete (Devine et al. 2010). The Census Bureau assumes death data have been complete since 1959 and birth data have been complete since 1985 (Devine et al. 2010). In addition to regularly published totals, the Census Bureau receives microdata files from NCHS containing detailed data on births and deaths each month.

The Census Bureau changed the way it calculated net international migration for the 2010 set of DA estimates (Bhaskar et al. 2010). The current method relies heavily on data from the American Community Survey (ACS) in which respondents are asked about the location of their Residence One Year Ago (ROYA). The total number of yearly immigrants was derived from this question in each year of the ACS, and then that total number was distributed to demographic cells (sex, age, and race) based on an accumulation of data over the last 5 years of the ACS. Five years of ACS data are used to provide estimates that are more reliable for small groups.

One of the major uncertainties in using DA estimates to assess the accuracy of census population counts is its assumptions about net international migration. The error of closure related to the 2000 Census count, at about 6.8 million people, made the importance of this assumption very apparent. See description of error of closure in 2000 Census at http://www.census.gov/popest/methodology/intercensal_nat_meth.pdf

Net international migration is a much smaller overall component than births but it is subject to higher relative error because of the uncertainty of some specific elements, especially emigration and undocumented immigration (Bhaskar et al. 2010). According to Bhaskar et al. (2010, p. 1), "The largest uncertainty in the Demographic Analysis (DA) estimates comes from the international migration component."

However, it is important to note that assumptions about net international immigration have minimal impact on the DA estimation for persons ages 0–4. Data from the 2010 ACS show only 1 % of children age 0–4 are foreign-born, compared to 20 % of prime working-age adults (age 25–44) (U.S. Census Bureau 2011). The DA estimates released in May 2012 assume a Net International Migration of only 244,000 out of a population of 21,172,000 for ages 0–4. Therefore, errors in this component of population change would not have a big impact on the final DA population estimate for the 0–4 age group.

Net native emigration is estimated using some data from censuses of other countries and a residual method based on the 2000 Census and the American Community Survey (Bhaskar et al. 2010). By any measure, the net native emigration for young children is very small.

Another reason DA is the preferred method for assessing the net undercount of young children is related to the quality of vital events data. Vital events data for younger people are of a higher quality than those for older people. Thus, the quality of DA estimates for younger people is likely to be better than that for older people, both in terms of total numbers and racial composition. Improvement in the birth certificate data over time is a major reason the Census Bureau is now producing DA estimates for Hispanics under age 20. In the five scenarios for 2010 DA estimates released in December 2010, the birth and death assumptions are identical for children (U.S. Census Bureau 2010). In comparing DA to DSE in 2000, Zeller (2006, p. 3201) also concludes, "Since the Demographic Analysis estimates for young children depended primarily on highly accurate recent birth registration data, the Demographic Analysis estimate is believed to be more accurate."

There are three major limitations to DA. First, it is only available for the nation as a whole. The fact that many people move after birth is a barrier to employing this method at the subnational level.

Second, DA estimates are only available for a few race/ethnic groups. Historically it has only been available for Black and Non-Black groups. This restriction is due to the lack of specificity and consistency for race data collected on the birth and death certificates historically. The only group that has been identified consistently over time is Blacks (African-Americans).

The 2010 DA estimates include data for Hispanics for the first time, but only for the population under age 20. Young Hispanics are included in the DA estimates in 2010 because Hispanics have been consistently identified in birth and death certificates since 1990.

The third limitation of the DA estimates is that they only supply net undercount/overcount figures. A zero net undercount could be the result of no one being missed (omissions) or double counted (erroneous enumerations) or it could be the results of ten percent of the population being missed and ten percent counted twice.

Despite these limitations, DA has been used for many decades, the underlying data and methodology are solid, and it has provided useful information for those trying to understand the strengths and weaknesses of the U.S. decennial census. According to Robinson (2000, p. 1), "The national DA estimates have become the accepted benchmark for tracking historical trends in net census undercounts and for assessing coverage differences by age, sex, and race (Black, all other)."

Using DA to Estimate the Black Population

One of the biggest challenges the Census Bureau faces is producing DA estimates for the Black population. As stated earlier, Black is the only race historically assessed using DA because Black is the only racial category for which data have been collected consistently in the birth and death certificates over time.

The Census Bureau faces multiple problems trying to make the decennial census racial categories consistent with the race data collected on birth and death certificates. For example, the "Some Other Race" category is a response category for the race question in the decennial census but not in birth or death certificates. Because the birth certificate data does not have a "some other race" category, the Census Bureau constructs a set of modified race categories from the decennial census responses in which respondents in the some other race category are distributed to Black and Non-Black categories. Thus for making comparisons between DA estimates and the decennial census counts for Blacks and Non-Blacks, one must use the 2010 Decennial Census modified race tabulations available on the Census Bureau's website. Population figures for modified race categories are available online at: http://www.census.gov/popest/data/national/totals/2011/index.html

For some groups, the modified race tabulations are substantially different from the unmodified tabulations. In the 2010 Census, the number of people age 0–17 in the Black alone category from the unmodified race tabulations was 10,841,000, but in the modified race tabulations the number in the Black alone category age 0–17 was 11,317,000, which amounts to a difference of 4.3 %. The Black alone or in combination population age 0–17 was 11,845,000 in the decennial census count, while on the modified file, it was 13,030,000, which amounts to a difference of 10 %. For the population age 0–4, the unmodified decennial census count for Black alone was 2,903,000, but the figure based on modified race concept was 3,055,000, which amounts to a 5 % difference. For age 0–4, the unmodified Black alone or in combination was 3,538,000, but it was 3,905,000 on the modified file, for a 10 % difference.

A second issue is the fact that decennial census respondents in 2000 and 2010 could mark more than one race. In 1997, the U.S. Office of Management and Budget (1997) updated Statistical Policy Directive 15 requiring federal data collection efforts to allow respondents to mark more than one race. Prior to the 2000 Census, respondents were only allowed to mark one race in the decennial census, which meant the race data from the decennial census and from vital events were consistent in this regard. This issue is further complicated by the fact that it wasn't until 2003 that the federal government issued new standard birth certificate and death certificate forms that allow parents to mark more than one race. However, birth and death certificate data are collected by states and states only changed to the new form slowly over time. Every year after 2003, a new group of states adopted the new birth certificate and death certificate forms, so each year from 2003 to 2010 the Census Bureau had to process some data from the old forms that allowed only one race to be selected and some data from the new forms that allowed more than one race to be selected. Some states changed forms in the middle of the year. The mixed data from the birth (and death) certificates had to be put into Black and Non-Black categories, based on both single-race and multiple-race reported by mother and fathers. In addition, for the DA release of May 2012, DA estimates were provided for "Black alone" as well as "Black alone or in combination," so birth certificate data had to be put into these two different racial categories.

A third issue is that birth certificate forms only record the race of the mother and father. Thus, the race of the child must be inferred from the race of the parent(s). This is further complicated by a significant level of missing data. While data on the race of mother is relatively complete, many birth certificates are missing the race of the father. In 2009, 19 % of birth certificate forms did not contain the race of the father (Martin et al. 2011).

When both parents report the same race, that is the race assigned to the child. When the two parents report different races on the birth certificate, the Census Bureau assigns newborns to a race category based on the reported race of their mother and father and on parent-child race relationships seen in the 2000 decennial census data (Ortman 2012). This is also an issue for Hispanic newborns, and a similar approach is used.

Mixed race parentage is a bigger statistical issue for young children than older people because increased rates of inter-marriage over time mean more children today are likely to have parents with different races and Hispanic status. One study found that about 15 % of marriages in 2010 involved spouses of different race or ethnicity compared to 7 % in 1980 (Wang 2012).

Assignment of race on death certificates is also a potential problem, but deaths contribute very little to the DA estimates for children (Aries et al. 2008).

Data Sources

In this study, I use the DA files that were released in May 2012 for all groups except Hispanics. The May 2012 DA update did not contain data for Hispanics, so I used the Hispanic data from the December 2010 DA release. For the 2010 Census counts, I used data for SF1 except for the Black/Non-Black figures for which I used the modified race data from the decennial census.

The DA program for 2010 continued the practice of producing estimates by age, sex, and Black and Non-Black. However, the 2010 DA analysis included two new facets. For the first time, the Census Bureau provided DA estimates for the Hispanic and Non-Hispanic populations under age 20. Also for the first time, the bureau produced DA estimates of "Black Alone" as well as "Black Alone or in combination."

I use the term children to refer to people age 0–17, and the term young children to refer to people age 0–4. I use the term adults to refer to people age 18 and over.

In the remainder of this study, the difference between the census counts and DA estimates are shown as the census count *minus* the DA estimate. Therefore, a negative number implies a net undercount and a positive number implies a net overcount. In converting the numbers to percentages or rates, the difference between the census and DA estimate is divided by the DA estimate. All estimates are shown rounded to the nearest thousand and percentages are shown to one decimal place for readability.

2010 Demographic Analysis Results

Figure 4.1 shows net undercounts and overcounts for the population age 0–84 by single years of age based on comparison of 2010 decennial census figures to the 2010 DA estimates.

The age-specific estimates from DA match the census counts closely except for three age groups. There is a large net undercount for people under age 10, particularly under age five, and a large net overcount for young adults (roughly age 18–24). There is also a large net overcount for people in their 1950s, 1960s and 1970s.

The overcount of 18-to-24-year-olds is widely believed to be due to the fact that many people in this age group are counted in the home of their parents as well as where they reside most of the time, for example a college dormitory. The overcount of those in their 50s, 60s and 70s is widely believed to be due to the fact that many of them have second homes (which leads to being counted twice in the census) and/

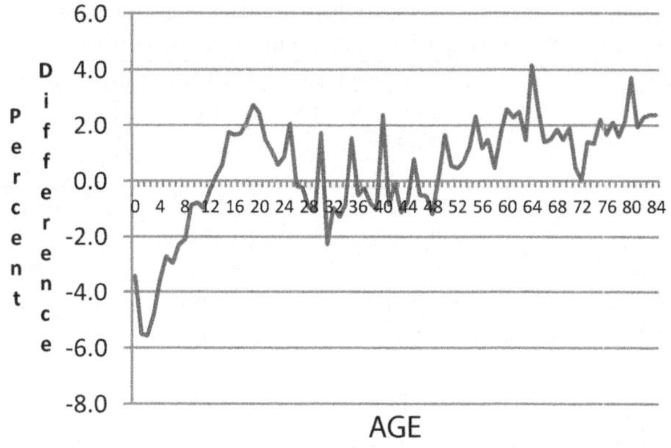

Fig. 4.1 Percent difference between 2010 census count and DA estimates by single year of age: 0–84

or are experiencing household changes related to retirement. On the other hand, there is no commonly accepted explanation for the net undercount of young children.

It is noteworthy that not only is the population of young children the only group to have a significant net undercount in the decennial census, the size of the error for age 0–4 is higher than the magnitude of the errors for other groups, regardless of direction.

2010 DA Estimates for Adults Compared to Children

In the 2010, there was a net overcount of only 0.1 % for the total population, however this overall figure masks important differences among age groups. There was a net undercount rate for children (people under age 18) of 1.7 % and a net overcount rate for adults (people age 18 and over) of 0.7 %. In population numbers, these reflect a net undercount of 1.3 million children and a net overcount of 1.7 million adults.

2010 DA Estimates for Single Year of Age for Children

There are big differences in net undercount and overcount rates for children based on their age. Figure 4.2 shows the net undercount and overcount rates for children by single year of age.

There are three key points that can be derived from Fig. 4.2. First, the highest net undercount rates are among the children under age 5. More than three-quarters of the 1.3 million person net undercount for the population age 0–17 can be accounted for by those age 0–4, where the net undercount is slightly under one million people (see Table 4.1).

Table 4.1 Difference between 2010 decennial census counts and DA estimates for people age 0–4, by sex, race, and Hispanic origin. (Source: Revised DA estimates released May 2012)

	2010 decennial census count (in 1000s)	2010 DA estimate (in 1000s)	Difference between decennial census count and DA estimate	Percent difference
Total	20,201	21,171	−970	−4.6
Female	9,882	10,353	−471	−4.5
Male	10,320	10,821	−501	−4.6
Black alone	3,055	3,195	−140	−4.4
Black alone or in combination	3,658	3,905	−247	−6.3
Hispanic[a]	5,114	5,528	−414	−7.5

[a] Except for data on Hispanics, which are from Middle Series of December 2010 DA release

Second, there is a net overcount rate for people age 14–17. The net overcount of children age 14–17 is completely accounted for by a high net overcount of Hispanics and Blacks in this age range (shown later).

Third, there is a very clear age gradient along the age range from age 1 to 17. The net undercount rate declines steadily from age 1 to 13, and there is a net overcount in the 14–17 age group.

Figure 4.2 makes it clear that people under age 18 should not be treated as a homogeneous age group with regard to census undercounts and overcounts. The data show that young children have a relatively high net undercount, while people age 14–17 have a net overcount. Analyses that fail to make a distinction among age groups of children are likely to find interpretation of findings difficult. The explanation for why young children experience a high net undercount is likely to be quite different from the explanation for why teens (age 14–17) have a high net overcount.

Undercount of Children by Sex

Undercount estimates by single year of age for males and females (Fig. 4.3) indicate that the same age gradient shown for both males and females is seen in the overall population age 0–17. Additionally, there are virtually no differences in net undercount rates between males and females at the youngest ages. When children enter the middle teens, however, the net overcount rate of males becomes noticeably higher than those of females.

The fact that males age 14–17 have a higher net overcount than females in the same age range is puzzling given the relative robust finding over many U.S. censuses that adult males have net undercounts while adult females have net overcounts. I suspect that one reason for this may be undetected net immigration from abroad, where males outnumber females, but this deserves further research.

Figure 4.4 shows net undercount rates for Black alone, Black alone or in combination, and Hispanic children. The age gradient seen for the total population of

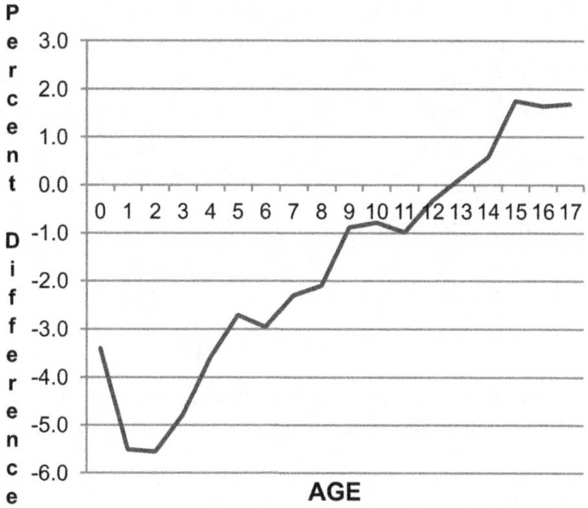

Fig. 4.2 Percent difference between 2010 census count and DA estimates by single year of age: 0–17

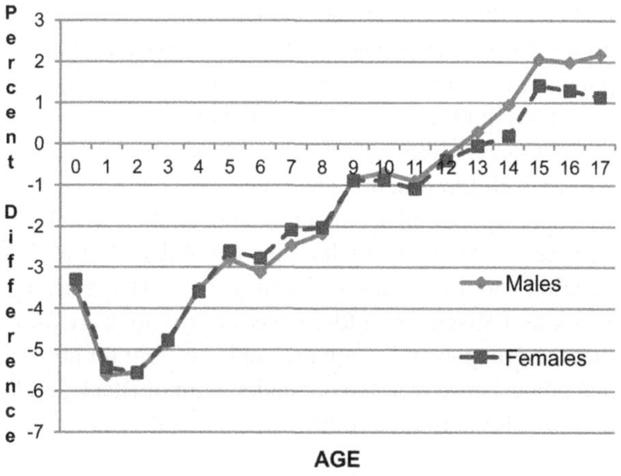

Fig. 4.3 Percent difference between 2010 census counts and DA estimates by sex and single year of age: 0–17

children is seen consistently among all the groups examined here, while levels and the exact age breaks differ slightly. For all groups, as one moves up in age, the net undercounts decrease, and net overcounts begin to occur in the early teen years.

The high net undercount of young children and the net overcount of 14-to-17-year-olds are both accounted for largely by the net undercounts and net overcounts of Hispanics and Blacks. Hispanics and Blacks have higher than average net undercount rates among children under age 5, but higher than average overcounts among children age 14–17. There was a net overcount rate of 1.5 % for the total population age 14–17 in the 2010 Census, but for Hispanics age 14–17 the net overcount rate was around 6 % and for Blacks (both Black alone and Black alone or in combination) age 14–17, it was around 4 %.

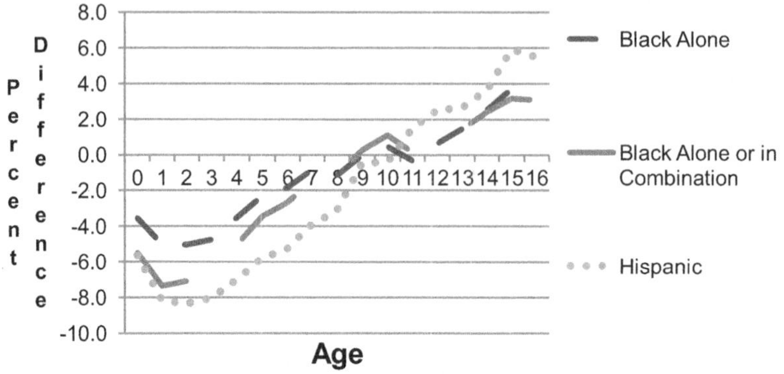

Fig. 4.4 Percent difference between 2010 census count and DA estimates for race and Hispanic groups by single year of age: 0–17

The Population Under Age 5

It is clear that children under age 5 have the highest net undercount rate of any age group in the 2010 Census. Table 4.1 shows that the net undercount rate for the total population under age 5 was 4.6 %, but this masks differences among groups. The net undercount rate for Black alone in this age range was 4.6 %, the net undercount rate for Black alone or in combination was 6.3 %, and the net undercount rate for Hispanic children in this age range was 7.5 %.

There was a total net undercount of slightly less than one million people under age 5 in the 2010 Census, including a net undercount of 247,000 Black alone or in combination and a net undercount of 414,000 Hispanics in this age range. Thus, young Black and Hispanic children account for about two-thirds of the net undercount in this age group even though they only account for about 40 % of the population in this age range. Moreover, the net undercount of Black and Hispanic children under age 5 accounts for about half of the total net undercount of all people under age 18.

Discussion

While the high net undercount rate for young children is clear, the reasons for such a high rate are not. A few of the potential reasons are discussed below.

It is possible that the way the decennial census data are collected and/or processed results in a high net undercount of young children. For example, the continuation form used by the Census Bureau to capture information on persons in large households may have a differential impact on young children. The 2010 decennial census form mail-out questionnaire only contains room for complete information for six people in the household. If there are more than 6 people in the household, the Census Bureau must follow-up to obtain complete information. Since respondents routinely list household member from oldest to youngest, the need to follow up with large households may affect children disproportionately. The 2010 American Community Survey shows that 10.1 % of young children live in households of seven or more people, compared to 3.5 % of adults. Therefore, any problem following up with these types of households would affect young children disproportionately.

It is possible that the way the Census Bureau imputes age to cases where age is not provided or the data provided are implausible may result in an underestimation of young children. Perhaps too many people had their age imputed as age 14–17 and too few had their age imputed as age 0–4.

It is also plausible that the living arrangements and/or locations of young children are the driving force behind their high net undercount rates. Research shows that the number of children living in high poverty neighborhoods increased by more than 1.5 million after 2000 (The Annie E. Casey Foundation 2012).

While speculation about these kinds of explanations abound, there is very little empirical research testing these ideas. Understanding why young children experience such a high net undercount in the decennial census will require a major research effort.

Conclusions

The very small net overcount for the total population reflected in the DA estimates masks important differences by age. There was a net overcount of 0.7 % for adults (people age 18+) but a net undercount of 1.7 % for children (people age 0–17). In addition, there are important differences in net undercount and net overcount rates for children by age. The net undercount rate for people under age 5 in the 2010 Census (4.6 %) is higher than any other age group.

There is a clear relationship between age and the net undercount. In all the groups examined here (males, females, Blacks, and Hispanics), young children (age 0–4) had the highest net undercount rate, but the net undercount rate diminished as children age and a net overcount rate occurs by the time children are 14–17 years old.

It is clear that children (people under age 18) should not be treated as a homogeneous group with regard to the likelihood of being undercounted or overcounted in the decennial census.

Examination of the inconsistency between the 2010 decennial census count and the DA estimates indicate that young children should be the focus of attention for those desiring a more complete count in the 2020 Census.

References

Anderson, B. A. (2004). *Undercount in China's 2000 census in comparative perspective*. PSC research report, no. 04-565, Population Studies Center, University of Michigan, Ann Arbor, MI.

Anderson, B. A., & Silver, B. D. (1985). Estimating census undercount from school enrollment data: An application to the Soviet Censuses on 1959 and 1970. *Demography, 22*(2), 289–308.

Aries, E., Schauman, W. S., Eschbach, K., Sorlie, P. D., & Backlund, E. (2008). The validity of race and Hispanic origin reporting on death certificates in the United States, National Center for Health Statistics, Vital and Health Statistics 2(148).

Bhaskar, R., Scopilliti, M., Hollman, F., & Armstrong, D. (2010). *Plans for producing estimates of net international migration for the 2010 demographic analysis estimates*. Census Bureau working paper no. 90. http://www.census.gov/population/www/documentation/twps0090/twps0090.pdf. Accessed 12 Dec 2011.

Coale, A. J. (1955). The population of the United States in 1950 classified by age, sex and color—a revision of census figures. *Journal of the American Statistical Association, 50,* 16–54.

Daponte, B. O., & Wolfson, L. J. (2003). How many American children are poor? Considering census undercount by comparing census to administrative data. Carnegie Mellon University, February 7.

Devine, J., Sink, L., DeSalvo, B., & Cortes, R. (2010). *The use of vital statistics in the 2010 demographic analysis estimates*. Census Bureau working paper no. 88. http://www.census.gov/population/www/documentation/twps0088/twps0088.pdf. Accessed 10 Dec 2011.

Edmonston, B. (2001). *Effects of census undercoverage on analyses of school enrollments: A case study of Portland public schools*. U.S. Census Monitoring Board, Report series report no. 05, February.

Goodkind, D. (2011). Child underreporting, fertility and sex ratio imbalance in China. *Demography, 48,* 291–316.

Hernandez, D., & Denton, N. (2001). Decennial Census Affects Children in Poverty, U.S. Decennial Census Monitoring Board, Presidential Members.

Martin, J. A., Hamilton, B. E., Ventura, S. J., et al. (2011). *Births: Final data for 2009*. National Vital Statistics System, Vol. 60, No. 1. Hyattsville, MD: National Center for Health Statistics.

O'Hare, W. P. (1999). *The overlooked undercount: Children missed in the decennial census*. Baltimore: The Annie E. Casey Foundation. Accessed 12 Dec 2011.

O'Hare, W. P. (2009). *Why are young children missed so often in the census*. KIDS COUNT working paper, December. http://www.aecf.org/~/media/Pubs/Other/W/WhoAreYoungChildrenMissedSoOftenintheCensus/final%20census%20undercount%20paper.pdf.

Ortman, J. M. (2012). *Estimating multiple-race births for the 2010 demographic analysis estimates*. Paper presented at the Applied Demography Conference, The University of Texas at San Antonio, San Antonio, TX.

Pitkin, J., & Park, J. (2005). *The gap between births and decennial census counts of children born in California: Undercount or transnational movement?* Paper presented at the Population Association of America Conference, Philadelphia, PA.

Price, D. O. (1947). A check on the underenumeration in the 1940 census. *American Sociological Review, 12,* 44–49.

Robinson, J. G. (2000). *Accuracy and coverage evaluation: Demographic analysis results*. U.S. Census Bureau, DSSD Census 2000 procedures for operations Memorandum Series B-4.

Robinson, J. G. (2010). *Coverage of population in census 2000 based on demographic analysis: The history behind the numbers*. Census Bureau working paper no. 91. http://www.census.gov/population/www/documentation/twps0091/twps0091.pdf.

Siegel, J. S., & Zelnik, M. (1966). An evaluation of coverage in the 1960 census of population by techniques of demographic analysis and by composite methods. In *Proceedings of the social statistics section of the American Statistical Association* (pp. 71–85). Washington, D.C.: American Statistical Association.

Statistics Canada. (2004). *2001 census technical report: Coverage*. Statistics Canada Catalogue no. 92-394-X. Ottawa, Ontario.

Statistics Canada. (2010). *2006 census technical report: Coverage*. Statistics Canada Catalogue no. 92-567-X Ottawa Ontario.

The Annie E. Casey Foundation. (2012). *Data snapshot on high poverty communities*. Baltimore: The Annie E. Casey Foundation. http://www.aecf.org/Newsroom/NewsReleases/HTML/2012Releases/DataSnapshotHig hPovertyCommunities.aspx. Accessed 5 Dec 2011.

U.S. Census Bureau. (2010). DA tables released at census bureau's December 6th, 2010 Conference. http://www.census.gov/coverage_measurement/demographic_analysis/.

U.S. Census Bureau. (2011). 2010 American Community Survey, Table B 06001. http://factfinder2.census.gov/faces/nav/jsf/pages/searchresults.xhtml?ref=top&refresh=t#none. (Available on Factfinder).

U.S. Office of Management and Budget (1997). *Revisions to the standards for the classification of federal data on race and ethnicity*. Statistical Policy Directive 15, Federal Register Notice October 30, 1997. http://www.whitehouse.gov/omb/fedreg_1997standards. Accessed 12 Dec 2011.

Wang, W. (2012). The rise of intermarriage, Pew Social and Demographic Trends, February, 16. http://pewresearch.org/pubs/2197/intermarriage-race-ethnicity-asians-whites-hispanics-Blacks. Accessed 12 Sept 2012.

West, K. (2012). *Using medicare enrollment file for the DA 2010 estimates*. Paper presented at the Applied Demography Conference at The University of Texas at San Antonio, Texas, January.

West, K., & Robinson, J. G. (1999). *What do we know about the undercount or children?* U.S. Census Bureau, Population Division working paper.

Zeller, A. (2006). *Inconsistency between accuracy and coverage evaluation revision II and demographic analysis estimates for children 0 to 9 years of age*. Paper delivered at the American Statistical Association annual conference, available in conference proceedings, p. 3201. http://www.amstat.org/sections/srms/Proceedings/y2006f.html. Accessed 12 Dec 2011.

Chapter 5
Mathematical Modeling and Projecting Population of Bangladesh by Age and Sex from 2002 to 2031

Md. Rafiqul Islam and M. Nazrul Hoque

Introduction

Census is the most important source of demographic data. However, most countries carry out their population census every 10 years. Public and private agencies use demographic data for different purposes and they need data for each and every year. Demographic data are also necessary to provide denominators to compute many types of rates and ratios, such as birth rates, death rates, school enrollment rates, labor force participation rates, dependency ratios, and sex ratios in non-census years. Demographic data play an important role in market analysis, public facility, and environmental planning and form a basis for determining the present and future markets for a variety of goods, services, and other aspects of private-sector planning and marketing efforts (Murdock and Ellis 1991). Demographic data are often critical elements in the analyses leading to city planning decisions of whether to build a new school, fire station, library, hospital, shopping mall, or highway (Siegel 2002). In order to achieve these goals, developed countries estimate their population in non-census years. In Bangladesh, the population census is carried out every 10 years. As far as we know, there are no population estimates in non-census years in Bangladesh. When there is no estimate, population projections can be used for current and future planning.

There are mainly two methods of carrying out population projections: the mathematical or trend extrapolation method and the cohort component method. The cohort component method is one of the most widely used techniques of

M. R. Islam (✉)
Department of Population Science and Human Resource Development,
University of Rajshahi, Rajshahi, Bangladesh
e-mail: rafique_pops@yahoo.com

M. N. Hoque
Hobby Center for Public Policy, University of Houston, Houston, TX, USA
e-mail: mnhoque@uh.edu

M. N. Hoque, L. B. Potter (eds.), *Emerging Techniques in Applied Demography,*
Applied Demography Series 4, DOI 10.1007/978-94-017-8990-5_5,

population projections in developed countries. In the cohort component method, the components of population change (fertility, mortality, and net migration) are projected separately for each birth cohort (persons born in a given year) and then combined to project the population. The base population is advanced each year by applying the projected survival rates by single years of age, sex, and race/ethnicity. Each year, net migration is computed by applying the net migration rates to each age, sex, and race/ethnicity cohort. Similarly, each year, a new birth cohort is computed by applying the projected fertility rates by age, sex, and race/ethnicity. However, cohort component projection techniques may not be appropriate for projecting the population of Bangladesh because computation and projection of fertility, mortality, and migration rates may not be possible due to a lack of vital statistics, namely births and deaths. A mathematical model may be more appropriate for projecting the population of Bangladesh because it needs minimum data (i.e., population counts for two time periods) and it assumes that the historical pattern of population change will apply to the future population change.

The main objective of this paper is to project population of Bangladesh by age and sex from 2002 to 2031 employing the exponential growth rate method so that the government and nongovernment agencies can use these data for short and long term planning.

This paper is divided into five sections. The introduction is included in the first section. The second section illustrates data and data sources of the study. Section three contains methods and various methodological issues in which data smoothing, model building, validation technique of model, F-test, and exponential growth rate method are described. Population projections by age and sex are presented in section four. The conclusions and concluding remarks of this study are given in section five

Data and Methods

To fulfill the objectives of this paper, the secondary data on population for male and female by 5 year age group have been obtained from the 1991 and 2001 censuses of Bangladesh (BBS 1993, 2003). These have been utilized as raw data in the present study and shown in Table 5.1. If the population of Bangladesh by age and sex is graphically plotted, it is observed that there is some sort of unexpected distortions in the data. It may be due to age heaping misreporting (i.e. tendency of the respondents to report certain ages at the expense of others). So, before going to fit the mathematical model to this data set, an adjustment is needed and important to mitigate these distortions. Therefore, an adjustment is made here using the Package Minitab Release 12.1 by the latest method of smoothing "4253H, twice" (Velleman 1980). Thereafter, the smoothed data are used to fit the mathematical model to population and these smoothed data have been provided in Table 5.1.

Table 5.1 Actual and smoothed population of Bangladesh by sex and age group in 1991 and 2001 and estimated growth rates between 1991 and 2001 (population in thousands)

1991					2001					
Age group	Actual		Smoothed		Actual		Smoothed		Annual growth rate	
	Male	Female	Male	Female	Male	Female	Male	Female	Male	Female
0–4	9,482	9,213	9,482	9,213	8,362	7,724	8,425	7,903	−0.0126	−0.0176
5–9	9,505	8,886	8,602	8,081	8,822	7,956	8,303	7,755	−0.0075	−0.0111
10–14	7,175	6,267	7,083	6,616	8,420	7,432	7,709	7,275	0.0160	0.0170
15–19	4,819	4,681	5,496	5,403	6,292	5,672	6,572	6,599	0.0267	0.0192
20–24	4,356	5,009	4,543	4,777	4,859	6,057	5,462	6,009	0.0109	0.0190
25–29	4,537	4,934	4,048	4,266	4,895	5,865	4,802	5,431	0.0076	0.0173
30–34	3,495	3,302	3,605	3,531	4,313	4,436	4,409	4,631	0.0210	0.0295
35–39	3,367	2,782	3,098	2,770	4,204	3,795	3,979	3,674	0.0222	0.0311
40–44	2,519	2,215	2,537	2,182	3,426	2,774	3,392	2,803	0.0308	0.0225
45–49	1,958	1,669	2,011	1,745	2,610	1,991	2,721	2,140	0.0287	0.0176
50–54	1,687	1,537	1,601	1,414	2,175	1,826	2,107	1,676	0.0254	0.0172
55–59	1,117	898	1,279	1,126	1,309	1,047	1,615	1,312	0.0159	0.0154
60–64	1,251	1,128	996	845	1,529	1,300	1,238	989	0.0201	0.0142
65–69	653	515	753	613	814	629	954	740	0.0220	0.0200
70–74	692	550	560	452	926	700	730	576	0.0291	0.0241
75–79	273	190	432	356	358	258	577	481	0.0271	0.0306
80+	430	365	379	325	581	496	525	452	0.0301	0.0307
Total	57,316	54,141	56,505	53,715	63,895	59,958	63,520	60,446	0.0109	0.0102

Model Building

Using the scatter plot of smoothed age structure of the population of Bangladesh by sex and age group, it appears that population is negatively exponentially distributed with respect to age. Therefore, a two-parameter negative exponential model is considered in this paper, and the mathematical configuration of the model is given below (Montgomery and Peck 1982):

$$y = e^{(-ax+b+u)}$$

Where x represents the middle value of the age group (in years); y represents the populations; a, b are unknown parameters; and u is the stochastic disturbance term of the model.

These models are fitted using the software STATISTICA. It is to be noted that other models, such as, Logistic, Gompertz, Makeham, linear, log linear, and semi-log linear, were also tried. but they seem to be worse fitted with respect to their coefficients of determination and corresponding shrinkage coefficients. For that reason, the findings of those models were not presented here.

Table 5.2 Information on model fittings and corresponding CVPP of these fitted models

Models	n	K	R^2	ρ^2_{cv}	Shrinkage	Parameters	*p*-value	Cal. F	Tab. F (at 1 % level)
1	17	1	0.97052	0.965	0.0062	a	0.0000	493.82	8.68 with
						b	0.0000		(1, 15) d.f.
2	17	1	0.94261	0.931	0.0121	a	0.0000	246.37	8.68 with
						b	0.0000		(1, 15) d.f.
3	17	1	0.96201	0.954	0.0079	a	0.0000	380.68	8.68 with
						b	0.0000		(1, 15) d.f.

Validation Technique of Model

To verify the validity of these models, the CVPP, ρ^2_{cv}, is applied. The mathematical formula for CVPP is known as:

$$\rho^2_{cv} = 1 - \frac{(n-1)(n-2)(n+1)}{n(n-k-1)(n-k-2)}\left(1 - R^2\right)$$

where n is the number of classes, k is the number of explanatory variables in the model, and the cross-validated R is the correlation between observed and predicted values of the dependent variable (Stevens 1996). The shrinkage of the model is equivalent to:

$$\left|\rho^2_{cv} - R^2\right|$$

where ρ^2_{cv} is CVPP and R^2 is the coefficient of determination in the model. Moreover, 1-shrinkage is the stability of R^2 of the model. The estimated CVPP analogous to their R^2 and information on model fittings are given in Table 5.2. It may be mentioned that CVPP was also employed as validation method by Islam (2003, 2004, 2007) and Islam et al. (2003, 2005).

F-test

To find out the measure of the overall significance level of the fitted models as well as the significance of R^2, the F-test is employed here. The F-test is given by

$$F = \frac{R^2/(l-1)}{(1-R^2)/(n-l)} \text{ with } (l-1,\ n-l) \text{ degrees of freedom (d.f.)}$$

where l = the number of parameters is to be estimated, n is the number of cases, and R^2 is the coefficient of determination of the model (Gujarati 1998).

Exponential Growth Rate Method

For the estimation of growth rate and projecting of population of Bangladesh, an exponential growth rate method is considered in this study and the mathematical form of this method is given by (Shryock et al. 1976):

$$P_{t_2}^{a-a+5} = P_{t_1}^{a-a+5} \exp\left\{r^{a-a+5}\left(t_2 - t_1\right)\right\} \tag{A}$$

where

$P_{t_1}^{a-a+5}$ is the predicted initial population at time t_1 in the age group a to a+5, $P_{t_2}^{a-a+5}$ is the predicted terminal population at time t_2 in the age group a to a+5, r^{a-a+5} is the intercensal annual growth rate in the age group a to a+5, and $\left(t_2 - t_1\right)$ is the time interval between intercensal period.

For the estimation of the annual growth rate, r^{a-a+5} is computed for different age groups from (A) as follows:

$$r^{a-a+5} = \frac{1}{\left(t_2 - t_1\right)} \ln\left(\frac{P_{t_2}^{a-a+5}}{P_{t_1}^{a-a+5}}\right) \tag{B}$$

Years 1991 and 2001 are considered as the initial and the terminal populations, respectively, in estimating the age specific intercensal annual growth rate by using Eq. (B). It should be mentioned here that the observed values for census 1991 and 2001 are used for the estimation of growth rate by age group. These estimated age specific intercensal annual exponential growth rates are presented in Table 5.1, and later these are used to project population for males and females of Bangladesh during the time interval 2002–2031.

Finally, the 2001 census population of Bangladesh by age and sex is considered as the base population, and the intercensal annual growth rate by age and sex during 1991–2001 obtained previously is used in this study, assuming fertility and mortality rates remaining constant during the projected period, are used to compute the projected population of Bangladesh by age and sex from 2002 to 2031. More specifically, the population of Bangladesh by age and sex is projected using Eq. (A) applying age specific growth rates to the 2001 base population by sex and age group from 2002 to 2031.

Results of Model Fittings and Discussion

The negative exponential model is assumed to fit the model to the population of Bangladesh in the 2001 census and the fitted models are presented in the following:

$$y = \exp(-0.02850x + 16.1319) \quad \text{for male} \tag{1}$$

t-stats (19.19726)(457.1148)

$$y = \exp(-0.02891x + 16.1027) \quad \text{for female} \tag{2}$$

t-stats (12.9477)(318.97)

$$y = \exp(-0.02869x + 16.8042) \quad \text{for both sexes} \tag{3}$$

t-stats (16.03024)(417.0224)

The information on model fittings and estimated CVPP, ρ^2_{cv}, corresponding to their R^2 of these models is shown in Table 5.2. From this table it appears that all the fitted models (1)–(3) are highly cross-validated and their shrinkages are 0.006193, 0.012053, and 0.007964, respectively. These imply that the fitted models (1)–(3) will be stable for more than 96, 93, and 95 %, respectively. Moreover, it is found that the parameters of the fitted model (1)–(3) are highly statistically significant with significance of variance explained. The stability for $R^2$of these models is more than 98 %.

The calculated values of F statistic for the models (1)–(3) are 493.82, 246.37, and 380.68, respectively, with (1, 15 d.f.), whereas the analogous tabulated values are only 8.68 at 1 % level of significance as is shown in Table 5.2. Therefore, from these statistics, it is seen that these models and their analogous R^2 values are highly statistically significant. Hence, the fits of these models are well suited to the data.

The base population and projected populations of Bangladesh by age and sex are presented in Table 5.3. Due to space limitation projected population data are provided for selected years. Single years projected population data can be obtained from the authors. Table 5.3 suggests that the major demographic pattern of the population of Bangladesh is downward in terms of age, but the population is increasing, i.e., upward trend with time during the projected period of 2002–2031. The projected populations of Bangladesh for both sexes can be obtained by adding the projected population of male and female by age group. The population of Bangladesh is projected to increase from 123.9 million in 2001 to 193.7 million in 2031, an increase of 56.39 % during the projection period. Male population will increase from 63.9 million in 2001 to 100.0 million in 2031, and female population will increase from 60.0 million in 2001 to 93.7 million in 2031, an increase of 56.47 and 56.3 %, respectively, during the projection period.

Conclusions and Concluding Remarks

In this study, it is observed that the age patterns of the population of Bangladesh in 2001 census follow a two-parameter negative exponential model. It is also observed that the age pattern of population is not smooth. Therefore, we smoothed the age distribution using Minitab software. We used an exponential growth rate method to project the population of Bangladesh by sex and age group from 2002 to 2031. It is

Table 5.3 Population in Bangladesh by sex and age group in 2001 and projected population by sex and age group from 2002 to 2030 (in thousands)

Age group	2001		2005		2010		2015		2020		2025		2030	
	Male	Female	Male	Female	Male	Female	Male	Female	Male	Female	Male	Female	Male	Female
0–4	8,362	7,724	7,952	7,198	7,468	6,591	7,013	6,035	6,586	5,526	6,184	5,059	5,808	4,633
5–9	8,822	7,956	8,563	7,612	8,249	7,203	7,947	6,815	7,657	6,449	7,376	6,102	7,106	5,774
10–14	8,420	7,432	8,977	7,957	9,724	8,665	10,534	9,436	11,412	10,275	12,362	11,190	13,392	12,185
15–19	6,292	5,672	7,000	6,125	7,999	6,742	9,140	7,422	10,444	8,169	11,934	8,993	13,636	9,899
20–24	4,859	6,057	5,076	6,535	5,361	7,186	5,662	7,903	5,980	8,690	6,316	9,556	6,671	10,508
25–29	4,895	5,865	5,046	6,285	5,241	6,852	5,444	7,471	5,655	8,145	5,874	8,880	6,101	9,682
30–34	4,313	4,436	4,692	4,992	5,212	5,786	5,790	6,706	6,431	7,773	7,145	9,010	7,937	10,443
35–39	4,204	3,795	4,594	4,297	5,134	5,019	5,737	5,861	6,410	6,846	7,163	7,996	8,003	9,339
40–44	3,426	2,774	3,874	3,035	4,518	3,397	5,270	3,801	6,145	4,254	7,167	4,761	8,358	5,328
45–49	2,610	1,991	2,928	2,137	3,381	2,334	3,903	2,549	4,506	2,784	5,203	3,041	6,007	3,321
50–54	2,175	1,826	2,408	1,956	2,734	2,132	3,104	2,324	3,525	2,533	4,002	2,761	4,544	3,010
55–59	1,309	1,047	1,395	1,113	1,510	1,202	1,634	1,298	1,769	1,402	1,915	1,513	2,074	1,634
60–64	1,529	1,300	1,657	1,376	1,832	1,477	2,025	1,586	2,239	1,702	2,475	1,828	2,736	1,962
65–69	814	629	889	681	993	753	1,108	832	1,237	920	1,381	1,016	1,542	1,123
70–74	926	700	1,040	771	1,204	870	1,392	981	1,611	1,107	1,863	1,249	2,155	1,409
75–79	358	258	399	292	457	340	523	396	599	461	686	538	786	627
80+	581	496	655	561	762	654	885	762	1,029	888	1,196	1,035	1,391	1,207
Total	63,895	59,956	67,145	62,922	71,777	67,201	77,112	72,178	83,235	77,925	90,243	84,527	98,247	92,082

expected that these population projections might be more useful for further research and can be useful in planning relating to socioeconomic, demographic, and health related issues by government and nongovernment organization. Furthermore, population projections are often used as a base for constructing other types of projections that are used for planning purposes, such as school enrollment projections, labor force projections, household projections, human services projection, projections of incidence of diseases/disorders, projections of consumer expenditures, and projections of health care personnel and costs. The Bangladesh government would be able to use the population projections as the base for computing other projections. Since there is no estimated population in non-census years in Bangladesh, these projections can be used as denominators for the estimation of various socio-economic, demographic, health related, and development indicators as well. Our projections suggest that the proportion of population that is 60 years of age or older is growing very fast and the government needs to target educational and disease prevention programs toward the needs of aging populations, namely health care.

References

Bangladesh Bureau of Statistics (BBS). (1993). *Bangladesh Population Census 1991*. National Report, Government of the People's Republic of Bangladesh, Dhaka.

Bangladesh Bureau of Statistics (BBS). (2003). *Bangladesh Population Census 2001*. National report, Government of the People's Republic of Bangladesh, Dhaka.

Gujarati, D. N. (1998). *Basic econometrics* (3rd ed.). New York: McGraw Hill, Inc.

Islam, Md. R. (2003). *Modeling of demographic parameters of Bangladesh—an empirical forecasing*. Unpublished Ph.D. Thesis, Rajshahi University.

Islam, Md. R. (2004). Indirect estimation of fertility parameters of Bangladesh. *Journal of Indian Anthropological Society, 39*(2), 195–202.

Islam, Md. R. (2007). Mathematical modeling of age specific marital fertility rates (ASMFRs) in rural area, Bangladesh. *Middle East Journal of Age and Ageing, 4*(4), 17–20.

Islam, Md. R., Islam, Md. N., Ali, Md. A., & Mostofa, Md. G. (2003). Construction of male life table from female widowed information of Bangladesh. *International Journal of Statistical Sciences, 2*, 69–82.

Islam, Md. R., Islam, Md. N., Ali, M. K., & Mondal, Md. N. I. (2005). Indirect estimation and mathematical modeling of some demographic parameters of Bangladesh. *The Oriental Anthropologist, 5*(2), 163–171.

Montgomery, D. C., & Peck, E. A. (1982). *Introduction to linear regression analysis*. New York: Wiley.

Murdock, S. H., & Ellis, D. (1991). *Applied demography: An introduction to basic concepts, methods, and data*. Boulder: Westview Press, Inc.

Shryock, H. S., Siegel J. S., & et al. (1976). *The methods and materials of demography*. New York: Academic Press, Inc.

Siegel, J. S. (2002). *Applied demography: Applications to business, government, law and public policy*. San Diego: Academic Press.

Stevens, J. (1996). *Applied multivariate statistics for the social sciences* (3rd ed.). New Jersey: Lawrence Erlbaum Associates, Inc.

Velleman, P. F. (1980). Definition and comparison of robust nonlinear data smoothing algorithms. *Journal of the American Statistical Association, 75*, 609–615.

Part II
Evaluation of Population Estimates Produced by New and Current Methods

Chapter 6
Sub-County Population Estimates Using Administrative Records: A Municipal-Level Case Study in New Mexico

Jack Baker, Adélamar Alcántara, Xiaomin Ruan, Daren Ruiz and Nathan Crouse

Introduction

The component method represents a long-standing alternative for estimating population change (Lotka 1956; Leslie 1945, 1948; Keyfitz and Caswell 2005; Sykes 1969; Shyrock and Siegel 1980; Smith et al. 2001; Bryan 2004). The method is accounting-based, typically relying in one form or another upon the capture of administrative data on the births, deaths, or migration events that constitute population change. The method is founded upon the well-known "population-balancing equation," which presents each of these components in a closed-form solution representing demographic change over a given time interval (Preston et al. 2003; Bryan 2004; Shyrock and Siegel 1980):

$$\textbf{Population Change} = \textbf{Births} - \textbf{Deaths} + \textbf{In-migration} - \textbf{Out-migration}$$

Provided that administrative data on each of these components of change are available, applications of the method may include either direct accounting of each component or formulation of rates of change for estimating population growth or decline over time (Shyrock and Siegel 1980; Bryan 2004; Keyfitz and Caswell 2005; Preston et al. 2003). While not always true (Smith and Lewis 1983; Smith and Mandell 1984; Smith and Cody 2013; Hoque 2010), it has been suggested that this method may out-perform alternatives because it measures population directly, rather than representing uncertain symptomatic indicators of growth or decline (Shyrock and Siegel 1980; Bryan 2004). In practice, the method may tend to be down-biased as its principal form of error will be inadequate surveillance (Shyrock and Siegel 1980; Preston et al. 2003; United Nations 1983). In spite of these limitations, the

J. Baker (✉) · A. Alcántara · X. Ruan · N. Crouse
Geospatial and Population Studies, University of New Mexico, Albuquerque, NM, USA
e-mail: gpsestimates@gmail.com

D. Ruiz
Bureau of Business and Economic Research, University of New Mexico,
Albuquerque, NM, USA

M. N. Hoque, L. B. Potter (eds.), *Emerging Techniques in Applied Demography*,
Applied Demography Series 4, DOI 10.1007/978-94-017-8990-5_6,

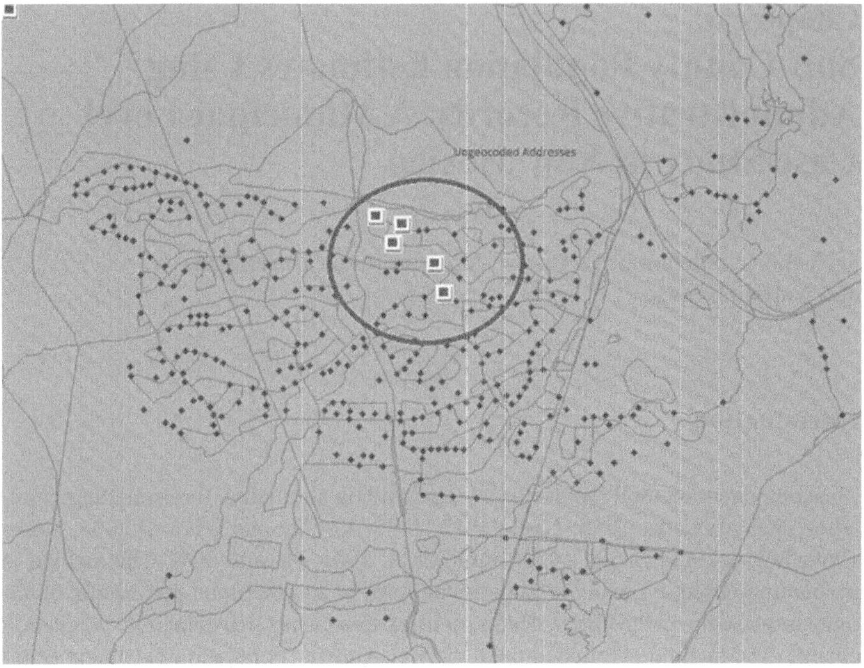

Fig. 6.1 Here, a handful of addresses within the area depicted exist and are contained within the address dataset used to make demographic estimates; however, they are ungeocoded and introduce bias into the estimation database

method is a robust and powerful procedure for modeling population change that has been widely utilized in a variety of settings (Shyrock and Siegel 1980; Preston et al. 2003; Keyfitz and Caswell 2005).

Until recently, applications of this method at the sub-county level have been challenged by a lack of available data on components of change at smaller geographic levels. Advancements in Geographic Information Systems (GIS) technology have reduced this limitation, however, opening the possibility of producing sub-county administrative records-based component estimates through geocoding of demographic data (Baker et al. 2012; Jarosz 2008; Swanson and Pol 2005; Bryan and George 2004). These positive developments have been complimented by the new availability of IRS tax return data at the zip-code level, which may allow small area estimation of net-migration. To date, we are unaware of research that has attempted to use these data directly in making small-area demographic estimates through the component method.

By far, the principal challenge in applying an ADREC-based procedure to estimating sub-county populations is incomplete geocoding of data on demographic events, which will negatively impact the accuracy of these estimates (Baker et al. 2012). At base, geocoding simply involves relating two strings of data representing an address—such as 1313 Mockingbird Lane—one of which contains spatial referencing information that permits its placement on an electronic map, as in Fig. 6.1

(Drummond 1995; Goldberg et al. 2007). Inherent limitations in this process of record matching means that at least some fraction of addresses in which demographic events occurred will fail to be referenced to electronic maps and associated with a set of municipal boundaries (Zandbergen 2009; Oliver 2005; Gilboa 2006; Baker et al. 2012). While some improvements are likely through remediation of address input data quality (misspellings, etc.) and the use of multiple computerized maps of road networks to improve overall coverage (Zandbergen 2009; Goldberg et al. 2007; Baker et al. 2012), it appears inevitable that at least some fraction of data will remain ungeocoded even after fairly intensive work. Previous studies have suggested that in urban areas, such as those that characterize the focus of this research, geocoding success rates will vary from as low as 75 % to as high as 90 % (Zandbergen 2009; Goldberg et al. 2007; Gilboa 2006; Oliver 2005). It is reasonable, therefore, to assume under-representation of between 10 and 25 % for a given component of change in any component estimate based on georeferenced data.

IRS tax return and exemption counts at the zip-code level are also subject to incompleteness. This incompleteness is not driven solely by geocoding issues (these data are reported in summary form by the IRS) or surveillance issues (Alcantara 1999) but by an incomplete series. In this research, tax return data were available only for a limited number of years (2002, 2004, 2005, 2006), requiring some form of remediation or imputation for missing years (2000, 2001, 2003, 2007–2010). With an inadequate length of this data series, time-series modeling of these data is out of the question and no other established methodology for dealing with such a data issue exists to our knowledge. This missing data issue is further complicated by the fact that IRS data at the zip-code level includes counts of returns and exemptions—not "migration flows" necessary to typical assessment of in and out-migration. As a final challenge, boundaries of zip-codes do not always coincide with municipal boundaries, introducing the necessity in some cases of "normalizing" zip-code level IRS data to municipal boundaries. Each of these limitations complicates the process of making sub-county municipal-level estimates using administrative records and must be addressed in this research.

This paper explores the use of these new forms of data for making sub-county total population estimates for municipalities in New Mexico, as well as estimates of demographic components of change (births, deaths, and net-migration). It addresses challenges introduced by incomplete vital records data, employing remediation procedures based on background research in geographic variation in geocoding success undertaken by the Geospatial and Population Studies unit at the University of New Mexico (described in Baker et al. 2012). It introduces the use of zip-code level IRS data for allocating county-level estimates of net-migration (available from the Census Bureau's Population Division: http://www.census.gov/popest/data/datasets.html). Though in this paper we focus on net-migration estimates, the Bureau's counts include information on migration from sources including the Internal Revenue Service, Medicare, and the American Community Survey (for net international migration). Additional challenges in geographic normalization of these estimates of net-migration from zip-codes to municipal boundaries are addressed and resolved using methods of spatial interpolation (Zandbergen and Ignizio 2010;

Voss et al. 1999; Flowerdrew and Green 1992; Tobler 1979). These data are used to make estimates of individual components of change (births, deaths, net-migration), which are aggregated to arrive at a sub-county ADREC-based component total population estimate series for the April 1, 2000, to April 1,2010, period. The April 1, 2010, estimates are evaluated against April 1, 2010,census counts using commonstatistical measures that capture aspects of accuracy, bias, and robustness (Tayman 1999; Smith and Sincich 1990; Smith 1987; Tayman et al. 1998)—which we consider as: (1) numerical closeness to Census 2010 counts, (2) the tendency of a set of estimates to be higher or lower than the census counts on average, and (3) the approximate standard deviation of errors about the 2010 census values across all municipalities. Results for this spatially remediated ADREC-based component estimate are compared to alternatives including holding the Census 2000 values constant, an "unremediated" ADREC-based estimate that does not attempt to correct for incomplete geocoding, and an April 1, 2010 vintage estimate using the Distributive Housing Unit Method (DHUM) published by the Census Bureau's Population Division (http://www.census.gov/popest/research/eval-estimates/eval-est2010.html#subcounty). The results are discussed in light of basic research in applied demography as well as with respect to methodological decisions about how to best estimate municipal-level populations in the post-2010 world.

Materials and Methods

Study Area: NM Characteristics

The population of New Mexico may serve as an important case study in population estimation methodologies. Its population comprises areas of recent, rapid growth as well as long-standing (sometimes on the order of hundreds to even thousands of years) "traditional" populations. New Mexico contains significant Native American tribal lands as well as historical Hispanic populations associated with the earliest Spanish colonial settlements and the *hacendado* and land grant systems (Esparza and Donelson 2008). This rural population is complemented by recent dramatic urban growth in the Albuquerque, Las Cruces, Santa Fe, and Farmington metro areas (to name a few) and the recent growth observed in New Mexico's *colonias* (Esparza and Donelson 2008). New Mexico's long-term population dynamics may be described as a mixture of these long-standing (and nearly stable) populations overlaid with recent, rapid growth in urban areas that is driven largely by positive net-migration. Certain parts of the state are also characterized by significant military (Clovis, Alamogordo) and student (Portales, Las Cruces, Albuquerque) populations. Together, these starkly contrasting sets of dynamics mean that much of the variation in success of population estimation methodologies, and the characteristics associated with this success, may be successfully studied within New Mexico.

The Component Method and Comparison Series

An accounting-based version of the component method was implemented in this study (Lotka 1956; Leslie 1945, 1948; Keyfitz and Caswell 2005; Shyrock and Siegel 1980; Bryan 2004). Address-level microdata on births and deaths were provided by the New Mexico Bureau of Vital Records. While these data are reported at the municipal level as summary counts, previous research by two independent agencies (Geospatial and Population Studies, University of New Mexico and the New Mexico Bureau of Vital Records) has suggested that self-reported municipal residence is over-reported, potentially biasing estimates of natural increase in unknown, and potentially unmeasurable, ways. Municipal-level estimates of births and deaths by year were based on geocoded input data, allocated to municipalities based on physical location using the methodology for geocoding described below. Estimates of net-migration were made using IRS tax exemption counts at the zip-code level, aggregated and normalized to municipal boundaries as necessary using the procedure also described below. The results included annual estimates of births, deaths, and net-migration. These were used to estimate a series, culminating in an April 1 Vintage estimate suitable for comparison with the 2010 census counts. Comparison sets were made that included: (1) a set based on holding the 2000 census values constant (after adjusting to 2010 boundaries), (2) a set ignoring spatial remediation of vital records inputs for incomplete geocoding, and (3) an April 1, 2010 vintage estimate of sub-county population made by the US Census Bureau using it's DHUM method (http://www.census.gov/popest/research/eval-estimates/eval-est2010.html#subcounty). The inclusion of sets 1 and 2 allows an evaluation of the marginal improvements associated with updating estimates at all since the previous census and that associated with spatial remediation for geocoding-based undercoverage in data on births and deaths. The third set allows a general comparison of how this alternative set of estimates might differ from the set issued by the Bureau during the last postcensal (2000–2010) series.

Database: Inputs, Georeferencing, and Remediation

Address-level microdata on births and deaths were geocoded to the street level using ESRI's Arc-GIS 9.3. These data were georeferenced through sequential presentation of addresses for geocoding to several electronic road network map files including (and in order of presentation): (1) vintage 2008 Dynamaps (Teleatlas) product (2) E911 road centerlines provided by the N.M. Division of Finance Administration (vintage 2010), (3) TIGER road networks from the U.S. Census Bureau (vintage 2010), and (4) local alternatives for specific jurisdictions (such as the City of Albuquerque or Las Cruces)—vintaged 2007–2010. At each step, only ungeocoded addresses remaining from the previous round were rematched. The successfully georeferenced addresses were located within zip-codes and zip-code level raising factors reflecting a 15,000,000 record experiment in geocoding conducted by GPS between 2008 and 2009 were used to "raise" the geocoded data, as reviewed in Baker et al. (2012). At the municipal level, these raising factors ([total addresses/ geocoded addresses]—(Horvitz and Thompson 1952; Popoff and Judson 2004) ranged from as low as 6.0% and as high as 23.0% (suggesting match rates overall between 77 and 94%, in line with that found in other studies—Zandbergen 2009).

IRS exemption counts were available at the zip-code level for years 2002, 2004, 2005, and 2006. These data did not provide information on "flows" of in and out migrants (which would permit a direct estimate of net-migration), so they were used simply to distribute the 2001–2009 postcensal county-level net-migration estimates from the U.S. Census Bureau (http://www.census.gov/popest/data/datasets.html) using the ratio: [(zip code exemptions/county exemptions)]. For years 2000, 2001, 2003, 2007–2010 (with years 2000 and 2010 fractioned at 0.25 to capture change only to April 1), an average of the ratios estimated for available years was used to complete the series. Since available data indicate that net-migration has been approximately stable throughout New Mexico during the recent recession, we do not anticipate the recession to bias our estimates. In cases where zip-code boundaries were not congruent with those of municipalities, a variant of the two-dimensional overlay method of areal interpolation was utilized (Flowerdrew and Green 1992; Zandbergen and Ignizio 2010; Tobler 1979; Voss et al. 1999). Specifically, in cases of intersection between zip-codes and municipal boundaries, the zip-code counts were allocated as "in" or "out" of the municipality based on the proportion of housing units in the area of intersection relative to the entire zip-code. Conceptually, this potentially improves upon straight two-dimensional areal interpolation by the use of ancillary data on housing density (Voss et al. 1999; Zandbergen and Ignizio 2010). As an upper-bound to potential distortions introduced by this method, Zandbergen and Ignizio (2010) working with 2010 census data at the *block group level* report a median overall error of 46.7% using simple areal weighting. These researchers compared a number of methods based on use of ancillary data, all of which substantially reduced the error associated with these estimates, most often in the range between 15.0 and 21.0%. It is well known that the transfer of data from smaller boundaries to larger ones (as in zip-codes to municipalities) introduces rather small amounts of error (Fisher and Langford 1995; Sadahiro 2000), while normalizing data from larger to smaller areas introduces much greater amounts of error (Simpson 2002). This previous research suggests that in this study we should anticipate errors that are much smaller in magnitude and proportional only to the amount of population added based on zip-code level estimates of net-migration. Since only 15 zip-codes required such normalization, and this normalization only affected estimates of net-migration, we anticipate the error associated with geographic normalization to be minimal.

Evaluating Estimates

Evaluation of estimates is accomplished primarily by descriptive comparisons between the April 1, 2010, vintage municipal estimates made using the ADREC component method and the April 1, 2010, census counts published in the Summary

Table 6.1 Evaluation measures

Error measure	Abbreviation	Concept captured
Mean absolute error	MAE	Low average error
Mean absolute percentage error	MAPE	Low average relative error
Mean algebraic error	MAIgE	Bias, both direction and magnitude
Mean algebraic percentage error	MALPE	
Percent > 5 % error	*	Low relative extreme errors
Percent > 10 % error	*	
Root mean squared error or deviation (numeric and percentage)	RMSE	Robusticity of the method across diverse geographies

* NA

File 1 data. While such *ex post-facto* evaluation strategies are the standard in applied demography (Tayman 1999; Smith and Sincich 1990; Smith 1987; Tayman et al. 1998), a number of researchers have highlighted the importance of considering net coverage errors in assessing the accuracy of a census itself when making comparisons and associated inferences (Fellegi 1968; Hogan 1992, 1993, 2004). From this perspective, bare comparisons between estimates and census counts ignore net-coverage errors associated with both the estimates base (in this case 2000) and the terminal estimate evaluated against the census (2010 in this study). In this case, estimates of net coverage for either the 2000 or 2010 censuses are unavailable at the municipal level, introducing a limitation to the proposed comparisons. While this criticism applies to the numeric accuracy of estimates of discrepancies between census values and population estimates, it remains true that these errors are constant across each method evaluated (errors on the census side do not change), and though this unmeasured variation may bias the overall magnitude of comparisons, it is not expected to bias the between-method comparisons that are the focus of this study.

With these caveats in mind, we compare each set of estimates against the April 1, 2010, municipal-level census counts. We make these comparisons following the suggestions of Cavanaugh (1981) that a successful population estimate will be characterized by low average errors, low average relative errors (after correcting for size-related differences across the set), few extreme relative errors, and an absence of bias for any specific population sub-group. Here, we quantify each of Cavanaugh's considerations using a specific measure of discrepancy (see Table 6.1). Low average error and low average relative error are considered using mean absolute error (MAE) and mean absolute percentage error (MAPE). Percentage errors become necessary because larger municipalities will have larger errors due to size alone; scaling them to a percentage measure facilitates comparisons between disparately-sized municipalities (Smith et al. 2001; Bryan 2004). Bias is assessed, both in absolute numeric terms and in percentage terms using the well-known mean algebraic numeric (MalgE) and percentage errors (MALPE) (Tayman 1999; Smith and Sincich 1990; Smith 1987; Tayman et al. 1998). Standard evaluation measures pursued in this research also include use of the Root Mean Squared Error (RMSE–Levinson 1947; Abraham and Ledolter 1983) measured in both numeric and percentage terms, as providing information on the robustness of the estimation method. In particular,

Table 6.2 Characteristics tested for association with error

Predictor	Data source
Municipal characteristics	
Size	Census 2000 and 2010
Greater than 50K in 2000	Census 2000
Over 20 % change 2000–2010	Census 2000 and 2010
Over 20 % loss 2000–2010	Census 2000 and 2010
Demographic characteristics	
Median age	Census 2010
Proportion Hispanic	Census 2010
Proportion college graduates	ACS, 2005–2009
Economic characteristics	
Proportion in poverty	ACS, 2005–2009
Proportion employed	ACS, 2005–2009
Proportion same house 1 year ago	ACS, 2005–2009
Median income	ACS, 2005–2009
Housing characteristics	
Commute less than 5 min	ACS, 2005–2009
Commute 5 to 10 min	ACS, 2005–2009
Commute 10 to 15 min	ACS, 2005–2009
Commute 15 to 20 min	ACS, 2005–2009
Commute 20 to 25 min	ACS, 2005–2009
Commute 25 to 30 min	ACS, 2005–2009
Commute greater than 30 min	ACS, 2005–2009
Proportion houses occupied	ACS, 2005–2009
Proportion houses owned	ACS, 2005–2009
Proportion of houses mobile homes	ACS, 2005–2009
Proportion of houses with mortgage	ACS, 2005–2009
Proportion houses built post 2005	ACS, 2005–2009
Proportion houses built pre 1950	ACS, 2005–2009

the RMSE is treated as a measure of how well the estimate set does across diverse types of municipalities included in this study. Finally, estimates of the effect of population estimation errors on specific sub-groups of municipalities are assessed using linear regression (Belsley et al. 1980; Neter et al. 1999). Summary comparisons were made using graphical charts and followed up analytically by regressing individual algebraic percentage errors (approximately normallydistributed and suitable for use in regression analysis) on a variety of municipal-level characteristics, each of which is listed, along with the data source from which it was drawn, in Table 6.2.

Marginal improvements associated with increasing levels of effort were also evaluated in this study. Hogan (2013, in this volume) has suggested that such an assessment might best be accomplished by dividing the error associated with the estimate set in question by the error associated with holding the 2000 census values constant. Here, we apply this suggestion in a slightly different manner by subtracting the percentage error associated with a given estimate from that associated with the Census 2000-constant series. This allows an intuitive residual of percentage

Table 6.3 Results for sub-county ADREC and alternative procedures (all cities, $n = 103$)

Method	Mean algebraic total error	Mean absolute total error	Mean algebraic percentage error	Mean absolute percentage error	Error >5%	Error >10%	Root mean squared error	Root Mean squared error (percents)	Marginal improvement (percentage points)
Census 2000	−1,881	2,110	0	12.19	71	46	10,544	16.42	*
ADREC No	−607	1,174	−7	13.59	79	51	5,364	17.95	1.40
ADREC Spatial	−653	1,189	−6	13.44	78	51	5,489	17.67	1.25
USCB DHUM	−152	561	2.52	10.37	58	31	1738	17.33	−1.82

* NA

points to be reported, quantifying the improvements associated with the sub-county ADREC-based estimates as well as the sub-county evaluation 2000–2010 estimates set released by the U.S. Census Bureau in February 2013. In the same vein, we also make comparisons between an unremediated ADREC-based component set (one subject to complete geocoding-based undercoverage) and the final set that incorporates remediation of incomplete geocoding (Baker et al. 2012).

Results

The results of this research (Tables 6.3 and 6.4) suggest complexity in the relationships observed between methodological choice and measures of estimation accuracy, bias, and robustness. When all 103 municipalities within the state are considered, the most accurate estimate set on average is, surprisingly, *holding the 2000 Census constant* (MAPE = 12.19%). An unremediated ADREC method (without adjustment for incomplete data) displayed a MAPE of 13.59%, and remediation of incomplete data on vital records did little to improve this at the municipal level (MAPE = 13.44%). The 2001–2010 DHUM evaluation estimates from the Census Bureau were significantly more accurate on average than ADREC-based alternatives (MAPE = 10.37%). The 2001–2010 DHUM estimates from the Census Bureau were also the least-biased alternative to a Census 2000 constant estimate, tending to slightly overestimate population (MALPE = 2.52%). The average marginal improvement over simply holding the 2000 census constant was positive for all estimates reported here (suggesting that error is actually increased on average) with the exception of the Census Bureau's DHUM-based evaluation estimates set. This last estimate reduced the overall error in the estimates by nearly two percentage points (MI = −1.82%) compared to the Census 2000 constant estimate. This

Table 6.4 Results for sub-county ADREC and alternative procedures (growth centers only: Albuquerque, Farmington, Las Cruces, Rio Rancho, Santa Fe, $n = 5$)

Method	Mean algebraic total error	Mean absolute total error	Mean algebraic percentage error	Mea mean absolute percentage error	Error >5%	Error >10%	Root mean squared error	Root mean squared error (percents)	Marginal improvement (percentage points)
Census 2000	−33,677	33,677	−21.29	21.29	5	4	47,362	24.11	*
ADREC No	−15,860	16,705	−8.66	9.90	4	2	23,910	16.36	−11.39
ADREC Spatial	−19,926	20,708	−10.17	11.32	4	2	24,494	16.48	−9.97
USCB DHUM	−2,001	5,659	0.40	4.99	1	1	7,386	6.70	−17.41

* NA

increase in accuracy may come at the cost of bias, however, as the DHUM-based evaluation estimate displayed a positive MALPE of 2.52 %.

The RMSE for each set of estimates suggests that the DHUM-based evaluation estimates were approximately equally robust as either of the ADREC estimates (remediated or not), or the strategy of holding the Census 2000 values constant. RMSE (in percents) were approximately equivalent for the ADREC alternatives (17.95 % and 17.67 %) and comparable to that associated with holding Census 2000 values constant (RMSE = 16.42 %), and the DHUM-based evaluation set returned an RMSE of 17.33 %. In absolute numeric terms, the same similarity was observed between the ADREC-based alternatives (5,364 and 4,489 for unremediated and remediated estimates), but were substantially lower for the DHUM-based evaluation estimates (RMSE = 1,738). In percentage terms, the RMSE for the DHUM-based evaluation estimates was the lowest of the non-Census 2000 alternatives, at 17.33 %. A relatively low numeric RMSE and a similar percentage-based RMSE suggested that the DHUM-based evaluation estimates might be less precise for smaller municipalities where numeric errors would be smaller in absolute terms but higher in percentage terms.

The results presented so far suggested that further comparisons between the ADREC-based methods and the Bureau's current housing-unit based methodology might be merited, more specifically by restricting comparisons to more rapidly growing municipalities where size and change-related effects were observed (Tables 6.5 and 6.6). We computed summary measures of error, bias, and precision for our five most dynamic municipalities (Albuquerque, Farmington, Las Cruces, Rio Rancho, and Santa Fe). Table 6.4 reports these results, which suggest that the ADREC-based methods might perform less well in these municipalities, while the DHUM-based evaluation estimates were observed to be much more accurate and robust than any other alternative considered. Errors for the ADREC-based estimates were between 9.90 % and 11.32 % (actually worse for the spatially remediated vari-

Table 6.5 Spatially-remediated ADREC estimates: Errors by size of municipality

Municipality size	Mean algebraic total error	Mean absolute total error	Mean algebraic percentage error	Mean absolute percentage error	Root mean squared error	Root mean squared error (percents)
< 1,000	−59	73	−11.43	21.80	128	27.42
1K–5K	−136	257	−8.92	13.61	348	17.23
5K–10K	−201	574	−2.90	7.96	632	8.88
10K–20K	−754	1,012	−5.89	7.81	1,220	9.21
20K–50K	−2,240	2,300	−7.80	7.98	3,477	11.68
50K+	−26,557	29,272	26.82	31.20	49,358	71.23

Table 6.6 Spatially-remediated ADREC estimates: Errors by percent change of municipality

Municipality size	Mean algebraic total error	Mean absolute total error	Mean algebraic percentage error	Mean absolute percentage error	Root mean squared error	Root mean squared error (percents)
>20 Loss	−56	56	28.06	28.06	1,319	23.68
10 to 20 Loss	−604	604	18.89	18.89	680	17.40
0 to 10 Loss	−463	478	10.81	12.48	1,230	10.04
0 to 10 Gain	42	360	−3.63	5.77	473	6.53
10 to 20 Gain	9,907	9,907	−10.45	10.45	16,982	11.29
>20 Gain	3,001	3,001	−30.31	30.31	7,020	38.12

ant), but were less than five percent (MAPE = 4.99 %) for the Bureau's DHUM-based evaluation estimates. Bias was similarly negative for all of the methods except for the which was only slightly positively biased (MALPE = 0.40 %). The DHUM-based estimates were only greater than 5 % and 10 % in one case (the City of Santa Fe, where the error was + 13.50 %), suggesting fewer relative extreme errors in this sub-set of municipalities as well. The RMSE of 7,386 persons or 6.70 % was approximately one-third to one-eighth of that observed in the Census 2000 constant or either the unremediated or remediated ADREC-based estimates. The results clearly suggest that utilizing a DHUM method in these rapidly growing municipalities makes for a more accurate, less biased, and more robust set of estimates. Using the ADREC-based estimates resulted in reductions in error (compared to holding the Census 2000 constant) of 9.97 (remediated) to 11.39 (unremediated) percent; however, using the DHUM estimate resulted in a marginal improvement of nearly 20 % (MI = 17.41 %).

Regression of percentage errors (signed) for the spatially remediated ADREC and the DHUM estimates on the set of municipal, demographic, socioeconomic, and housing characteristics listed in Table 6.2 suggested few statistically significant associations. A notable exception was an increase in error in association with the proportion of the population living in poverty in the ADREC-based estimate. For each one percent increase in this proportion, the estimation error was suggested to increase by nearly one-fouth percent in the spatially remediated ADREC method

(Beta = 0.2498, p = 0.0207). No other demographic, socioeconomic, or housing characteristic was significantly associated with the magnitude of error in the spatially remediated ADREC estimate. Similar results characterize the regression focused upon the extrapolated DHUM estimate, where a nearly 1.0 % (Beta = −0.8769, p = 0.002) decrease in error was associated with a 1.0 % increase in the proportion of housing built prior to 1950. This may reflect the importance of stability in housing stock in driving estimation accuracy in a method that relies upon this data source in its estimating procedure (Brown 2008; Baer 1990; Smith and Lewis 1983; Bryan 2004).

Discussion

The objectives of this research have been to provide basic background on the potential of making sub-county (municipal) population estimates using administrative records to estimate components of change and to inform methodological decision-making by the U.S. Census Bureau's Population Division. Currently, the Bureau makes sub-county estimates using its Distributive Housing Unit Method (http://www.census.gov/popest/methodology/index.html; Swanson and McKibben 2010; Harper et al. 2003) in which the share of housing unit stock (weighted by the average persons per household and occupancy rates from the previous census) are used to "share-out" county household population estimates, with the resulting estimate augmented by data on Group Quarters. While previous research has suggested this method is acceptably accurate (Harper et al. 2003), similar to the results reported here for the Bureau's 2001–2010 DHUM-based evaluation estimates for sub-county areas released in February 2013, it does not provide a mechanism for estimating components of population change such as births, deaths, and net-migration. This limitation has motivated the current effort, which suggests that on average, a sub-county ADREC-based method is feasible but may come at the cost of reduced accuracy, increased bias, and less overall robustness. The results, however, also suggest that, with further methodological development aimed especially at more rapidlychanging municipalities, an ADREC-based estimate might be tuned to match the performance of the Bureau's current method. The results of this study are likely to hold true in many Western states characterized by increasing urbanization coupled with lingering regional centers of long-term growth (an example in New Mexico would be the well-known City of Roswell). This study encompasses a wide range of diverse types of municipalities, ranging between the military "base-towns" of Clovis and Alamogordo, to sprawling and rapidly-growing suburban areas such as the City of Rio Rancho, to municipalities with highly-concentrated student populations (the cities of Portales, Las Vegas, Las Cruces, and Albuquerque) and newly-incorporated *colonias* such as Sunland Park. This diversity suggests that the results of this study may be of broader applicability, though this study was not specifically designed to center upon a nationallyrepresentative sample of municipalities or to draw general nationwide inferences.

Table 6.7 Regression Results: Statistically Significant Associations with Percentage Error

Predictor		Coefficient (p-value)
	Municipal characteristics	
Size	n.s.	
Greater than 50K in 2000	n.s.	
Over 20 % Change 2000–2010		*0.090298 (0.017)*
Over 20 % Loss 2000–2010		*0.19632 (0.001)*
	Demographic characteristics	
Median age	n.s.	
Proportion Hispanic	n.s.	
Proportion college graduates	n.s.	
	Economic characteristics	
Proportion in poverty		*0.2427 (0.051)*
Proportion employed	n.s.	
Proportion same house 1 year ago	n.s.	
Median income	n.s.	
	Housing characteristics	
Commute less than 5 min	n.s.	
Commute 5 to 10 min	n.s.	
Commute 10 to 15 min	n.s.	
Commute 15 to 20 min	n.s.	
Commute 20 to 25 min	n.s.	
Commute 25 to 30 min	n.s.	
Commute greater than 30 minutes	n.s.	
Proportion houses occupied	n.s.	
Proportion houses owned	n.s.	
Proportion of houses mobile homes	n.s.	
Proportion of houses with mortgage	n.s.	
Proportion houses built post 2005	n.s.	
Proportion houses built pre 1950	n.s.	

While the results suggest that ADREC-based municipal estimates may not systematically misestimate specific sub-groups of the overall population (with the potential exception of the poor, see Table 6.7), a significant limitation of this study is an inability to estimate the accuracy, bias, or robustness of any individual estimate of a component of change (birth, death, or net migration) in a direct sense. In the absence of any type of "gold-standard" for *ex post facto* comparisons, the contribution of mis-estimation in any component to overall estimation errors will remain unclear. This inevitable uncertainty will continue to pose a challenge to research on sub-county estimation using the component method; however, a simple sensitivity analysis of how updating estimates of each component over time contributes to reductions in estimation error provides some useful insights. Table 6.8 presents the results of a follow-up analysis in which the marginal reduction in errors associated with estimating each component of change—proceeding from a model based on births alone, to one including deaths, and then one encompassing estimates of net-migration—is estimated. Estimating only births actually *increases* error in esti-

Table 6.8 Effect on estimate accuracy by component estimated

Estimate or component	Mean absolute percentage error	Root mean squared error (percents)	Marginal improvement (percentage points)
Census 2000 constant	12.19	16.42	*
Births only	18.08	24.05	−5.89
Births and deaths	12.41	16.90	5.67
Births, deaths, & net-migration	13.44	17.67	−1.03

* NA

mates and reduces their robustness. A births-only estimation model would increase the MAPE to over 18.00%, compared to 12.19% using the Census 2000 values only. The RMSE would be observed to swell to over 24.00% in this model. Including deaths in the estimate drastically reduces the average errors back to 12.41% (MAPE) while also reducing the RMSE to 16.90%, comparable to the 16.42% observed in the Census 2000 constant model as well as its 12.19% error. Including net-migration comes at a minor cost to accuracy and robustness (MAPE = −13.44% and RMSE = 17.67%), but allows estimation of components of change within a largely accurate and generally precise model. While this model is approximately 3.0% less accurate on average to the DHUM-based evaluation estimates, a focus on reducing error in large and quicklychanging municipalities could close this gap with a method that provides component of change estimates.

The performance of the sub-county ADREC-based component estimates reported in this research is best considered in light of previously reported research on municipal-level estimation. First, Harper et al. (2003) report similar accuracy in evaluating April 1, 2000, sub-county DHUM-based estimates, with MAPEs ranging between a high of 35.1% in the smallest municipalities (< 100—see their Table 6.1) to a low of only 4.0% in those between 50K and 100K persons. Errors in municipalities over 100K are slightly higher (4.3%). This linear reduction in error as population size increases was not observed in evaluating the sub-county ADREC method described here, where size-related errors display a u-shaped distribution (Tables 6.5 and 6.6); however, the final overall accuracy of 12.40% in that study is comparable to the MAPEs reported here for both ADREC (remediated or not) as well as the Bureau's 2001–2010 DHUM-based evaluation estimates. From this perspective, the sub-county estimates presented here are similarly accurate to those reported in previous Census Bureau evaluations of estimates error at the municipal level. In contrast, all of the estimates reported here were substantially less accurate than estimates made using the component or housing unit methods in Texas (Hoque 2010–1990 Vintage) or Florida (Smith and Cody 2013–2010 Vintage). They are similar, however, to those reported previously for Florida using the HUM in comparison to the results of special censuses conducted in the state (Smith and Lewis 1983). It remains unclear why New Mexico estimates appear to have greater errors than those reported in studies in Texas and Florida, but it is likely that these discrepancies relate to subtle issues of surveillance within the state. For example, Alcantara (1999) has suggested that IRS tax records may under-report migration in general due to undercoverage in this data source that she argued to be linked to poverty (and a need to either not file tax returns due to low income or in an attempt to evade taxation) and a high proportion of migration that remains undocumented in tax records (Alcantara 1999).

While the results of this study suggest that a sub-county ADREC-based component estimate represents a feasible alternative with relatively accurate and robust estimation capabilities, a large part of the decision to implement and use the procedure in the Census Bureau's official estimates will depend on the perceived importance of estimating components of population change. A housing unit-based estimate is less data intensive, requiring no electronic address matching or specific remediation procedures associated with incomplete geocoding. To implement the method described here, a zip-code level database on geocoding success (certainly possible using the Bureau's Master Address File—see Swanson and McKibben 2010) would be required to develop remediation factors for adjusting geocoding-based estimates of births and deaths. The current method is suggested to be more accurate than an ADREC-based alternative—though potentially less robust—raising the question about whether the benefits associated with such a series would indicate a cost-offset. The ADREC-based method appears to struggle in rapidly changing areas, suggesting that further methodological attention in these areas specifically may be required.

In spite of these challenges, the research reported here commends further investigation of the potential for making sub-county ADREC-based population estimates. The results here mirror those of other studies in terms of relationships between size and estimation accuracy, robustness, and bias (Hoque 2010; Harper et al. 2003; Smith and Mandell 1984; Smith and Cody 2013, suggesting that the challenges associated with making sub-county estimates using administrative records are far from insurmountable. If progress can be made in improving the performance of a sub-county ADREC-based estimate in larger municipalities and those which are changing rapidly, then the method may prove to provide a high quality alternative with an added advantage of including estimates of components of population change. Acceptable versions of weighted estimates may accomplish these objectives and suggest new avenues for the Census Bureau and other agencies involved in estimating sub-county populations.

Acknowledgements This research was funded in part by support from the U.S. Census Bureau, RFQ 10-002245RT (Services to Support 2010 Postcensal Estimates Program). The paper was greatly improved by the comments of Howard Hogan, Chief Demographer of the U.S. Census Bureau, and Paul Zandbergen, Associate Professor of Geography at the University of New Mexico. The paper also benefitted greatly from the comments of two anonymous referees. Ongoing suggestions from colleagues including Stan Smith, David Swanson, Nazrul Hoque, Mohammed Shahidullah, Eddie Hunsinger, Jan Vink, Webb Sprague, Qian Tsai, Jeff Hardcastle, RisaProehl, Matt Hesser, Susan Strate, Nicholas Nagle, Joe Francis, Warren Brown, Ken Hodges and others were valued. Ongoing and numerous comments, insights, and suggestions on population estimates research were provided by members of the Federal State Cooperative Program on Population Estimates and by Census Bureau staff especially including Jason Devine, Victoria Velkoff, Tiffany Yowell, and Rodger Johnson.

References

Abraham, B., & Ledolter, J. (1983). *Statistical methods for forecasting*. New York: Wiley.

Alcantara, A. (1999). *Assessment of IRS tax returns migration coverage in New Mexico*. Paper presented the Estimates Methods Conference, U. S. Bureau of the Census, Suitland.

Baer, W. C. (1990). Aging of the housing stock and components of inventory change. In D. Myers (Ed.), *Housing demography: Linking demographic structure and housing markets* (pp. 249–273). Madison: University of Wisconsin.

Baker, J., Alcantara, A., Ruan, X. M., & Watkins, K. (2012).The impact of incomplete geocoding on small area population estimates. *Journal of Population Research, 29,* 91–112.

Belsley, D. A., Kuh, E., & Welch, R. (1980). *Regression diagnostics: Identifying influential data and sources of colinearity*. New York: Wiley.

Brown, W. (2008). *Changes to the housing unit stock: Loss of housing units*. Presentation at the New York State Data Center Affiliate Meeting. May 15, 2008. New York: West Point.

Bryan, T. (2004). Population estimates. In J. Siegel & D. Swanson (Ed.), *The Methods and materials of demography*. New York: Springer.

Bryan, T., & George, M. V. (2004). GIS. In J. Siegel & D. Swanson (Ed.), *The methods and materials of demography*. New York: Springer.

Cavanaugh, F. (1981). The Census Bureau's 1980 census test of population estimates. In: *Small-area population estimates-methods and their accuracy and new metropolitan area definitions and their impact on the private and public sector*. Series GE-41, No. 7. Washington, D.C.: Government Planning Office.

Drummond, W. J. (1995). Address matching: GIS technology for mapping human activity patterns. *Journal of the American Planning Association, 61*(2), 240–251.

Esparza, A., & Donelson, A. (2008). *Colonias in Arizona and New Mexico: Border poverty and community development solutions*. Tucson: University of Arizona Press.

Fellegi, I. P. (1968). *Coverage check of the 1961 census of population*. Technical memorandum (Census Evaluation Series). No. 2, Dominion Bureau of Statistics.

Fisher, P. F., & Langford, M. (1995). Modeling the errors in areal interpolation between zonal systems using monte carlo simulation. *Environment and Planning A, 27,* 212–214.

Flowerdrew, R., & Green, M. (1992). Developments in areal interpolation methods and GIS. *The Annals of Regional Science, 26,* 67–78.

Gilboa, S. M. (2006). Comparison of residential geocoding methods in a population-based study of air quality and birth defects. *Environmental Research, 101,* 256–262.

Goldberg, D. W., Wilson, J. P., & Knoblock, C. A. (2007). From text to geographic coordinates: The current state of geocoding. *URISA Journal, 19*(1), 33–46.

Harper, G., Coleman, C., & Devine, J. (2003). Evaluation of 2000 subcounty population estimates. Population Estimates Branch, Population Division. U.S. Census Bureau.

Hogan, H. (1992). The 1990 post-enumeration survey: An overview. *The American Statistician, 46,* 261–269.

Hogan, H. (1993). The 1990 post-enumeration survey: Operations and results. *Journal of the American Statistical Association, 88,* 1047–1060.

Hogan, H. (2003). The accuracy and coverage evaluation: Theory and design. *Survey Methodology, 29*(2), 129–138.

Hoque, N. (2010). An evaluation of small area population estimates produced by component method II, ratio correlation, and housing unit methods for 1990. *The Open Demography Journal, 3,* 18–30.

Horvitz, D. G., & Thompson, D. J. (1952). A generalization of sampling without replacement from a finite universe. *Journal of the American Statistical Association, 47,* 663–685.

Jarosz, B. (2008). Using assessor parcel data to maintain housing unit counts for small area population estimates. In S. Murdock & D. Swanson (Ed.), *Applied demography in the 21st century* (pp. 89–101). New York: Springer.

Keyfitz, N., & Caswell, H. (2005). *Applied mathematical demography* (2nd ed.). New York: Springer.

Leslie, P. (1945). The use of matrices in certain population mathematics. *Biometrika, 33*(3), 183–212.
Leslie, P. (1948). Some further notes on the use of matrices in population mathematics. *Biometrika, 35*(3–4), 213–245.
Levinson, N. (1947). The wiener RMS (root mean square) error criteria for filter design and prediction. *Journal of Mathematical Physics, 25,* 261–278.
Lotka, A. J. (1956). *Elements of mathematical biology*. New York: Dover.
Neter, J., Kutner, M., Wasserman, M., & Nachtshem, C. (1999). *Applied linear statistical models* (4th ed.). New York: McGraw-Hill.
Oliver, M. N. (2005). Geographic bias related to geocoding in epidemiologic Studies. *International Journal of Health Geographics, 4*(29), Online.
Popoff, C., & Judson, D. (2004). Selected general methods. In J. S. Siegel & D. Swanson (Ed.), *The methods and materials of demography*.(2nd ed., pp. 644–675). New York: Springer.
Preston, S., Hueverline, P., & Guillot, M. (2003). *Demography: Measuring and modeling population processes*. New York: McGraw Hill.
Sadahiro, Y. (2000). Accuracy of count data transferred through the areal weighting interpolation method. *International Journal of Geographical Information Science, 14,* 25–50.
Shyrock, H., & Siegel, J. (1980). *The methods and materials of demography* (Vol. II). Washington, D.C.: U.S. Bureau of the Census.
Simpson, L. (2002). Geography conversion tables: A framework for conversion of data between geographical units. *International Journal of Population Geography, 8,* 69–82.
Smith, S. (1987). Tests of forecast accuracy and bias for county population projections. *Journal of the American Statistical Association, 82*(400), 991–1003.
Smith, S., & Cody, S. (2013). Making the housing unit method work: An evaluation of 2010 population estimates in florida. *Population Research and Policy Review, 32*(2), 221–242.
Smith, S., & Lewis, B. (1983). Some new techniques for applying the housing unit method of local population estimation: Further evidence. *Demography, 20*(3), 407–413.
Smith, S., & Mandell, M. (1984). A comparison of population estimation methods: Housing unit versus component II, ratio correlation, and administrative records. *Journal of the American Statistical Association, 79*(386), 282–289.
Smith, S., & Sincich, T. (1990). The relationship between length of the base period and population forecast errors. *Journal of the American Statistical Association, 85*(410), 367–375.
Smith, S., Tayman, J., & Swanson, D. (2001). *State and local population projections: Methodology and analysis*. New York: Plenum.
Swanson, D., & McKibben, J. (2010). New directions in the development of population estimates in the United States. *Population Research and Policy Review, 29*(6), 797–818.
Swanson, D., & Pol, L. (2005). Contemporary developments in applied demography within the United States. *Journal of Applied Sociology, 21*(2), 26–56.
Sykes, M. (1969). Some stochastic versions of the matrix model for population dynamics. *Journal of the American Statistical Association, 64,* 111–130.
Tayman, J. (1999). On the validity of MAPE as a measure of forecast accuracy. *Population Research and Policy Review, 18*(4), 299–322.
Tayman, J., Schafer, E., & Carter, L. (1998). The role of population size in the determination and prediction of population forecast errors: An evaluation using confidence intervals for subcounty areas. *Population Research and Policy Review, 17*(1), 1–20.
Tobler, W. R. (1979). Smooth pycnophylactic interpolation for geographical regions. *Journal of the American Statistical Association, 74,* 519–530.
United Nations. (1983). *Manual X*. New York: UN Population Division.
Voss, P. R., Long, D. D., & Hammer, R. B. (1999). *When census geography doesn't work: Using ancillary information to improve the spatial interpolation of demographic data*. Center for Demography and Ecology, University of Wisconsin, Madison. Working Paper No. 99–26.
Zandbergen, P. (2009). Geocoding quality and implications for spatial analysis. *The Geography Compass, 3*(2), 647–680.
Zandbergen, P., & Ignizio, D. (2010).Comparison of dyasymetric mapping techniques for small area population estimates. *Cartography and Geographic Information Science, 37*(3), 199–214.

Chapter 7
Housing-Unit Method in Comparison: The Virginia Case

Qian Cai and Rebecca Tippett

Introduction

The housing unit (HU) method is widely used for making sub-state population estimates. It is an intuitive, appealing method for the production of small-area population estimates, but in past comparisons, the HU method did not perform as well as alternative methodologies in estimating the population of Virginia's 134 counties and county-equivalent independent cities (Cai and Spar 2008). The HU method typically produced overestimates, and persons-per-household (PPH) estimates were critical for overall estimates accuracy. Smith and Mandell (1984) argue that improvements in the data and techniques used to estimate the components of the HU method can improve estimates and yield results comparable to other estimation methods.

This study draws on recently available data from the 2006–2010 American Community Survey (ACS) to examine whether using the more recent ACS PPH and occupancy rate estimates to derive household population improves the overall estimates. After choosing the best input variables for the HU method, we subsequently evaluate the population estimates produced by three different methods: the HU method, the ratio-correlation (RC) method, and the administrative records (AdRec) method used by the U.S. Census Bureau. Using 2010 census data for 134 counties in Virginia, we compare the precision, bias, and distribution of errors of these three sets of estimates. In addition, we explore the accuracy of averaging estimates produced by two different methods, an approach often suggested and applied in the estimates field (e.g., Hoque 2012). We conclude that while HU is a highly practical and valuable method for sub-county population estimates, it does not perform nearly as well as AdRec or RC for Virginia's county population estimates.

Q. Cai (✉) · R. Tippett
Demographics & Workforce Group, Weldon Cooper Center for Public Service,
University of Virginia, Charlottesville, VA, USA
e-mail: qc6q@cms.mail.virginia.edu

M. N. Hoque, L. B. Potter (eds.), *Emerging Techniques in Applied Demography*,
Applied Demography Series 4, DOI 10.1007/978-94-017-8990-5_7,

Estimation Methodologies

In the field of small area population estimates, three methodological approaches are commonly applied, the component method, the ratio-correlation method, and the housing unit method. Each has unique features and multiple variations.

Component Method

The first approach, the component method, estimates population utilizing the major components of population change: births, deaths, and migration. Variations of the component method are used by the Census Bureau and by many states that produce their own population estimates, such as Arizona, Oregon, Texas, and Wisconsin. For any time period, population is estimated using the equation

$$\boldsymbol{P_t = P_0 + B - D + NM}$$

where $\boldsymbol{P_t}$ equals the population for the estimate period; $\boldsymbol{P_0}$ equals the population in the base period; $\boldsymbol{B}$ equals births occurring between $\boldsymbol{P_0}$ and $\boldsymbol{P_t}$; $\boldsymbol{D}$ equals deaths occurring between $\boldsymbol{P_0}$ and $\boldsymbol{P_t}$; and $\boldsymbol{NM}$ equals net migration occurring between $\boldsymbol{P_0}$ and $\boldsymbol{P_t}$.

Variations of this method are largely determined by ways of estimating migration, among which is the administrative records method. AdRec estimates migration by examining the place of residence recorded on matched sets of federal income tax returns at two consecutive years. If the address on the return of the filer and any dependents changes from year one to year two, in-migrants to the receiving county and out-migrants from the sending county are recorded.

AdRec is the method used by the Census Bureau for its state and county population estimates; it is one of the best estimating methods and produces highly accurate estimates. The Bureau's collaborative efforts with the Federal State Cooperative for Population Estimates and the National Center for Health Statistics in collecting vital statistics data, as well as their careful, extensive research into estimating migration have resulted in high quality estimates that closely capture population change due to births, deaths, and migration. Many states do not produce their own county-level population estimates and rely on the AdRec estimates from the Census Bureau.

Ratio-Correlation Method

The second approach, the ratio-correlation method, uses linear regression to estimate population based on a set of symptomatic indicator variables that capture population dynamics, such as births, school enrollments, driver's licenses, housing, voter registrations, and Medicare enrollments. RC is used by many states in their county population estimates, such as Texas, North Carolina, and Washington, and has been implemented in Virginia for decades. The population estimates are developed using a multiple regression equation

$$Y = \beta_0 + \beta_1 X_1 + \beta_2 X_2 \ldots + \beta_n X_n + e$$

where Y equals the dependent variable to be estimated (population); β_0 equals the intercept to be estimated; $\beta_1 - \beta_n$ are the coefficients to be estimated; $X_1 - X_n$ are the independent variables; and e is the error term.

In the ratio-correlation method, the resulting estimate is not a population total. Rather, it is the percentage of the state's total household population that will be allocated to the locality. The dependent and independent variables are represented as double ratios.

First, *single ratios (SR)* are constructed for both base and estimating years. The base year is the most recent decennial census and the estimating year is the year for which estimates are being produced:

$$SR_{indicator} = \frac{Locality\ Total_{ind}}{State\ Total_{ind}}$$

Next, a *double ratio (DR)* is constructed to compare the locality's share of the indicator in the estimating year to its share of the state total in the base year.

$$DR_{indicator} = \frac{Estimating\ Year\ SR_{ind}}{Base\ Year\ SR_{ind}}$$

These double ratios measure change in the locality's share of the state total for each indicator. A double ratio less than one indicates that the locality's share of the state total for that variable has fallen relative to its share in the base year; a double ratio greater than one indicates the locality's share of that variable has grown relative to the base year.

The key source of variation in the RC method is the selection of systematic indicator variables available to the estimates producer and included in the model. The Virginia estimates are produced using five indicator variables for each locality: total housing stock; school enrollment in grades 1–8; 3-year aggregate of births; 3-year aggregate of deaths; total licensed drivers. We use the Census Bureau's AdRec-derived state population estimate minus statewide estimated group quarter (GQ) population as the statewide control total. The final step in obtaining an estimate of the total population for a county is the addition of the GQ population estimate to the estimated household population.

Our office annually collects data on the group quarters population in federal and state prisons, local jails, juvenile justice facilities, state mental health facilities, and college dormitories. For the 2010 population estimates, these GQ counts were combined with the 2000 census counts of nursing home and military group quarters residents to create a GQ estimate for each locality.

Housing Unit Method

The third approach, the housing unit method, estimates population through changes in total housing stock, persons per household (PPH), occupancy rate, and people living in group quarters (such as college dormitories, nursing homes, prisons, and military barracks). The HU method is used to estimate county-level population by some states, such as Florida, New Hampshire, and Texas, and is used by the Census Bureau and many state agencies to estimate sub-county population. For any time period, the population is estimated using the equation

$$\boldsymbol{P_t = (HU_t \times OCC_t \times PPH_t) + GQ_t}$$

where $\boldsymbol{P_t}$ equals the population; $\boldsymbol{HU_t}$ equals the number of housing units; $\boldsymbol{OCC_t}$ equals the household occupancy rate; $\boldsymbol{PPH_t}$ equals the persons-per-household; and $\boldsymbol{GQ_t}$ equals the group quarters population.

Variations of this method largely come from ways of estimating housing units (such as building permits or utility hookups), occupancy rates, and PPH. In 2008, Cai and Spar found that the best housing unit method estimates for Virginia were produced by a model with updated housing stock, estimated PPH based on percent change between the latest two censuses, and a constant occupancy rate.

Housing units are estimated by the equation

$$\boldsymbol{HU_t = HU_0 + BP_0^t + MH_{t-0}}$$

where $\boldsymbol{HU_t}$ equals housing units on the estimate date; $\boldsymbol{HU_0}$ equals housing units in the base period; $\boldsymbol{BP_0^t}$ equals cumulative building permits issued between the base period and the estimate date (6-month lag); and $\boldsymbol{MH_{t-0}}$ equals the estimated difference in mobile/manufactured homes between the base period and estimate date.[1]

Estimated PPH for 2010 was derived by first calculating the percentage change in PPH between 1990 and 2000 for each locality. This percentage was then used to update the 2000 PPH to 2010, with the assumption that the percentage change in PPH between 1990 and 2000 held constant for the next decade.

$$\boldsymbol{PPH_{2010} = \left(1 + \frac{PPH_{2000} - PPH_{1990}}{PPH_{1990}}\right) \times PPH_{2000}}$$

Occupancy rate for 2010 in each county was held constant to the occupancy rate in the most recent census.

$$\boldsymbol{OCC_{2010} = OCC_{2000}}$$

[1] Housing unit estimates are typically produced for July 1 and were linearly interpolated between July 1, 2009, and July 1, 2010, to obtain an estimate for April 1, 2010.

This study evaluates two model specifications to identify the best input variables for the HU method:

1. HU1, or "2007 best," used the most accurate model specification from the 2007 study.
2. HU2 drew on the newly available 5-year ACS data and used 2006–2010 ACS PPH and occupancy estimates.

We use the Census Bureau's state population estimate (minus statewide estimated group quarters population) as the statewide control total. This estimate was summed with the GQ population to create a total population estimate.

Evaluation Measures

We constructed population estimates for April 1, 2010, for each of Virginia's 134 localities using the ratio-correlation and housing-unit methodologies. We evaluate the accuracy and precision of these estimates by comparing them to the census counts for the same date. In the following formulas, EST refers to the calculated population estimate, CEN is the decennial census population count, and *n* is the total number of localities for which estimates have been prepared.

We use mean absolute percent error (MAPE) measured as

$$MAPE_{est} = \frac{\sum \frac{|EST - CEN|}{CEN}}{n} \times 100$$

as a measure of precision. MAPE gives the overall average error when the direction of the error (over or underestimate) is ignored. The bias of the estimates are indicated by the mean algebraic percent error (MALPE) measured as

$$MALPE_{est} = \frac{\sum \frac{EST - CEN}{CEN}}{n} \times 100$$

A positive MALPE indicates that the estimates tend to be higher than the census counts, indicating a tendency for the method to overestimate, while a negative MALPE indicates a tendency to underestimate. Last, we examine extreme errors greater than 5 and 10 %, measured as total count of errors larger than ± 5 and ± 10 %, respectively. These measures provide an indication of the occurrence of extreme errors.

Table 7.1 Accuracy of VA county population estimates by housing-unit model specification, 2010

Methodology	MAPE	MALPE	Extremes	
			>5%	>10%
HU1	3.73	0.39	31	8
HU2	4.21	1.22	34	12

What are the Best Input Variables for the House Unit Method?

We compared two HU model specifications to determine the best ways to measure occupancy rates and persons-per-households in the HU method. HU1 or "2007 best" used the most accurate model specification from the Cai and Spar (2008) evaluation, while HU2 drew on the recently available 2006–2010 ACS for PPH and occupancy rate. Each HU method was evaluated based on its accuracy in estimating total population, which includes household population based on the HU method plus the estimated group quarters population.

As Table 7.1 shows, estimates based on ACS PPH and occupancy rate (HU2) are less accurate than the "2007 best" (HU1) on all evaluation measurements. HU2 has a MAPE of 4.21 while HU1 is, on average, more accurate, with a MAPE of 3.73. Both HU1 and HU2 have positive MALPEs, indicating a tendency to overestimate population (Starsinic and Zitter 1968), with the positive bias more pronounced for HU2. Last, the incidence of extreme errors, particularly for errors greater than 10%, is much higher for HU2.

The poor performance of HU2 compared to HU1 may seem counter-intuitive, since the more current ACS should do a better job of capturing changes in both PPH and occupancy rates than the past Census data. The failure of the ACS data may be linked to the declining accuracy of the population and housing unit estimates used as control totals for the 2006–2010 ACS. Both PPH and occupancy rate are controlled by the population and housing totals; therefore, they are influenced by the accuracy of these two estimates.

How Well Do the Three Methods Perform?

Prior research found that the HU method was less accurate than the RC and AdRec methods in producing county estimates for Virginia (Cai and Spar 2008). To evaluate whether these findings still held true, estimates from three methods—HU, RC, and AdRec—were compared to the 2010 Census counts. For the purposes of this comparison:

- The HU estimates are those produced by HU1, with estimated PPH based on percent change and constant occupancy rate.

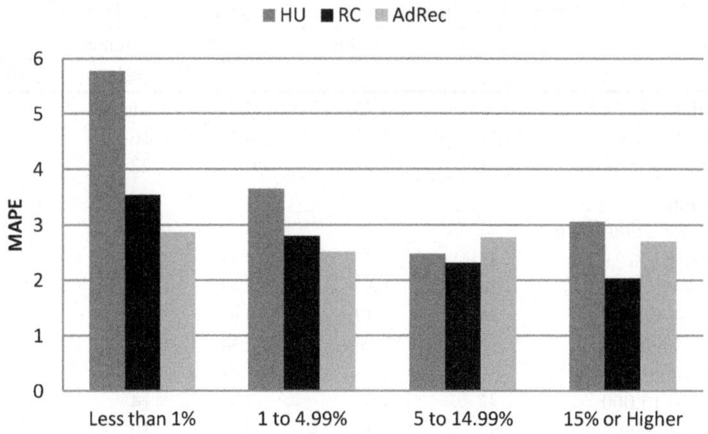

Fig. 7.1 MAPE by 2000–2010 growth rate and estimating methodology

- The RC estimates are based on an estimating model that includes five independent variables: housing stock, births, public school enrollment for grades 1–8, driver's licenses, and state income tax exemptions.
- The AdRec estimates are the Census Bureau's "pure" estimates. They are the estimates derived directly from the method, without subsequent adjustments from the challenge process, obtained from the Census Bureau for the purposes of this research. This comparison allows evaluation of the best method for producing estimates.

Table 7.2 presents the accuracy measures of these three estimating methodologies for all Virginia's localities overall, as well as by growth rate and 2010 population size. Both RC and AdRec performed better than HU, across all accuracy measures. While RC and AdRec both produce highly accurate estimates with minimal bias, the RC estimates slightly outperform those produced by AdRec. Compared to AdRec, the ratio-correlation estimates have a lower MAPE (2.66 versus 2.72), a lower MALPE (0.17 versus −0.25), and a tendency to produce a smaller proportion of extreme errors.

Virginia's counties vary widely in their growth patterns and total population. Evaluation by growth rate and population size shows that AdRec performs most consistently across size and growth categories, with no discernible patterns in precision, bias, or extreme errors. RC is increasingly accurate for faster growing and larger counties; as growth rate and size increase, MAPE and the presence of extreme errors declines. HU is consistently the least accurate in most categories. These patterns for the RC and HU methods are similar to evaluations of estimation methodology in other states (Hoque 2012).

Figures 7.1 and 7.2 present MAPE by methodology and by growth rate and population size, respectively. Figure 7.1 shows that both HU and RC perform less well when estimating slow-growing or declining populations (growth rate of less than 1 %).

Table 7.2 Accuracy measures by estimating methodology, growth rate, and population size, 2010

Methodology	*n*	MAPE	MALPE	Extremes	
				>5%	>10%
Housing unit	*134*	3.73	0.39	31	8
Ratio-correlation	*134*	2.66	0.17	16	2
Administrative records	*134*	2.72	−0.25	22	3
Housing-unit					
Growth rate, 2000–2010					
Less than 1%	*35*	5.77	5.11	13	6
1 to 4.99%	*28*	3.65	−0.43	7	1
5 to 14.99%	*36*	2.47	−0.93	4	0
15% or higher	*35*	3.06	−2.31	7	1
Total population, 2010					
Less than 15,000	*37*	4.95	2.44	14	6
15,000–49,999	*62*	3.49	0.13	10	2
50,000–100,000	*20*	2.70	−1.64	4	0
100,000 or more	*15*	3.08	−0.85	3	0
Ratio-correlation					
Growth rate, 2000–2010					
Less than 1%	*35*	3.54	2.49	7	1
1 to 4.99%	*28*	2.80	−0.05	5	1
5 to 14.99%	*36*	2.30	−0.65	3	0
15% or higher	*35*	2.03	−1.14	1	0
Total population, 2010					
Less than 15,000	*37*	3.06	0.81	6	0
15,000–49,999	*62*	2.70	0.59	10	2
50,000–100,000	*20*	2.33	−1.47	0	0
100,000 or more	*15*	1.92	−1.00	0	0
Administrative records					
Growth rate, 2000–2010					
Less than 1%	*35*	2.86	1.34	7	1
1 to 4.99%	*28*	2.50	−0.27	3	1
5 to 14.99%	*36*	2.77	−0.68	6	0
15% or higher	*35*	2.70	−1.36	6	1
Total population, 2010					
Less than 15,000	*37*	3.24	−0.53	9	1
15,000–49,999	*62*	2.42	0.49	9	2
50,000–100,000	*20*	2.94	−1.71	3	0
100,000 or more	*15*	2.36	−0.64	1	0

Figure 7.2 shows that, across all methods, smaller populations, defined here as less than 15,000, are prone to greater estimate errors than larger populations, a finding consistent with other estimates evaluation research (Smith and Cody 2013). Both figures clearly display the improved accuracy of RC as growth rates and total population size increase and the relative consistency of AdRec method across categories.

Estimates of the total population that fall within 2% of the Census counts are generally regarded as "high accuracy." Figures 7.3a, b, c show localities with

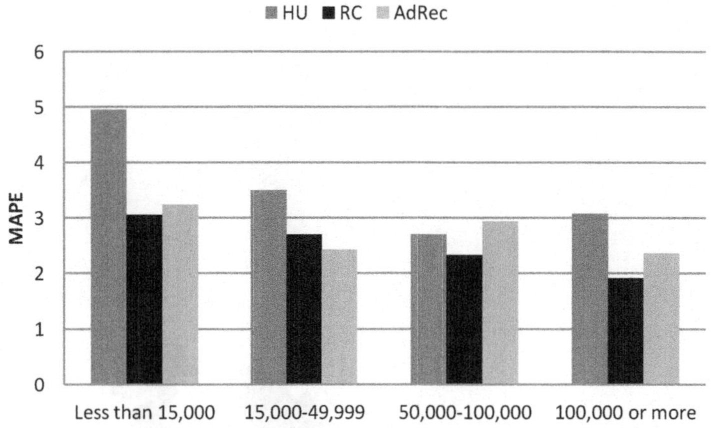

Fig. 7.2 MAPE by 2010 population size and estimating methodology

estimates within ±2% of 2010 Census count by the HU (3a), RC (3b), and AdRec (3c) methods. While there is substantial overlap between the methods, especially between RC and AdRec, the number of localities with estimates within ±2% of 2010 Census counts is substantially lower for the HU estimates. Among Virginia's 134 localities, only 51 have estimates in this range under the HU method, compared to 62 and 64 with RC and AdRec, respectively.

Does Averaging Two Methods Improve Accuracy?

Theoretically, estimates produced by different methods should track each other closely, as they measure the same population. In reality, estimates produced by different methods can differ significantly, largely due to variations in data input quality and specific methodological limitations. When such occasions arise, averaging is often suggested as a way to mitigate potential large errors by one, or both, methods and is commonly employed in states that produce their own estimates (e.g., Hoque 2012). Two averages were examined to see if they performed better than the estimates by the single better method:

1. RC and HU.
2. AdRec and HU.

RC and AdRec estimates were not averaged because, practically, it would not be feasible for either the Bureau or the Cooper Center to incorporate the other's estimates in a timely manner.

Table 7.3 shows the accuracy measures for averaging both RC and AdRec with HU and the performance of the methods on their own. While averaging HU and RC produced good estimates overall, they are not as good as estimates produced by

Fig. 7.3 **a** Localities with estimates within ±2 % of 2010 census count, housing unit method. **b** Localities with estimates within ±2 % of 2010 census count, ratio-correlation method. **c** Localities with estimates within ±2 % of 2010 census count, administrative records method

the RC method alone. The average has slightly higher MAPE (2.80 versus 2.66), MALPE (0.17 versus 0.28), and a greater incidence of extreme errors than RC alone.

Averaging HU and AdRec produced slightly better results than AdRec alone, especially in terms of reducing bias and number of localities with errors larger than 5 %. This may be because the AdRec method's tendency to underestimate total population (MALPE of −0.25) is counterbalanced by the HU method's tendency to overestimate total population (MALPE of 0.39).

Table 7.3 Accuracy measures for averages

	MAPE	MALPE	Extremes	
			>5%	>10%
Average, RC and HU	2.80	0.28	19	3
RC alone	2.66	0.17	16	2
Average, AdRec and HU	2.71	0.07	15	3
AdRec alone	2.72	−0.25	22	3

Discussion

This case study provided a comprehensive evaluation of three methods for county population estimates, as well as the value of averaging more than one method's results. The findings have multiple implications for the methodological choices for the estimates programs.

First, while HU is a highly practical and valuable method for sub-county population estimates, results from this study and prior work indicate that it does not perform nearly as well as AdRec or RC for Virginia's county population estimates. One major reason may be that, other than housing stock, which is drawn from administrative data, two key components of the HU method, PPH and occupancy rate, often need to be estimated without reliable methods or techniques. This subsequently compounds the estimates errors and makes it difficult to identify the error sources. In comparison, the RC and AdRec methods draw almost entirely on administrative data that reflect population change. As such, they more directly capture the dynamics of population change and the potential error sources are more readily identifiable.

While the availability of the ACS data offers promise for potential improvements in PPH and occupancy rate, both our evaluation and other empirical evidence indicate that, in its current form, the ACS data fall short of providing reliable data for use in post-censal population estimates production. Swanson and Hough's (2012) evaluation of the PPH estimates in the ACS finds that the nature of the ACS survey, and the presence of both sampling and non-sampling error, leads to volatility in the PPH estimates that is inconsistent with demographic theory. That is, demographic theory typically predicts PPH will trend consistently in one direction or another, following broader societal or population changes, and not fluctuate significantly from year-to-year as it does in the ACS.

Although a number of states produce HU estimates for county population, most incorporate them into their overall estimates process via averaging, a method employed in Texas (Hoque 2012). Among states that produce county-level population estimates, the HU method performs consistently well in Florida. Over the course of decades (Smith and Lewis 1980; Smith and Mandell 1984; Smith 1986), Florida has tailored the HU method to produce highly accurate estimates at the state, county, and subcounty level (Smith and Cody 2013). Their work offers suggestions on how to refine and improve the HU method, if the resources and data are available to estimates producers. For example, they advocate the use of utility hook ups and not just building permits to estimate housing units (see also Starsinic and Zitter 1968), and disaggregating housing units by type and applying type-specific occupancy rates and PPH (Smith and Lewis 1980).

Based on the evaluation of the performance of the three methodologies in Virginia, RC alone is preferred for Virginia's county estimates. The evaluation of averaging suggests that the Census Bureau and other states may want to evaluate averaging AdRec and HU estimates to see if the results for Virginia hold true for the entire country. If the benefit of averaging is positive, but minimal, it is perhaps still better to use AdRec alone, as the costs of producing a parallel set of HU estimates far exceed the benefit of minimally improved accuracy.

References

Cai, Q., & Spar, M. (2008). *An evaluation of housing unit-based estimates in Virginia*. Charlottesville: Weldon Cooper Center.

Hoque, N. (2012). Evaluation of small area population estimates produced by housing unit, ratio-correlation, and component method II compared to 2000 census counts. *Canadian Studies in Population, 39*(1–2), 91–108.

Smith, S. K. (1986). A review and evaluation of the housing unit method of population estimation. *Journal of the American Statistical Association, 81,* 287–296.

Smith, S. K., & Cody, S. (2013). Making the housing unit method work: An evaluation of 2010 population estimates in Florida. *Population Research and Policy Review, 32*(2), 221–242.

Smith, S. K., & Lewis, B. (1980). Some new techniques for applying the housing unit method of local population estimation. *Demography, 17,* 323–339.

Smith, S. K., & Mandell, M. (1984). A comparison of population estimation methods: Housing unit versus component II, ratio correlation, and administrative records. *Journal of the American Statistical Association, 79*(386), 282–289.

Starsinic, D. E., & Zitter, M. (1968). Accuracy of the housing unit method in preparing population estimates for cities. *Demography, 5,* 475–484.

Swanson, D. A., & Hough, G. C. Jr. (2012). An evaluation of persons per household (PPH) estimates generated by the American Community Survey: A demographic perspective. *Population Research and Policy Review, 31*(2), 235–266.

Chapter 8
On the Ratio-Correlation Regression Method of Population Estimation and Its Variants

David A. Swanson and Jeff Tayman

Introduction

Regression-based methods for estimating population date back to Snow (1911) who published, "The application of the method of multiple correlation to the estimation of post-censal populations" in the *Journal of the Royal Statistical Society*. Snow's paper represents the first published description of the use of multiple regression in the estimation of population. It also discusses other methods, pointing out their strengths and weaknesses, describing the model framework and the data used in the regression application, and applying it to districts in the United Kingdom. In addition to being the first published report in English of the use of regression for population estimates, it set the stage for subsequent papers by discussing it relative to other methods. A discussion is published with the paper that contains many important insights that are today commonplace in the use of multiple regression, not only for making population estimates but also for general use.

One of the insights (Snow 1911, p. 625) is given by David Heron who suggests that a shortcoming acknowledged by Snow was the need to "control" the sum of the estimates for individual districts to an estimate for the whole country (estimate for the whole country/sum of estimates for individual districts). Another is provided by G. Udny Yule who contributed substantially to the development of multiple regression as a modern analytic technique (Stigler 1986, pp. 345–361). Yule (Snow 1911, p. 621) noted that Snow demonstrated that a multiple regression model built using data over one decade had coefficients that could be used for the subsequent decade with the insertion of the new set of values for the independent variables. Yule also agreed with Snow that ex post facto tests using variables constructed on relative (percent) change would perform better than variables constructed on

J. Tayman (✉)
Department of Economics, University of San Diego, San Diego, CA, USA
e-mail: jtayman@san.rr.com

D. A. Swanson
Department of Sociology and Center for Sustainable Suburban Development,
University of California Riverside, Riverside, CA, USA

M. N. Hoque, L. B. Potter (eds.), *Emerging Techniques in Applied Demography*,
Applied Demography Series 4, DOI 10.1007/978-94-017-8990-5_8,

absolute change (Snow 1911, p. 622). Finally, among many comments that are useful still today for those interested in regression based methods for estimating population are Greenwood's remarks on the impact of skewed distributions (Snow 1911, p. 626); Baines' comments on using ratios (Snow 1911, p. 626); and the importance of data quality, something mentioned by virtually all discussants (Snow 1911, pp. 621–629).

Snow's (1911) seminal paper is based on the premise that the relationship between symptomatic indicators and the corresponding population remains unchanged over time. His work and the insights provided by the discussants of his paper have led to three related but distinct approaches: ratio-correlation, difference-correlation, and average-ratio methods. The main objectives of this paper are to synthesize the sizable literature on regression models for population estimation, provide a comprehensive evaluation of these models, show their connection to synthetic methods, and demonstrate their advantages for point and interval estimates of population.

Ratio-Correlation and its Variants

The most common regression-based approach for estimating total population is the ratio-correlation method. Introduced and tested by Schmitt and Crosetti (1954) and again tested by Crosetti and Schmitt (1956), this multiple regression method involves relating changes in several variables known as symptomatic indicators on the one hand to population changes on the other hand. Symptomatic indicators reflect the variables related to population change that are available and of them, those that yield an optimal model. Examples of symptomatic variables that have been used for this purpose are births, deaths, school enrollment, tax returns, motor vehicle registrations, employment, and registered voters. The ratio-correlation method is appropriate where a set of areas (e.g., counties) are structured into a geographical hierarchy (e.g. the populations of counties within a given state sum to the total state population). It proceeds in two steps. The first is the construction of the model and the second is its implementation; using the model to create estimates for postcensal years.

Because the method looks at change, population data from two successive censuses are needed to construct the model, along with data for the same years representing the symptomatic indicators. During its implementation step, the ratio-correlation method requires symptomatic data representing the year for which an estimate is desired and an estimate of the population for the highest level of geography (e.g., the state) that is independent of the ratio-correlation model.

The ratio-correlation method expresses the relationship between (1) the change over the previous intercensal period (e.g., 2000–2010) in an area's share (e.g., a given county) of the total for the parent area (e.g., the state) for several symptomatic series and (2) the change in an area's share of the population of the parent area. The method can be employed to make estimates for primary or secondary political, administrative, and statistical divisions of a country (Bryan 2004). In the United

States, the variables selected usually differ from state to state and because of the small number of counties in some states, states may be combined and estimated in one regression equation.

In general terms, the ratio-correlation model is formally described as follows (Swanson and Beck 1994):

$$P_{i,t} = a_0 + \sum (b_j) \times S_{i,j,t} + \varepsilon_i \tag{8.1a}$$

where,

a_0 = the intercept term to be estimated
b_j = the regression coefficient to be estimated
ε_i = the error term
j = symptomatic indicator ($1 \leq j \leq k$)
i = subarea ($1 \leq j \leq n$)
t = year of the most recent census

and,

$$P_{i,t} = \frac{\left(P_{i,t} / \sum P_{i,t}\right)}{\left(P_{i,t-z} / \sum P_{i,t-z}\right)} \tag{8.1b}$$

$$S_{i,j,t} = \frac{\left(S_{i,t} / \sum S_{i,t}\right)_j}{\left(S_{i,t-z} / \sum S_{i,t-z}\right)_j} \tag{8.1c}$$

where,

z = number of years between the two censuses
P = population
S = symptomatic indicator.

Once a ratio-correlation model is estimated, population estimates for time $t+k$ are developed in a series of six steps. First, $(S_{i,t+\kappa} / \sum S_{i,t+\kappa})_j$ is substituted into the numerator of Eq. (8.1c) for each symptomatic indicator j and $(S_{i,t} / \sum Si,t)_j$ is substituted into the denominator of Eq. (8.1c) for each symptomatic indicator j, which yields $S_{i,j,t+k}$. Second, the updated model with the preceding substitution of symptomatic data for time $t+k$ is used to estimate $P_{i,t+\kappa}$. Third, $(P_{i,t} / \sum P_{i,t})$ is substituted into the denominator of $P_{i,t+k}$, which yields $P_{i,t+k} = (P_{i,t+k} / \sum \boldsymbol{P}_{i,t+k})/(P_{i,t} / \sum P_{i,t})$, where $\sum \boldsymbol{P}_{i,t+k}$ represents the independently estimated population of the "parent" area at time $t+k$. Fifth, since $P_{i,t+k}$, $(P_{i,t} / \sum P_{i,t})$ and $\sum \boldsymbol{P}_{i,t+k}$ are all known values, the equation $P_{i,t+k} = \left(P_{i,t+k} / \sum \mathbf{P}_{\mathbf{i,t+k}}\right) / \left(P_{i,t} / \sum P_{i,t}\right)$, is manipulated to yield an estimate of the population of area i at time $t+k$:

$$P_{i,t+k} = P_{i,t+k} \times \left(P_{i,t} / \sum P_{i,t}\right) \times \sum \mathbf{P}_{\mathbf{i,t+k}}. \tag{8.1d}$$

As Eq. (8.1d) shows, an independent (exogenous) estimate of the population for the "parent" geography ($\Sigma \boldsymbol{P}_{i,\,t+k}$) of the i subareas is required when using the ratio-correlation model to generate population estimates. The sixth and final step is to effect a final "control" so that the sum of the i subarea population estimates is equal to the independently estimated population for the parent of these i subareas: $\Sigma P_{i,\,t+k} = \Sigma \boldsymbol{P}_{i,\,t+k}$, which is accomplished as follows:

$$P_{i,t+\underline{k}} = \left(P_{i,t+k} / \sum P_{i,t+k}\right) \times \sum \mathbf{P}_{i,t+k}. \tag{8.1e}$$

As an empirical example of ratio-correlation model, we use data for the 39 counties of Washington State. Using Excel, we construct a ratio-correlation model using 1990 and 2000 census data in conjunction with three symptomatic indicators: (1) registered voters; (2) registered automobiles, and (3) public school enrollment in grades 1–8. The raw 1990, 2000, and 2005 input data for this model are provided in Appendix Tables 8.2, 8.3, 8.4, 8.5. We use 2005 symptomatic indicators to construct a set of county estimates for 2005. The results of these calculations are shown in Appendix Table 8.6. A summary of the regression model and its characteristics is provided in Exhibit 8.1.

Exhibit 8.1 1990–2000 Ratio-correlation model, Washington State Counties

$$P_{i,t} = 0.195 + (0.0933 \times \text{Voters}) + (0.3362 \times \text{Autos}) + (0.3980 \times \text{Enroll})$$

$$[p < 0.001] \qquad [p = 0.14] \qquad [p < 0.001] \qquad [p < 0.001]$$

where,

$$P_{i,\,t} = (P_{i,2000} / \Sigma P_{i,2000}) / (P_{i,1990} / \Sigma P_{i,1990})$$
$$S_{i,1,t} = (\text{Voters}_{i,2000} / \Sigma \text{Voters}_{i,2000}) / (\text{Voters}_{i,1990} / \Sigma \text{Voters}_{i,1990})$$
$$S_{i,2,t} = (\text{Autos}_{i,2000} / \Sigma \text{Autos}_{i,2000}) / (\text{Autos}_{i,1990} / \Sigma \text{Autos}_{i,1990})$$
$$S_{i,3,t} = (\text{Enroll}_{i,2000} / \Sigma \text{Enroll}_{i,2000}) / (\text{Enroll}_{i,1990} / \Sigma \text{Enroll}_{i,1990}).$$

$r^2 = 0.794$
adj $r^2 = 0.776$

Although the coefficient for voters is not statistically significant, we elected to retain this symptomatic indicator to have a model with three independent variables, a feature that, as explained later, can assist in dealing with "model invariance." The amount of "explained variance" ($r^2 = 0.794$) is typical for a ratio-correlation model. Do not be alarmed that this level is not sufficient to have a "good model." That is, neither believe that a good ratio-correlation model should have a very high level of explained variance (e.g., $r^2 > 0.9$) nor expect a very high level of explained variance. This is the case because the structure of the ratio-correlation model reflects the "stationarity" achieved by taking ratios over time (Swanson 2004). Note that the coefficients approximately sum to 1.0. This also is a universal feature of the ratio-correlation model, one that can be exploited in a model with three symptomatic indicators as discussed shortly.

In using this model to construct a set of county population estimates for 2005, we follow the six steps just described. First, we substitute $(S_{i,2005}/\sum S_{i,2005})_j$ into the numerator of the model for each symptomatic indicator j and $(S_{i,2000}/\sum S_{i,2000})_j$ into the denominator of the model for each symptomatic indicator j, which yields $S_{i,j,2005}$. Second, the updated model with the preceding substitution of symptomatic data for 2005 is used to estimate $P_{i,2005}$. Third, $(P_{i,2000}/\sum P_{i,2000})$ is substituted into the denominator of $P_{i,2005}$, which yields $P_{i,2005}=(P_{i,2005}/\sum \mathbf{P}_{i,2005})/(P_{i,2000}/\sum P_{i,2000})$, where $\sum \mathbf{P}_{i,2005}$ represents the independently estimated population of the state or the parent area of the 39 counties. Fifth, since $P_{i,2005}$, $(P_{i,2000}/\sum P_{i,2000})$ and $\sum \mathbf{P}_{i,2005}$ are all known values, the equation $P_{i,2005} = (P_{i,2005}/\sum \mathbf{P}_{i,2005})/(P_{i,2000}/\sum P_{i,2000})$ is manipulated to yield an estimate of the population of county i in the year 2005:

$$\mathrm{P}_{i,2005} = \mathrm{P}_{i,2005} \times \left(\mathrm{P}_{i,2000} / \sum \mathrm{P}_{i,2000}\right) \times \sum \mathbf{P}_{i,2005}.$$

The sixth and final step is to control the 2005 population estimates of the 39 counties so that they sum to the independently estimated 2005 population for the state of Washington:

$$\mathrm{P}_{i,2005} = \left(\mathrm{P}_{i,2005} / \mathrm{P}_{i,2005}\right) \times \sum \mathbf{P}_{i,2005}.$$

The final "controlled" 2005 population estimates are shown in the last column of Appendix Table 8.6, which also shows the steps for obtaining these estimates.

An acute observer may notice that except when $k=z$, the use of the model for estimating population corresponds to a shorter length of time than that used to calibrate the model. For example, if one constructs a model using 2000 and 2010 data, it corresponds to a 10 year period of change in both population shares and shares of symptomatic variables. However, in using this model to estimate the population in 2013, the time period now corresponds to a 3 year period of change in both population shares and shares of symptomatic variables. Swanson and Tedrow (1984) addressed this temporal inconsistency by using a logarithmic transformation. They called the resulting model the "rate-correlation" model.

The rate-correlation model is one of several variants of the basic ratio-correlation regression technique. Another is known as the "difference-correlation" method. Similar in principle to the ratio-correlation method, the difference-correlation method departs from it in terms of the construction of the variables used to reflect change over time. Rather than making ratios out of the proportions at two points in time, the difference-correlation method employs the *differences* between proportions (Schmitt and Grier 1966; O'Hare 1980; Swanson 1978a). Another variant was proposed by Namboodiri and Lalu (1971). Known as the "average regression" technique, they evaluated the simple, unweighted average of the estimates provided by several simple regression equations, each relating the population ratio to one symptomatic indicator ratio. This approach is very similar averaging several censal ratio estimates. Using the insights provide by Namboodiri and Lalu (1971), Swanson and

Prevost (1985) demonstrated that the ratio-correlation model can be interpreted as a demographic form of "synthetic estimation" composed of a set of weighted censal ratio estimates, with the regression coefficients serving as the weights. We cover this topic toward later in the paper.

Bryan (2004) observes that one shortcoming of the ratio-correlation method and related techniques is that substantial time lags can occur in obtaining the symptomatic indicators needed for producing a current population estimate. That is, suppose that a current (2014) estimate is desired, but the most current symptomatic indicators are for 2012. What can one do? One solution to this problem is "lagged ratio-correlation," which was introduced by Swanson and Beck (1994). In this variant of ratio-correlation method, the symptomatic indicator ratios precede the population ratios by lagging them by "*m*" years in model construction:

$$S_{i,j,t-m} = \frac{\left(S_{i,t-m} / \sum S_{i,t-m}\right)_j}{\left(S_{i,(t-m)-z} / \sum S_{i,(t-m)-z}\right)_j} \tag{8.1f}$$

where,

m = number of years that symptomatic indicators precede the population.

When the lagged ratio-correlation is used to estimate a population, the only change to the six steps described earlier is that $\left(S_{i,(t-m)+k} / \Sigma S_{i,(t-m)+k}\right)_j$ is substituted into the numerator of Eq. (8.1c) in place of $\left(S_{i,t+k} / \Sigma S_{i,t+k}\right)_j$ and $\left(S_{i,(t-m)} / \Sigma S_{i,(t-m)}\right)_j$ into the denominator of Eq. (8.1c) in place of $\left(S_{i,t} / \Sigma S_{i,t}\right)_j$.

Uncertainty in Ratio-Correlation Estimates

Because ratio-correlation and its variants are grounded in regression, they are connected to the inferential and other statistical tools that come with it (Swanson 1989; Swanson and Beck 1994). In using these tools, it is important to be aware of several qualifications. The first is that within this framework, "uncertainty" is generally based on the "frequentist" view of sample error. As discussed by Swanson and Beck (1994), the construction of confidence intervals around estimated values implies, for example, that one perceives (whether implicitly or explicitly) the following: (1) the data used in model construction are a random sample drawn from a universe; (2) the model would fit perfectly were it not for random error; and (3) any subsequent observations of independent variables placed into the model and used to generate dependent variables are drawn from the same universe. Since a given model is constructed from data using observations from all known cases (e.g., all 39 counties in Washington), the "universe" represented by the county data is a "super-population." As noted by D'Allesandro and Tayman (1980), this means that the observed values are a random manifestation of all the possible observations that could have occurred.

Technically speaking, this makes it difficult to interpret confidence intervals in an actual estimation application or an ex post facto test because we can never observe the regression surface for this super-population (specifically, the set of county populations forming the expected values of this regression surface). What we do observe is a census count. This census count has two distinct uses. First, it must be viewed as an estimator during the model construction phase (as are all of the symptomatic indicators). However, when we use a given model to estimate the number of persons, we must view the number that is (or could be) generated by a complete enumeration as a parameter. Thus, in using the term "confidence intervals," one (implicitly or explicitly) assumes that a census count is used to generate an estimate. Consequently, when a confidence band is placed around an estimate, the band is an interval estimator for a parameter (Swanson and Beck 1994).

Given these qualifications, Swanson and Beck (1994) conducted ex post facto examinations on estimates produced by the lagged ratio-correlation model and their "forecast intervals" for total populations of the 39 counties in Washington State in 1970, 1980, and 1990. For the 1970 set of county population projections, they found that the 66 % forecast intervals contained the 1970 census figure in more than two-thirds of the counties (30 of 39), as did the 1990 results (31 of 39 counties). For the 1980 set, the 66 % forecast interval contained the 1980 census figure in just less than two-thirds (24 of the 39 counties). Swanson and Beck (1994) argued that these findings are of interest from an application standpoint because if the 66 % forecast intervals contained substantially less than two-thirds of the actual county populations, one would have a misplaced sense of accuracy in the ability of the given models to accurately estimate and project county populations. Since the intervals did contain close to two-thirds of the actual county population figures in both 1970 and 1990 and nearly two-thirds in 1980, they argued that the results of this case study revealed an intuitively appealing view of the accuracy of these particular models (Swanson and Beck 1994).

The findings by Swanson and Beck (1994) suggest that, among other useful features, one can construct intervals around the estimates produced by ratio-correlation and its variants that are both statistically and substantively meaningful. Table 8.1 shows 66 % confidence intervals for 2010 county estimates in Washington state based on the ratio-correlation model shown in Exhibit 8.1. These results further support the efficacy of regression-based intervals in accurately measuring the uncertainty of these county population estimates. Sixty-two percent of the county census counts fall within the intervals, close to the expected 66 %. Moreover, the intervals appear valid across a wide range of population sizes.

Table 8.1 Sixty-six percent confidence intervals for population estimates, Washington State Counties, 2010[a]

County	Lower limit	Point estimate	Upper limit	2010 census	Outside interval	
					Lower	Upper
Adams	19,223	20,006	20,790	18,728	x	
Asotin	21,379	22,326	23,273	21,623		
Benton	171,103	177,658	184,214	175,177		
Chelan	71,078	74,172	77,265	72,453		
Clallam	68,856	71,738	74,620	71,404		
Clark	429,504	445,660	461,816	425,363	x	
Columbia	4,203	4,391	4,579	4,078	x	
Cowlitz	97,492	101,687	105,883	102,410		
Douglas	41,645	43,484	45,324	38,431	x	
Ferry	7,832	8,155	8,479	7,551	x	
Franklin	72,086	75,116	78,146	78,163		x
Garfield	2,191	2,304	2,418	2,266		
Grant	89,121	92,596	96,071	89,120	x	
Gig Harbor	69,129	72,162	75,194	72,797		
Island	76,105	79,356	82,607	78,506		
Jefferson	27,450	28,665	29,879	29,872		
King	1,886,466	1,966,293	2,046,121	1,931,249		
Kitsap	240,308	250,729	261,151	251,133		
Kittitas	39,129	40,634	42,140	40,915		
Klickitat	20,154	21,024	21,894	20,318		
Lewis	73,452	76,549	79,645	75,455		
Lincoln	10,443	10,917	11,391	10,570		
Mason	57,086	59,315	61,543	60,699		
Okanogan	41,373	43,164	44,955	41,120	x	
Pacific	21,341	22,288	23,236	20,920	x	
Pend Oreille	12,253	12,781	13,309	13,001		
Pierce	802,867	834,243	865,619	795,225	x	
San Juan	15,932	16,562	17,191	15,769	x	
Skagit	114,358	118,968	123,578	116,901		
Skamania	11,053	11,492	11,932	11,066		
Snohomish	698,084	725,177	752,271	713,335		
Spokane	467,506	486,378	505,250	471,221		
Stevens	47,729	49,651	51,573	43,531	x	
Thurston	247,038	256,439	265,839	252,264		
Wahkaikum	4,235	4,407	4,579	3,978	x	
Walla Walla	60,606	63,116	65,626	58,781	x	
Whatcom	194,600	202,102	209,603	201,140		
Whitman	41,263	43,258	45,252	44,776		
Yakima	250,615	260,797	270,980	243,231	x	
Washington State	6,626,288	6,895,760	7,165,236	6,724,540		
				% outside	38 %	

[a] Based on the ratio-correlation model from Exhibit 8.1

Shortcomings of Regression-Based Techniques

Given that the input data are of good quality, the accuracy of the regression-based techniques largely depends upon the validity of the central underlying assumption that the observed statistical relationship between the independent and dependent variables in the past intercensal period will persist in the current postcensal period. The adequacy of this assumption (that the model is invariant) is dependent on several conditions (Swanson 1980; Mandel and Tayman 1982; McKibben and Swanson 1997; Tayman and Schafer 1985).

In an attempt to deal with model invariance, Ericksen (1973, 1974) introduced a method of post-censal estimation in which the symptomatic information is combined with sample data by means of a regression format. He considered combining symptomatic information on births, deaths, and school enrollment with sample data from the Current Population Survey. Swanson (1980) took a different approach to the issue of model invariance and presented a mildly restricted procedure for using a theoretical causal ordering and principles from path analysis to provide a basis for modifying regression coefficients in order to improve the estimation accuracy of the ratio-correlation method of population estimation.

Ridge regression also represents a method for dealing with model invariance. Swanson (1978b) and D'Allesandro and Tayman (1980) examined this approach to multiple regression and found that it offered some benefits. Ridge regression also represents a way to deal with another possible problem with the regression approach, which is multicollinearity: a condition whereby the independent variables are all highly correlated. This condition can result in type II errors (finding that given coefficients are not shown to be statistically significant when in fact they are) when one evaluates the coefficients associated with the symptomatic indicators used in a given model. One also can use the standard diagnostic tools associated with regression to evaluate and this issue and overcome it without resorting to ridge regression (Fox 1991). Swanson (1989) demonstrated another way to deal with model invariance by using the statistical properties of the ratio-correlation method in conjunction with the Wilcoxon matched-pairs signed rank test and the "rank-order" procedure (Swanson 1980).

Judgment is also important in the application of ratio-correlation, as the analyst must take into account the reliability and consistency of coverage of each variable (Tayman and Schafer 1985). The increasing availability of administrative data allows many possible combinations of variables. High correlation coefficients for two past intercensal periods would suggest that the degree of association of the variables is not changing very rapidly. In such a case, the regression based on the last intercensal period should be applicable to the current postcensal period. Furthermore, it is assumed that deficiencies in coverage in the basic data series will remain constant, or change very little, in the present period (Tayman and Schafer 1985).

In addition to the issue of time lags in the availability of symptomatic indicators, Bryan (2004) notes two other shortcomings of regression-based techniques: (1) the use of multiple and different variables (depending on the place being estimated) and the averaging of multiple estimates makes it difficult to decompose error; and (2) may compromise the comparability of estimates between different subnational areas. In regard to decomposing error, this is a feature of all estimation methods that do not directly include the components of population change. In regard to comparability, we note that this is an issue when different regression models are used (e.g., the ratio-correlation model used to estimate the populations of the 75 counties of Arkansas is different from the ratio-correlation model used to estimate the populations of the 39 counties of Washington state).

In regard to the issue of decomposing error, McKibben and Swanson (1997) argue that at least some of the shortcomings in accuracy of population estimates would be better understood by linking these methods with the substantive socioeconomic and demographic dynamics that underlie the changes in population that the methods are designed to measure. They provide a case study of Indiana over two periods, 1970–1980 and 1980–1990, which were selected because model coefficients showed substantial change between these two decades. The authors link these changes to Indiana's transition to a post-industrial economy and describe how this transition operated through demographic dynamics that ultimately affected the estimation model.

Ratio-Correlation and Synthetic Estimation

Before describing synthetic estimation and its relationship to the ratio-correlation method, it is important to realize that synthetic estimation emerged from the field of survey research, as statisticians grappled with the problem of trying to apply survey results for a large area (e.g., the United States.) to subareas (e.g., states) while maintaining validity and avoiding excessive costs. Thus, as Swanson and Pol (2008, p. 322) observe, there are two distinct traditions in regard to "small area estimates," (1) demographic and (2) statistical:

> Demographic methods are used to develop estimates of a total population as well as the ascribed characteristics—age, race, and sex—of a given population. Statistical methods are largely used to estimate the achieved characteristics of a population—educational attainment, employment status, income, and marital status, for example. Among survey statisticians, the demographer's definition of an estimate is generally termed an "indirect estimate" because unlike a sample survey, the data used to construct a demographic estimate are symptomatic indicators of population change (e.g., enrollment, births, deaths) and do not directly represent the phenomenon of interest. Among demographers, the term "indirect estimate" has a different meaning.

So, in the field of demography a direct estimate refers to the measurement of demographic phenomena using data that directly represent the phenomena of interest, while among statisticians, it is used to describe estimates obtained by survey sampling. In terms of an indirect estimate, demographers usually use this term in referring to the measurement of demographic phenomena using data that do not directly represent the phenomena of interest (e.g., a child/woman ratio instead of a crude birth rate). Among survey statisticians, this term refers to an estimate not based on a sample survey, for example, a model-based estimate (Schaible 1993).

As a bit of history on the emergence of synthetic estimation, Ford (1981) notes that the problem of constructing county or other small area estimates from survey data has been an important topic, and large-scale surveys and even complete census counts were often used to solve the problem. Because of the resource needs of this approach, attention turned to possible alternatives for obtaining small area information in the 1970s (NCHS 1968; Ford 1981). One alternative that gained a lot of attention was synthetic estimation, which according to Ford (1981) emerged from a 1978 workshop on Synthetic Estimates for Small Area Estimates co-sponsored by the National Institute on Drug Abuse (NIDA) and the National Center for Health Statistics (NCHS). This same workshop resulted in a monograph edited by Steinberg (1979).

In the "Introduction" to the NIDA/NCHS monograph, Steinberg (1979) cites "The Radio Listening Survey," discussed in Hansen et al. (1953), as an early implementation of the synthetic method. In this survey, questionnaires were mailed to about 1,000 families in each of 500 county areas, and personal interviews were conducted with a sub-sample of the families in 85 of these county areas who were mailed questionnaires (Hansen et al. 1953, pp. 483–484). Knowing in advance that the mail-out portion would yield a low level of responses (about 20% of those mailed questionnaires responded), the data collected in the personal interviews were used to obtain estimates not affected by non-response. The relationships between the data in the 85 county areas that were collected from the personal interviews and from the mailed questionnaires were then applied to the county areas for which only mail-out/mail-back was done to improve the estimates for these areas (Hansen et al. 1953, p. 483). While the radio listening study did not use the hallmark of synthetic estimation, which is taking information from a "parent" area and applying it to its subareas, the idea behind this study is similar.

In most cases, synthetic estimation is used to estimate "achieved characteristics" and often relies on estimates made by demographers of total populations and their ascribed characteristics (e.g., age, race, sex) in developing the estimates (Causey 1988; Cohen and Zhang 1988; Gonzalez and Hoza 1978; Levy 1979). However, it need not be confined to this use. Before we turn to a demographic interpretation of synthetic estimation, it is useful to discuss its statistical interpretation.

Cohen and Zhang (1988) provide an informal statistical definition of a synthetic estimator that we adapt. First, assume that one is interested in obtaining estimates of an unknown characteristic, x_i over a set of i sub-regions ($i=1,\ldots,n$). Second, suppose one has census counts p_i, ($i=1,\ldots,n$), for each of the sub-regions and both a census count, P, and a "known" value of X, for the parent region, where $\sum p_i = P$ and $\sum x_i = X$, respectively. Third, suppose that the estimated values of x_i for the subareas must sum to the known value X for the parent area. In this case, Cohen and Zhang (1988, p. 2) define the statistical synthetic estimate as:

$$x_i = (X/P) \times p_i. \tag{8.2}$$

Equation (8.2) shows that the estimated characteristic (x_i) for a given subarea i is found by multiplying the known value of population for sub-area i, p_i, by the "known" ratio of the characteristic (X) to population (P) for the parent area. It is inevitably the case that the "known" value of X for the parent area is taken from a sample survey (NCHS 1968). Cohen and Zhang (1988) go on to show how the basic idea given in Eq. (8.2) can be extended to include demographic subgroups (e.g., by age, race, sex). Similar examples are provided by Levy (1979).

Exhibit 8.2 contains a simple example that shows how Eq. (8.2) is applied. Suppose we have 50,000 people in a parent area ($P=50{,}000$) and 1,000 have a characteristic ($X=1{,}000$) that we are interested in estimating for its three subareas, which have 30,000, 15,000, and 5,000 people. The synthetic method would yield estimates of characteristic x for the subareas of 600, 300, and 100, respectively. From a statistical perspective, synthetic estimates are generally held to be "biased." That is, there is a difference between the estimator's expected value and the true value of the parameter being estimated (e.g., Weisstein 2011). The bias occurs because the ratio of x_i to p_i in a given subarea i is usually not the same as the ratio for the parent area. That is, $X/P \neq x_i/p_i$.

Exhibit 8.2 Example of synthetic estimation

Sub-area	Sub-area population	Parent areas ratio (X/P)	Sub-area estimate of characteristic (x)
1	30,000	1,000/50,000	600
2	15,000	1,000/50,000	300
3	5,000	1,000/50,000	100

With this introduction to systematic estimation, we now turn to how synthetic estimation works from the standpoint of demographers. The key difference for demographers is, that unlike for statisticians, it is the population of area i (p_i) that is "unknown" rather than some characteristic (x_i) of this population. To implement synthetic estimation, demographers find "characteristics" that are available for both the parent area and its subareas, known as "symptomatic indicators," per our earlier discussion. For demographers, Eq. (8.2) becomes:

$$p_i = \frac{(s_{j,i})}{(\mathbf{S}_j / \mathbf{P})} \tag{8.3}$$

where,

$\boldsymbol{P}$ = population of the parent area
$\boldsymbol{S}_j$ = value of symptomatic indicator j for the parent area
$s_{j,i}$ = value of symptomatic indicator j for subarea i ($1 \leq i \leq n$)
p_i = estimated population for subarea i.

As is the case for the synthetic estimators used by statisticians (Eq. (8.2)), the basic form of the synthetic estimator used by demographers (Eq. (8.3)) can be expanded. One expansion puts the synthetic estimation process in motion using a regression framework:

$$p_{i,t} = a_0 \times (\mathbf{P}_t) \times (p_{i,t-z}/\mathbf{P}_{t-z}) + b_j \times [(s_{j,i,t})/((s_{j,i,t-z}/p_{i,t-z}) \times (\mathbf{S}_{j,t}/(\mathbf{S}_{j,t-z}/\mathbf{P}_{t-z})))] + \varepsilon_i \tag{8.4}$$

where,

a_0 = the intercept term to be estimated
b_j = the regression coefficient to be estimated for symptomatic indicator j
ε_i = the error term
$s_{j,i}$ = symptomatic indicator ($1 \le j \le k$) in subarea i ($1 \le i \le n$)
t = year of the most recent census
z = number years to the census preceding the most recent census
$\boldsymbol{P}$ = population of the parent area
$\boldsymbol{S}_j$ = value of symptomatic indicator j for the parent area
p_i = estimated population for subarea i.

Once the preceding regression model is estimated, it can be used to estimate the population of each area i for k years subsequent to the last census (time $= t$):

$$p_{i,t+k} = [a_0 \times (\mathbf{P}_{t+k}) \times (p_{i,t}/\mathbf{P}_t)] + [b_j \times ((s_{j,i,t+k})/((s_{j,i,t}/p_{i,t}) \times (\mathbf{S}_{j,t+k}/(\mathbf{S}_{j,t}/\mathbf{P}_t))))] \tag{8.5}$$

Equations (8.4) and (8.5) can be algebraically manipulated to become the bivariate form (i.e., a regression model with only one independent variable) of the ratio-correlation model discussed earlier. First, borrowing from Eq. (8.1a), we show the simple bivariate ratio-correlation regression model is algebraically equivalent to Eq. (8.5):

$$P_{i,t} = a_0 + b_j \times S_{i,j,t} + \varepsilon_i \tag{8.6}$$

where,

a_0 = the intercept term to be estimated
b_j = the regression coefficient to be estimated
ε_i = the error term
j = symptomatic indicator ($1 \le j \le k$)
i = subarea ($1 \le j \le n$)
t = year of the most recent census

and,

$$P_{i,t} = \frac{(P_{i,t}/\sum P_{i,t})}{(P_{i,t-z}/\sum P_{i,t-z})} \tag{8.7}$$

$$S_{i,j,t} = \frac{(S_{i,t}/\sum S_{i,t})_j}{(S_{i,t-z}/\sum S_{i,t-z})_j} \tag{8.8}$$

where,

z = number of years between each census for which data are used to construct the model

P = population

S = symptomatic indicator.

As was shown earlier, a set of population estimates is done in a series of six steps, which lead to the estimation version of Eq. (8.6), which is algebraically equivalent to Eq. (8.5):

$$\mathrm{P}_{\mathrm{i,t+}} = \left(P_{\mathrm{i,t+k}}\right) \times \left(\mathrm{P}_{\mathrm{i,t}} / \sum \mathrm{P}_{\mathrm{i,t}}\right) \times \sum \mathbf{P}_{\mathbf{i,t+k}}. \tag{8.9}$$

As discussed by Swanson and Prevost (1985), these equations show that the ratio-correlation model can be viewed as a regression method that uses synthetic estimation (taking a ratio of change for a given "rate" in a parent area and a "censal-ratio" to estimate a current population for area i). Note that the intercept term, a_0, shown in Eq. (8.5) serves as a "weight" applied to an estimate of p_i at time $t+k$ ($p_{i,t+k}$), based on the proportion of the population in area i at the time of the last census t ($p_{i,t}$) multiplied by the total of the parent area at time $t+k$ ($\boldsymbol{P}_{t+k}$). The regression coefficient, b_j, shown in Eq. (8.5) also serves as a weight. In this case it is applied to the "synthetic estimate" based on symptomatic indicator s_j. As Swanson (1980) and Swanson and Prevost (1985) observe, the regression coefficients in a ratio-correlation model sum to 1.00 (or very nearly so), which means, as shown in Eq. (8.5), the estimate of p_i can be viewed as a weighted average of synthetic estimates based on j symptomatic indicators.

A strength of sample-based methods aimed at generating what the statisticians refer to direct estimates is they offer a well-understood approach that is less costly than full enumerations along with estimates of their precision. A weakness is the cost of sample surveys often precludes using them to develop usable information for small areas unless they are supplemented by other methods such as synthetic estimation (Ghosh and Rao 1994; Platek et al. 1987; Rao 2003). Jaffe (1951, p. 211) notes that while sample surveys are cheaper than full enumerations, "demographic procedures" are cheaper than sample surveys; however, he also notes that the "direct estimates" resulting from sample surveys can only be used for current estimates since it is impossible to interview past or future populations. He further observes that only "demographic procedures" can provide past, current, and future estimates. We note, however, that these same 'demographic procedures' can be improved by using the statistical tools and perspectives that have emerged from sampling, as this discussion of synthetic estimation illustrates.

Conclusion

Regression-based methods have limited application in the preparation of estimates of population composition, such as age and sex for small geographic areas. It is possible, of course, to apply the age distribution at the last census date to a pre-assigned current total for the area, or to extrapolate the last two census age distributions to the current date and apply the extrapolated distribution to the current total. Spar and Martin (1979), however, found that the ratio-correlation method was more accurate than other methods in estimating the populations of Virginia counties by race and age. Swanson (1978a) also found regression-based methods useful for estimation small highly-concentrated populations, such as those identified on the basis of race or ethnicity.

While the regression-based methods have limitations, they also have strong advantages given the availability of good quality data to implement and test them. Among their many advantages is the fact that regression has a firm foundation in statistical inference, which leads to the construction of meaningful measures of uncertainty around the estimates it produces, as demonstrated by Swanson and Beck (1994) and shown in this paper. No population technique other than those based on survey samples has this characteristic. Further, as suggested by Snow (1911) and those who discussed his ground-breaking use of multiple regression for population estimation, it is important to use variables that represent some measure of relative change over time, which the ratio-correlation method does. Although ratio-correlation is inherently a cross-sectional model rather than a time series, Swanson (2004) suggests that one of the reasons for its consistently good performance may be due to the fact that the formation of the change in ratios provides some of the benefits associated with "stationarity," which is an essential characteristic of time series models (Smith et al. 2001, pp. 172–176). In this context, it is worth noting that the ratio-correlation approach is conceptually similar to using cohort change ratios to project a population by age (Hamilton and Perry 1962, Smith et al. 2001, pp. 127–129, Swanson and Tayman 2013, Swanson and Tedrow 2013).

The basic assumption underlying the regression methods discussed here is the same as those underlying any trend extrapolation method—in terms of the change in a variable of interest specified by a particular method—the future will be just like the past. This is the source of model invariance and one must always ask in using a regression-based method what sort of changes are expected to occur over time and how can they be accommodated? These questions can be set in terms of spatial and temporal heterogeneity, spatial autocorrelation, spatial dependence, and spatial interaction. Some progress toward answering these questions appears to have been made (D'Allesandro and Tayman 1980; Ericksen 1973; Mandel and Tayman 1982; McKibben and Swanson 1997; Swanson 1978b; Swanson 1980; Tayman and Schafer 1985), but more work is needed. A factor favoring the success of these endeavors is that these regression models are firmly embedded in the theory, substance, and issues of spatial demography (Voss 2007).

Appendix

1990–2000 Ratio-Correlation Model: Data, Computations, and 2005 EstimatesWashington State Counties

Table 8.2 Registered voters, 1990, 2000 and 2005

	Number			Proportion			Ratios	
County	1990	2000	2005	1990	2000	2005	2000/1990	2005/2000
Adams	5,553	6,098	6,477	0.002500	0.001967	0.001846	0.786800	0.938485
Asotin	8,597	12,987	11,805	0.003870	0.004190	0.003365	1.082687	0.803103
Benton	53,452	75,315	85,586	0.024062	0.024299	0.024396	1.009850	1.003992
Chelan	24,043	32,803	37,395	0.010823	0.010583	0.010659	0.977825	1.007181
Clallam	28,085	39,068	43,520	0.012643	0.012604	0.012405	0.996915	0.984211
Clark	88,903	167,584	207,611	0.040021	0.054067	0.059179	1.350966	1.094549
Columbia	2,256	2,671	2,542	0.001016	0.000862	0.000725	0.848425	0.841067
Cowlitz	34,503	49,643	53,914	0.015532	0.016016	0.015368	1.031161	0.959540
Douglas	11,320	16,855	16,994	0.005096	0.005438	0.004844	1.067111	0.890769
Ferry	2,486	3,856	4,088	0.001119	0.001244	0.001165	1.111707	0.936495
Franklin	13,228	16,321	21,235	0.005955	0.005266	0.006053	0.884299	1.149449
Garfield	1,537	1,670	1,524	0.000692	0.000539	0.000434	0.778902	0.805195
Grant	21,391	29,970	32,760	0.009629	0.009669	0.009338	1.004154	0.965767
Gig Harbor	29,613	32,038	36,647	0.013331	0.010336	0.010446	0.775336	1.010642
Island	24,325	38,265	43,688	0.010950	0.012345	0.012453	1.127397	1.008748
Jefferson	11,413	17,330	21,165	0.005138	0.005591	0.006033	1.088167	1.079056
King	765,692	1,001,339	1,082,406	0.344688	0.323059	0.308535	0.937250	0.955042
Kitsap	82,518	125,219	138,956	0.037147	0.040399	0.039609	1.087544	0.980445
Kittitas	12,836	16,417	19,817	0.005778	0.005297	0.005649	0.916753	1.066453
Klickitat	7,943	11,717	12,163	0.003576	0.003780	0.003467	1.057047	0.917196
Lewis	27,990	40,913	38,007	0.012600	0.013200	0.010834	1.047619	0.820758
Lincoln	5,495	6,656	6,642	0.002474	0.002147	0.001893	0.867825	0.881695
Mason	18,108	27,238	31,083	0.008152	0.008788	0.008860	1.078018	1.008193

Table 8.2 (continued)

	Number			Proportion			Ratios	
County	1990	2000	2005	1990	2000	2005	2000/1990	2005/2000
Okanogan	14,987	18,159	20,066	0.006747	0.005859	0.005720	0.868386	0.976276
Pacific	9,906	12,697	13,195	0.004459	0.004096	0.003761	0.918592	0.918213
Pend Oreille	4,851	6,903	7,486	0.002184	0.002227	0.002134	1.019689	0.958240
Pierce	229,449	325,079	405,023	0.103290	0.104879	0.115450	1.015384	1.100792
San Juan	6,919	9,228	11,246	0.003115	0.002977	0.003206	0.955698	1.076923
Skagit	38,696	55,780	63,185	0.017420	0.017996	0.018011	1.033065	1.000834
Skamania	3,946	5,586	6,305	0.001776	0.001802	0.001797	1.014640	0.997225
Snohomish	196,968	303,110	352,238	0.088668	0.097792	0.100404	1.102901	1.026710
Spokane	165,189	209,404	251,184	0.074362	0.067559	0.071599	0.908515	1.059800
Stevens	14,406	25,481	28,414	0.006485	0.008221	0.008099	1.267695	0.985160
Thurston	79,381	119,016	137,742	0.035735	0.038398	0.039263	1.074521	1.022527
Wahkaikum	1,944	2,455	2,592	0.000875	0.000792	0.000739	0.905143	0.933081
Walla Walla	20,614	24,411	29,279	0.009280	0.007876	0.008346	0.848707	1.059675
Whatcom	60,874	90,987	106,094	0.027403	0.029355	0.030242	1.071233	1.030216
Whitman	18,842	25,273	21,082	0.008482	0.008154	0.006009	0.961330	0.736939
Yakima	73,148	94,011	97,052	0.032929	0.030331	0.027664	0.921103	0.912070
Washington State	2,221,407	3,099,553	3,508,208	1.00000	1.00000	1.00000	n/a	n/a

Table 8.3 Registered automobiles, 1990, 2000, and 2005

	Number			Proportion			Ratios	
County	1990	2000	2005	1990	2000	2005	2000/1990	2005/2000
Adams	7,476	9,144	12,064	0.002643	0.002774	0.003036	1.049565	1.094448
Asotin	8,964	10,375	11,853	0.003169	0.003147	0.002983	0.993058	0.947887
Benton	62,203	80,977	103,288	0.021993	0.024563	0.025997	1.116855	1.058380
Chelan	31,360	39,153	40,826	0.011088	0.011876	0.010275	1.071068	0.865190
Clallam	29,592	35,697	43,880	0.010463	0.010828	0.011044	1.034885	1.019948
Clark	139,958	183,053	238,323	0.049484	0.055526	0.059983	1.122100	1.080269
Columbia	2,226	2,186	2,602	0.000787	0.000663	0.000655	0.842440	0.987934
Cowlitz	47,555	52,461	59,836	0.016814	0.015913	0.015060	0.946414	0.946396
Douglas	12,107	13,008	23,100	0.004281	0.003946	0.005814	0.921747	1.473391
Ferry	1,943	2,384	2,767	0.000687	0.000723	0.000696	1.052402	0.962656
Franklin	24,762	27,518	35,678	0.008755	0.008347	0.008980	0.953398	1.075836
Garfield	1,247	1,263	1,413	0.000441	0.000383	0.000356	0.868481	0.929504
Grant	28,154	35,188	42,352	0.009954	0.010674	0.010660	1.072333	0.998688
Gig Harbor	32,097	33,310	38,934	0.011348	0.010104	0.009799	0.890377	0.969814
Island	28,462	37,675	47,153	0.010063	0.011428	0.011868	1.135645	1.038502
Jefferson	10,170	14,459	18,982	0.003596	0.004386	0.004778	1.219689	1.089375
King	975,138	1,083,380	1,227,244	0.344770	0.328624	0.308885	0.953169	0.939934
Kitsap	101,075	125,716	152,831	0.035736	0.038134	0.038466	1.067103	1.008706
Kittitas	13,174	16,405	20,690	0.004658	0.004976	0.005207	1.068270	1.046423
Klickitat	8,351	9,820	11,859	0.002953	0.002979	0.002985	1.008805	1.002014
Lewis	34,157	36,164	39,820	0.012077	0.010970	0.010022	0.908338	0.913582
Lincoln	5,632	5,566	6,025	0.001991	0.001688	0.001516	0.847815	0.898104
Mason	18,893	25,701	34,352	0.006680	0.007796	0.008646	1.167066	1.109030
Okanogan	15,046	18,420	21,622	0.005320	0.005587	0.005442	1.050188	0.974047
Pacific	9,204	10,214	12,270	0.003254	0.003098	0.003088	0.952059	0.996772
Pend Oreille	4,486	5,709	7,157	0.001586	0.001732	0.001801	1.092055	1.039838

Table 8.3 (continued)

	Number			Proportion			Ratios	
County	1990	2000	2005	1990	2000	2005	2000/1990	2005/2000
Pierce	308,937	349,476	436,245	0.109228	0.106007	0.109798	0.970511	1.035762
San Juan	5,917	8,063	10,736	0.002092	0.002446	0.002702	1.169216	1.104661
Skagit	49,147	66,322	81,691	0.017376	0.020118	0.020561	1.157804	1.022020
Skamania	3,104	4,149	5,032	0.001097	0.001259	0.001267	1.147675	1.006354
Snohomish	278,326	332,324	412,919	0.098405	0.100805	0.103927	1.024389	1.030971
Spokane	202,904	231,030	277,551	0.071739	0.070079	0.069857	0.976861	0.996832
Stevens	12,789	16,866	20,268	0.004522	0.005116	0.005101	1.131358	0.997068
Thurston	104,118	121,894	163,196	0.036812	0.036974	0.041075	1.004401	1.110916
Wahkaikum	1,513	1,634	2,080	0.000535	0.000496	0.000524	0.927103	1.056452
Walla Walla	22,549	24,258	29,277	0.007972	0.007358	0.007369	0.922980	1.001495
Whatcom	70,164	90,938	115,773	0.024807	0.027584	0.029139	1.111944	1.056373
Whitman	16,285	17,061	20,277	0.005758	0.005175	0.005104	0.898750	0.986280
Yakima	99,187	117,751	141,179	0.035069	0.035718	0.035533	1.018506	0.994821
Washington State	2,828,372	3,296,712	3,973,145	1.00000	1.00000	1.00000	n/a	n/a

Table 8.4 School enrollment, Grades 1–8, 1990, 2000, and 2005

County	Number			Proportion			Ratios	
	1990	2000	2005	1990	2000	2005	2000/1990	2005/2000
Adams	2,277	2,417	2,482	0.004073	0.003614	0.003749	0.887307	1.037355
Asotin	2,212	2,183	2,077	0.003957	0.003265	0.003138	0.825120	0.961103
Benton	15,296	18,719	19,064	0.027361	0.027991	0.028803	1.023025	1.029009
Chelan	6,567	8,268	7,930	0.011747	0.012364	0.011981	1.052524	0.969023
Clallam	6,439	6,424	5,899	0.011518	0.009607	0.008912	0.834086	0.927657
Clark	30,613	42,803	46,759	0.054759	0.064006	0.070644	1.168867	1.103709
Columbia	521	381	389	0.000932	0.000570	0.000588	0.611588	1.031579
Cowlitz	10,538	11,789	11,373	0.018850	0.017628	0.017182	0.935172	0.974699
Douglas	3,285	3,979	4,067	0.005876	0.005950	0.006145	1.012594	1.032773
Ferry	896	816	736	0.001603	0.001220	0.001111	0.761073	0.910656
Franklin	5,760	6,980	8,701	0.010303	0.010438	0.013146	1.013103	1.259437
Garfield	311	295	241	0.000556	0.000441	0.000364	0.793165	0.825397
Grant	8,281	10,776	10,846	0.014813	0.016114	0.016386	1.087828	1.016880
Gig Harbor	8,129	7,778	7,155	0.014541	0.011631	0.010810	0.799876	0.929413
Island	5,803	6,433	5,909	0.010380	0.009620	0.008928	0.926782	0.928067
Jefferson	2,145	2,282	1,933	0.003837	0.003412	0.002921	0.889236	0.856096
King	145,005	173,328	170,347	0.259379	0.259188	0.257361	0.999264	0.992951
Kitsap	23,320	27,470	25,376	0.041714	0.041077	0.038339	0.984729	0.933345
Kittitas	2,637	2,907	2,964	0.004717	0.004347	0.004478	0.921560	1.030136
Klickitat	2,370	2,365	1,984	0.004239	0.003536	0.002997	0.834159	0.847568
Lewis	8,124	7,901	7,682	0.014532	0.011815	0.011605	0.813033	0.982226
Lincoln	1,466	1,475	1,341	0.002622	0.002206	0.002027	0.841342	0.918858
Mason	4,448	5,281	5,074	0.007956	0.007897	0.007666	0.992584	0.970748
Okanogan	4,449	4,895	4,021	0.007958	0.007320	0.006075	0.919829	0.829918
Pacific	2,069	2,068	1,817	0.003701	0.003092	0.002746	0.835450	0.888098
Pend Oreille	1,150	1,242	1,110	0.002057	0.001857	0.001677	0.902771	0.903069
Pierce	70,118	85,065	84,043	0.125424	0.127203	0.126973	1.014184	0.998192

Table 8.4 (continued)

County	Number			Proportion			Ratios	
	1990	2000	2005	1990	2000	2005	2000/1990	2005/2000
San Juan	949	1,175	1,126	0.001698	0.001757	0.001700	1.034747	0.967558
Skagit	9,713	12,035	12,072	0.017374	0.017997	0.018239	1.035858	1.013447
Skamania	877	835	748	0.001569	0.001248	0.001130	0.795411	0.905449
Snohomish	56,030	73,759	73,322	0.100224	0.110296	0.110775	1.100495	1.004343
Spokane	43,219	48,216	46,975	0.077308	0.072101	0.070970	0.932646	0.984314
Stevens	3,898	3,938	3,754	0.006973	0.005888	0.005672	0.844400	0.963315
Thurston	20,459	23,806	24,096	0.036596	0.035599	0.036404	0.972757	1.022613
Wahkaikum	287	318	302	0.000513	0.000476	0.000456	0.927875	0.957983
Walla Walla	5,650	6,082	6,027	0.010107	0.009095	0.009106	0.899871	1.001209
Whatcom	14,297	17,695	17,575	0.025574	0.026460	0.026552	1.034645	1.003477
Whitman	3,079	3,120	2,891	0.005508	0.004666	0.004368	0.847131	0.936134
Yakima	26,359	31,436	31,688	0.047150	0.047008	0.047875	0.996988	1.018444
Washington State	559,046	668,735	661,898	1.00000	1.00000	1.00000	n/a	n/a

Table 8.5 Total population 1990 and 2000

	Number		Proportion		Ratio
County	1990	2000	1990	2000	2000/1990
Adams	13,603	16,428	0.002795	0.002787	0.997138
Asotin	17,605	20,551	0.003617	0.003487	0.964059
Benton	112,560	142,475	0.023129	0.024172	1.045095
Chelan	52,250	66,616	0.010736	0.011302	1.052720
Clallam	56,464	64,525	0.011602	0.010947	0.943544
Clark	238,053	345,238	0.048915	0.058573	1.197445
Columbia	4,024	4,064	0.000827	0.000690	0.834341
Cowlitz	82,119	92,948	0.016874	0.015770	0.934574
Douglas	26,205	32,603	0.005385	0.005531	1.027112
Ferry	6,295	7,260	0.001293	0.001232	0.952823
Franklin	37,473	49,347	0.007700	0.008372	1.087273
Garfield	2,248	2,397	0.000462	0.000407	0.880952
Grant	54,758	74,698	0.011252	0.012673	1.126289
Gig Harbor	64,175	67,194	0.013187	0.011400	0.864488
Island	60,195	71,558	0.012369	0.012141	0.981567
Jefferson	20,146	25,953	0.004140	0.004403	1.063527
King	1,507,319	1,737,034	0.309721	0.294706	0.951521
Kitsap	189,731	231,969	0.038986	0.039356	1.009491
Kittitas	26,725	33,362	0.005491	0.005660	1.030778
Klickitat	16,616	19,161	0.003414	0.003251	0.952255
Lewis	59,358	68,600	0.012197	0.011639	0.954251
Lincoln	8,864	10,184	0.001821	0.001728	0.948929
Mason	38,341	49,405	0.007878	0.008382	1.063976
Okanogan	33,350	39,564	0.006853	0.006712	0.979425
Pacific	18,882	20,984	0.003880	0.003560	0.917526
Pend Oreille	8,915	11,732	0.001832	0.001990	1.086245
Pierce	586,203	700,820	0.120452	0.118902	0.987132
San Juan	10,035	14,077	0.002062	0.002388	1.158099
Skagit	79,555	102,979	0.016347	0.017471	1.068759
Skamania	8,289	9,872	0.001703	0.001675	0.983558
Snohomish	465,642	606,024	0.095679	0.102818	1.074614
Spokane	361,364	417,939	0.074252	0.070908	0.954964
Stevens	30,948	40,066	0.006359	0.006798	1.069036
Thurston	161,238	207,355	0.033131	0.035180	1.061845
Wahkaikum	3,327	3,824	0.000684	0.000649	0.948830
Walla Walla	48,439	55,180	0.009953	0.009362	0.940621
Whatcom	127,780	166,814	0.026256	0.028302	1.077925
Whitman	38,775	40,740	0.007967	0.006912	0.867579
Yakima	188,823	222,581	0.038799	0.037763	0.973298
Washington State	4,866,692	5,894,121	1.00000	1.00000	n/a

Table 8.6 Population estimates, 2005

	Proportions				
	Estimated			2005 Population	
County	2000	2005/2000[a]	2005[b]	Uncontrolled[c]	Controlled[d]
Adams	0.002787	1.086296	0.003028	18,943	18,475
Asotin	0.003487	0.965916	0.003368	21,071	20,550
Benton	0.024172	1.065724	0.025761	161,172	157,191
Chelan	0.011302	0.924204	0.010445	65,351	63,737
Clallam	0.010947	1.035677	0.011338	70,935	69,183
Clark	0.058573	1.090261	0.063860	399,534	389,664
Columbia	0.000690	0.998584	0.000689	4,308	4,202
Cowlitz	0.015770	0.979367	0.015444	96,625	94,238
Douglas	0.005531	1.359950	0.007522	47,064	45,901
Ferry	0.001232	0.989464	0.001219	7,625	7,437
Franklin	0.008372	1.092101	0.009143	57,204	55,791
Garfield	0.000407	0.951779	0.000387	2,422	2,362
Grant	0.012673	1.018336	0.012906	80,743	78,748
Gig Harbor	0.011400	1.001349	0.011416	71,420	69,656
Island	0.012141	1.051574	0.012767	79,874	77,901
Jefferson	0.004403	1.095443	0.004823	30,177	29,432
King	0.294706	0.974204	0.287104	1,796,237	1,751,863
Kitsap	0.039356	1.027072	0.040421	252,893	246,646
Kittitas	0.005660	1.062829	0.006016	37,638	36,708
Klickitat	0.003251	1.016264	0.003304	20,670	20,159
Lewis	0.011639	0.942366	0.010968	68,620	66,925
Lincoln	0.001728	0.936698	0.001618	10,126	9,876
Mason	0.008382	1.103328	0.009248	57,860	56,431
Okanogan	0.006712	1.001189	0.006720	42,046	41,007
Pacific	0.003560	1.012494	0.003605	22,552	21,995
Pend Oreille	0.001990	1.048110	0.002086	13,052	12,730
Pierce	0.118902	1.058160	0.125817	787,160	767,714
San Juan	0.002388	1.106619	0.002643	16,535	16,127
Skagit	0.017471	1.038749	0.018148	113,544	110,739
Skamania	0.001675	1.026895	0.001720	10,761	10,495
Snohomish	0.102818	1.047737	0.107727	673,979	657,329
Spokane	0.070908	1.025751	0.072734	455,051	443,810
Stevens	0.006798	1.019002	0.006927	43,337	42,266
Thurston	0.035180	1.106022	0.038910	243,435	237,421
Wahkaikum	0.000649	1.057515	0.000686	4,292	4,186
Walla Walla	0.009362	1.029116	0.009634	60,277	58,788
Whatcom	0.028302	1.066692	0.030189	188,876	184,210
Whitman	0.006912	0.987798	0.006828	42,716	41,661
Yakima	0.037763	1.010508	0.038160	238,744	232,846
Washington State	1.00000	n/a	1.02533	6,414,869	6,256,400

[a] Computed from estimated regression equation and 2005/2000 symptomatic indicators
[b] 2000 proportion × estimated 2005/2000 proportion
[c] Estimated 2005 proportion × State control total (6,256,400)
[d] Uncontrolled population × adjustment factor (6,256,400/6,414,869)

References

Bryan, T. (2004). Population estimates. In J. S. Siegel & D. A. Swanson (Eds.), *The methods and materials of demography*, (2nd ed., pp. 523–560). Amsterdam: Elsevier.

Causey, B. (1988). *Evaluation of census ratio estimation and synthetic estimation*. Statistical Research Division report no. Census/SRD/RR/88/15, http://www.census.gov/srd/papers/pdf/rr88-15.pdf.

Cohen, M., & Zhang, X. (1988). *The difficulty of improving statistical synthetic estimation*. Statistical Research Division report no. CENSUS/SRD/RR-88/12. Washington, DC: U. S. Bureau of the Census, http://www.census.gov/srd/papers/pdf/rr88-12.pdf.

Crosetti, A., & Schmitt, R. (1956). A method of estimating the inter-censal population of counties. *Journal of the American Statistical Association, 5,* 587–590.

D'Allesandro, F., & Tayman, J. (1980). *Ridge regression for population estimation: Some insights and clarifications*. Staff document No. 56. Olympia. Washington: Office of Financial Management.

Ericksen, E. (1973). A method for combining sample survey data and symptomatic indicators to obtain population estimates for local areas. *Demography, 10,* 137–160.

Ericksen, E. (1974). A regression method for estimating population changes of local areas. *Journal of the American Statistical Association, 69,* 867–875.

Ford, B. (1981). *The development of county estimates in North Carolina*. Staff report AGES 811119. Agriculture statistical reporting service, Research Division. Washington, DC: U.S. Department of Agriculture.

Fox, J. (1991). *Regression diagnostics*. Quantitative applications in the social sciences, no. 79. Newbury Park: Sage Publications.

Ghosh, M., & Rao, J. N. K. (1994). Small area estimation: An appraisal. *Statistical Science, 9,* 55–76.

Gonzalez, M., & Hoza, C. (1978). Small area estimation with application to unemployment and housing estimates. *Journal of the American Statistical Association, 73,* 7–15.

Hamilton, C. H., & Perry, J. (1962). A short method for projecting population by age from one decennial census to another. *Social Forces, 41,* 163–170.

Hansen, M., Hurwitz, W., & Madow, W. (1953). *Sample survey methods and theory, volume I: Methods and applications*. New York: Wiley.

Jaffe, A. J. (1951). *Handbook of statistical methods for demographers: Selected problems in the analysis of census data, preliminary edition, second printing*. Washington, DC: U.S. Government Printing Office.

Levy, P. (1979). Small area estimation: Synthetic and other procedures, 1968–1978. In J. Steinberg (Ed.), *Synthetic estimates for small areas: Statistical workshop papers and discussion. NIDA research monograph 24* (pp. 4–19). Rockville: U.S. Department of Health, Education, and Welfare, Public Health Service, Alcohol, Drug Abuse, and Mental Health Administration, National Institute on Drug Abuse.

Mandel, M., & Tayman, J. (1982). Measuring temporal stability in regression models of population estimation. *Demography, 19,* 135–146.

McKibben, J., & Swanson, D. A. (1997). Linking substance and practice: A case study of the relationship between socio-economic structure and population estimation. *Journal of Economic and Social Measurement, 24,* 135–147.

Namboodiri, N. K., & Lalu, N. (1971). The average of several simple regression estimates as an alternative to the multiple regression estimate in post-censal and inter-censal population estimation: A case study. *Rural Sociology, 36,* 187–194.

National Center for Health Statistics. (1968). *Synthetic state estimates of disability*. PHS publication no. 1759. U.S. Public Health Service. Washington, DC: U.S. Government Printing Office.

O'Hare, W. (1980). A note on the use of regression methods in population estimates. *Demography, 17,* 341–343.

Platek, R., Rao, J. N. K., Särndal, C. E., & Singh, M. P. (Eds.). (1987). *Small area statistics: An international symposium*. New York: Wiley.

Rao, J. N. K. (2003). *Small area estimation*. New York: Wiley-Interscience.

Schaible, W. (1993). *Indirect estimators: Definition, characteristics, and recommendations*. Proceedings of the survey research methods section, American Statistical Association Vol. I (pp. 1–10). Alexandria, VA: American Statistical Association, http://www.amstat.org/sections/srms/proceedings/y1993f.html.

Schmitt, R., & Crosetti, A. (1954). Accuracy of the ratio-correlation method for estimating post-censal population. *Land Economics, 30,* 279–281.

Schmitt, R., & Grier, J. (1966). A method of estimating the population of minor civil divisions. *Rural Sociology, 31,* 355–361.

Smith, S. K., Tayman, J., & Swanson, D. A. (2001). *State and local population projections: Methodology and analysis*. New York: Kluwer.

Snow, E. C. (1911). The application of the method of multiple correlation to the estimation of post-censal populations. *Journal of the Royal Statistical Society, 74*, 575–629. (pp. 621–629 contain the discussion).

Spar, M., & Martin, J. (1979). Refinements to regression-based estimates of post-censal population characteristics. *Review of Public Data Use, 7,* 16–22.

Steinberg, J. (1979). Introduction. In J. Steinberg (Ed.), *Synthetic estimates for small areas: Statistical workshop papers and discussion NIDA research monograph 24* (pp. 1–2). Rockville: U.S. Department of Health, Education, and Welfare, Public Health Service, Alcohol, Drug Abuse, and Mental Health Administration, National Institute on Drug Abuse.

Stigler, S. (1986). *The history of statistics: The measurement of uncertainty before 1900*. Cambridge: The Belknap Press of Harvard University.

Swanson, D. A. (1978a). An evaluation of ratio and difference regression methods for estimating small, highly concentrated populations: The case of ethnic groups. *Review of Public Data Use, 6,* 18–27.

Swanson, D. A. (1978b). *Preliminary results of an evaluation of the utility of ridge regression for making county population estimates*. Presented at the annual meeting of the Pacific Sociological Association, Spokane, WA.

Swanson, D. A. (1980). Improving accuracy in multiple regression estimates of county populations using principles from causal modeling. *Demography, 17,* 413–427.

Swanson, D. A. (1989). Confidence intervals for postcensal population estimates: A case study for local areas. *Survey Methodology, 15,* 271–280.

Swanson, D. A. (2004). Advancing methodological knowledge within state and local demography: A case study. *Population Research and Policy Review, 23,* 379–398.

Swanson, D. A., & Beck, D. (1994). A new short-term county population projection method. *Journal of Economic and Social Measurement, 21,* 25–50.

Swanson, D. A., & Pol, L. (2008). Applied demography: Its business and public sector components. In Y. Zeng (Ed.), *The encyclopedia of life support systems, demography volume* (pp. 321–348). Oxford: UNESCO-EOLSS Publishers.

Swanson, D. A., & Prevost, R. (1985). A new technique for assessing error in ratio-correlation estimates of population: A preliminary note. *Applied Demography, 1,* 1–4.

Swanson, D. A., & Tayman, J. (2013). *Measuring uncertainty in population forecasts: A new approach*. Presented at the EUROSTAT/UNECE work session on Demographic Projections, Rome, Italy, October 29–31.

Swanson, D. A., & Tedrow, L. (1984). Improving the measurement of change in regression models used for county population estimates. *Demography, 21,* 373–381.

Swanson, D. A., & Tedrow, L. (2013). *Exploring stable population concepts from the perspective of cohort change ratios*. Presented at the annual conference of the Canadian Population Society, Victoria, British Columbia, Canada, June 5–7.

Tayman, J., & Schafer, E. (1985). The impact of coefficient drift and measurement error on the accuracy of ratio-correlation population estimates. *The Review of Regional Studies, 15,* 3–10.

Voss, P. (2007). Demography as a spatial social science. *Population Research and Policy Review, 26,* 457–476.

Weisstein, E. W. (2011). Estimator bias. From MathWorld, a Wolfram web resource, http://mathworld.wolfram.com/EstimatorBias.html.

Chapter 9
Assessing Accuracy in Postcensal Estimates: Statistical Properties of Different Measures

Howard Hogan and Mary H. Mulry

Introduction

Over 30 years ago, the National Research Council Committee on National Statistics (CNSTAT) published its influential *Estimating Population and Income of Small Areas* (Panel on Small-Area Estimates of Population and Income 1980). This was at the height of General Revenue Sharing when the visibility of the U.S. Census Bureau postcensal estimates was high.

The CNSTAT report articulated four "considerations of accuracy" for the postcensal estimates:

1. Low average error,
2. Low average relative error,
3. Few extreme relative errors, and
4. Absence of bias for subgroups.

One needs to recall the situation in federal statistics and particularly the census to understand the context surrounding the CNSTAT report. First, 1980 was at the very beginning of the controversy, which was legal, political, and statistical, concerning the census undercount and how statistical estimates should account for that error. Several developments since 1980 are important.

In 1980, the most recent estimate of net national census undercount was 2.5% for the 1970 Census (Siegel 1974), which was later revised to 2.7% (Hogan and Robinson 1993). More importantly, the only estimates of undercount for sub-national areas were for states, which were the demographically derived Developmental Estimates (U.S. Census Bureau 1977). We now have three well-executed post-enumeration surveys

---

This report is released to inform interested parties and encourage discussion of work in progress. The views expressed on statistical, methodological, and operational issues are those of the authors and not necessarily those of the U.S. Census Bureau.

H. Hogan (✉) · M. H. Mulry
U.S. Census Bureau, Washington, D.C., USA
e-mail: howard.r.hogan@census.gov

M. N. Hoque, L. B. Potter (eds.), *Emerging Techniques in Applied Demography*, Applied Demography Series 4, DOI 10.1007/978-94-017-8990-5_9,

(1990, 2000, and 2010). These can be used to improve the assessment of the accuracy of the postcensal estimates.

Equally important, the issue of correcting the census base for the population estimates for undercount was still being debated in 1980. In other words, the goal of the estimates was explicitly to measure the population as accurately as possible. However, in 1990 and again in 2000, the U.S. Census Bureau considered and rejected the idea of changing the census base for the population estimates program (U.S. Census Bureau 1991, 2001). The goal of the estimates program then became measuring not the level of population but the change in population since the most recent census.

Finally, one important result of the statistical debate over census undercount adjustment was serious thinking and research on measures of accuracy, especially measures implied by the uses of the estimates to allocate fixed resources, i.e. federal money.

This paper discusses the measures designed to reflect the four principles outlined in the CNSTAT report and also makes a few suggestions as to how better to assess the accuracy of the postcensal estimates. The goal is to take advantage of some of what has been learned during the past three decades.

We see the measures of accuracy principally as a tool for statisticians and demographers to assess different estimation methods, and only secondarily as a tool to communicate accuracy to data users. A full understanding of the statistical properties of different accuracy measures is important to making informed decisions about current and future estimation methods.

Background

The four principles outlined in the CNSTAT report still guide the assessment of estimates produced by the Postcensal Estimates Program and used in fund allocations. The program has quantified the principles with measures that are listed below (Yowell and Devine 2012).

First, we need some notation. Let

N = Number of areas.
y_i = Estimated population for area i.
$Y = \sum y_{i.}$
t_i = Target (or True) population value for area i.
$T = \sum t_{i.}$

(1) Low average error Three measures assess the average error in different ways. However, in each of these measures, average is measured across areas (states, counties, etc.).

- Mean Absolute Proportional Error (MAPE)

$$\sum \frac{\left(|y_i - t_i|/t_i\right)}{N}$$

MAPE treats percentage error the same for large areas and small areas. An error of 1 % has the same contribution regardless of the size of the area, whether it occurs in California or Rhode Island. In addition, an underestimate has the same contribution as an overestimate. However, when MAPE is very small, the expected proportional error has to be small for a *place* selected at random. MAPE is often expressed as percentage rather than a proportion.

- Mean Algebraic Proportional Error (MALPE)

$$\sum \frac{(y_i - t_i)/t_i}{N}$$

MALPE allows over- and under-estimates to offset. However, the off-setting is done at the place level. Again, MALPE is often expressed as a percentage. An over-estimate in a large state may offset an under-estimate in a small state. A 1 % over-estimate in California may offset a 1 % under-estimate in Rhode Island.

- Root Mean Square Error (RMSE)

$$\sum \left(\frac{(y_i - t_i)^2}{N} \right)^{1/2}$$

RMSE is a common measure for evaluating the quality of an estimate. In a set of estimates, squaring the error for an area puts greater weight on the larger errors. However, a small percentage error in a large state may swamp a large percentage error in a small area.

(2) Low average relative error

- Total Absolute Error of Shares (TAES)

$$\sum |y_i/Y - t_i/T|.$$

TAES sums the absolute values of the errors in the areas' shares where an area's share is defined by its portion of the population. The first term is the share, as measured by the estimates of the total population of each place, while the second term is the share from the true or target distribution. Although the Census Bureau uses "Total" error in its reports, dividing by the number of areas quickly yields the average error.

(3) Few extreme relative errors

- Number of areas with large absolute percentage error

$$\sum I_{\alpha,i}$$

where

$$I_{\alpha,i} = 1 \text{ if } \left(\frac{|y_i - t_i|}{t_i} \right) > \alpha,$$
$$0, \text{ otherwise.}$$

The number of areas with absolute relative percentage error above a specified threshold α aims to measure extreme relative errors. The values of α currently in use are 5% and 10%.

(4) Absence of bias for subgroups This is assessed by applying the above measures to areas grouped by size at the beginning of the decade and percent population growth during the decade, both as measured by the census.

In assessing accuracy of the postcensal estimates for the year of the next census, the new census result serves as the target or measure of truth.

These measures have played and will continue to play an important role in assessing post-censal estimates. We believe that the current measures are valuable on two counts. First, the measures do quantify important aspects of accuracy. Secondly, after 30 some years of use, the measures are relatively well accepted and well understood. Importantly in the current discussion, the Federal State Cooperative Program for Population Estimates (FSCPE) partners discussed the current measures and accepted them before the results were known.

However, the measures have several important limitations. All measures emphasize the place rather than the individual or person. The statistical basis underlying these measures is not clear, or at least not clearly articulated. What is being minimized and why? Although not a direct criticism of the theoretical measures, the impacts of errors in the target population are also not often well articulated. We address these issues in the remainder of this paper.

Measure of Equity

The first point concerns whether the current measures adequately assess the issue of fairness in the use of the estimates in allocating a fixed amount to areas or other entities, called a "fixed pie" allocation. In an important paper published soon after the NRC report, Ivan Fellegi (1980) addressed the issue of which measures of accuracy flow from specific uses of the data. Of the issues he addressed, the most relevant in this context is the use of the estimates of population size to divide a fixed total amount of money equally among areas *per capita*. The amount each unit should receive

$$a_i = \left(\frac{t_i}{T}\right) A$$

where:

y_i = Estimated population for area i.
$Y = \sum y_i$
t_i = Target (or True) population for area i.
$T = \sum t_i$
a = Amount (dollars) that should go to area i.
A = Total (dollar) amount.

The amount that should be distributed per capita equals:

$$X = \frac{A}{T}$$

However, when the distribution of funds is based on estimates, the amount actually distributed per capita to area i equals:

$$x_i = \left[\left(\frac{y_i}{Y}\right)A\right]\left(\frac{1}{t_i}\right)$$

The term in brackets denotes the amount that area i will get, which is divided by its true (or target) population. That is, the amount is allocated by the measured share, but the per capita amount for each place is determined by its true population.

Both the error in the per capita amount for area i and the error in the total amount for area i depend on the error in the share for area i. The true share for area i is t_i/T while the share for area i based on the estimates is y_i/Y. We show below why the error in the share is important.

The per capita error is:

$$d_i = X - x_i = \frac{A}{T} - A\left(\frac{y_i}{Y}\right)\left(\frac{1}{t_i}\right)$$

$$= \frac{A}{Y}\left(\frac{Y}{T} - \frac{y_i}{t_i}\right) \qquad (9.1)$$

Fellegi defined equity as "a numerical measure of the extent to which legislative intent is complied with." Although the details of the intent of legislation are often complex, one dimension is equal treatment of all individuals. That is, if a person did not know the jurisdiction where he/she would be living, which allocation would he/she choose? This concept is known as "interpreting equity as impersonality." For details regarding the interpretation of equity, see discussions by Spencer (1980a, 1980b)

Motivated by the premise of equitable treatment of all people, Fellegi suggested a measure of accuracy that treats all individuals equally regardless of jurisdiction. This measure relates the percentage error to the per capita error. First, we define proportional error in population as

$$e_i = \frac{(t_i - y_i)}{t_i} \qquad \textit{for area } i,$$

$$E = \frac{(T - Y)}{T} \qquad \textit{for the areas combined.}$$

Then Fellegi drew on the convention of squared error combined with weighting the squared error by the area's proportion of the whole, called its share, to suggest the following sum over all the areas as a measure of error:

$$\sum \frac{t_i}{T}(d_i)^2 = \sum \frac{t_i}{T}\frac{A^2}{Y^2}\left(\frac{Y}{T}-\frac{y_i}{t_i}\right)^2 \tag{9.2a}$$

$$= \frac{A^2}{TY^2}\sum t_i\left(\left(1-\frac{y_i}{t_i}\right)-\left(1-\frac{Y}{T}\right)\right)^2 \tag{9.2b}$$

$$= \frac{A^2}{T^3}\frac{1}{(1-E)^2}\sum t_i(e_i-E)^2 \tag{9.2c}$$

by using that $Y = T - T(T-Y)/T$.

Fellegi's measure also has appeared in the literature as Eq. (9.2a) (Mulry and Hogan 1986) in the form of

$$\frac{A^2}{TY^2}\sum t_i\left(\frac{Y}{T}-\frac{y_i}{t_i}\right)^2 \tag{9.3}$$

In addition, the measure also may be formulated in terms of error in the shares by noticing that Eq. (9.2a) equals

$$\sum \frac{t_i}{T}A^2\left(\frac{t_i}{Tt_i}-\frac{y_i}{Yt_i}\right)^2 = \frac{A^2}{T}\sum \frac{1}{t_i}\left(\frac{t_i}{T}-\frac{y_i}{Y}\right)^2. \tag{9.4}$$

The interpretation of the Eq. (9.4) is that the squared error in shares is weighted by the inverse of the size of the area (Alho and Spencer 2005, Chap. 4, p. 359).

For our analysis, we are going to use Fellegi's measure as expressed in Eq. (9.3) but drop the constant A^2/T that does not depend on the set of estimates under evaluation. We call this measure Weighted Proportional Squared Error (WPSE)

$$\frac{1}{Y^2}\sum t_i\left(\frac{Y}{T}-\frac{y_i}{t_i}\right)^2$$

Equation (9.4) shows that WPSE may be formulated in terms of error in shares. It is related to but not equivalent to Total Absolute Error of Shares (TAES)

$$\sum \left|\frac{\mathrm{y_i}}{\mathrm{Y}}-\frac{\mathrm{t_i}}{\mathrm{T}}\right|.$$

Table 9.1 Target population size of counties in Tables 9.2 and 9.3

County	Target size
Loving County	100
Jones County	1,000
Yuma County	10,000
Ashtabula County	100,000
Salt Lake County	1,000,000
Los Angeles County	10,000,000

The difference is that TAES focuses on equity across jurisdictions, while WPSE focuses on equity across all people.

To gain a more intuitive understanding of the nature of the different measures, we constructed a simple example shown in Table 9.1. We focus on six hypotheical counties, successively larger by factors of 10, with population sizes ranging from 100 people to 10 million. The county names are included to suggest that while this example includes only six rather than 3,019 counties, it is realistic in term of the range of county size actually observed in the United States. The order of magnitude in the example is comparable to that of the real counties with the same name.

Now assume that the estimates program underestimates the population size of one of these counties by exactly 10 %, while the estimates for other counties are precisely correct. How does this affect each measure? Table 9.2 illustrates this. Since the measures have different scales and we wish to understand the relative impact of an error, we have, in Table 9.3, scaled the measures relative to the error measure for a county size 100,000, which is "Ashtabula" in the example. As expected, the relative impact of a 10 % error on MAPE and MALPE is constant. Missing 10 people in "Loving County" has the same impact as missing a million in "Los Angeles County." This seems to give too little importance to errors in large counties. On the other hand, we have the RMSE. Missing 10 % of any county has an effect roughly proportional to its population size.

With the exception of "Los Angeles County," each of the two accuracy measures based on shares (TAES and WPSE) gives approximately the same relative importance to errors in the different size categories. Further, these impacts on the error measures are roughly proportional to the population size. However, this is not strictly the case, as illustrated by "Los Angeles County." Note that an error in any one county affects both its estimate (y_i) and the estimated total (Y), that is both numerator and denominator are affected. For counties that are a small part of the total, the effect on Y is quite literally negligible. However, in our example, "Los Angeles County" is proportionally very large and an error there affects greatly the estimated total population.

Table 9.2 Measures for when one county has 10 % error and the other counties have no error

No.	Scenarios for error in counties						Measures of error for data set for each scenario				
							TAES	WPSE	MAPE	MALPE	RMSE
	Loving	Jones	Yuma	Ashtabula	Salt Lake	Los Angeles	$\Sigma\lvert y_i/Y-t_i/T\rvert$	$\Sigma(t_i(y_i/t_i-Y/T)^2)/Y^2$ (× 10 billion)	$\Sigma(\lvert y_i-t_i\rvert/t_i)/n$	$\Sigma((y_i-t_i)/t_i)/n$	$\text{sqrt}\Sigma((y_i-t_i)^2)/n$
1	10 %	0	0	0	0	0	0.000002	0.000008	0.0167	−0.0167	4.08
2	0	10 %	0	0	0	0	0.000018	0.000081	0.0167	−0.0167	40.82
3	0	0	10 %	0	0	0	0.000180	0.000809	0.0167	−0.0167	408.25
4	0	0	0	10 %	0	0	0.001785	0.008042	0.0167	−0.0167	4,082.48
5	0	0	0	0	10 %	0	0.016529	0.075055	0.0167	−0.0167	40,824.83
6	0	0	0	0	0	10 %	0.019780	0.097814	0.0167	−0.0167	408,248.29

Table 9.3 Measures relative to the value of the measure when only error is a 10 % error in a county of size 100,000 (Ashtabula)

No.	Scenarios for error in counties						Measures of error for data set for each scenario				
							TAES	WPSE	MAPE	MALPE	RMSE
	Loving	Jones	Yuma	Ashtabula	Salt Lake	Los Angeles	$\Sigma \lvert y_i/Y - t_i/T \rvert$	$\Sigma(t_i(y_i/t_i - Y/T)^2)/Y^2$ (× 10 billion)	$\Sigma(\lvert y_i - t_i \rvert/t_i)/n$	$\Sigma((y_i - t_i)/t_i)/n$	$\text{sqrt}\Sigma((y_i - t_i)^2)/n$
1	10 %	0	0	0	0	0	0.001	0.001	1.000	1.000	0.001
2	0	10 %	0	0	0	0	0.010	0.010	1.000	1.000	0.010
3	0	0	10 %	0	0	0	0.101	0.101	1.000	1.000	0.100
4	0	0	0	10 %	0	0	1.000	1.000	1.000	1.000	1.000
5	0	0	0	0	10 %	0	9.258	9.333	1.000	1.000	10.000
6	0	0	0	0	0	10 %	11.079	12.163	1.000	1.000	100.000

Assessment of Bias

Another analysis of the current methods concerns the assessment of bias. As statisticians we consider bias as the difference between the expected value of a measure and its true value. Ideally and conceptually, to measure bias one would need to run the population estimates program over a series of realizations, the so-called "super-population" model. This cannot be done as we have only one set of estimates and one set of true populations for each decade. However, we must keep in mind that just because a method over- or under-estimated a set of places during a particular decade does not mean that the method was *a priori* biased.

Clearly a method that systematically short-changed some groups would be unacceptable statistically and politically. The current approach to assessing the effect of a set of estimates on subgroups is by applying the measures to subsets of the jurisdictions, most importantly, jurisdictions sorted by:

- Population size at the start of the period
- Population growth during the period

The use of population size at the start of the period provides information about the error in areas of comparable size. Grouping areas by the amount of growth tends to show the bias in estimates for the areas with large growth or large decline. However, both of these groupings tend to be somewhat correlated with the estimates.

We argue that a more complete assessment of *bias* would examine subgroups defined using variables independent from, and thereby uncorrelated with, what we are trying to measure. For example, if areas that grew fast in the previous decade tended to be underestimated in the current decade, then we would have evidence of bias.

Assessments of the error in the estimates should focus on regional variations and other characteristics that cause variations in accuracy of the data used in forming the estimates. The characteristics that are candidates for consideration include:

- Census divisions (Northeast, Mid-Atlantic, South-Atlantic)
- Metro/Non-metro counties
- Counties with high completeness in the Master Address File (MAF) vs. other areas
- Areas with high percentage of permanent single family dwellings vs. those with high percentage of multi-unit, mobile, and other non-standard dwellings
- Areas with high immigrant populations, as measured at the beginning of the period

The goal is to design methods so that, at the beginning of the period, no person or mayor could predict that his/her jurisdiction would be disadvantaged. Some work has been done in this area (see for example Bolender et al. 2012). However, it has not been given the prominence that it deserves.

The choice of measures is also important. In one sense simply the "error of closure" presents a possible measure of "bias." The current measures emphasize the place rather than the person. However, this can become less important if the analysis is performed by place size. To the extent that places are divided finely by population size, so that all places being compared are of roughly equal size, our criticism of MAPE or MALPE greatly lessens.

When applying relative measures, it is important to pay attention as to "relative to what?" Consider any of the relative error measures, such as:

$$\sum\left|\frac{y_i}{Y}-\frac{t_i}{T}\right|$$

In applying these to sub-groups it is important to decide whether t_i and T refer to the total population or only to the sub-group. The latter would be justified only if there were a program, for example aid to large cities or to rural areas, that only targeted the sub-group.

Considering Census Net Undercount and Its Estimation

The above discussion ignored the choice of a target or truth population. In much of the current discussion, the census measure is assumed to be the "best approximation" of truth, whether it is the true level or true change. However, the census suffers errors of its own. If we focus on population totals, these errors are coverage errors, i.e. net undercount or net overcount. For sub-groups, content errors also play a role because they may lead to misclassifications.

The definition of census undercount is easy to formulate, but measurement is more difficult. Following Spencer (1980c) and continuing the notation described earlier in this paper, define proportional census undercount as

$$u_i = \frac{(t_i - c_i)}{t_i}$$

and

$$U = \frac{(T - C)}{T},$$

where C and c_i denote the national and local census numbers.

Consider the current measurement of Mean Absolute Percent Error (MAPE)

$$\sum\left(\frac{|y_i - t_i|}{t_i}\right).$$

Currently MAPE is assessed by substituting the census count c_i for t_i

$$\sum\left(\frac{|y_i - c_i|}{c_i}\right).$$

When we account for the census undercount rate, the current MAPE becomes

$$\sum\left(\frac{\left|(y_i - t_i) + u_i t_i\right|}{(t_i - u_i t_i)}\right).$$

Notice that when y_i is larger than t_i and area i has a census undercount, u_i is positive, causing the contribution from area i to the MAPE to be greater than it should be. And when the same area i has a census overcount, u_i is negative, and the contribution from area i to the MAPE to be less than it should be. However, when y_i is less than t_i, the error in the contribution of area i to the MAPE depends on whether area i has an undercount or overcount and on the relative size of the undercount and the difference between y_i and t_i. One would have to know the configuration of the sizes of the areas and the undercount rates to know whether the MAPE would be too large or too small. However, an assumption that MAPE is unbiased in the presence of census undercount is not supported.

Census undercount also affects Mean Algebraic Percent Error (MALPE) when using

$$\sum\left(\frac{(y_i - c_i)}{c_i}\right)$$

to assess

$$\sum\left(\frac{(y_i - t_i)}{t_i}\right).$$

When we include the effect of the undercount rate, the current MALPE becomes

$$\sum\frac{((y_i - t_i)+u_i t_i)}{(t_i - u_i t_i)}.$$

Since MALPE has both positive and negative terms, derivations showing whether census undercount or overcount would tend to exaggerate or minimize measured MALPE are not possible without a specific set of sizes of areas and their census errors. Nevertheless, census error certainly would affect the comparison of estimators and comparisons of improvement in estimates over two or more decades.

A statistical assessment of the effect of census errors on the evaluation of population estimates accuracy is possible. Clearly, we do not know the true undercount for each of the states and each of the counties. However, for Census 2000 and now for the 2010 Census, we have an estimate of the census error for states. These estimates are subject to error, including sampling error. Sampling error is estimated, so it is possible to correct the *measures of accuracy* to account for the effect of census undercount and its own estimation errors. We emphasize that we are discussing correcting the "measures of accuracy" and not the estimates themselves.

How to Focus Better on the Estimation of Population Change

The above discussion has focused on estimating the population level, which was the focus of much of the 1980 CNSTAT report. However, during the following decades, the goal of the population estimates program has been to measure, not the population level, but the change in population since the previous census. Following both the 1990 and 2000 censuses, the Census Bureau reviewed the issue of whether to correct the population base used by the estimates program for census undercount. The decision was to accept the most recent census as the starting point for the population estimates. Thus, a proper assessment of the population estimates program must be how well it carries out its currently assigned mission, to estimate the true change in the population.

Again, following Spencer (1980c), we consider the goal of measuring the true change in the national population between censuses, but the following derivations also apply to areas. We want to measure

$$\text{True change} = T_{10} - T_0,$$

where the subscript 10 now refers to the current census and the subscript 0 refers to most recent past census. Since we do not know the true population sizes in the two census years, we instead measure the change in the two census counts, $C_{10} - C_0$. When we account for undercount in both censuses, we find

$$C_{10} - C_0 = T_{10} - T_0 - (u_{10}T_{10} - u_0T_0).$$

So, the estimate of change in the population based on the two censuses is biased by the difference in their undercounts.

The estimate of the change in the population between censuses from the postcensal estimation program is $Y_{10} - Y_0$. The error Δ in measuring change between censuses using the postcensal estimates equals

$$\Delta = (Y_{10} - Y_0) - (T_{10} - T_0). \tag{9.5}$$

Because the postcensal estimate is used throughout the decade to measure the population size, the error in the postcensal estimate in the year of the recent census, relative to that census, $Y_{10} - T_{10}$, known as the error of closure, is also of interest. We form an estimate of error of closure by

$$Y_{10} - C_{10}.$$

Equation (9.5) aids us in showing that undercount in the censuses at the beginning of the decade and the end of the decade also affect the estimate of error of closure based on the census count. Notice that the error of closure equals

$$Y_{10} - C_{10} = Y_{10} - T_{10} + u_{10}T_{10}$$

Using Eq. (9.5), we substitute for Y_{10} and find

Table 9.4 Net change in DA estimate of census undercoverage and error of closure. (Source for Error of Closure: Jones-Putoff and Yowell 2012)

Census year	DA estimate undercoverage	Net change in undercoverage	Error of closure
	(%)	(%)	(%)
1970	2.71		
		−1.49	−2.15
1980	1.22		
		0.43	0.59
1990	1.65		
		−1.53	−2.45
2000	0.12		
		−0.22	−0.10
2010	−0.10		

Sources for DA estimates of census undercoverage: 1970–2000 from The Demographic Analysis Research Team (2010). 2010 from Mayol-Garcia and Robinson (2011)

$$\begin{aligned} Y_{10} - C_{10} &= \Delta + Y_0 + (T_{10} - T_0) - T_{10} + u_{10}T_{10} \\ &= \Delta + (Y_0 - T_0) + u_{10}T_{10} \\ &= \Delta + u_{10}T_{10} - u_0T_0 \end{aligned} \tag{9.6}$$

since the starting point of the estimates is set to equal the census count ($Y_0 = C_0$). Therefore, the estimate of the error of closure is the sum of the error in the estimate of change between censuses and the difference in the two census undercounts.

In 1980, very little data were available to illustrate the effect of census undercount on estimates of change between censuses. Fortunately, now we have data available on the undercount in five consecutive censuses. Table 9.4 shows the estimated undercoverage for the U.S. population in the 1970 to 2010 censuses based on Demographic Analysis (DA), which uses vital records to form estimates. A negative undercoveage estimate indicates an overcount. In addition, Table 9.4 contains the net change in DA estimates of census undercount and the estimated error of closure.

Figure 9.1 shows a plot of the net change in DA estimates of census undercoverage versus the estimated error of closure from Table 9.4. The two variables are highly correlated with a correlation coefficient of 0.99. The relationship appears to be linear and Eq. (9.6) lends credence to the appearance. A simple regression fit would be:

$$\text{Error of Closure} = 0.05365 + 1.539^{*} \quad \text{Change in Coverage.}$$

Notice that since the data are in percentages, the intercept is close to zero and the error of closure tends to be about 1.5 times the change in coverage between censuses. The coefficient of the variable Change in Coverage being greater than 1 implies that the error Δ in measuring change possibly is related to the change in census cover-

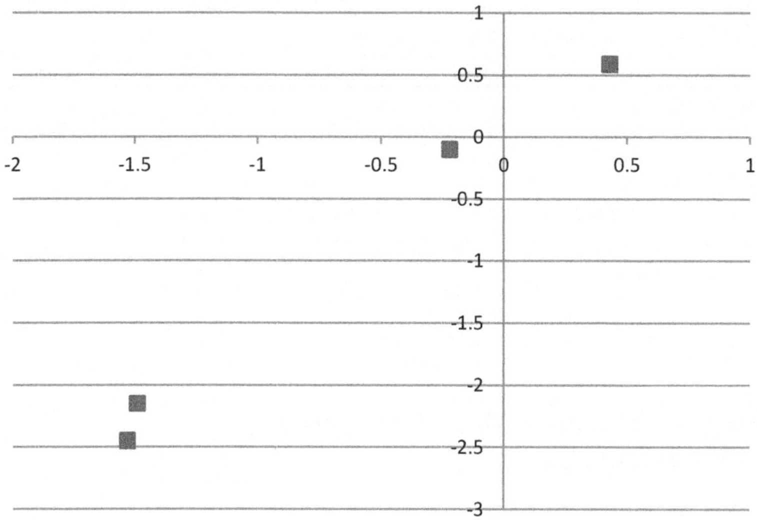

Fig. 9.1 Net change in DA estimates of census undercoverage vs. error of closure. (Source: Table 9.4)

age, but that is a topic for another investigation. We emphasize that with just four data points, the model describes only the relationship in the data used in the fit. No inferences may be made to other situations.

At the national level, the estimate of net census undercount was 1.65 % in 1990 and 0.12 % in 2000, resulting in a net change in coverage of around − 1.53 %. Therefore, if the population estimates program had correctly estimated the rate of change in the 1990s, it would have measured an "error" of approximately one and a half percent. Of course, there is considerable uncertainty around both numbers. Looking at the next decade, the Demographic Analysis produced a range of error for its estimates 2010 population indicating its 2010 Census undercount estimate of −0.10 % could range from −0.9 % (overcount) to 1.4 % (undercount). Coupling these with the 2000 estimate implies a range for the estimated change the change in undercount of −0.78 to 1.52 %.

Much more important than the change in census coverage at the national level is the change in coverage at the state and county level. We now have the 2010 Census Coverage Measurement estimates for state and county coverage. Assessing the effect of the level and change in local coverage on the estimate error of the postcensal estimates should be possible, although beyond the scope of this paper.

Looking forward, we should note that while the net national coverage errors in the past two censuses seem to be both small and relatively similar, that might not be true for the next census. Locking the assessment of error into a paradigm of census completeness may not work well for the long run.

Table 9.5 Measures of relative change in the measures of error for the population estimates program estimates in 2010 relative to their value in 2000

	TAES	WPSE	MAPE	MALPE	RMSE
Previous census					
State	0.053	2,692.179	8.557	8.535	19,585.323
County	0.085	107.801	8.430	−3.681	37,210.850
Population estimates					
State	0.007	37.956	0.973	0.548	1,517.311
County	0.018	6.682	2.909	−1.277	7,191.661
Relative improvement					
State	13.3 %	1.4 %	11.4 %	6.4 %	7.7 %
County	21.1 %	6.2 %	34.5 %	34.7 %	19.3 %

Making the Measures More Transparent and Understandable

In assessing different population estimation methods, the demographer will use several of the methods discussed here. However, comparing what the different measures are saying is difficult. Since each measure (MAPE, MALPE, etc.) has its own scale, the reader becomes quickly lost in understanding which improvements are "important" and which are not. Fortunately, there is an easy approach that also has additional benefits. This is to scale each measure of accuracy for a set of estimates relative to the measure for using the previous census instead. Therefore, a measure of relative improvement is

$$\text{Relative Improvement} = \frac{\text{Measure of error for estimate}}{\text{Measure of error using last census}}$$

This way of measuring change in the measures has two added benefits. First, it focuses on how well the estimate measures change. Predicting that Los Angeles County will be big and Loving County small takes no skill. Just using the previous census will predict that. How much better, as measured by each formula, does the estimates program do than just using the previous census? The relative improvement measures the "value added" of the population estimates program. Table 9.5 gives several measures of relative change. The population estimates program does surprisingly well.

Summary and Conclusion

The population estimates program of the U.S. Census Bureau produces amazingly good estimates by whatever statistical measure, but especially as measured by usefulness to the federal government, the states, and the academic and business communities. The staff spends considerable effort to improve the estimates and to understand their error structure. In this paper, we have offered some analysis of the current measures and suggestions for alternative measures. We emphasized that a set of measures should:

- Take account of the general uses of the data.
- Take account for how well change is measured.
- Take account of the effect of census coverage.
- Express the results in terms of accuracy relative to simply using the previous census.

Our general message, however, is that the choice of measures cannot be casually made. While we agree with the general criteria of the 1980 National Academy report, we think that demographers must consider their choice of measures carefully. Failure to do so can lead them to adopt estimation methods that minimize the criteria, but do not serve the user well.

References

Alho, J. M., & Spencer, B. D. (2005). *Statistical demography and forecasting*. New York: Springer.

Bolender, B C., Dokko, I., Lewis, J. (2012). *Metropolitan and Nonmetropolitan Counties: Evaluation of Postcensal Population Estimates and Census 2010 Results*. Poster presented at the Population Association Annual Meetings, 2–3 May, 2012, San Francisco, CA.

Fellegi, I. (1980). *Should the Census Count Be Adjusted for Allocation Purposes—Equity Considerations*. Conference on Census Undercount: Proceedings of the 1980 Conference. U.S. Department of Commerce, Washington, DC, pp. 193–203.

Hogan, H., & Robinson, J. G. (1993). *What the Census Bureau's Coverage Evaluation Programs Tell Us about Differential Undercount*. Proceedings of the U.S Census Bureau 1993 Research Conference on Undercounted Ethnic Populations, 5–7 May, 1993. U.S. Census Bureau, Washington, DC.

Jones-Putoff, A., & Yowell., T. (2012). *2010 Estimates Evaluations: Overview and County Results*. Paper presented at the 2010 Estimates Evaluations: Research, Results, and Direction Conference. 30 March, 2012, Suitland, MD.

Mayol-Garcia, Y., & Robinson, J. G. (2011). *2010 Census Counts Compared to the 2010 Population Estimates by Demographic Characteristics*. Paper presented at the 2012 Southern Demographic Association Annual Meeting, 10–12 October, 2012, Williamsburg, VA.

Mulry, M. H., & Hogan, H. (1986). *Research Plan on Census Adjustment Standards*. Proceedings of the section on Survey Research Methods. American Statistical Association, Alexandria, VA, pp. 566–570. http://www.amstat.org/sections/SRMS/Proceedings/papers/1986_106.pdf. Accessed 3 October 2012.

Panel on Small-Area Estimates of Population and Income. (1980). *Estimating Population and Income of Small Areas*. Committee on National Statistics, National Research Council. National Academy Press, Washington, DC.

Siegel, J. S. (1974). Estimates of coverage of the population by sex, race, and age in the 1970 census. *Demography, 11*(1), 1–23

Spencer, B. D. (1980a) *Implications of Equity and Accuracy for Undercount Adjustment: A Decision-Theoretic Approach*. Conference on Census Undercount: Proceedings of the 1980 Conference. U.S. Department of Commerce, Washington, DC, pp. 204–216.

Spencer, B. D. (1980b). *Benefit-cost analysis of data used to allocate funds*. New York: Springer-Verlag.

Spencer, B. D. (1980c). *Effect of biases in census estimates on evaluation of postcensal estimates. Appendix I in estimating population and income of small areas* (pp. 232–236). Washington, DC: National Academy Press.

The Demographic Analysis Research Team. (2010). *The Development and Sensitivity Analysis of the 2010 Demographic Analysis Estimates*. Report dated 16 December, 2010. Population Division. U.S. Census Bureau, Washington, DC.

U.S. Bureau of the Census. (1977). *Developmental estimates of the coverage of the population of states in the 1970 census: demographic analysis. Current population reports, Series P-23, No. 65*. Washington, DC: U.S. Government Printing Office.

U.S. Bureau of the Census. (1991). *Technical Assessment of the Accuracy of Unadjusted Versus Adjusted 1990 Census Counts*. Report of the Undercount Steering Committee, 21 June, 1991. U.S. Census Bureau, Washington, DC.

U.S. Bureau of the Census. (2001). *Report of the Executive Steering Committee for Accuracy and Coverage Evaluation Policy on Adjustment for Non-Redistricting Uses*. U.S. Census Bureau, Washington, DC. http://www.census.gov/dmd/www/pdf/Recommend2.pdf. Accessed 3 October 2012.

Yowell, T., & Devine, J. (2012). *Overview and county level results. Population division*. Washington, DC: U.S. Census Bureau.

Chapter 10
Using Tax Data to Estimate the Number of Families and Households in Canada

Julien Bérard-Chagnon

Background

For over 50 years, Statistics Canada has been producing national and provincial/territorial census family[1] estimates annually. Household estimates[2] are also produced every year and are used mainly for weighting a number of major Statistics Canada household surveys, such as the Survey of Household Spending. In both cases, these estimates are produced for various characteristics, such as family type and family and household size.

The methods used for estimating such concepts need to be reviewed regularly to incorporate the changes occurring in Canadian society, such as the increase of unmarried couples, or to take advantage of new data sources.

Recently, the lack of consistency between family and household estimates proved to be another motivator for conducting an extensive review of the methods. In spite of the strong intrinsic links between the family and household concepts, the estimates were traditionally conducted independently using separate methods. These issues justified the development of a new integrated method that produces accurate and consistent family and household estimates.

The purpose of this article is, firstly, to present the new methodology adopted by Statistics Canada to estimate both the number of families and the number of households and, secondly, to show how it compares to previous methods. To do this, useful concepts will first be introduced, followed by explanations of the previous methodologies. Then, the administrative file behind the new method, the T1 Family File (T1FF), will be presented with the new methodology. Lastly, comparisons will be drawn between the new methodology and the previous ones.

[1] For ease of reading, the term "family" designates census families.

[2] For ease of reading, the term "household" designates private households only.

J. Bérard-Chagnon (✉)
Statistics Canada, Ottawa, Ontario, Canada
e-mail: Julien.Berard-Chagnon@statcan.gc.ca

M. N. Hoque, L. B. Potter (eds.), *Emerging Techniques in Applied Demography*, Applied Demography Series 4, DOI 10.1007/978-94-017-8990-5_10,

Definition of Concepts

Before continuing, the concepts of family and household must be clarified. The definitions used for Canada's Population Estimates Program (PEP) are identical to those used for the 2006 Census (Statistics Canada 2010a).

A census family refers to a married or unmarried couple (with or without children of either or both spouses) or a lone parent of any marital status with at least one child living in the same dwelling. A couple may be of the opposite or same sex. Headship of the family is shared by both spouses in the case of a couple, while the parent of a lone-parent family is given headship of the family.

A household refers to a person or a group of persons who occupy the same dwelling and do not have a usual place of residence elsewhere in Canada. Headship of the household is shared by the maintainers of the household as reported in the Census. A maintainer is a person of the household who pays, for instance, the rent, mortgage, taxes, or electricity of the dwelling.

It is important to note that a head of a family is not automatically a head of the household and vice versa. For example, let's take a couple with two children (regardless of their age) who live with the wife's mother. This will be considered a census family of four persons (two parents and two children; the wife's mother is considered to be a non-family person) whose headship will be shared by the two parents. If the maintainers reported in the Census are the two parents and the wife's mother, those three persons will share be the headship of the household.

Previous Methods

In the past, families and households were estimated using two very different methods. This section will describe the previous methods and their main limitations.

Families were estimated using the component method (Statistics Canada 2007). Firstly, all factors that can affect family numbers were therefore isolated and estimated separately to obtain the estimated number of families. Secondly, family characteristics (family type and size, age groups of spouses, etc.) were extrapolated based on trends from the last two censuses. Using this method raised a number of issues. Many of the components were very difficult to estimate due to the lack of appropriate data, and the effect of certain demographic events on family numbers was difficult to break down. For instance, marriage may help form a family if both spouses were not already heads of family (e.g. they were living with their respective parents), dissolve a family if both spouses were already heads of family (e.g. two lone-parents getting married), or have no effect at all on the number of families where one of the two spouses was already the head of a family. Since no information on the head of family status of individuals was available in most data sources used, all these events had to be modelled on a series of sometimes very strong assumptions, especially for Census net undercoverage,[3] and numerous data sources.

Statistics Canada's household estimates were previously produced using headship rates. These rates were calculated by province or territory of residence and age group of the household head using the last two censuses. They were then extrapolated logistically and applied to the estimated population to obtain an estimated number of households. Distribution by household size was extrapolated separately based on the last two censuses and applied to the estimated number of households. This method primarily assumed that there was no Census net undercoverage of households, meaning that all households were fully accounted for by the Census. Given that Canadian censuses usually have a population net undercoverage of around 2.5 %, this assumption is likely false. This method also relied heavily on the quality of the extrapolation assumptions for both the number and the characteristics of households.

T1 Family File

The search for alternative methods quickly led to the use of a new data source, the T1 Family File (T1FF). This file is created at Statistics Canada using tax data from the Canada Revenue Agency (CRA). It has been produced annually since 1982 and contains a wide range of demographic information, such as the place of residence, age, sex, marital status, and family type and size. The T1FF population originates from three sources. The largest portion is derived from personal income tax returns. Spouses who did not file a tax return but were declared as dependants on their spouse's return are added to the file and their characteristics are imputed according to those of their spouse. Lastly, children are added to the file and linked to their parents by using information from the Canada Child Tax Benefit (CCTB),[4] Vital Statistics, or a historical file created from the T1FF from previous years. This procedure produces a file that contains basic information on census families and that has a coverage rate hovering around 96.0 %, which is considered to be very good.

[3] For the 1991 and 1996 censuses, Statistics Canada produced an official estimate of census net undercoverage of families. However, this estimate was no longer available as of 2001. In order to continue to take into account census net undercoverage in family estimates, a method based on the correlation between the net undercoverage of individuals and families from the 1991 and 1996 censuses was used to estimate the family net undercoverage for 2001.

[4] CCTB is a federal program aimed at helping eligible families with the cost of raising children under age 18 by sending them monthly payments. It is possible to link children from this program to their parents with their social insurance number (SIN) to add them as dependants on the T1FF. However, families with high incomes will not receive CCTB payments. For that reason, CCTB doesn't cover all children (although around 90 % of the children are present on the file). Children not covered by the CCTB are added to the T1FF with Vital Statistics or with an historical file created from the T1FF from previous years.

In addition to good coverage, another asset of the T1FF is its annual nature, which makes it possible to base estimates on the changes observed rather than on the extrapolation of past trends. However, as it will be shown later, adjustments will be applied to the T1FF in order to correct its limitations. Note that the T1FF contains information on individuals and families but not on households. It is nonetheless possible to use this file to estimate the number of households by drawing on the correlation between families and households.

New Method

The new family and household estimation method is based T1FF data. Family heads can be derived from the T1FF since this file has the information on the spouses and their children if any. These will serve as the base of the new estimates, to which four separate adjustments will be applied:

- Firstly, we will adjust T1FF data for their coverage with PEP's population estimates.
- Secondly, we will compare T1FF family heads with those of the Census of Canada to correct the bias of the T1FF.
- Thirdly, we will use PEP's population estimates to move the reference date of the estimates to July 1.
- Lastly, we will add a certain number of families and households to take into account Census net undercoverage of families and households.

The equation can be summarized as follow:

$$EST = H^{T1FF} \times CA \times BA \times RDA + CNUA \tag{10.1}$$

Where:

EST	Estimates of families or households
H^{T1FF}	T1FF family heads
CA	Coverage adjustment
BA	Bias adjustment
RDA	Reference date adjustment
CNUA	Census net undercoverage adjustment

Each step of this equation will be expanded upon in the following paragraphs.

Coverage Adjustment of the T1FF

The first step is to apply a coverage adjustment to the T1FF family heads. This adjustment is needed due to the very nature of tax data, which are not specifically

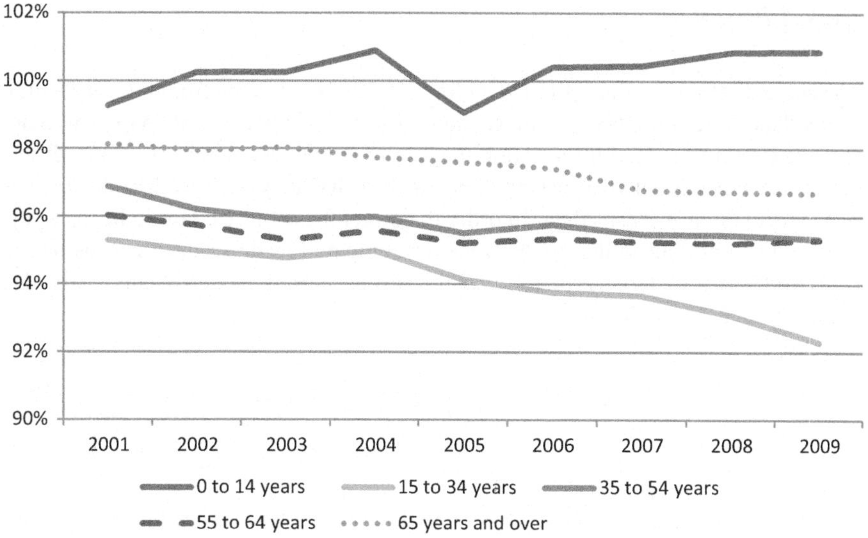

Fig. 10.1 T1 Family File (*T1FF*) coverage rate (in percentage) by year and age group, 2001 to 2009, Canada

made for demographic accounts. The T1FF population, by province, age and sex, is compared to PEP's population estimates to obtain an inflation ratio. Population estimates used for this adjustment are as of January 1st because this date is closer to the moment where Canadian filers fill their income tax. This rate is then applied to T1FF heads of family to adjust them for coverage:

$$CA(p,a,s) = \frac{P_{t+n}^{PEP}(p,a,s)}{P_{t+n}^{T1FF}(p,a,s)} \tag{10.2}$$

Where

P_{t+n}^{PEP} estimated population (from the PEP) for year $t+n$ according to province p, age a (single year of age up to 100+ years) and sex s at January 1

P_{t+n}^{T1FF} T1FF population for year $t+n$ according to province p, age a (single year of age up to 100+ years) and sex s.

The following chart shows the changes in T1FF coverage for certain age groups (Fig. 10.1).

The file's coverage changes slightly from year to year. It varies particularly from one age group to another and in time. Overall, the T1FF coverage rate hovers around 96.0% and has dropped slightly in the past few years from 97.0% in 2001 to 95.6% in 2009. It is generally higher for children aged 0 to 14 and is even sometimes slightly above 100%. T1FF coverage is lower for young adults aged 15 to 34, particularly single men, even though it remains at above 92.0% for this age group. In spite of these variations, T1FF coverage is very good.

Bias Adjustment

The second step is to adjust T1FF data for bias. This bias stems from the very nature of tax data since some tax incentives may influence whether people will or will not file a tax return or what information they will include. Moreover, there are differences in concepts between tax and census data that may also lead to differences between T1FF and census data. In order to correct these biases, family heads of the T1FF corresponding to the census year are compared to those from census on the basis of their characteristics so as to create census correction coefficients, marked ε, that are calculated as follows:

$$ {}_{i}\varepsilon_{t}(X) = \frac{{}_{i}H_{t}^{Cens.}(X)}{CA(p,a,s,) \times H_{t}^{T1FF}(Y)} \tag{10.3} $$

Where

${}_{i}H_{t}^{Cens.}$ census heads for families (i = CF) or households (i = HH) for census year t

X estimated domains available in the Census and for which family and household estimates are produced (province, age group [15–24, 25–34 up to 75+ years] and sex of head, family type and size, age structure of children, and household size)

$H_{t}^{T1FF.}$ T1FF heads of families for census year t;

Y estimated domains available in the T1FF, which is a subset of X (province, age group and sex of head, family type and size, and age structure of children).

A coefficient equal to one means that the T1FF is not biased compared to the census for this domain.

From Families to Households

Since the T1FF does not have information on households, estimates for the latter must be based on family estimates. Census correction coefficients are tools that enable this transition. For households, the calculation of census correction coefficients can be broken down as follows:

$$ {}_{HH}\varepsilon_{t}(X) = \frac{{}_{CF}H_{t}^{Cens.}(X)}{AH_{t}^{T1FF}(Y)} \times \frac{{}_{HH}H_{t}^{Cens.}(X)}{{}_{CF}H_{t}^{Cens.}(X)} = \frac{{}_{HH}H_{t}^{Cens.}(X)}{AH_{t}^{T1FF}(Y)} \tag{10.4} $$

Where:

AH_{t}^{T1FF} T1FF family heads adjusted for coverage. These are obtained by multiplying coverage adjustment of the T1FF calculated in the first step (Eq. 10.2) to the T1FF family heads.

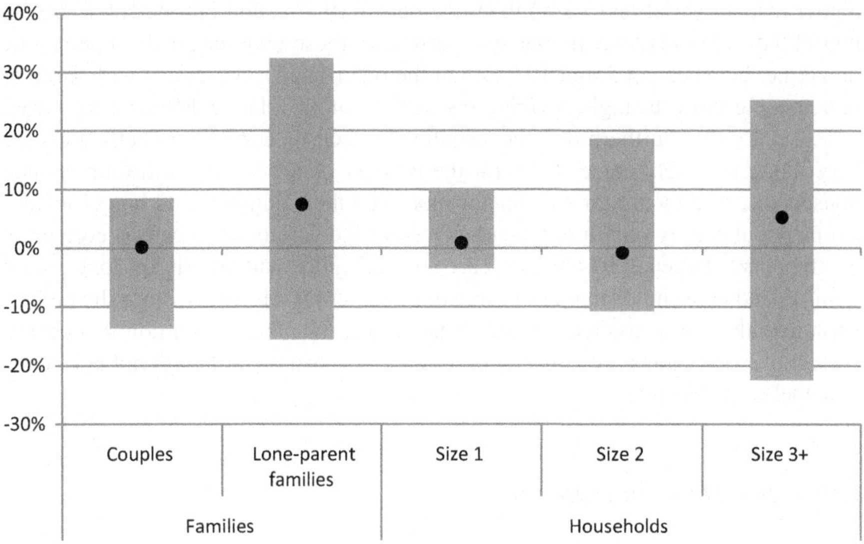

Fig. 10.2 Percentiles 10 and 90 and median of relative variations (in percentage) between the 2001 and 2006 census correction coefficients for families by type and for households by size. (Notes: Relative variations are weighted according to the number of heads in 2001 in order to reflect the size of the population of each domain. Maximum and minimum values are not shown because of extreme variations that come from coefficients calculated from very small numbers of heads)

In comparing census family heads to those from the T1FF, the first ratio of the equation represents a bias adjustment for families. The second term represents the ratio observed in the census of the number of household heads for each family head. T1FF families to which household census correction coefficients are applied are therefore first adjusted for bias and then for the relationship between households and families to obtain an estimate of the number of households.

These coefficients remain constant until the next Census. Chart 2 evaluates this assumption by comparing the coefficient values for 2006 with those for 2001. Percentiles 10 and 90 (this range will be referred to as the 10-90 percentile range) and the median of relative variations are shown in Chart 2. For the assumption of the model to be respected, the variations between 2001 and 2006 must be relatively slight (Fig. 10.2).

For families, the median variation is very close to zero (0.2 %) among couples, but is more pronounced for lone-parent families (7.5 %). The 10th and the 90th percentile reveal that 80 % of the relative differences go from − 13.7 to 8.5 % for couples and from − 15.6 to 32.3 % for lone-parent families, which represents a much wider interval.[5] As for households, those that have three or more people have a

[5] Changes were made in the processing of children from lone-parent families in the T1FF for 2006. These changes had an impact on the number of lone-parent families and, thus, on the census correction coefficients for 2006.

higher median variation (5.3 %) than one-person (0.9 %) and two-person (−0.8 %) households. Households with just one person are those with the smallest percentile range, i.e. between −3.5 and 10.2 %. On the other hand, households with three or more people show the highest variations, as 80 % of the relative differences go from −22.4 to 25.3 %. Furthermore, the variations in census correction coefficients are very much inversely correlated with the number of heads, for both families and households, as they are far smaller for more populous domains and bigger for domains populated by only a few heads. Overall, the variations in census correction coefficients between 2001 and 2006 are not negligible, particularly for lone-parent families and households that have three or more people. However, since the highest variations then to be associated with smaller domains, the assumption that census correction coefficients are constant between two censuses, although not perfect, is nonetheless acceptable.

Reference Date Adjustment

The third step is to adjust for the reference date. Family and household estimates are generally produced for July 1. However, applying census correction coefficients to T1FF family heads moves the reference date to Census Day, which is generally in the middle of May. To correct this shift, headship rates are calculated using population estimates. The particularity of the headship rates of this adjustment is that the portion that represents the census net undercoverage is removed from population estimates. Bear in mind that population estimates are calculated using the component method on the basis of the most recent census, which is adjusted for census net undercoverage. In 2006, the adjustment amounted to 868,657 people, or 2.7 % of the Canadian population. These individuals are subtracted from the headship rate numerator and denominator. The decision to subtract them from the headship rates was made to isolate everything related to census net undercoverage, the step requiring the most modelling, as the last step in the method. The reference date adjustment for year *t*+*n*, marked *RDA*, is calculated as follows:

$$RDA_{t+n} = \frac{P^{PEP}_{t+n(July)}(p,ag,s) - P^{CNU}_{t}(p,ag,s)}{P^{PEP}_{t+n(CD)}(p,ag,s) - P^{CNU}_{t}(p,ag,s)} \tag{10.5}$$

Where:

P^{CNU}_{t} estimated census net undercoverage of population for census year *t* according to province *p*, age group *ag* (15–24, 25–34 up to 75+ years) and sex *s*

CD Census Day of year *t*+*n* (usually around the middle of May).

Canada's population growth between mid-May and June 30 is generally between 0.15 and 0.25 % (Statistics Canada 2011). This adjustment is thus necessary in order to reflect this growth.

Census Coverage Adjustment

The fourth and last step is the census net coverage adjustment. Some people are not counted in the census, which leads to undercoverage. Conversely, some people are counted more than once, which leads to overcoverage. The difference between undercoverage and overcoverage is called net undercoverage. It is usually positive, meaning that the undercoverage is more marked than the overcoverage. The presence of a net undercoverage for the population suggests that there is probably one for families and households as well. The census correction coefficients of the second step, calculated on the basis of the census, therefore omit a certain number of families and households.

In order to take that into account, a demographic adjustment was calculated using census coverage studies. Because census undercoverage far exceeds overcoverage in Canadian censuses, the adjustments for 2001 and 2006 censuses were exclusively based on undercoverage data. However, as will be demonstrated, census overcoverage was also considered indirectly.[6] Undercoverage is estimated by the Reverse Record Check (RRC), a combination of administrative linkages and a sample survey (Statistics Canada 2010b). The design of the RRC aims at estimating the undercoverage of individuals, not families and households, hence the need to develop this demographic adjustment. In short, this adjustment is divided into four main steps. First, the RRC is used to calculate probabilities that the missed population is in a particular family stratum (adult in a couple category with children, adult in a couple category without children, single parent, child, etc.) by age group, sex, marital status, and household size. These probabilities are then applied to census net undercoverage of population to obtain estimates of census net undercoverage of families. This step allows for the indirect inclusion of census overcoverage in the adjustment. Census net undercoverage of households is obtained from household to family headship ratios derived from the census and applied to the family net undercoverage estimates. Lastly, calibration is done on the basis of family and household size to reconcile the total with that of the population net undercoverage. This adjustment assumes that the individuals added by the net undercoverage all belong to the families and households that are also added by the net undercoverage. Although it likely leads to a certain overestimation of the net undercoverage, this assumption is necessary due to a lack of information on partially enumerated families and households and because it is preferable to not making the adjustment. These estimates are kept constant until the next census. Producing these estimates is the step of the new method that requires the most modelling. This is why it was deemed preferable to isolate it from the three other steps, particularly the calculation of census correction coefficients, which enables any necessary improvements to be made more easily.

Table 10.1 shows the net undercoverage estimates for families and households for the 2006 Census.

[6] Research will be done to improve the adjustment for the 2011 Census. One very possible improvement is the use of overcoverage data in order to derive families and households undercoverage and overcoverage independently.

Table 10.1 Estimated family and household net undercoverage by size and age group of the head, 2006, Canada

Age groups (years)	Families			Households			
	Size 2	Size 3+	Total	Size 1	Size 2	Size 3+	Total
15 to 24	18,518	4,895	23,413	15,455	22,222	17,008	54,685
25 to 34	41,322	24,448	65,770	41,812	49,141	47,132	138,085
35 to 44	25,295	34,541	59,836	49,136	28,164	47,206	124,506
45 to 54	2,615	3,691	6,306	9,568	3,363	6,501	19,432
55 to 64	2,056	126	2,182	6,197	3,092	2,937	12,226
65 to 74	−2,904	−1,916	−4,820	−2,001	−1,783	−2,352	−6,136
75 and over	−2,028	−2,759	−4,787	−3,435	−1,503	−2,789	−7,727
Total	84,874	63,026	147,900	116,732	102,696	115,643	335,071

In 2006, approximately 150,000 families and 335,000 households were added to reflect the census net undercoverage. This represents a net undercoverage rate of 1.6 % for families and 2.6 % for households. The net undercoverage rate for households is very close to that of the population (2.7 %) and the deviation from that of families can be explained by the fact that a large part of the missed population is not part of a census family (e.g. people living alone). The age structure of heads follows that of the population net undercoverage, which is higher among young adults and slightly negative among older people. Moreover, compared to census figures, lone-parent families and smaller families and households are overrepresented in this adjustment. These results are consistent with what is known about the missed and overrepresented population and represent a sensible assumption for the purpose of the new method to estimate families and households presented in this paper.

To summarize, the new method is based on T1FF family heads, corrected for T1FF coverage, bias, reference date, and census net undercoverage. The complete equation for estimating the number of families and households for year $t+n$ is as follows:

$$
{}_iEST_{t+n}(X) = H_t^{T1FF}(Y) \times \frac{P_{t+n}^{\ PEP}(p,a,s)}{P_{t+n}^{\ T1FF}(p,a,s)} \times_i \varepsilon_t(X) \times \frac{P_{t+n(July)}^{PEP}(p,a,s) - P_t^{CNU}(p,a,s)}{P_{t+n(CD)}^{PEP}(p,a,s) - P_t^{CNU}(p,a,s)} +_i CNUA_t(X) \tag{10.6}
$$

Comparison of Methods

It is possible to compare estimates produced with the new method against those produced with previous methods—the component method for families and the headship rate method for households — by comparing them with the 2006 Census figures, adjusted for family and household net undercoverage using the above method.

The estimates from the new method should more closely resemble the adjusted figures from the 2006 Census.

For families, the families taken directly from the T1FF will be added to the comparisons. This will measure the effect of the adjustments made to T1FF families by the new method.[7]

For households, it is also worth adding estimates from a third method to the comparisons. For the purposes of this exercise, this method is called the adjusted headship rate method and consists in using estimates from the headship rate method to which the household net undercoverage estimates from the new method are added.[8] The idea here is to control for net undercoverage during the comparison.

Comparative Indicators

The first quality indicator is relative error (RE), which will be used to compare the aggregated totals. It is calculated as follows:

$$ {}_iRE_t(X) = 100 \times \frac{{}_iEST_t(X) - {}_iA\_Cens_t(X)}{{}_iA\_Cens_t(X)} \tag{10.7} $$

Where:

A_Cens_t adjusted census figures for census year t.

Then, to take into account each estimated domain, three other quality indicators will be used: mean percent error (MPE), mean absolute percent error (MAPE), and weighted mean absolute percent error (WMAPE). The formulas are as follows:

$$ {}_iMPE_t = 100 \times \frac{\sum_{j=1}^{n} {}_iRE_t(X_j)}{n} \tag{10.8} $$

$$ {}_iMAPE_t = 100 \times \frac{\sum_{j=1}^{n} \left| {}_iRE_t(X_j) \right|}{n} \tag{10.9} $$

[7] Given that the new method is based on T1FF families, for which various adjustments are made, the addition of T1FF families to the comparisons will make it possible to measure the added value of these adjustments. Furthermore, assessing the quality of the T1FF with regard to families will also be possible.

[8] The headship rate method makes the assumption that there is no census net undercoverage for households. Consequently, it is expected that this method underestimates the number of households during comparisons. However, estimation of household net undercoverage is not intrinsic to the new method. It can therefore be applied to the headship rate method estimates to compare this method with the new one, thereby enabling to control for the effect of household net undercoverage.

$$ {}_iWMAPE_t = 100 \times \frac{\sum_{j=1}^{n} \left| {}_iRE_t\left(X_j\right) \right| \times {}_iCens_t\left(X_j\right)}{\sum_{j=1}^{n} {}_iCens_t\left(X_j\right)} \tag{10.10} $$

Where:

n number of estimated domains.

The MPE is the average relative error for each estimated domain. As such, it provides an idea of the net impact of the differences between estimates and census figures. However, its major shortcoming is that it takes into account the direction of the errors in its formula: positive errors can cancel out negative errors to provide a false idea of accuracy. For instance, a relative error of 20 % in one domain will cancel out in part a relative error of −25 % from another domain. The MAPE works around this problem by taking the absolute values of the relative errors. Therefore, in reference to the previous example, the errors of 20 and −25 % would be added instead of being cancelled with this indicator. However, the MAPE also has a significant analytical limitation. Like the MPE, the MAPE assumes that each relative error has the same weight in calculating the indicator. It is preferable that a high relative error from a populous domain contribute more to the indicator than the same relative error for a less populous domain. Therefore, if the domain with the 20 % error has 100 people, it is desirable that it counts more than an domain with a −25 % error but only 5 people. In addition to taking absolute error values, the WMAPE enables the size of each domain to be considered in its calculation by adding a weight to each relative error. Where the MPE can be seen as being a bias indicator, the MAPE also considers variance (or amplitude) and the WMAPE also considers domain size. In all cases, it is preferable that the indicator be as close to zero as possible. The combined use of these three indicators therefore highlights the strengths and weaknesses of each method, after painting a general picture using relative errors.

Each of these indicators will be calculated for each category of household size and for each family type for families. For households, for each size category (1 people, 2 people, and 3 people or more), the domains studied are the province or territory (13 groups) and the heads' age group (7 groups), for a total of 91 relative errors per size category. For families, the comparisons exclude Canada's three territories (Yukon, Northwest Territories, and Nunavut) since the previous method produced estimates only for the ten provinces. For each family type (couple or lone-parent), the domains studied are the province (10 groups) and the size (2 people, 3 people, 4 people, 5 people, and 6 people or more), for a total of 50 relative errors per family type.

Families

Chart 3 shows the relative errors for each method according to family type in relation to the adjusted 2006 Census data (Fig. 10.3).

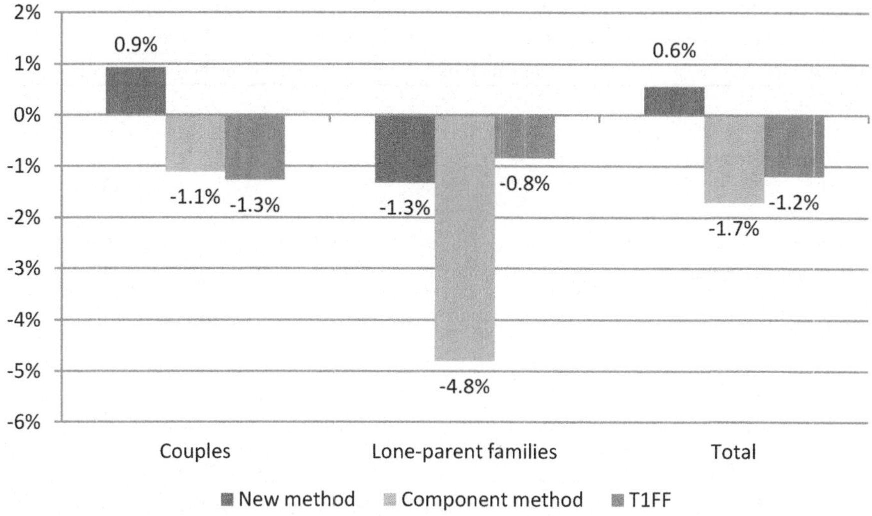

Fig. 10.3 Relative errors (in percentage) for family estimates by type and method, 2006

In 2006, considering census net undercoverage, there were a total of 7,556,000 couples and 1,461,000 lone-parent families in Canada. For all families, the new method had estimates that were closest to the adjusted census figures (0.6 %), compared to the T1FF (− 1.2 %) and the component method (− 1.7 %). The new method is also the most accurate for couples (0.9 %). In contrast, the T1FF (−0.8 %) is the method closest to adjusted census data for lone-parent families. The component method considerably underestimates lone-parent families (−4.8 %), a direct consequence of the extrapolation of past trends.

Table 10.2 compares the MPE, MAPE, and WMAPE for the three methods by family type.

The new method presents a far lower MPE than the other two methods (1.3 % compared to 6.5 and 13.8 %) for all families and for lone-parent families (1.4 % compared to 5.4 and 27.5 %). The T1FF has a very marked average relative error for lone-parent families. This means that, although the T1FF estimates the total number of lone-parent families relatively well, it tends to overestimate certain smaller domains, which is particularly the case for lone-parent families of six people or more.

The following indicator, the MAPE, paints a picture similar to the MPE. The new method has the lowest MAPE (7.3 %), well ahead of the component method (14.4 %) and the T1FF (17.3 %), not only for total families, but also for the two family types. The T1FF has by far the highest MAPE for lone-parent families (28.5 %), which reinforces the idea that, although the total number of lone-parent families is close to that of the census, the T1FF does not estimate this family type as well for larger lone-parent families. Even though it is not as accurate as the new method (2.1 %), the T1FF fares far better (6.0 %) for couples than for lone-parent families.

Lastly, the WMAPE also abounds in the other two indicators, in that the new method is far more accurate not only for the total number of families (1.6 % com-

Table 10.2 Mean percent error (*MPE*), mean absolute percent error (*MAPE*), and weighted mean absolute percent error (*WMAPE*) for family estimates by method and family type

Family type	New method	Component method	T1FF
MPE			
Couples	1.1	7.6	0.2
Lone-parent families	1.4	5.4	27.5
Total	1.3	6.5	13.8
MAPE			
Couples	2.1	11.4	6.0
Lone-parent families	12.5	17.3	28.5
Total	7.3	14.4	17.3
WMAPE			
Couples	1.5	6.1	4.5
Lone-parent families	2.5	5.8	4.6
Total	1.6	6.0	4.5

pared to 6.0 and 4.5 %), but also for the two family types. In the three cases, the T1FF is positioned between the new method and the component method. The large variations between the MAPE and the WMAPE of the three methods suggest that the very marked relative errors occurred particularly for domains with few families. This is especially true for lone-parent families in the T1FF, as the MAPE (28.5 %) is substantially higher than the WMAPE (4.6 %).

The new method therefore produces estimates that are far closer to the adjusted 2006 Census than the component method. Moreover, it also yields more accurate results than those taken directly from the T1FF. This shows the relevance of the adjustments made to T1FF families in the new method.

Households

Chart 4 shows the relative errors for each method by household size (Fig. 10.4).

For all households, the adjusted headship rate method (0.002 %) and the new method (−0.01 %) yield estimates that are very close to the adjusted 2006 Census figures. Not surprisingly, the headship rate method presents a total relative error of −2.6 %, which roughly corresponds to the household net undercoverage estimate.

When comparing the methods by household size, the picture tends to change. The weakness of the headship rate method, based on extrapolations of trends, becomes apparent as it tends to overestimate one-person households, while underestimating two-person households and even more so those with three or more people. The adjusted headship rate method also overestimates the number of one-person households, since the household net undercoverage estimate is added to the existing overestimation from the headship rate method. The underestimation of two-person households and those with three or more people from the adjusted headship rate method is less than the headship rate method, but still relatively high for households with three or more people.

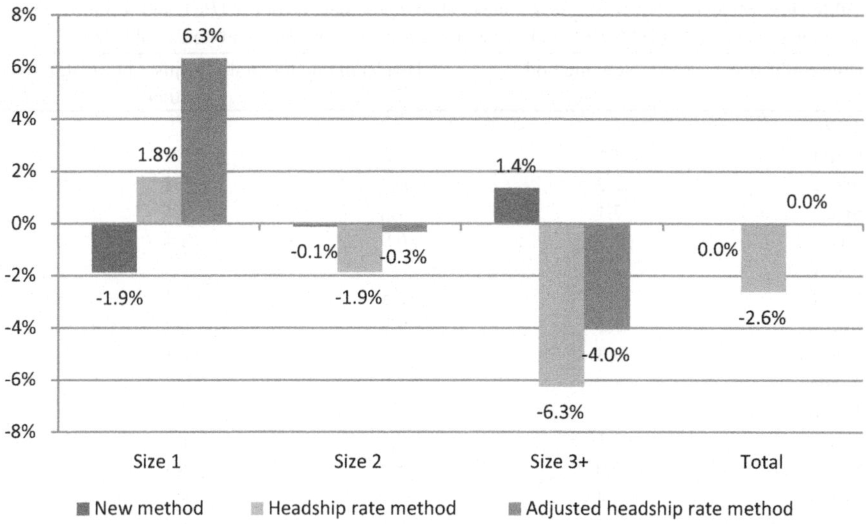

Fig. 10.4 Relative errors (in percentage) for household estimates by size and method, 2006

Table 10.3 compares the MPE, MAPE, and WMAPE for the three methods by household size.

The headship rate method has the lowest MPE (−0.9 %), compared to the new method (2.7 %) and the adjusted headship rate method (3.4 %). This result is interesting in that the headship rate method has the most marked total relative error in Chart 4. For this method (−7.8 %) and the new method (7.1 %), most of the average relative error is attributable to households with three or more people, whereas for the adjusted headship rate method, households with just one person accounted for the largest portion of this indicator (13.0 %). Inversely, for the headship rate method, the average relative error was particularly low for two-person households (−0.4 %), in spite of the fact that this method had the most marked total relative error of the three methods in Chart 4.

As for the MAPE, the headship rate method, which yielded the lowest MPE, is the least accurate method (11.8 %), just behind the adjusted headship rate method (11.6 %) and far behind the new method (8.7 %). We can now see that good results from the headship rate method were in fact derived from cancellations of errors of opposite directions rather than from accurate estimates. These cancellations are naturally reflected in the adjusted headship rate method, which means that the MAPEs for the two methods are very similar. For the three methods, two-person households are those with the lowest MAPE (7.1 %, 9.8 %, and 8.3 %, respectively).

Lastly, also considering the size of the domains, the WMAPE shows that the new method is even more accurate than the others (2.7 % compared to 5.1 % for the adjusted headship rate method and 6.1 % for the headship rate method). Furthermore, the new method stands out particularly from the two other methods for one-person

Table 10.3 Mean percent error (*MPE*), mean absolute percent error (*MAPE*), and weighted mean absolute percent error (*WMAPE*) for household estimates by method and household size

Household size	New method	Headship rate method	Adjusted headship rate method
MPE			
Size 1	3.5	5.5	13.0
Size 2	−2.3	−0.4	−2.4
Size 3+	7.1	−7.8	−0.4
Total	2.7	−0.9	3.4
MAPE			
Size 1	9.6	12.5	14.8
Size 2	7.1	9.8	8.3
Size 3+	9.3	13.3	11.5
Total	8.7	11.8	11.6
WMAPE			
Size 1	2.1	6.6	4.7
Size 2	1.9	5.9	4.3
Size 3+	4.4	5.8	6.7
Total	2.7	6.1	5.1

(2.1 % compared to 6.6 % and 4.7 %) and two-person (1.9 % compared to 5.9 % and 4.3 %) households.

These results therefore suggest that the new method produces better results than the headship rate method. Moreover, even when the headship rate method is adjusted for census net undercoverage, the new method still yields more accurate results.

Conclusion

The purpose of this article was to present Statistics Canada's new family and household estimation method. This method replaces the component method used for families and the headship rate method used for households. It is based on data from the T1FF, a file created using various Canadian tax data. The T1FF has the advantage of being produced annually, which enables recent data to be used instead of extrapolating trends from previous censuses, and has very good coverage. Four adjustments are made to T1FF data: an annual coverage adjustment using population estimates, a 5-year bias adjustment using census data, an adjustment for the reference date, and an adjustment for census coverage. Moreover, households can be estimated on the basis of T1FF individuals and families. This method yields results that are closer to the adjusted 2006 Census figures than the previous methods for both families and households. It can be concluded that the new method is a notable improvement of family and household estimates.

References

Statistics Canada. (2007). Population and Family Estimation Methods at Statistics Canada, Statistics Canada, Statistics Canada Catalogue no 91–528.

Statistics Canada. (2010a). 2006 Census Dictionary, Statistics Canada, Statistics Canada Catalogue no 92–566.

Statistics Canada. (2010b). 2006 Census Technical Report: Coverage, Statistics Canada, Statistics Canada Catalogue no 92–567.

Statistics Canada. (2011). Quarterly Demographic Estimates: April to June 2011, Statistics Canada, Vol. 25, no. 2, Statistics Canada, Statistics Canada Catalogue no 91–002.

Part III
Labor Market, Household, and Poverty

Chapter 11
Comparing Immigrant Education Levels and Resultant Labor Market Outcomes: The European Versus the Native Born Experience in the United States

Cristina Bradatan and Laszlo J. Kulcsar

Background

This study focuses on the influence the education level has on the life course of European immigrants in the United States. While the boats brought a large number of European immigrants from the beginning of the U.S. history to the first part of the twentieth century, now Europeans have become few among the millions of newcomers arriving from other continents, such as Asia and Central and South America. There are about 5 million European born persons currently living in the United States (Malone et al. 2003), and they have a higher than average level of education. The United Kingdom, Germany, Poland, and Russia continue to send most of the European immigrants to the United States, while countries such as Italy, Greece, and Romania send a disproportionately large number of educated immigrants.

In this paper we examine European immigrants who supposedly[1] do not suffer the effect of racial discrimination, making it possible to highlight the influence of other factors (such as education, immigration history, occupation, etc.) on the lives of immigrants. Some of the questions to be addressed in the paper are: How does the U.S. immigration policy select immigrants? Which are the demographic characteristics of those highly educated as opposed to those with a low education? Where do these European immigrants settle down in the United States? Does the nationality play a similarly strong role for the well educated as for the low educated? Are the skilled immigrants likely to do better than the low skilled immigrants in the U.S. job market?

[1] Recent research argues that, although the Southern European immigrants who came at the beginning of the twentieth century were able to assimilate well in the mainstream society (in terms of wage, education level, and marriage patterns), certain European origin groups are still disadvantaged in terms of access to elite groups/organizations (Alba and Abdel-Hady 2005).

C. Bradatan (✉)
Texas Tech University, Lubbock, TX, USA
e-mail: cristina.bradatan@ttu.edu

L. J. Kulcsar
Kansas State University, Manhattan, KS, USA

M. N. Hoque, L. B. Potter (eds.), *Emerging Techniques in Applied Demography*, Applied Demography Series 4, DOI 10.1007/978-94-017-8990-5_11,

Table 11.1 Proportion of foreign born persons at various levels of education. (Source: current population survey, 2000–2008, authors' computations)

Years of education	Percentage foreign born (%)
Total population	12.5
Less than high school	25.8
High school	10.1
Some college	7.9
College (4+ years)	13.3

The foreign born population of the United States is increasing, with more than 900,000 legally admitted immigrants every year. Most of this immigration comes from family-sponsored visas; some are based on employment, refugee status, or the Diversity Visa Program. U.S. immigrants come from a variety of countries and ethnic groups and enter the country with different levels of human capital.

Compared to the native born, immigrants fall into the extremes of educational attainment. Twenty-one percent of the 1992–1996 legal immigrants had 17 or more years of education, while only 7% of the native group attained the same level of education. According to the U.S. Census Bureau, one in every four astronomers, two in every five medical scientists, and one in every five doctors working in the United States in 2000 were foreign born (Kaushal and Fix 2006). At the same time, only 15% of the native born have not completed high school, while 34% of the legal immigrants are in this educational group (Jasso et al. 2000). Table 11.1 shows the proportion of foreign born persons in the U.S. population at various levels of education.

Education acquired either in the country of origin or in the United States plays a significant role in shaping the life course of immigrants. Some authors (Borjas 1992) argue that the educational differences between immigrant groups tend to affect not only the first generation immigrants, but also their children and grandchildren—second and third generations, while other students of migration (Alba et al. 2001) disagree with this. While the level of education generally determines the type of job and level of income an immigrant would attain, foreign education does not bring the same rewards as U.S. education. Immigrants with degrees from U.S. institutions tend to have higher incomes than immigrants with the same level of education achieved abroad (Zhang and Xie 2004). Some of the immigrants without U.S. degrees end up in dead end jobs, with little or no connection to their abilities and educational level.

Immigrants obviously understand these dynamics, and one way to compensate for the lack of immediate rewards has been a higher than average occupational mobility (Green 1999). This mobility allows immigrants to speed up promotion and career advancement. At the same time, a prerequisite for such mobility is having weak social ties in the host country. For highly skilled immigrants, this is coupled with the international or transnational nature of many positions, and subsequently it affects their incorporation and identity formation as well.

Policies also affect the type of immigrants a country receives. The U.S. immigration policy changed dramatically during the twentieth century. The beginning of the century was marked by the adoption of several laws aimed at controlling the number, national origin, and other characteristics of immigrants coming to the United States. The Immigration Act of 1917, for example, banned the immigration of "idiots," "homosexuals," "feeble-minded persons," and "insane persons," as well as people coming from most of Asia and Pacific Islands. In 1921, the Emergency Quota Act was adopted, limiting the number of immigrants coming to the United States to 3 % of the number of residents from the same country already living here in 1890. This was followed by the 1924 Immigration Act, which limited the percentage to 2 %. These laws were abolished through the Immigration and Nationality Act in 1965 and replaced by an immigration system based on family connections and skills, followed by the 1980 Refugee Act, which defined U.S. policy toward refugees. Currently, an alien can use four different channels to settle down as a permanent resident: family connections, employment, diversity visa program, and refugee status (Martin and Midgley 2003). While the ethnicity of the immigrants is overemphasized in the literature on immigration, the immigration channels vis-à-vis the educational background are relatively under researched (Jasso et al. 2000). The way immigrants get admitted to the United States is partly determined by education and other demographic characteristics and it is a good predictor for how the life of the immigrant will unfold (Jasso et al. 2000). For example, those admitted based on family connections (family-sponsored immigration) have a lower than average level of education and settle down close to their family, most often in ethnic enclaves. This makes sense as these immigrants tend to follow a primary immigrant already in the country. Immigrant communities, or 'ethnic enclaves,' are mostly constituted by the low educated immigrants and even though the ethnic homogeneity of these communities is most often discussed, there is also a class/education homogeneity that keeps people in the enclave because of the lack of opportunities outside. It has to be noted, though, that ethnic enclaves are also selective for nationality and culture and not typical for all countries sending a large number of emigrants to the United States.

Those immigrants who have a higher than average level of education (in comparison with U.S. citizens), however, go where their jobs are, no matter whether any co-ethnics are there. Their occupation, and not their ethnicity, has an important effect on their friendship networks and plays an important role in defining their identity. It might be that, rather than 'Chinese,' 'Mexican,' 'Indian,' or 'Hungarian,' an immigrant who is a physician would most probably define him/herself as a 'physician' and would have contacts within the group of physicians, not necessarily within his/her ethnic group.

On the one hand, the societal integration of highly educated immigrants tends to be easy: they have good English skills (many of them complete their studies in the United States before getting a job) and often they do not stay attached to any ethnic group. On the other hand, educated immigrants have the means to maintain a transnational profile, by keeping in touch with the country of origin. Africans, for example—the most highly educated group of immigrants in the United States (Butcher 1994)—tend to separate themselves from the African-Americans by emphasizing their African origins in the education of their off-springs (Lieberson and Waters 1988).

The migration of highly educated workers has been facilitated by the internationalization of markets and professions. This internationalization influences how migrants think of themselves and what type of identities they are comfortable with. Interestingly, this process can support both the weak and the strong ties of the migrant experiences mentioned above. If the main identity is that of a transnational professional, the migrant may not look for co-ethnics or co-nationals. At the same time, internationalization of certain occupations can help maintain strong ties to the country of origin as the migrant might not feel any disconnection, especially if his or her home social network consists of similarly trained professionals. Thus, internationalization can be a two-way street, and the traditional brain drain concept could be substituted with the concept of brain mobility (Ouaked 2002).

The incorporation of highly skilled immigrants has been discussed by Portes and Borocz (1989). They differentiated between various forms of skilled immigrant incorporation based on the extent to which the immigrants are incorporated in a market position corresponding with their expertise. In countries like the United States with a flexible job market and long traditions of immigration, skilled immigrants may have better opportunities to be judged based on their skills rather than their immigrant status. This would suggest that their identity formation will be less pressured by the need for fitting in, and it is relatively easy for them to maintain an international professional profile.

As Iredale (2001) noted, the trends lead toward more internationalization of the labor market, especially in high technology occupations such as computer science and higher education. This means that understanding the dynamics of immigrant incorporation for highly skilled immigrants and those who are not subjected to racial profiling will be increasingly important. Our study contributes to this effort and helps prepare for the incorporation challenges of tomorrow.

Data and Results

As the number of European immigrants is relatively small in comparison with other immigrant groups, we have to use databases that include large samples of Europeans in order to have a decent number of subjects of interest. We use the March Supplement of the Current Population Survey 2000–2008 (pooled data) from the Minnesota Population Center as our first source of data. This dataset includes information for about 5,782 European immigrants. We also use the New Immigrant Survey database to analyze the patterns of emigration for European-born permanent resident immigrants—that is, what immigration channels do they use to get their green cards. Aggregate level data from the Homeland Security/Office of Immigration and Survey of Doctorate Recipients (1995) is also used to put the analyses into the general context of U.S. immigration.

The foreign born population living in the United States is relatively young, and its proportion in the labor force has been increasing in the past years. In 2007, for example, 15.7 % of the U.S. population aged 16 and over (24.0 million) were foreign born, up from 15.3 % in 2006. Their rate of unemployment is lower but

Table 11.2 Immigrants' region of birth at various levels of education. (Source: current population survey, 2000–2008, authors' computations)

	Total (%)	Less than high school (%)	College (4 years +) (%)
Central, South America, and Mexico	49.7	79.1	20.4
Asia	25.7	9.0	48.1
Europe	16.0	7.9	20.3
Other regions	8.6	4.0	11.2
Total	100	100	100

the difference is not significant when compared with that of natives—4.3 % of the foreign born were unemployed in 2007, while the percentage for natives was 4.7 %. Generally, there is a difference in earnings between the natives and the foreign born in the United States, with native born earning more than foreign born persons, but the gap decreases with the level of education, and the foreign born persons with college degrees have earnings that are very similar to earnings of native born persons (U.S. Bureau of Labor Statistics 2009). In 2011, the earnings of a foreign born person with less than a high school education was 83.9 % of a native in the same educational category. The same ratio for those with a bachelor's degree or higher was 99.8 % (http://www.bls.gov/news.release/pdf/forbrn.pdf).

The ethnic composition of immigrants varies by levels of education, with immigrants coming from Latin America being overrepresented among the low educated immigrants and Asians being the majority among the immigrants with higher education. Table 11.2 presents the ethnic distribution of immigrants at various levels of education.

Among the foreign born, a small percentage of those with low education are Europeans, while more than one in five immigrants with 4+ years of advanced education come from Europe. In Table 11.3, we included some general information about the European born immigrants living in the United States in 2000.

In the following, we will focus on the differences in income between native born persons and European immigrants. Europeans have generally higher incomes than the native born: using the Current Population Survey data 2000–2008, we compared White native born persons with foreign born and European immigrants in the United States. Previous studies of ethnic/racial groups of immigrants in the United States argue for comparing these groups with the native group of the race (Butcher 1994). In Table 11.4 we present some information on immigrants who received a wage, 2000–2008.

Foreign born, generally, and Europeans in particular, tend to reside in metropolitan areas more so than the native born persons do (92 versus 69.4 %). Also, a larger percentage of Europeans as well as total foreign born persons live in the central part of cities (37.5 versus 20.5 %).

We adjusted the earnings for inflation and we included (a sub-sample) only those who declared that they worked and earned a wage and who declared the amount as well. Our results show that White immigrants in general, and European immigrants in particular, have higher mean incomes than the native Whites (Table 11.5). While

Table 11.3 European born persons living in the United States, 2000. (Source: U.S. Census Bureau, 2000 U.S. Census)

	European born
Total European-born population	4,915,555
Entered U.S. between 1990 and 2000	33%
Entered U.S. between 1980 and 1989	14%
Entered U.S. before 1980	53%
Median age (years)	50
Currently in college or graduate school	315,505
No high school diploma (age 25 and over)	23.5%
Bachelor's degree or higher (age 25 and over)	29.2%

Table 11.4 Native born persons and foreign born Whites who received a wage, 2000–2008. (Source: current population survey, 2000–2008, authors' computations)

	Native born	Foreign born	European born
Mean age	43.3	44.5	44.9
% Female	41.6%	38.9%	41.0%
% Own the house	75.5%	66.0%	68.2%
% Metro area	69.4%	91.8%	92.0%
% Central city	20.5%	37.7%	37.5%
% Married	60.6%	64.4%	63.7%
% Living in the same house 1 year ago	86.6%	85.7%	87.1%
% No high school diploma	4.5%	6.7%	5.8%
% 4 years college or more	34.7%	47.7%	46.0%
Number of cases	282,341	10,196	5,782

Table 11.5 Mean income for native born and foreign born Whites, 2000–2008. (Source: current population survey, 2000–2008, authors' computations)

	Native born	Foreign born	European born
Less than high school	20,400	23,180	24,980
High school	31,500	30,680	32,100
Some college	36,000	34,500	35,001
College and above	55,281	60,000	59,000
Total	38,948	42,000	41,600
Number of cases	282,341	10,196	5,782

this result might come from the fact that immigrants have a higher level of education than the natives (47.7% of White foreign born and 46% of European born persons who had a wage income during 2000–2008 have four or more years of college, while 34.7% of native born persons are in this educational group), breaking down the income on educational levels shows that immigrants without a high school diploma and those who have college and above are those who have higher earnings than the native born population. Those with a high school diploma or some college actually earn less than the native born.

The youngest (mean age 41) and the highest educated group among the European immigrants are those coming from former Soviet Union: 64.8 % of them have four years of college and above, and only 2.7 % do not have a high school diploma. However, those coming from Western Europe have the highest income ($44,517). There are two possible explanations for this discrepancy: (1) late arrival in the United States of the former USSR born residents and (2) a more general difficulty in achieving incomes similar to the Western European born.

The first explanation of lower incomes for people coming from the former USSR countries might be related to their late arrival in the United States. Studies show that after a number of years spent in the host country (10–15 years), immigrants are able to close the gap with their native born comparable groups (Borjas 1994, 1999; Chiswick 1978) and, in some cases, they even surpass the native born (Chiswick 1978) in terms of occupational and income attainment. Their trajectories follow a U shape (a decrease followed by an increase), more pronounced for highly skilled migrants (Barrett and Duffy 2008).

Most of the immigrants coming from former USSR countries came after 1990 (71.7 %), while most of the Western Europeans (70.4 %) and about half of the Eastern Europeans (56.6 %) came before 1990. The larger immigration of educated residents from the former USSR into the United States after 1990 was influenced by the U.S. immigration regulations following the fall of the iron curtain. In 1992, the Soviet Scientists Immigration Act (SSIA), Public Law 102–509, was enacted to facilitate the settlement of former USSR scientists coming to the United States. This law set aside immigration visas for scientists and engineers from the independent states of the former Soviet Union and the Baltic States with expertise in nuclear, chemical, biological, or other high-technology fields or defense projects. The law was modified several times in the following years, changing the number of visas and the evidence eligible subjects had to submit in order to establish their expertise/work experience in the required fields. Those who were eligible to apply for this type of visa did not need to have a job in the United States in order to immigrate (U.S. Citizenship and Immigration Services, http://www.uscis.gov).

The second explanation might be related to the very fact of coming from a specific country (in this case, former USSR countries) where the governments do not spend a lot on education. These results are confirmed by what Mattoo et al. (2008) found using census data: that U.S. immigrants from Eastern Europe and Latin America tend to have significantly lower occupational attainment for their level of education in comparison to U.S. natives and other groups of immigrants

Using the New Immigrants Survey 2003 data, we employed all the variables enumerated above (education, education in the United States, immigration channels, European origin) as well as other control variables (gender, age) to study the effects they have on income. As a dependent variable we used the natural logarithm of wage income and we included in the analysis only those immigrants who declared having a wage income (Table 11.6).[2]

[2] We also did a separate analysis using total income, and the results were similar.

Table 11.6 Influence of various variables on legal immigrants' wage income. (Source: NIS 2003 pilot project data, authors' computations)

	Model 1		Model 2		Model 3		Model 4	
	B	St.err.	B	St.err.	B	St.err.	B	St.err.
Gender (0- Male, 1-Female)	-.572 ***	.067	-.511***	.065	-0.5***	.056	-0.45***	.053
Year born	-.015***	0.003	-.024***	.003	-0.016***	.003	-0.014***	.003
Years school completed			0.094***	.007	0.11***	.006	0.067***	.006
% Years of education in the US			1.120***	.173	-0.17	.154	0.18	.148
Already in the US					1.8***	.058	1.62***	.056
Employment based immigration (1-yes)							1.103***	.063
European/former USSR origin (1- yes)							0.2**	.067
R^2	0.033		0.113		0.342		0.407	
R^2 adjusted	0.032		0.111		0.341		0.406	
Mean VIF	1		1.049		1.077		1.15	
Durbin Watson	1.93		1.939		1.908		1.902	
Number of cases	2758		2753		2753		2753	

***: $p<0.001$
**: $p<0.01$

Some of the results were expected—such as the differences in wages between men and women, which remains strong in all models. Some others were not expected: for example, percentage of years of education in the US is an important predictor in model one, but it becomes insignificant once we control for whether the immigrant was already in the United States when s/he got the green card. However, this might be a statistical artifact due to a strong relationship between percentage of years of education in the United States and U.S. residence before getting a green card. Employment-based immigration is a strong predictor for higher wages—in other models (results not shown), we controlled for immigration channels and all the other methods (family based, diversity, refugee) are not significant. Only employment based-immigration made a difference. Being European has advantages for immigrants in gaining a better income. We also tried this case with several other options (using Asians and Hispanics as predictors) and while Hispanics had a significant advantage in a model where we did not control for whether the immigrant was already in the United States before becoming a permanent resident, the advantage disappeared once we controlled for this variable. However, those immigrants coming from Europe or the former USSR countries tend to keep a significant advantage even when we control for all the other variables.

Developed countries encourage skilled migrants to come as short time workers, but few of them allow such migrants to settle permanently (Iredale 2001). The United States is one of these few countries allowing skilled workers to settle permanently if they prove to be useful and not in the position of becoming a public charge. In 2006, approximately 1,560 European-born persons received a PhD in the United States, a similar number to the Indians (1,742). Although there is increasing public pressure toward limiting migration, this pressure manifests mainly in regard to illegal migrants and the migration of low skilled workers. The need for skilled migrants seemed to increase over the past years, and various agencies lobby toward more relaxed policies toward highly educated migrants. However, the bulk of immigration visas are set aside for family based immigration, so a relatively small number of immigrants come to the United States based on employment visas.

The highly skilled professionals come to the United States using two channels: temporary work visas (such as H1B) and immigrant visas. The number of visas available every year is subject to change. A person admitted based on the H1B can stay up to six years in the United States but during this period he or she can apply for permanent residency through various tracks specifically designed for highly skilled workers. There is a given number (quota) of immigrant visas reserved every year for those with advanced degrees (Master's and PhD) (priority workers—E1 and professionals and persons with extraordinary ability—E2) (U.S. Department of State, http://travel.state.gov/visa/immigrants/types/types_1323.html#first)

Conclusions

In this paper we focused on the education and labor market outcomes of European immigrants living in the United States. While Europeans no longer represent a large segment of recent immigration waves, there are about 5 million European-born persons living currently in the United States. They tend to be concentrated among the highly skilled immigrants, as they have generally higher than average levels of education and wages. While the current discourse usually focuses on skilled Asian immigrants, the number of European-born immigrants who get advanced degrees (PhD) in the United States is in fact similar to the number of persons born in India. Interviews conducted with several highly educated European immigrants (not discussed in detail here) show that many came to the United States to complete their education and later decided to stay here either because of job market insufficiencies back home or because of family reasons (getting married in the United States). For many, the United States became 'home' to some extent, but at the same time they continue to keep strong ties to their countries of origin, by traveling there frequently, speaking the native language at home, and remaining informed about their country of origin. While many have an extensive and strong network of friends, including other immigrants, these other immigrants are not necessarily from the same ethnic group or country of origin, but rather people with similar levels of education.

While most of the Western Europeans came to the United States before 1990s, many of the Eastern European immigrants came after the fall of communism in Europe. While those coming from former USSR countries represent the youngest and most educated group, the Western Europeans have the highest mean income, most probably because many came earlier and are older, having more opportunities for career advancement. Our results show that, after controlling for variables such as gender, age, education, and channel of immigration, being a European or former USSR born immigrant living in the United States is an advantage, and it leads to higher wage incomes than for other immigrants.

This study has indicated that despite their relatively low number, European immigrants still have a significant impact on the American economy and society because they are concentrated in high-end occupations and positions. The historic ties between the United States and Europe are still dynamic. On the other hand, European immigration itself has changed. More recent immigrants from Eastern Europe are different in terms both of their immigration and of their integration experiences. For many of these immigrants, the United States as a destination competes with Western Europe, especially after the large-scale eastern expansion of the European Union over the past decade. Given the current state of academia and the research and development job market in the former communist countries, we can expect a continuous flow of immigrants from that region as long as these immigrants perceive that their training pays its dividends and their integration will be easy in the United States. Further research is needed to analyze this immigrant flow in order to better understand the motivation and networks of Eastern European immigrants.

References

Alba, R., & Abdel-Hady, D. (2005). Galileo's children: Italian Americans' difficult entry into the intellectual elite. *The Sociological Quarterly, 46*(1), 3–18.

Alba, R. D., Lutz, A., & Vesselinov, E. (2001). How enduring are the inequalities among European immigrant groups in the US? *Demography, 38*(3), 349–356.

Barrett, A., & Duffy, D. (2008). Are Ireland's immigrants integrating into its labor market? *International Migration Review, 42,* 597–619. doi:10.1111/j.1747-7379.2008.00139.x.

Birrell, B., & Healy, E. (2008). How are skilled migrants doing? *People and Place, 16*(Suppl 1), 1–19.

Borjas, G. J. (1992). Ethnic capital and intergenerational mobility. *Quarterly Journal of Economics, 107*(428), 123–150.

Borjas, G. J. (1994). Long–run convergence of ethnic skills differentials: The children and grandchildren of the Great Migration. *Industrial and Labor Relations Review, 47*(4), 553–573.

Borjas, G. J. (1999). *Heaven's door. Immigration policy and the American economy.* Princeton: Princeton University Press.

Butcher, K. F. (1994). Black immigrants in the United States: A comparison with native Blacks and other immigrants. *Industrial and Labor Relations Review, 47*(2), 265–284.

Chiswick, B. R. (1978). The effect of Americanization on the earnings of foreign-born men. *Journal of Political Economy, 86*(5), 897–921.

Green, D. (1999). Immigrant occupational attainment: Assimilation and mobility over time. *Journal of Labor Economics, 17*(1), 49–79.

Iredale, R. (2001). The migration of professionals: Theories and typologies. *International Migration, 39*(5), 7–26.

Jasso, G., Massey, D. S., Rosenzweig, M. R., & Smith, J. P. (2000). The new immigrants survey pilot: Overview and new findings about US immigrants at admission. *Demography, 37*(1), 127–138.

Kaushal, N., & Fix, M. (2006). The contribution of high-skilled immigrants. Migration Policy Institute. http://www.migrationpolicy.org. Accessed 5 May 2014.

Liberson, S., & Waters, M. C. (1988). *From many stands: Ethnic and racial groups in contemporary America.* New York: Russell Sage.

Malone, N., Kaari, F. B., Joseph, M. C., & Cynthia, J. D. (2003). The Foreign Born Population: 2000, Census 2000 Brief. http://www.census.gov/prod/2003pubs/c2kbr-34.pdf. Accessed 5 May 2014.

Martin, P., & Midgley, E. (2003). *Immigration: Shaping and reshaping America.* Population Reference Bureau.

Mattoo, A., Neagu, I. C., & Ozden, C. (2008). Brain waste? Educated immigrants in the US labour market. *Journal of Development Economics, 87,* 255–269.

Ouaked, S. (2002). Transatlantic roundtable on high-skilled migration and sending countries issues. *International Migration, 40,* 153–166. doi:10.1111/1468-2435.00209.

Portes, A., & Borocz, J. (1989). Contemporary immigration: Theoretical perspectives on its determinants and modes of incorporation. *International Migration Review, 23*(3), 606–630. (Special Silver Anniversary Issue: International Migration an Assessment for the 90's).

U.S. Bureau of Labor Statistics. (2009). *Foreign born workers: Labor force characteristics in 2008.* http://www.bls.gov/news.release/archives/forbrn_03262009.pdf. Accessed 10 March 2012.

Zheng, Z., & Xie, Y. (2004). Asian-Americans' earnings disadvantaged reexamined: The role of place of education. *American Journal of Sociology, 109*(5), 1075–1108.

Chapter 12
Childbearing and the Labor Market: Time and Space Dynamics

Elena Kotyrlo

Introduction

During the twentieth century, a dramatic decline in fertility was observed in developed countries that was associated with the introduction of contraceptives and increased female labor market participation. Despite the overall downward trend, the variation in total fertility rates (TFR) differs from one country to another. Fertility varies as a consequence of economic events and changes in the cost of raising children. In this paper, fertility time and space dynamics in Sweden are analyzed, particularly in relation to the labor market.

The short-run effects of these factors can be assessed by examining two effects of earnings in which children are regarded as "normal goods" in the maximization of household utility (Becker and Barro 1988; Becker 1960). *The income effect* assumes that a larger income encourages families to have more children. Childbearing can be viewed as "household production" and is considered *a substitute* for female labor market participation. Thus, higher wages raise the opportunity cost of having a child.

Current income and changes in expected earnings contribute to the effect of earnings, implying that a higher income helps a family to deal with the direct costs of childbearing. Thus, in the present study, we anticipated that the postponement or acceleration of childbearing occurs in the short run in Sweden because the Swedish completed cohort fertility rate is rather constant, but the variation in total fertility rate is about 10% higher than in other Nordic countries during the studied period.

In the long run, the age structure of the population may affect the total fertility rates and economic explanation of this phenomenon. This principle, known as the Easterlin hypothesis (Easterlin 1966), relates to a negative response of fertility to increasing labor market tightness caused by increasing numbers of people of working age. According to this hypothesis, decisions about childbearing, which presumably primarily concern the young generation, are made on the basis of the income potentials of the young generation compared to previous generations.

E. Kotyrlo (✉)
Ageing and Living Conditions Center, Demographic Data Base,
Umeå University, Umeå, Sweden
e-mail: elena.kotyrlo@umu.se

M. N. Hoque, L. B. Potter (eds.), *Emerging Techniques in Applied Demography*, Applied Demography Series 4, DOI 10.1007/978-94-017-8990-5_12,

Labor mobility, which has exhibited a positive trend over the last few decades in Sweden (Eliasson et al. 2007), contributes to the space dynamics of fertility. Growing flows of in- and out-migrated people increase the probability of finding a partner, which may lead to marriage or cohabitation and having a child. In addition, these labor flows generate earning flows across space and affect families' income potentials for childbearing.

New econometric instruments, such as spatial econometrics for panel data, allow a more in-depth study of these problems than previously possible by taking into account the diffusion of fertility norms and the influence of economic factors across space. Municipalities can be considered as open demo-economic systems. Interactions between adjacent municipal labor markets, resulting from the flow of in- and out-migrated people, affect the labor market equilibrium as well as the spatial income distribution. In particular, a gain in local labor market tightness, caused by the entry of a large young generation, can be smoothed by increasing labor mobility, but it would worsen the situation in surrounding labor markets. Thus, the inverted Easterlin hypothesis is expected to be supported in the spatial dimension when considering income potential coupled with tightness of surrounding labor markets; increasing tightness reduces peoples' opportunities to find a good job or compete for higher earnings.

The spatial effect of earnings can be explained in terms of the influence of the average annual income per capita in surrounding municipalities on the total fertility rate in a certain municipality. This includes the effect of migrants, whose earnings are considered statistically to be in the place (municipality) of work, despite the fact that they may have their families in other municipalities.

One important study that measured fertility in the spatial dimension is that of Waldorf and Franklin (2002), who tested the Easterlin hypothesis by assuming the fertility among 18 Italian regions was governed by spatial diffusion. Two types of spatial diffusion between units are considered, namely space interaction of fertility norms and labor mobility, which both influence fertility.

The purpose of the present work is to study how the labor market situation, as measured by household earnings, influences fertility, taking into account dynamics in time and space. Space diffusion is assessed by global and local spillover effects. Transition of fertility norms across municipalities gives a first-order spatial autocorrelation. Influence of the relative cohort sizes in surrounding municipalities on fertility norms in a given one and cross-municipal influence of the space diffusion of income generated by labor mobility are assumed to be a local form of spillover. Time dynamics are examined by considering a second-order serial autocorrelation of total fertility rates and testing the direct effect of the Easterlin hypothesis and the effect of current earnings in a given municipality. Measurement of space diffusion is based on two types of weight matrices to avoid multi-correlation among the explanatory variables. The row-standardized contiguity weight matrix is used for lagged total fertility rates, whereas matrices with spherical distances weighted by population size are applied for estimating the influence of average annual income per capita and relative cohort size on fertility rates.

The main contribution of this paper is the analysis of influence of earnings on fertility with taking into account spatio-temporal dynamics. In contrast to previous studies, the present work considers the Easterlin hypothesis in terms of the long-run impact of earnings and, at the same time, assesses the relationship between current earnings and fertility. The use of panel data allows space diffusion of fertility norms to be monitored as a function of time in "three dimensions." The effects of earnings on fertility are related to factors such as skill characteristics of labor markets and labor flows. In contrast to other papers, municipal level data is analyzed, which gives more detailed results than studies at national or regional levels. The theoretical contribution of the paper is in the application of stationarity conditions in the SAR(2,1) model and the derivation of the long-run effects of the explanatory variables in direct, spatial, and total forms.

The paper is structured as follows. Section two describes the main econometric methods for dynamic models of space and time; previous studies of fertility in spatial diffusion; studies of the Easterlin hypothesis for Sweden; and results concerning the impact of earnings on fertility in Sweden. Section three explains the methods used for estimation and post-estimation interpretation, e.g., to evaluate the short- and long-run effects within and across municipalities as well as total effects. A stationarity condition for the estimated model is also discussed. Section four describes the data set. Section five details the empirical specification. In section six, the results are presented, and the final section provides a summary.

Previous Literature

Spatial econometrics of panel data has gained increasing popularity as a new, rapidly growing branch of econometrics, since in many cases, the importance of nearest neighbors on social and economic behavior and activity seems self-evident. The derivation of the estimated model approach to estimation and post-estimation analysis, as well as interpretation of the model and results, have been detailed in earlier papers by Anselin (2002), Brueckner (2003), Elhorst (2001), LeSage and Pace (2010), and Yua et al. (2008). Brueckner (2003) classified spatial interactions according to a spillover model, whereby spatial units reciprocally affect each other, or a resource-flow model, in which they share some limited resources. Labor mobility may be considered from both points of view. It exhibits a spillover effect when labor mobility increases matching of couples and, consequently, fertility. It can also be interpreted as a model of common resource sharing, such as a total earning potential of the labor market. It is useful that, analytically, both models give rise to a spatially lagged econometric specification (Anselin 2002, p. 250), since it is not possible to attribute labor mobility to purely one effect.

Elhorst (2001) has provided a thorough analysis of first-order autoregressive panel data models in both space and time, including a taxonomy of the models, approaches for estimation and determining stationarity in the time conditions, and a spatial equilibrium correction model, which provides the static long-run equilibrium relationship between endogenous and explanatory variables.

The paper of Yua et al. (2008) gives a better understanding of the general approach for employing stationary time conditions in spatial modeling. LeSage and Pace (2010) have provided an interpretation of the direct, the indirect (spatial), and the total effects, which has been accepted by other researchers as a standard approach for spatial models. The interpretation can be problematic because the indirect effect is specific for each pair of spatial units and the size of the effects matrix depends on the number of units. Thus, LeSage and Pace (2010) suggested measuring the spatial effect compared to the direct and total effects. The average direct effect is interpreted as a mean of diagonal elements. The indirect effect for unit i of a variable x is defined as the sum of off-diagonal elements $j=1,\ldots,N$ of row i and the average indirect effect is the mean of $i=1,\ldots,N$ indirect effects. The average total effect is calculated as the sum of the average direct and indirect effects.

Several studies have considered spatial diffusion of fertility from the perspective of spreading knowledge about contraception (Bongaarts and Watkins 1996; Weeks et al. 2004; Woods 1984). These papers have mainly focused on developing countries or historically remote time periods of developed countries. There are substantially fewer papers reporting investigations of space dynamics of fertility in developed countries (de Castro 2007; McNicoll 1980; Waldorf and Franklin 2002).

The Easterlin hypothesis for cross-sectional and panel data is a popular approach for interpreting the effects of earnings on fertility. Macunovich (1998) reviewed 185 published articles incorporating 76 empirical analyses of the Easterlin hypothesis and concluded that the results were mixed. Such ambiguous results may be due to testing the Easterlin hypothesis in the absence of other controls and the assumption that household income and male earnings are interchangeable. Waldorf and Byun (2005) performed a meta-analysis of 334 empirical papers to test the Easterlin hypothesis, and their research showed a more robust negative effect despite positive effects being more frequent. A negative effect or inverted Easterlin hypothesis implies that a more numerous young generation than parental generation is related to a higher total fertility rate when the young generation is of fertility age.

The importance of the relative cohort size, R, as an indicator of relative economic status depends on the age range defining the young generation. Researchers have varied the upper boundary from 29–34 years in order to maximize the correlation between fertility and age structure. Waldorf and Byun (2005) concluded that the use of a broad age range for the young cohort increases the likelihood of a negative correlation.

Several cross-sectional studies have tested the Easterlin hypothesis in different countries, such as Artzrouni and Easterlin (1982), Baird (1987), Pampel (1993), Wright (1989) and Sevilla (2007). Most of these papers (except Artzrouni and Easterlin (1982) and Baird (1987)) have reported that the inverted Easterlin hypothesis, i.e., a positive relationship between fertility and the proportion of the young generation, applies for Sweden.

Pampel (1993) concluded that the institutional structure, such as family policy, together with increased female labor force participation, influence the relative economic status of the cohort, which explains the negative effect of the cohort size. Hence, the relative cohort size positively influences fertility only when it is associated with poor opportunities for employment, higher wages, and promotion. Pampel proposed that state policies to keep unemployment at a minimum and guarantee jobs, as well as policies against sex discrimination in the labor market, an effective child-care system, and the length of maternity leave, helped to explain the insignificance of the cohort size effect on fertility. This conclusion is important for understanding the effect of earnings on fertility in Sweden, where family policy plays a major role in reducing the costs associated with raising children. The substitution effect on childbearing is weakened in Sweden not only because maternity benefits are closely related to a woman's pre-birth earnings, encouraging women to be employed before childbearing, but also because women are able to return to the labor market despite having small children due to the supportive child-care system. Studies based on Swedish micro-data support the positive effect of earnings on fertility (Andersson 1999; Hoem 2000).

The skill level of the labor force also affects the studied relationships. On the one hand, women who achieve higher levels of education generally receive higher salaries, which increase the opportunity costs of childbearing and, consequently, reduce the demand on children. Thus, the proportion of high- and low-skilled women employed in a local economy will affect the fertility rate. On the other hand, Andersson et al. (2003) found that women with university education have a higher probability of having a third birth than women with lower education levels. This may in part be due to the family policy in Sweden, where women with a university education generally have better opportunities than others to combine work and family as a result of higher salaries and more flexible working hours. Education and childbearing have been shown to be highly related from a household productivity or investment point of view (Becker and Barro 1988). Thus, the status of university cities is usually controlled in regression analyses of fertility (Andersson et al. 2003; Westerberg 2006).

Research Strategy

Three different hypotheses are tested in this paper. The first is the Easterlin hypothesis, which assumes that the dynamics of age structure affect the tightness of the labor market and considers the role of income potential of the young generation relative to the older generation in explaining decisions concerning childbearing. The cohort ratio is the main explanatory variable. The second hypothesis concerns the short-run effect of earnings, in which the present income potential of households is compared to their earnings in the recent past and expected earnings in the future. This hypothesis predicts an increase in total fertility rates during macroeconomic boom periods or better family policy regimes and local labor market conditions. The main explanatory variable considered in the second hypothesis is income. The third hypothesis concerns spatial effects on the relationship between fertility and age structure and between fertility and current earnings. The existence of autocorrelation of fertility rates across municipalities, generated by labor movements and "earnings' flow," is presumed. The hypotheses are considered assuming the spatial diffusion of fertility rates. The endogenous variable in the model is the annual total fertility rate within a certain municipality.

In the assumption of employing only conditional spatial terms in the model, our research strategy is based on the Arellano-Bond linear dynamic panel-data estimation for LAG type of spatial modeling instead of the maximum likelihood method. This assumption is reasonable since childbearing is a lagged process in relation to factors affecting decisions concerning fertility. The model is estimated for different sets of municipal variables as discussed further below.

Spatial reaction functions can be incorporated into a lag model as either a global form of spillovers or spatial autocorrelation or as a local form of spillovers, using spatial lag as an explanatory variable. Global and local form spillovers can be combined in one model, but in such a case, the problem of multicollinearity arises since exogenous variables are included explicitly in a local form and implicitly in a global form. To avoid this problem, distinct weight matrices can be used for lagged-dependent and explanatory variables.

The model, in which fertility has a spatio-temporal lag structure and the spatial influence of age structure and income are extracted, has a linear form. The weighted lagged total fertility rate (**W·TFR**) reflects the recent space-autoregressive dependence of fertility rates due to the possible balancing of age-gender inequality and interactions between people living in different municipalities who potentially form matches during work and leisure. Even though both the cohort ratio R and income I are implicitly included in the specification via the global form of spillover **W·TFR**, their spatial influence may be extracted by incorporating local-form spillovers or spatially weighted variables **V·R** and **V·I**.

Several types of matrices for summarizing the spatial morphology of fertility across municipalities are empirically tested on the best approximation of diffusion of fertility rates, using incomes and cohort ratios as the main explanatory variables. As a result of this test, two approaches suggested by Waldorf and Franklin (2002) and based on a matrix of contiguity **W** and a set of matrices $\mathbf{V}(t)$ with spherical distances between municipalities weighted by population are chosen for use in the model. These approaches are convenient for reducing multicollinearity and, in the latter case, for taking into account of the influence of larger (in terms of population size) cities.

The row-standardized matrix W is constructed under the assumption that fertility is a spatial stationary process, where the covariation of fertility rates in two municipalities is purely a function of the distance between them. Here, $w_{ij} = 1/k_i$, if municipalities defined by indices i and j $(i, j = 1,\ldots, N)$ share a common border, where k_i is the number of municipalities bordering i and N is the total number of municipalities, otherwise $w_{ij} = 0$.

Row-standardized weight matrices $\mathbf{V}(t)$ based on spherical distances between municipalities are used to summarize the spatial morphology due to the influence of cohort ratio and incomes on fertility:

$$v_{ij}(t) = \frac{Pop_j(t) / d_{ij}}{\sum_k Pop_k(t) / d_{ik}} \tag{12.1}$$

where d_{ij} is the spherical distance between municipalities identified by the indices i and j. A standard approach (Anselin 2002) was employed to construct the weight matrix for the situation where a variable potentially affects the spatial interaction, i.e., in our case, the population size of the municipalities. In a panel data analysis, larger cities cannot be controlled directly by using a dummy variable or incorporating population size (approximately constant for a given unit) into the model. The set of v_{ij}, $j=1,\ldots,N$ for a given i allows higher weights to be ascribed to larger cities, and thus dynamics associated with the size of the municipality are captured in the weight coefficients.

The corresponding panel data matrices have the form $\mathbf{W}_{NT} = \mathbf{I}_T \otimes \mathbf{W}_N$[1] and $\mathbf{V}_{NT} = \mathbf{I}_T \otimes \mathbf{V}_N(t)$, $t=1,\ldots,T$, where $T=28$ for the period 1981–2008, and $\mathbf{I}_T$ is an identity matrix of dimension T.

Data

Municipality level data for 276 municipalities over the period 1981–2008 are included in the analysis (Statistics of Sweden)[2]. A description of variables and descriptive statistics are presented in Tables 12.2 and 12.3. The dependent variable *TFR* (Statistics of Sweden) is defined as the sum of the age-specific fertility rate (*SFR*) for women aged 16–49 years living in the municipality, as given by Eq. 12.2.

$$TFR = \sum_{i=16}^{49} SFR_i \tag{12.2}$$

Based on previous results by Macunovich (1998) and Waldorf and Byun (2005), the cohort ratio (R) is defined as the number of men aged 35–64 years divided by the number of men of aged 15–34 years and is calculated as a 3-year smoothed cohort ratio as shown in Eq. 12.3. The mean age of men at the birth of their first child, which increased from 26.66 in 1970–31.46 in 2006, is also examined.

$$R_{jt} = \sum_{\tau=t-2}^{t} M_{35-64,j\tau} \Big/ \sum_{\tau=t-2}^{t} M_{15-34,j\tau} \tag{12.3}$$

Whereas R measures the relative effect of earnings between generations, the average income responds to the effect of earnings in the short-run dynamics and across municipalities. The average income per capita in each municipality for people aged 20 and above is deflated by CPI (1981 = 100) and converted to a logarithm because of its log-normality ($\ln(I)$). It is assumed to be strongly positively correlated with the average earnings. Income in the data could not be separated by gender, thus only

[1] $\otimes$ is a Kronecker product.

[2] Appendix A3 provides some information about constructing data with respect to restructuring of municipalities in 1992.

the mean household effects of earnings on fertility could be measured. The proportion of relative net migration and relative total flow of in-/out-migrated women in the age range 16–49 years is considered in the specifications. Preliminary analysis suggested that the relative total flow of in-/out-migrated women is the most highly correlated variable to total fertility rates among the other variables characterizing migration.

To allow for different skills characteristics of local labor markets, the proportion of women with a primary and secondary education of 9 years and less (ISCED97 1) (in the age range 16–49 yrs), the proportion of women with post-graduate education (ISCED97 6), and the proportion of women with post-secondary education of 3 years or more (ISCED97 5A) (aged 20–49 yrs) are included in the model. Thus, boundary skill groups are taken into account in the model.

There are several reasons that can cause the cohort ratio to appear insignificant after including control variables, even though the correlation between them is not high. A larger young generation is obviously connected with greater mobility as the acquisition of education is a key reason for the relocation of young adults. In addition, a higher proportion of the young generation compared to other age groups correlates to a greater proportion of low-skilled people due to a larger number of people aged 16 through 19 who have not completed their education. However, the proportion of highly skilled people may also be greater among the young generation, particularly, due to increasing accessibility of educational programs over time.

The status of marriage or divorce on fertility was not examined because Hoem et al. (2006) have already published conclusions about the insignificance of these factors on fertility. The proportion of employed women was also not taken into account because of a lack of data for the entire period. However, previous studies have provided a justification for including this information in the analysis (Berinde 1999; Westerberg 2006). Following earlier papers, variables such as size of labor force, mean age at first birth, and earned income quintiles are expected to be important. These variables are included in some of the specifications.

It is important to eliminate business cycle components from the analysis. Gross domestic product (GDP) in constant prices for Sweden (indexmundi.com) was considered a suitable variable for reflecting business activity changes.

Empirical Specifications

Space dynamics are taken into account in the model through lagged terms. Residuals are assumed to be not spatially autocorrelated. The total fertility rate dynamics are considered to involve a stationary process with a cyclical component, which required incorporating at least two time lags. Both explanatory variables of interest – income and the cohort ratio—also contain cyclical components. The cyclical component of income is related to business cycles, whereas the cyclical component of the cohort ratio can be explained by demographic cycles. The cohort ratio exhibited a trend associated with aging of the population. Preliminary analysis of the data on income, migration, and educational levels showed that they also followed some trends. These findings support the use of a model that incorporates explanatory variables as lags. This is achieved by applying the Arellano-Bond method of estimation for panel data models with a spatially lagged dependent variable. This method is based on the generalized method of moments (GMM), which allows the evaluation of asymptotically efficient estimates under the assumption of autocorrelation between explanatory variables and errors when a stationary process is considered.

The cyclical component of income is modeled using two different approaches. The first approach involved a model with time-specific fixed effects, whereas the second approach employed GDP growth as a control variable for time and business cycles. The development of the spatial first-order and serial second-order panel data model SAR (2,1) for the estimation is presented below in explicit vector form (12.4). It combines global and local forms of spillovers:

$$\mathbf{TFR}_t = \varphi_1\mathbf{TFR}_{t-1} + \varphi_2\mathbf{TFR}_{t-2} + \gamma\mathbf{W}_{NT}\mathbf{TFR}_{t-1} + \pi\mathbf{R}_{t-1} + \nu\mathbf{V}_{NT}\mathbf{R}_{t-1} + \theta\ln\mathbf{I}_{t-1} + \vartheta\mathbf{V}_{NT}\ln\mathbf{I}_{t-1}\mathbf{X}_{t-1}\beta + \varepsilon_t \tag{12.4}$$

where π and θ are parameters associated with the cohort ratio and log-income, respectively, v and ϑ are time-space autoregressive parameters of the local form of spillovers, φ_k and γ are parameters associated with the time- and space-lagged total fertility rate, respectively, and ε_t is a normally distributed, reciprocally independent vector of errors of size N.

The short-run effect of the lagged *TFR* is described by $\frac{\partial\mathbf{TFR}_t}{\partial\mathbf{TFR}_{t-1}} = \gamma\mathbf{W}' + \varphi\mathbf{I}_N$. The marginal effects of the cohort size ratio and log-income on fertility are $\frac{\partial\mathbf{TFR}_t}{\partial\mathbf{R}_{t-1}} = \nu\mathbf{V}' + \pi\mathbf{I}_N$ and $\frac{\partial\mathbf{TFR}_t}{\partial\ln(\mathbf{I}_{t-1})} = \vartheta\mathbf{V}' + \theta\mathbf{I}_N$, respectively. The first term in these expressions corresponds to spillover or indirect effects, whereas the second term reflects a direct effect of a lagged variable on fertility rate.

The long-run effects presented in Eqs. 12.5, 12.6, and 12.7 are derived in Appendix 5. Equations 12.5 and 12.6 give the long-run spatial effects under conditions of a non-zero parameter of the spatially lagged variable. If local spillover parameters v and ϑ are insignificant, Eq. 12.7 can be used to estimate the long-run effects of the cohort ratio and earnings by substituting π and θ in place of β. These formulae imply that even if the short-run spillover effect is absent or the parameter of the spatially weighted variable is equal to zero, the non-zero long-run indirect effect exists in the presence of direct effect. Interpretation of the results and the estimated values of average direct, indirect (spatial), and total effects are given in the next section.

$$\frac{\partial\mathbf{TFR}}{\partial\mathbf{R}} = \left[\left(\left(1-\sum_{k=1}^{2}\varphi_k\right)\mathbf{I}_N - \gamma\mathbf{W}\right)^{-1}\left(\nu\mathbf{V} + \pi\mathbf{I}_N\right)\right]' \tag{12.5}$$

$$\frac{\partial \mathbf{TFR}}{\partial \ln(\mathbf{I})} = \left[\left(\left(1 - \sum_{k=1}^{2} \varphi_k \right) \mathbf{I}_N - \gamma \mathbf{W} \right)^{-1} \left(\vartheta \mathbf{V} + \theta \mathbf{I}_N \right) \right]^{\prime} \tag{12.6}$$

$$\frac{\partial \mathbf{TFR}}{\partial \mathbf{X}} = \left[\left(\left(1 - \sum_{k=1}^{2} \varphi_k \right) \mathbf{I}_N - \gamma \mathbf{W} \right)^{-1} \beta \right]^{\prime} \tag{12.7}$$

We consider linear coefficients of elasticity $e = b\frac{\bar{x}}{\bar{y}}$ where b represents the estimate of the parameter for explanatory variable x. The average value of the endogenous variable y alters by e percent when x changes by one percent. Assuming a stationarity condition for *TFR*, the bounds for autoregressive parameters of the model are defined by Eq. 12.8,

$$\left| \frac{\varphi_1 + \gamma \mu_i \pm \sqrt{(\phi_1 + \gamma \mu_i)^2 + 4\varphi_2}}{2} \right| < 1 \tag{12.8}$$

where $\{\mu_i\}$, $i = 1,\ldots,N$ is a set of eigenvalues of the matrix W. The proof of the inequality is shown in Appendix 6. The estimated models are tested for the absence of serial autocorrelation in residuals. Wald values, which are used for accepting or rejecting the hypothesis that each parameter is equal to 0, are shown for each model in Table 12.4.

Results

The results of the estimation for two sets of variables and two types of cyclical component of income are presented in Table 12.4. The basic specification for the period 1981–2008 included the relative cohort size R, log(I), and the proportions of in-/out-migrated women aged 16–49 years. A more detailed specification for the period 1985–2008 included the same explanatory variables and, in addition, the educational levels of women, i.e., the proportion of women aged 16–49 years with more than 3 years post-secondary education and the proportion of women aged 16–49 years with less than 9 years education.

The main finding is that the parameter of the weighted lagged *TFR* is significant and positive in both specifications. This suggests that a spatial positive autocorrelation of *TFR* applies across municipalities. It means that declining or rising fertility in one municipality affects neighboring municipalities in the same direction. However, the factors generating this spatial autocorrelation could not be extracted separately. Estimated values of the parameters for one specification of the time-specific model, presented in column 8 in Table 12.4, are shown in Table 12.1 and discussed in detail below.

For the specification shown in Table 12.1, the parameter of the spatially lagged *TFR* is greater than the time-lagged variable (0.032 and 0.430, respectively). This

Table 12.1 Estimates of time-space dynamics in the model describing TFR as a SAR (2,1) process

Variables			The average short-run effect			The average long -run effect		
	Coeff.	St. dev.	Direct	Indirect	Total	Direct	Indirect	Total
$TFR_{t-}1$	0.032*	0.015	0.032	0.014	0.046	0	0	0
Weighted$TFR_{t-}1$	0.430***	0.032						
$TFR_{t-}2$	0.086***	0.014	0.086	–				
$\ln(I_{t-}1)$	−0.319*	0.154	−0.319	0	−0.319	−0.382	−0.323	−0.706
Weighted $\ln(I_{t-}1)$	0.328	0.272						
$R_{t-}1$	−0.042	0.065	–	–	–	–	–	–
Weighted $R_{t-}1$	−0.708	0.610						
(The relative total flow of out-/in-migrated women aged 16–49)$_{t-1}$	1.328**	0.526	1.328	–	–	1.594	1.343	2.937
(The proportion of women aged 16–49 years with more than 3 years post-secondary)$_{t-}1$	0.978***	0.281	0.978	–	–	1.174	0.989	2.163
(The proportion of women aged 16–49 years with less than 9 years education)$_{t-}1$	1.067***	0.274	1.067	–	–	1.281	1.079	2.360
Intercept	1.798***	0.541	1.798	–	–	–	–	–
Number of observations	–	6322						–
Wald χ^2	–	9615						–
Stationarity Accepted								

*$p<0.05$; **$p<0.01$; ***$p<0.0001$

result may be wrongly interpreted as showing a larger role of the indirect effect in fertility dynamics than the direct effect. However, the average short-run effect of interactions between municipalities, calculated according to the LeSage and Pace approach (2010), is 0.014, which is less than the time-lagged parameter or the direct effect. Thus, the indirect effect and the direct effect in the short run explain 0.014 and 0.032% of relative changes in total fertility rates, respectively. This means that both reduction and growth of fertility occur in related municipalities on average because of demographic, economic, or other reasons. In this case, the long-run effect is absent as the process is considered to be stationary.

Overall, the results weakly support a direct effect according to the inverted Easterlin hypothesis for the analyzed period (1981–2008) because the estimate of the cohort ratio parameter is significant for all the specifications that did not include other labor market characteristics (labor force skills and mobility). However, for the specification considered in Table 12.1, the parameter for the cohort ratio is not significant. For example, for specification 5 (Table 12.4), the estimated parameter of the cohort ratio is equal to −0.198, which explains a 0.16 % reduction in *TFR* when *R* increases by 1 %. The spatially lagged term is not significant in all specifications. However, taking into account the equilibrium condition in the long run, the direct effect explained 0.19 %, indirect effect 0.16 %, and total effect 0.35 % of the relative change in fertility.

The income parameter is negative in each of the specifications, but the spatially lagged income is found to be insignificant. For the considered specification in Table 12.1, the direct effect of incomes in the short run is equal to −0.319, whereas it is −0.382 for the long run. Thus, there appears to be a negative direct effect of earnings on total fertility rates, or equivalently, a dominant substitution effect between wages (labor market) and childbearing (viewed as household production), despite the strong Swedish family policy supporting fertility. This effect manifests as a postponement or acceleration of childbearing in the short run. The direct short-run effect can be attributed to 0.67 % of the variation in fertility. However, consideration of the total long-run effect increased total fertility rates by up to 1.49 % (the long-run direct and indirect effects are 0.81 and 0.68 %, respectively).

Among the control variables tested, the most important is the sum of in- and out-migrated people in the population, i.e., the relative total flow. A high degree of labor mobility in both directions may reflect several processes, such as changes in age-gender structure, levels of education in a municipality, the number of matches resulting in cohabitation and marriage, and increasing demand and supply values in the labor market over time. The main factor cannot be extracted, but evidently, internal migration is positively related to childbearing, giving significant direct, indirect, and total effects in the long run of 1.594, 1.343, and 2.937, respectively. Since the numbers of in- and out-migrated people compared to the size of the population is rather low, the total long-run effect only captured 0.001 % of the relative changes in fertility.

Municipalities with a large proportion of women with educational levels higher or lower than the mean level exhibited the highest total fertility rates. This result agrees with previous papers (Andersson et al. 2003; Berinde 1999) and probably reflects the low opportunity cost of childbearing that women with low educational levels experience. The positive estimate for the contribution of highly educated women can be attributed to the higher benefits they receive during maternity leave and greater opportunities for flexibility in distributing their time between employment and taking care of a child. In comparison, the long-run effects of the proportions of high and low educated women on total fertility rates are higher by almost two fold and totally explained 0.105 % and 0.054 % of the long-run variation in fertility, respectively.

Substituting estimates of the autoregressive parameters and boundary eigenvalues for **W** in Eq. 12.8 proves that the process, described in the model, is stationary.

In contrast to a previous study for Italy (Waldorf and Franklin 2002), where total fertility rates are linked to changes in the average age of first births, no such relationship is found for Sweden.

Conclusions

There is no doubt that changes in fertility can be explained by economic factors. A large number of papers have provided theoretical and empirical explanations of reproductive behavior, considering female employment and alternative investment choices, such as gaining an education.

The present paper makes an important contribution by reporting an analysis of the relationship between changes in childbearing and several factors that are important for settlements located near to each other. The space autoregressive component was found to be positively significant in all of the specifications employed. This suggests that, for a given municipality, the whole set of factors that can affect total fertility rates cause it to change in the same direction as in surrounding municipalities.

The main aim of this paper was to empirically test the relationship between fertility and earnings in time and space dimensions. The findings support the inverted Easterlin hypothesis. The results revealed a short-run direct effect and long-run direct and indirect effects. In the short run, earnings negatively affect fertility within municipalities, but an indirect effect across space was not found. The specification of the model allows the long-run spatial effect to be evaluated in addition to the direct effect. The results indicated that the long-run spatial effect was negative, which can be explained by a dominant substitution effect governing the choice between female labor supply and childbearing as a household's production, despite the fact that family policy in Sweden provides good opportunities to combine them both.

A stationarity condition was adopted in the present study in the form of an inequality, which defined bounds for the autoregressive parameters by considering the unit root of the weight matrix for the spatially autoregressive parameter. Using these conditions, the stationarity of fertility in time and space dynamics, measured by total fertility rates, was empirically proved.

The observed long-run effects of the explanatory variables in the SAR (2,1) model derived in this paper imply that direct, indirect, and total effects should be considered. It was empirically shown that the spatial effect in the long run almost doubles the influences of the log-income and cohort ratio on fertility compared to the short run. Thus, the results clearly show that spatial disturbances are important in modeling fertility processes.

Appendix 1

Table 12.2 List of variables

Total fertility rate (TFR)	Total fertility rate by region, gender and period: The data are based on the Historical Population and Multi-Generation registers. The Multi-Generation Register is updated continuously with links between mother/child and father/child. The statistics could differ slightly from official statistics depending on yearly corrections to the registers. Thus, the whole series is updated each year for the entire period.
Relative cohort size (*R*)	The number of men aged 35–64 years divided by the number of men of aged 15–34 years smoothed over 3 years.
The proportion of women aged 16–49 years with a given level of education 9 years (ISCED97 1) of education post-graduate education (ISCED97 6) post-secondary education of more than 3 years (ISCED97 5A)	Women aged 16–49 years with a given level of education/total number of women aged 16–49 Level of educational attainment by region, gender, age, income class and time: The classification by level of educational attainment follows the Swedish National Educational classification (SUN)
Income	Total and average income for residents in Sweden on 31/12 in thousands
Income_CPI	Income adjusted by CPI to the basic level in 1981
Numbers of in- and out-migrated women	Numbers of in- and out-migrated women by region, age and time. When calculating age-specific rates per 1,000 of the mean population, the mean population for the year of birth should be used. Age refers to the age attained by the end of the year, i.e., in principle, the number of years since birth
The relative balance of in-/out-migrated women aged 16–49 years	(In-migrated women aged 16–49 years—out-migrated women aged 16–49 years)/Total number of women aged 16–49 years
The relative flow of in-/out-migrated women aged 16–49 years	(In-migrated women in aged 16–49 years + out-migrated women aged 16–49 years)/Total number of women aged 16–49 years
Mean age of woman at birth of the first child (AAFB)	Mean age at birth of the first child by region and time: The data were based on the Historical population register and the Multi-Generation Register.
Population size (100 thousand)	Mean population (by year of birth)
Gross domestic product (GDP) in constant prices	Annual percentages of constant price GDP are year-on-year changes; the base year is 1990

Appendix 2

Table 12.3 Descriptive statistics for 276 municipalities during 1970–2008

Variable	Obs	Mean	Std. Dev.	Min	Max
Total fertility rate (TFR)	7452	1.929	0.301	0.91	3.31
Mean age at birth of the first child, female parents (AAFB)	7452	26.596	1.525	22.33	33.07
Mean age at birth of the first child, male parents (AAFB)	40	29.113	1.566	26.66	31.46
Income to CPI, 1981 = 100 %	4968	58.189	9.427	39.770	180.705
The relative net migration of in-/out-migrated women aged 16–49 years	7422	−0.001	0.006	−0.022	0.042
The relative total flow of in-/out-migrated women aged 16–49 years	7422	0.061	0.019	0.023	0.205
Relative cohort (*R*)	7452	1.572	0.249	0.952	2.369
The proportion of women aged 16–49 years with less than 9 years education	7452	0.044	0.046	0.101	0.231
The proportion of women with post-graduate education	7452	0.002	0.003	0.004	0.047
The proportion of women aged 16–49 years with more than 3 years post-secondary education	7452	0.094	0.064	0.030	0.456
Population size (100 thousands)	7452	0.312	0.566	0.028	8.026
GDP in constant prices[a]	28	2.375	1.825	−2.058	4.66

[a] data for the period 1981–2008

Appendix 3 The municipality restructuring in 1992

In 1992, municipality reform was performed in Sweden, which resulted in the number and boundaries of municipalities being changed. The municipalities that were established or annulled as a consequence of this reform were excluded from the present analysis. Thus, the total number of municipalities included was 276. Weight matrices based on spherical distances were unchanged by the reform because the municipal center had the same geographical coordinates. Weight matrices based on contiguity were changed, but the change in boundaries was not so large as to give misleading results. After the reform, the individual municipal populations changed by more than 2 % in only 9 municipalities (only in Vaxholm and Värmdö did the population change by more than 3 %), but the total change in population was not more than 5 %. The variables used were merged by Statistics Sweden (SCB).

Appendix 4

Table 12.4 GMM estimates for *TFR*. The model with time-specific fixed effects for the period 1981-2008.

Variables	No spatial effects				SAR				SAR with exogenous spatial interaction effect							
	1		2		3		4		5		6		7		8	
	Coeff.	St. dev.	Coeff.	St. dev.	Coeff.	St. dev.	Coeff.	St. dev.	Coeff.	St. dev.	Coeff.	St. dev.	Coeff.	St. dev.	Coeff.	St. dev.
$TFR_{t-}1$	0.095***	0.015	0.044**	0.016	0.033*	0.015	0.033*	0.015	0.033*	0.015	0.037*	0.015	0.044**	0.016	0.032*	0.015
$TFR_{t-}2$	0.148***	0.014	0.100***	0.015	0.084***	0.014	0.086***	0.014	0.084***	0.014	0.092***	0.015	0.100***	0.015	0.086***	0.014
Weighted $TFR_{t-}1$	–	–	–	–	0.422***	0.032	0.431***	0.032	0.423***	0.032	–	–	–	–	0.430***	0.032
$\ln(I_{t-}1)$	0.961***	0.100	0.120	0.130	−0.708	0.194	−0.220*	0.130	−0.759***	0.200	−0.848***	0.203	−0.017	0.156	−0.319*	0.154
Weighted $\ln(I_{t-}1)$	–	–	–	–	–	–	–	–	0.306	0.269	0.247	0.274	0.398	0.279	0.328	0.272
$R_{t-}1$	−0.225***	0.063	−0.014	0.066	−0.215*	0.059	−0.050	0.065	−0.198***	0.061	−0.251***	0.062	−0.011	0.067	−0.042	0.065
Weighted $R_{t-}1$	–	–	–	–	–	–	–	–	−0.660	0.597	−0.458	0.608	−0.639	0.625	−0.708	0.610
(The relative flow of in/out-migrated women aged 16-49 $\text{years})_{t-}1$	2.398***	0.550	1.889***	0.537	1.435**	0.518	1.320**	0.526	1.444**	0.518	1.902***	0.528	1.893***	0.537	1.328**	0.526
(The proportion of women aged 16-49 years with more than 3 years of post-secondary $\text{education})_{t-}1$	–	–	1.677***	0.265	–	–	1.078***	0.263	–	–	–	–	1.500***	0.284	0.978***	0.281

Table 12.4 (continued)

Variables	No spatial effects				SAR				SAR with exogenous spatial interaction effect							
	1		2		3		4		5		6		7		8	
	Coeff.	St. dev.	Coeff.	St. dev.	Coeff.	St. dev.	Coeff.	St. dev.	Coeff.	St. dev.	Coeff.	St. dev.	Coeff.	St. dev.	Coeff.	St. dev.
(The proportion of women aged 16-49 years with less than 9 years of education)$_{t-1}$	–	–	1.498***	0.272	–	–	1.095***	0.268	–	–	–	–	1.428***	0.279	1.067***	0.274
Intercept	−2.076***	0.349	1.105*	0.472	4.126***	0.828	1.740***	0.463	4.185***	0.991	5.299***	1.005	0.946*	0.551	1.798***	0.541
Number of observations	6596		6322		6596		6322		6596		6596		6322		6322	
Wald χ^2	8406		9007		9963		9612		9936		9388		9007		9615	

*$p<0.05$; **$p<0.01$; ***$p<0.0001$

Appendix 5 The Long-Run Effect of an Explanatory Variable in the SAR (2,1) Model

Consider the model SAR (2,1) with a second-order autoregressive disturbance, a first-order spatial disturbance weighted by a spatial weights matrix **W** of size $N \times N$, and a first-order lagged common factor weighted by some spatial matrix **V** of size $N \times N$.

$$\mathbf{y}_t = \varphi_1 \mathbf{y}_{t-1} + \varphi_2 \mathbf{y}_{t-2} + \gamma \mathbf{W} \mathbf{y}_{t-1} + \eta \mathbf{x}_{t-1} + \delta \mathbf{V} \mathbf{x}_{t-1} + \boldsymbol{\varepsilon}_t, \tag{12.9}$$

where ε_t is a "white noise" vector of size $N \times 1$, y_t is a vector of size $N \times 1$ of observations of an endogenous variable for every spatial unit at time t, x_t is a vector of explanatory variables at time t, and φ, γ, δ and η are parameters. If $\mathbf{y}_t$ converges to equilibrium, the equilibrium condition is given by the following equation:

$$\left((1-\varphi_1-\varphi_2)\mathbf{I} - \gamma \mathbf{W}\right)\mathbf{y} = (\eta \mathbf{I} + \delta \mathbf{V})\mathbf{x} \tag{12.10}$$

where I is the identity matrix of size $N \times N$.

Thus, the long-run impact of x on y yields"

$$\frac{\partial \mathbf{y}}{\partial \mathbf{x}} = \left[\left((1-\varphi_1-\varphi_2)\mathbf{I} - \gamma \mathbf{W}\right)^{-1}(\eta \mathbf{I} + \delta \mathbf{V})\right]' \mathbf{y} \tag{12.11}$$

Appendix 6 Stationarity Condition in the SAR(2,1) Model

Consider the following stationarity condition in the SAR(2,1) model described in Appendix 5:

$$\mathbf{y}_t = \varphi_1 \mathbf{y}_{t-1} + \varphi_2 \mathbf{y}_{t-2} + \gamma \mathbf{W} \mathbf{y}_{t-1} + \eta \mathbf{x}_{t-1} + \delta \mathbf{V} \mathbf{x}_{t-1} + \boldsymbol{\varepsilon}_t \tag{12.12}$$

The vector auto-regression form (VAR) for this model yields:

$$\begin{pmatrix} \mathbf{y}_t \\ \mathbf{y}_{t-1} \end{pmatrix} = \begin{pmatrix} \varphi_1 \mathbf{I} + \gamma \mathbf{W} & \varphi_2 \mathbf{I} \\ \mathbf{I} & 0 \end{pmatrix} \begin{pmatrix} \mathbf{y}_{t-1} \\ \mathbf{y}_{t-2} \end{pmatrix} + \begin{pmatrix} (\eta \mathbf{i} + \delta \mathbf{V})\mathbf{x}_{t-1} \\ \mathbf{0} \end{pmatrix} + \begin{pmatrix} \boldsymbol{\varepsilon}_t \\ \mathbf{0} \end{pmatrix} \tag{12.13}$$

where **i** is a vector of units. Let matrix **A** be defined as

$$\mathbf{A} = \begin{pmatrix} \varphi_1 \mathbf{I} + \gamma \mathbf{W} & \varphi_2 \mathbf{I} \\ \mathbf{I} & \mathbf{0} \end{pmatrix} \tag{12.14}$$

The stationarity condition implies $|\lambda_i| < 1$ when λ_i $(i = 1,...,2n)$ is a characteristic root of the matrix **A**, or a root of the characteristic equation $|\mathbf{A} - \lambda \mathbf{I}| = 0$, which is a polynomial in λ.

The matrix $\mathbf{A} - \lambda \mathbf{I} = \begin{pmatrix} \varphi_1 \mathbf{I} + \gamma \mathbf{W} - \lambda \mathbf{I} & \varphi_2 \mathbf{I} \\ \mathbf{I} & -\lambda \mathbf{I} \end{pmatrix}$ has a property of block matrix, described by Silvester (2000, p. 463). Accordingly,

$$|\mathbf{A}-\lambda\mathbf{I}| = \begin{vmatrix} \varphi_1\mathbf{I}+\gamma\mathbf{W}-\lambda\mathbf{I} & \varphi_2\mathbf{I} \\ \mathbf{I} & -\lambda\mathbf{I} \end{vmatrix} = |(\varphi_1\mathbf{I}+\gamma\mathbf{W}-\lambda\mathbf{I})(-\lambda\mathbf{I})-\varphi_2\mathbf{I}| \quad (12.15)$$

$$= |\lambda^2\mathbf{I}-(\varphi_1\mathbf{I}+\gamma\mathbf{W})\lambda-\varphi_2\mathbf{I}|$$

Let **M** be a matrix containing the characteristic roots $\{\mu_i\}$ $(i=1,..., N)$ of the weight matrix **W** of size $N \times N$. According to the basic properties of a block matrix, $|\mathbf{M}|=|\mathbf{W}|$, and there exists a nonsingular matrix **R** of characteristic vectors of size $n \times n$ such that $\mathbf{RMR}'=\mathbf{W}$, $\mathbf{RR}'=\mathbf{I}$. Using this decomposition and the given properties, the characteristic equation for **A** can be transformed as follows:

$$|\lambda^2\mathbf{I}-(\varphi_1\mathbf{I}+\gamma\mathbf{W})\lambda-\varphi_2\mathbf{I}| = |\lambda^2\mathbf{RIR}^{-1}-(\varphi_1\mathbf{RIR}^{-1}+\gamma\mathbf{RMR}^{-1})\lambda-\varphi_2\mathbf{RIR}^{-1}|$$

$$= |\mathbf{R}[\lambda^2\mathbf{I}-(\varphi_1\mathbf{I}+\gamma\mathbf{M})\lambda-\varphi_2\mathbf{I}]\mathbf{R}^{-1}| = 0 \quad (12.16)$$

Since **R** is a nonsingular matrix and $\lambda^2\mathbf{I}-(\varphi_1\mathbf{I}+\gamma\mathbf{M})\lambda-\varphi_2\mathbf{I}$ is a diagonal matrix, the determinant is equal to zero and λ is a root of the polynomial $\lambda^2-(\varphi_1+\gamma\mu_i)\lambda-\varphi_2$.

Thus,

$$\lambda_j = \frac{\varphi_1+\gamma\mu_i \pm \sqrt{(\varphi_1+\gamma\mu_i)^2+4\varphi_2}}{2}, j=1,...,2n \quad (12.17)$$

Finally, the stationarity condition can be written as Eq. 12.8.

Acknowledgments I would like to thank my supervisor and co-supervisor, Magnus Wikström and Niklas Hanes, who directed me in this research. My sincere gratitude is also extended to Kurt Brännäs, who helped me with application of spatial econometrics. I appreciate Kirk Scott and other senior researchers and participants of the conference for Ph.D. students in economic demography in Mölle, Sweden, 2010, for valuable comments on an earlier version of the paper. I also want to thank participants of the 1st Nordic Winter Conference in Hemavan, Sweden, 2011, 6th International Conference on Population Geographies in Umeå, Sweden, 2011, and participants of the Applied Demography Conference in San Antonio, Texas, USA, 2012, for comments on my presentations of the research. Acknowledged with gratitude for its financial support is the Graduate School in Population Dynamics and Public Policy at Umeå University.

References

Andersson, G. (1999). Childbearing trends in Sweden 1961–1997. *European Journal of Population, 15,* 1–24.

Andersson, G., Duvander, A., & Hank, K. (2003). *Do child care characteristics influence continued childbearing in Sweden? An investigation of the quantity, quality, and price dimension.* MPIDR Working Paper WP 2003–013 May 2003.

Anselin, L. (2002). Under the hood. Issues in the specification and interpretation of spatial regression models. *Agricultural Economics, 27,* 247–267.

Artzrouni, M. A., & Easterlin, R. A. (1982). Birth history, age structure, and post World War II fertility in ten developed countries: An exploratory empirical analysis. *Genus, 38*(3–4), 81–99.

Baird, A. J. (1987). A note on the Easterlin model of fertility in northwestern Europe and the United States: 1950–1981. *International Journal of Comparative Sociology, 23*(1–2), 57–68.

Becker, G. S. (1960). An economic analysis of fertility. In Universities-National Bureau (Ed.), *Demographic and economic change in developed countries* (pp. 209–240). New York: Columbia University Press.

Becker, G. S., & Barro, R. J. (1988). A reformulation of the economic theory of fertility. *The Quarterly Journal of Economics, 103*(1), 1–25.

Berinde, D. (1999). Pathways to a third child in Sweden. *European Journal of Population, 15,* 349–378.

Bongaarts, J., & Watkins, C. S. (1996). Social interactions and contemporary fertility transitions. *Population and Development Review, 22*(4), 639–682.

Brueckner, J. K. (2003). Strategic interaction among governments: An overview of empirical studies. *International Regional Science Review, 26*(2), 175–188.

de Castro, M. C. (2007). Spatial demography: An opportunity to improve policy making at diverse decision levels. *Population Resource Policy Review, 26,* 477–509.

Easterlin, R. A. (1966). On the relation of economic factors to recent and projected fertility changes. *Demography, 3,* 135–153.

Elhorst, J. P. (2001). Dynamic models in space and time. *Geographical Analysis, 33*(2), 119–140.

Eliasson, K., Westerlund, O., Åström, J. (2007). Flyttning och pendling i Sverige. Fritzes, Stockholm. 219 p.

Hoem, B. (2000). Entry into motherhood in Sweden: The influence of economic factors on the rise and fall in fertility, 1986–1997. *Demographic Research, 2*(4). http: //www.demographic-research.org/Volumes/Vol2/4. Accessed 18 Nov 2009.

Hoem, J. M., Neyer, G., Andersson, G. (2006). *Educational attainment and ultimate fertility among Swedish women born in 1955–59.* MPIDR Working Paper WP 2006–004. March 2006.

LeSage, J. P., & Pace, R. K. (2010). Spatial econometric models. In M. M. Fisher & A. Getis (Eds.), *Handbook of applied spatial analysis: Software, tools, methods and applications* (pp. 355–376). Heidelberg: Springer.

Macunovich, D. J. (1998). Fertility and the Easterlin hypothesis: An assessment of the literature. *Population Economy, 11,* 53–111.

McNicoll, G. (1980). Institutional determinants of fertility change. *Population and Development Review, 6*(3), 441–462.

Pampel, F. C. (1993). Relative cohort size and fertility: The socio-political context of the Easterlin effect. *American Sociological Review, 58,* 496–514.

Sevilla, J. P. (2007). *Fertility and relative cohort size.* Arbetsrapport. Institutet för Framtidsstudier, 2007:11.

Silvester, J. R. (2000). Determinants of block matrices. *The Mathematical Gazette, 84*(501), 460–467.

Waldorf, B., & Byun, P. (2005). Meta-analysis of the impact of age structure on fertility. *Journal of Population Economy, 18,* 15–40.

Waldorf, B., & Franklin, R. (2002). Spatial dimension of the Easterlin hypothesis: Fertility variations in Italy. *Journal of Regional Science, 42*(3), 549–578.

Weeks, J. R., Getis, A., Hill, A. G., Gadalla, M. S., & Rashed, T. (2004). The fertility transition in Egypt: Intraurban patterns in Cairo. *Annals of the Association of American Geographers, 94*(1), 74–93.

Westerberg, T. (2006). *More work, less kids—he relationship between market experience and number of children.* Umeå Economic Studies. No. 683.

Woods, R. (1984). Social class variations in the decline of marital fertility in late nineteenth-century London. *Geografiska Annaler: Series B, Human Geography, 66*(1), 29–38.

Wright, R. E. (1989). The Easterlin hypothesis and European fertility rates. *Population and Development Review, 15*(1), 107–122.

Yua, J., de Jong, R., & Lee, L. (2008). Quasi-maximum likelihood estimators for spatial dynamic panel data with fixed effects when both n and T are large. *Journal of Econometrics, 146,* 118–134.

Chapter 13
Household Expenditure on Medical Care and Health in Australia

Farhat Yusuf and Stephen R. Leeder

Introduction

Financial barriers to healthcare are of fundamental concern to health policy makers who seek to develop systems that manifest equity of access to essential care. Most universally accessible systems, supported by public finance, aim to overcome these barriers. But many economically advanced countries have found that the financial demands of such systems exceed the political, and to some extent economic, will to pay.

According to the estimates prepared by the Australian Institute of Health and Welfare (AIHW), the total expenditure on health in Australia was $ 121.4 billion in 2009–2010 (throughout this study $ refers to the Australian dollar). Just less than 44 % of this cost was contributed by the federal government, 26 % by the state and the local governments, and the remaining 30 % by other sources (AIHW 2011). Among the other sources, the major contributors were the co-payments and other out-of-pocket charges paid for by the individual patients.

While there have been many studies on health expenditure in Australia at an aggregate level (see for example: AIHW 2011; Ang 2010; Butler and Smith 1992; Polder et al. 2005; Schofield 2000; Sharma and Srivastava 2011; Smith 2001), few studies have been conducted about the distribution of health expenditure at micro levels such as the individual patients or their households (see for example: Barrett and Conlon 2003; Jones et al. 2008; Yusuf and Leeder 2013).

In this paper we have sought to establish the pattern of total household expenditure on medical care and health, as well as the expenditure on certain relevant goods and services purchased by households. Expenditure patterns have also been analysed in relation to important demographic and socio-economic characteristics

F. Yusuf (✉) · S. R. Leeder
Menzies Centre for Health Policy, Sydney School of Public Health,
The University of Sydney, Sydney, Australia
e-mail: farhat.yusuf@sydney.edu.au

F. Yusuf
Department of Marketing and Management, Macquarie University, Sydney, Australia

M. N. Hoque, L. B. Potter (eds.), *Emerging Techniques in Applied Demography,*
Applied Demography Series 4, DOI 10.1007/978-94-017-8990-5_13,

of households, which may have an influence on the expenditure levels. In the context of this study, household expenditure on medical care and health refers only to the out-of-pocket expenditure, unless stated otherwise.

The study is primarily based on the analysis of the most recent Household Expenditure Survey (HES) conducted by the Australian Bureau of Statistics (ABS).

After a brief review of the system of medical care and health in Australia, the methodology of HES is described, followed by the presentation of findings and a brief discussion on our results and their implications for future policy.

The System of Medical Care and Health in Australia

In Australia, public hospitals are supported through taxation, collected federally and distributed to the six states and two territories that manage them. Private hospital care is mainly funded through private health insurance, which is available to those able and willing to pay. Both the private health insurance premiums and stays in private hospitals receive subsidies from the federal government in recognition that patients treated in the private system do not call upon the public system for care. Private hospitals provide much elective surgery while care of patients with chronic or serious medical problems predominate in the public hospitals. For those conditions that might be managed in both sectors, there are very few comparative data and no compelling evidence of differences in health outcomes.

Most doctors and allied health professionals are private practitioners, charging fees for service to the patients who consult them, whether in the community or in hospital. An increasing cadre of salaried medical staff, however, is found in the public hospitals. Patients recoup the fees they pay for care outside hospital through the Medical Benefits Scheme (MBS), one of the important elements of Medicare—the publicly funded payment system for healthcare in Australia. Medicare is supported principally from general tax revenue and in part through an additional income-based levy of 1.5 % of taxable income. Unless the medical practitioner chooses to bill Medicare directly, each patient is asked to contribute to the cost of care by private practitioners. This may be small, as when consulting a general practitioner, or can be thousands of dollars when consulting, and being treated by, an eminent specialist.

Beside the MBS, Medicare includes subsidies for pharmaceuticals that have passed rigorous cost-effectiveness assessment. The Pharmaceutical Benefits Scheme (PBS), which lists the drugs available for subsidised prescription, allows each patient to obtain whatever is prescribed for them at a modest cost—around $ 35.40 per item prescribed for 1 month. A safety net operates so that if annual expenditure on prescription drugs exceeds a certain amount (around $ 1,400 in 2009–2010) the co-payment per prescription falls to $ 5.80.

Pharmaceuticals not included on the PBS fall entirely to the patient to pay for, as do dental expenses that are only partially publicly funded for those who are not privately insured. Limited claims can be made on private health insurance for dental care and allied health services, such as physiotherapy, but those without private insurance must meet the full cost.

Australia also has a system of healthcare cards that are available on a needs basis and are means-tested (i.e., available only to those individuals/families that qualify under criteria of income and assets). More details are provided by Jones et al. (2008) or the website of the Australian Department of Human Services (Centrelink):

http://www.centrelink.gov.au/internet/internet.nsf/payments/conc_cards_hcc.htm.

In summary, the Australian healthcare system is a blend of private and public services, funded from taxation and through private contributions with hospital care available to all freely at the point of care. Essential medicines are subsidised from tax revenues. Out-of-pocket payments are a significant component in financing healthcare in Australia.

For a more comprehensive description of the healthcare system and policies see: ABS (2010), AIHW (2011) or the website of the Australian Department of Health and Ageing:

http://www.health.gov.au/internet/main/publishing.nsf/Content/health-historic-pubs-hfsocc-occpahsfv1.htm.

Methodology of HES

The period of HES data collection spanned 1 year starting from July 2009. The survey involved interviewing the usual residents of a sample of private dwellings in both urban and rural areas of Australia. Private dwellings included houses, flats, home units, etc., as well as long-stay caravan parks, but excluded non-private dwellings such as hotels, boarding houses, and other institutions. The survey also excluded people living in very remote areas, which accounted for about 3 % of the population, as well as foreign diplomatic or defense force staff (ABS 2011).

Household was defined as a person or group of persons living together and having common provision for food and other essentials of living. Usual residents were those who regarded the dwelling as their own or main home, and therefore others present in the dwelling were considered to be visitors and excluded from the survey.

The sample was selected using a multistage, stratified probability sampling design. Within each household a person aged 15 or over was selected as the "reference person," if he or she was the first sole person in the household to fulfill one of the following criteria:

- was a partner in a registered or *de facto* marriage, or
- a lone-parent with dependent child (ren), or
- the person with the highest income, or
- the eldest person

Personal interviews were conducted in the selected households to obtain data on characteristics of households and their members and various items of income and expenditure.

In addition to the reference person, identified spenders in the households were each issued with a diary to record expenditure on every good and service purchased during a specified week. Subsequent to completing these diaries, spenders were issued another diary to do the same for a second week. The diaries were intended to be kept up-to-date on a daily basis to reduce errors due to recall.

Apart from the expense diaries, information was collected for the purchase of large ticket items (such as white goods, motor vehicles, and insurance) that otherwise may be missed because of the 2 reference periods of 1-week each.

Detailed information was collected on more than 400 expenditure items classified under 17 major groups. One of these groups was the expenditure on medical care and health. Under this group, information was collated for out-of-pocket expenditure on each of the following 22 categories related to medical care and health:

1	=Hospital, medical, and dental insurance
2	=Ambulance insurance
3	=Sickness and personal accident insurance
4	=GP (general practitioner) doctors' fees
5	=Specialist doctors' fees
6	=Dentists' fees
7	=Opticians' fees (including spectacles)
8	=Physiotherapists' and chiropractors' fees
9	=Other health practitioners' fees
10	=Medicines, pharmaceutical products, and therapeutic appliances not fully defined
11	=Medicines and pharmaceutical products
12	=Prescription medicines
13	=Non-prescribed pain relievers
14	=Sunscreens
15	=Non-prescribed ointments and lotions, not elsewhere classified (NEC)
16	=Medicines and pharmaceutical products NEC
17	=Surgical dressings
18	=Therapeutic appliances and equipment (excluding hire)
19	=First aid supplies, therapeutic appliances, and equipment NEC
20	=Hospital/nursing home fees
21	=Hire of therapeutic appliances
22	=Other medical care and health expenses NEC

Considering the size of estimates for each expenditure category and their relative standard errors, a smaller set of 13 categories was created for detailed analysis as follows:

Private health insurance	
1	=Hospital, medical, and dental
2–3	=Ambulance/sickness/personal
Health practitioners' fees	
4	=GP doctors' fees
5	=Specialist doctors' fees
6	=Dentists' fees
7	=Opticians' fees
8	=Physio/chiropractors' fees
9	=Other health practitioners' fees
Medicine, pharmaceutical and therapeutic products	
12	=Prescription medicines
10–11, 13–16	=Other pharmaceuticals
17–19	=First aid/therapeutic products
Other medical care and health expenses	
20	=Hospital/nursing home fees
21–22	=Other health-related expenses

Confidentialised unit records of the 9,774 individual households were available to the authors through an arrangement between the ABS and the University of Sydney. These records included the characteristics of households and the average weekly expenditure on various goods and services purchased by the household members. These estimates of weekly household expenditure did not refer to any particular week. They were derived by ABS for each expenditure item by dividing the reported expenditure for all members of the household on that item by the number of weeks in the relevant recall/reference period[1]. In the context of healthcare expenditure, the recall periods were 12 months for expenditure categories 1–3, 3 and 20 months for expenditure categories 4–9, and 2 periods of 1-week each for expenditure categories 10–19, 21 and 22.

For each record a weighting factor was available to enable the compilation of national estimates from the sample data. Since these estimates were subject to sampling errors, 60 replicate weights were also made available for each household to facilitate the estimation of standard errors (*SE*) (see Appendix). These are shown preceded by ± for estimates presented in various tables. The *SEs* are also indicated in Figs. 13.1, 13.2, 13.3, 13.4. The relative standard error (*RSE*) of an estimate ($\hat{Y}$) was defined as:

$$RSE(\hat{Y}) = \frac{SE(\hat{Y}) * 100}{\hat{Y}}$$

Estimates with an *RSE* between 25 and < 50 % have been marked with a single asterisk (*), and those with $RSE \geq 50\,\%$ with a double asterisk (**). The former estimates should be treated with caution while the latter estimates are too unreliable.

[1] The file provided by the ABS had the average weekly expenditure reported on various items. These were converted into annual estimates by multiplying them by 52.17857.

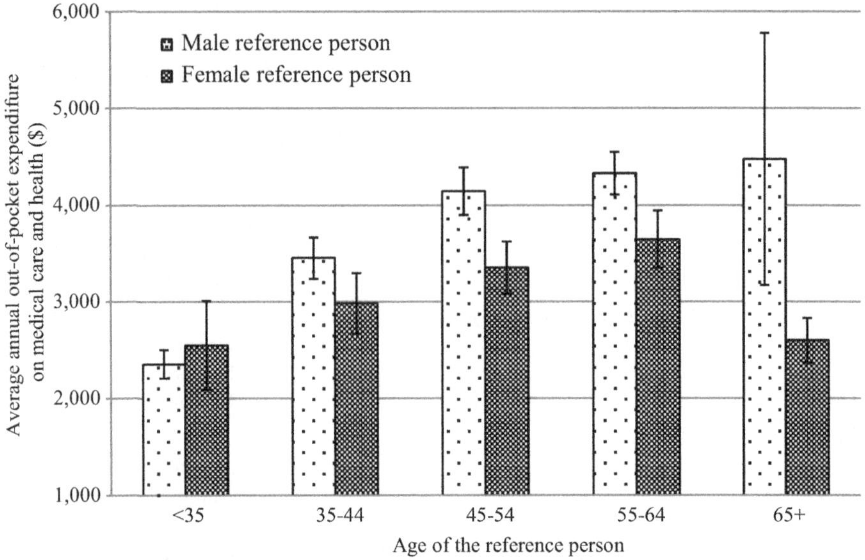

Fig. 13.1 Average annual out-of-pocket household expenditure on medical care and health by age and sex of the reference person. (The *RSE* for males 65+ was 29 % and therefore the estimate should be treated with caution)

ABS with its long experience of conducting sample surveys made every effort to minimise non-sampling errors. However, some may still have occurred.

It was noted that just over 10 % of the households reported no expenditure on medical care and health during the various reference periods. These households were not much different in terms of their social, economic and demographic characteristics compared to those who reported expenditure.

Findings

Profile of Households

According to the HES, the estimated number of households in Australia was nearly 8.4 million in 2009–2010 (Table 13.1). About one-third of the households consisted of couple-with-children[2]. The next largest group was that of couple-only, followed

[2] Among couples living with children, 71 % had only their dependent children living with them, 19 % had only their non-dependent children living with them, while the remaining 10 % had both dependent and non-dependent children living with them.

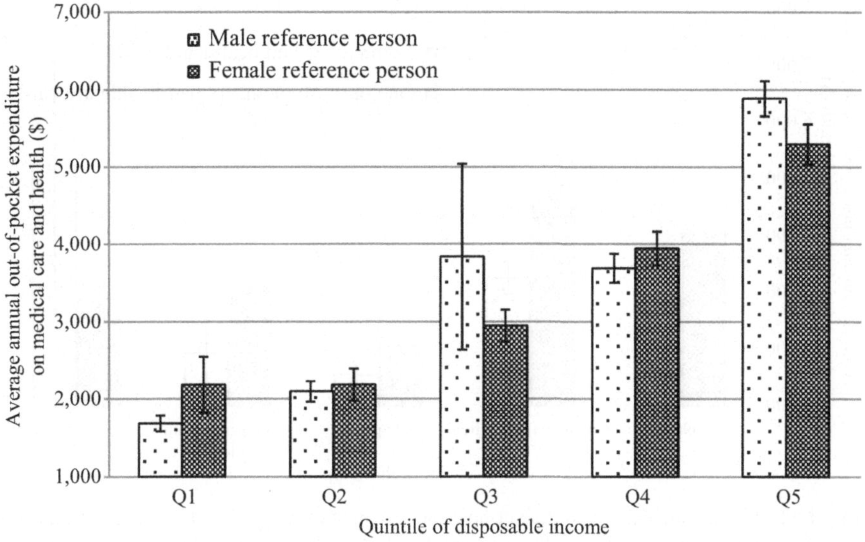

Fig. 13.2 Average annual out-of-pocket household expenditure on medical care and health by quintile of the household disposable income. (The *RSE* for males for Q3 was 31 % and therefore the estimate should be treated with caution)

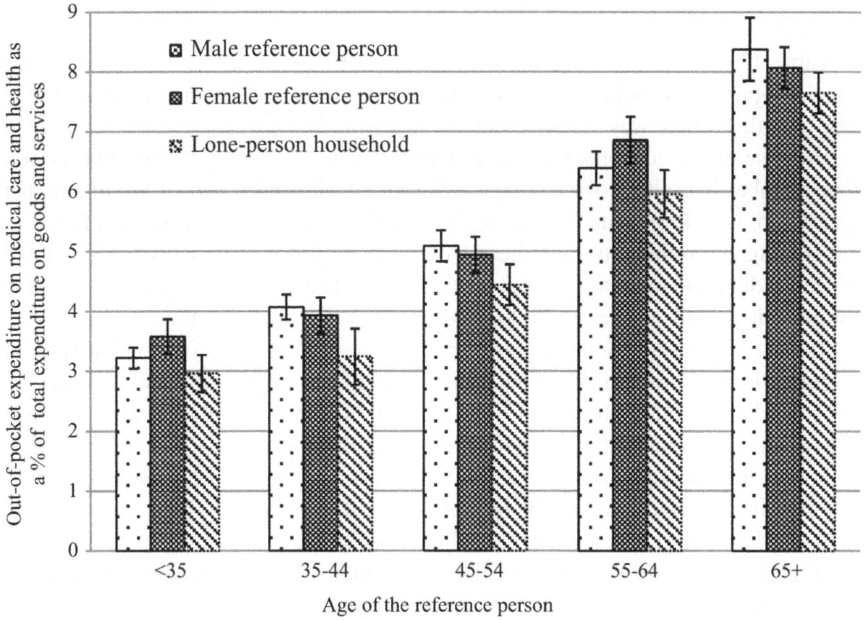

Fig. 13.3 Out-of-pocket expenditure on medical care and health as a % of the total expenditure on goods and services by age and sex of the household reference person

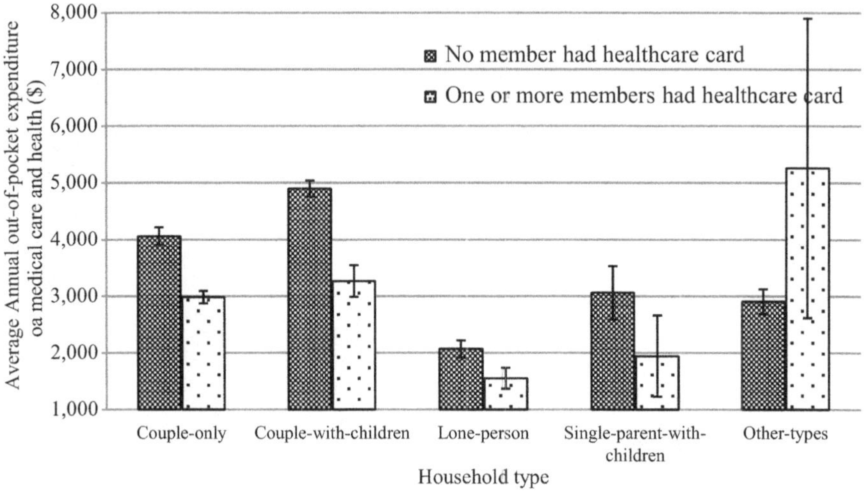

Fig. 13.4 Average annual out-of-pocket household expenditure on medical care and health by household type and access to a healthcare card. The *RSE* for other-type of households where one or more members had a healthcare card was >50 % and therefore this estimate is very unreliable

by lone-person households and those consisting of single-parent-with-children. These four categories accounted for 88 % of all households. The remainder, other-types, consisted of other-couples, other-one-family, multiple family and group households.

Table 13.1 also shows that the average size of households varied between one (for lone-person households) and just over five (for multiple-family households). The overall average was 2.56 persons per households.

Because of the economies of scale it can be assumed that the consumption of a four-member household, for example, will not be four times that of a one-member household. OECD (undated) suggested a scaling method so that a scaling factor of 1.0 is assigned to the household head (reference person in the context of HES), 0.5 for each additional member, and 0.3 for each child. These scaling factors were used to estimate the equalized average household size shown in the last column of Table 13.1.

Table 13.2 shows characteristics of households in Australia. The median age for all reference persons was 49 years, while those of the couple-only and lone-person households was much older: just over 58 years. Couple-with-children, single-parent-with-children and other-types of households had somewhat younger reference persons—median ages in the range 41–45 years. The reference persons of other-one-family and multiple-family households were somewhat older with median ages of 54 and 50 years respectively, while those of the group households consisted mainly of younger people—the median age of their reference persons was just under 29 years.

Most of the households had a male reference person. The only exception was the single- parent-with-children households, where reference persons were predominantly females.

Table 13.1 Number, standard error (*SE*), percentage, average size and equalized average size of households. (Household Expenditure Survey 2009–2010)

Household type	Number of households (in 000's)	%	Household size	
			Average	Equalized average
All households	8,399±26	100	2.56±0.008	1.68±0.004
Couple-with-children	2,699±19	32	3.95±0.015	2.24±0.006
Couple-only	2,210±18	26	2.00±0.000	1.50±0.000
Lone-person	2,055±20	25	1.00±0.000	1.00±0.000
Single-parent-with-children	518±9	6	3.10±0.057	1.77±0.021
Other-types	916±19	11	2.97±0.045	1.95±0.019
Other-couples	142±7	2*	3.23±0.078	2.12±0.039
Other-one-family	363±12	4*	2.31±0.055	1.66±0.027
Multiple-family	146±9	2*	5.18±0.091	2.89±0.039
Group	265±7	3*	2.50±0.070	1.75±0.003

Estimates marked with an asterisk (*) are percentages based on numerators with *RSE* between 25 and <50%. These estimates should be treated with caution

The three groups that ranked rather low on the income scale were the lone-persons and single-parent-with children households. The majority of the first group was in the lowest income quintile, while nearly half of the second was in the bottom two quintiles. Their median annual disposable incomes were around $ 28,000 and $ 45,000, respectively; these were substantially lower than the national median of about $ 62,000. Couple-only and other-one-family households had incomes similar to the national levels, while the other-types households had much higher median incomes.

As noted earlier, the government pays pensions and certain allowances that are related to the age, disability, unemployment and other factors that affect a person's earning capacity. These allowances are generally means-tested, that is, they depend reciprocally on the current income and/or assets of the household. Allowances are paid for individuals, including the age pension, disability, or unemployment allowance; others are for families. The HES asked questions from the reference person about the sources and amounts that constituted household income. Disposable income was estimated by the ABS by deducting appropriate income tax liabilities. The highest proportion of those not receiving government assistance were couples-with-children, other-couples, and group households. On the other hand, single-parent-with-children and lone-person households derived substantial proportions of their incomes from government pensions and/or allowances.

In Australia certain groups of individuals are provided healthcare cards by the government. The eligibility criteria are somewhat similar to other government pensions and allowances. However, retired defence personnel and their spouses are eligible for a Department of Veteran Affairs gold card that provides even more entitlements compared to the ordinary healthcare card and are not subjected to the income and asset tests. Benefits from these cards are usually available only to the individuals to whom they have been issued and not the other members of the household.

Table 13.2 Percentage distributions of households by type and characteristics. (HES 2009–2010)

		Household type								
Characteristics	All households	Couple-only	Couple-with-children	Lone-person	Single-parent-with-children	Other-types	Other-couples	*Other-one-family*	*Multiple-family*	*Group*
Age of household reference person										
<35	21	23	15	17	27	37	37	20	20	71
35–44	20	8	36	12	38	12	13	10	18	12
45–54	20	12	32	14	26	17	18*	24	25	3*
55–64	18	24	12	21	6*	17	17*	21	26	7*
65+	21	34	5*	36	2*	16	15*	25	11*	7*
Sex of household reference person										
Male	60	70	72	47	11	56	72	40	71	61
Female	40	30	28	53	89	44	28	60	29	39
Quintile of disposable income										
Q1 (lowest 20 %)	20	17	3*	53	18	4*	1*	7*	<1*	5*
Q2	20	25	11	23	41	18	9	27	4*	17
Q3	20	19	21	16	27	25	15	32	16	24
Q4	20	22	30	6*	11*	24	27	21	27	26
Q5 (highest 20 %)	20	18	35	3*	3*	30	47	14*	53	29
Govt. pension/allowances as a proportion of the total household income										
Zero %	59	61	72	48	13	67	80	51	65	82
<25 %	10	7	15	6	22	5	4*	7*	12*	1*
≥25 %	30	32	13	45	64	27	15*	41*	22*	17
One or more household member has a healthcare card										
Yes	42	40	25	50	79	49	48	63	64	31
No	58	60	75	50	21	51	52	37	36	69

Column totals may not add to 100 because of rounding

Estimates marked with an asterisk (*) are percentages based on numerators with *RSE* between 25 and <50 %. These estimates should be treated with caution

In the HES, a question was asked as to the number of household members who possessed a healthcare card. The majority of households with one or more healthcare cards were those of the single-parent-with-children, multiple-family and other-one-family households, while the lowest proportion of healthcare card holders were couple-with children households.

Out-of-Pocket Expenditure by Household Type

According to the HES, the annual out-of-pocket expenditure on medical care and health incurred by an average Australian household was $ 3,422 ± 161. This accounted for just over 5 % of the total household expenditure on goods and services ($ 64,477 ± 582). Table 13.3 shows that while couples-with-children households spent, on average, the largest amount, the lone-person and single–parents-with-children households spent significantly less on medical care and health.

When expressed as a percentage of the total household expenditure on goods and services, it was highest (close to 7 %) for couple only and lowest for single parent with children (3.1 %). For all other categories it fluctuated around 5 %.

As expected, the overall expenditure on a per capita basis was 26 % lower than that calculated using the equalised household size. However, the differential varied according to the household type, being zero % for the lone-person households, 25 % for couple-only households, and 31 to 41 % for all other household types. Despite Medicare, 54 % of all Australian households had private health insurance. The highest prevalence of private health insurance was among couple-only and couple-with-children households (62 %), followed by lone-person households (44 %) and lowest (24 %) among the single-parent-with-children households. The other-type of households were only 2 % below the national average of 54 %.

Excluding the cost of private health insurance premiums resulted in a 40 % decline in the out-of-pocket expenses, from $ 3,422 ± 161 to $ 2,037 ± 159 (Tables 13.3 and 13.4). The reduction was somewhat higher for couple-with-children

Table 13.3 Average annual out-of-pocket expenditure on medical care and health per household, per capita and per capita (equalized) by household type. (Household Expenditure Survey 2009–2010)

Household type	Per household	Per capita	Per capita (equalized)
All households	3,422 ± 161	1,515 ± 60	2,048 ± 85
Couple-only	3,626 ± 98	1,813 ± 52	2,417 ± 70
Couple-with-children	4,482 ± 127	1,184 ± 33	2,024 ± 54
Lone-person	1,814 ± 121	1,814 ± 127	1,814 ± 127
Single-parent-with-children	2,179*	839*	1,340*
Other-types	4,116*	1,483*	2,156*

Estimates marked with an asterisk (*) had *RSEs* between 25 and <50 %. These estimates should be treated with caution

Table 13.4 Comparison of the average annual out-of-pocket expenditure on medical care and health excluding the cost of private health insurance premiums for all, privately insured and uninsured households by household type. (Household Expenditure Survey 2009–2010)

Household type	All households	With private health insurance	Without private health insurance
All households	2,037 ± 159	2,707 ± 283	1,248 ± 68
Couple-only	2,049 ± 77	2,379 ± 128	1,506 ± 87
Couple-with-children	2,426 ± 93	2,983 ± 133	1500 ± 117
Lone-person	1,153 ± 116	1,436 ± 139	935 ± 187
Single-parent-with-children	1,610*	4,108**	825 ± 113
Other-types	3,087*	4,740**	1,375 ± 162

Estimates marked with a single asterisk (*) had *RSEs* between 25% and <50% and should be treated with caution, while those marked with a double asterisk (**) had *RSEs* of ≥50% and are very unreliable

and couple-only households (46 % and 43 %, respectively), about 36 % for lone-person households, and much lower for the remaining two household types. When the cost of private health insurance was subtracted from total household expenditure on medical care and health, insured households spent $ 2,707 ± 283 compared to $ 1,248 ± 68 for the uninsured ones (Table 13.4).

Excluding the cost of private health insurance, the combined out-of-pocket expenditure on all other health related goods and services was nearly twice for those households that opted for private health insurance compared to those that did not. In case of the most disadvantaged group, single parent with children, the ratio was nearly 5:1. Given the rather low prevalence of private health insurance among these households (nearly 24 %), it could be assumed that some of these households may have incurred unusual health expenses during the reference periods of this study.

Out-of-Pocket Expenditure by Other Characteristics of Households

Figure 13.1 shows that households with male reference persons spent more than those with female reference persons, probably because of the gender gap in income—the median disposable income was around $ 73,000 and just under $ 60,000 per annum for households with male and female reference persons, respectively.

The out-of-pocket expenditure among households with male reference persons increased monotonically with age. It was also the case for households with female reference persons, except for a drop in expenditure among female reference persons aged 65+. Further analysis revealed that 62 % of female reference persons aged 65+ were in lone-person households compared to 39 % of those aged 55–64. On the contrary, 30 % of the 55–64 year old female reference persons were living in couple-only households, *vis-à-vis* 23 % of the 65+ year old female reference persons. Thus, the changed circumstances, most probably because of widowhood, may explain this sudden drop, which was statistically significant.

Apart from the stage of life cycle as reflected by the age of reference person, another important factor is the level of household income. All the households were divided into five equal groups (quintiles) depending upon their disposable income from all sources. Figure 13.2 shows the average annual out-of-pocket expenditure by income quintile for households with male and female reference persons. The positive association between income and expenditure is quite obvious. Those in the top 20 % of the income distribution seem to spend more than three times those households in the bottom 20 %.

As expected, the prevalence of private health insurance showed a similar positive association with income quintile, that is, those in the top quintile, Q5, had a much higher prevalence (54 %) compared to those in the bottom quintile, Q1, (32 %). The trend was quite similar among the households with either male or female reference persons.

Figure 13.3 reveals a strong positive relationship between age of the household reference person and the out-of-pocket expenditure on medical care and health as a proportion of the total household expenditure on goods and services. Again this relationship holds irrespective of the sex of the household reference person.

Although the above positive relationship between age and the out-of-pocket expenditure on medical care and health pertains only to the household reference persons, it is likely to be true for the general population as well. This proposition was tested by using the data for lone-person households only, and thus avoiding the confounding effect of the household composition and size.

The average annual out-of-pocket expenditure on medical care and health for those households that received no government assistance was highest (just under $ 3,900). Households that received government assistance showed lower expenditures: 15 % drop for those with government assistance under 25 % of their disposable income and 34 % drop for those getting even more assistance. In terms of their economic circumstances, the last group of households was probably most disadvantaged as, for the majority of them, government support was the main source of income. Most of the households receiving less than 25 % of their income were getting government allowances that were not means tested.

The negative association between the out-of-pocket expenditure on medical care and health and the extent of government financial support was observed among all household types and irrespective of the age and sex of reference persons.

Households where one or more member had a government issued healthcare card had a substantially smaller out-of-pocket expenditure on medical care and health *vis-à-vis* those that did not. The former type of households, on the average, spent $ 2,806 ± 373 per annum, which was only 74 % of the latter, that spent $ 3,860 ± 85 per annum. It is possible that patients with a healthcare card are more likely to be bulk-billed by their doctors, that is, the doctor charges only the Medicare rebate. This is less likely to happen for consultations with specialist doctors.

Figure 13.4 shows that for most household types the out-of-pocket expenditure for healthcare card holders was substantially less than for those households in which none of the members had a healthcare card. The only exceptions were the couple-only households and other types of households—both appeared to show differences that were statistically not significant at 5 % level

Purchase of Goods and Services for Medical Care and Health

Table 13.5 shows the range of medical care and health related goods and services purchased and the annual out-of-pocket expenditure on each for various household types. Given below is an overview based on the data for all household types combined.

Of the total out-of-pocket medical care and health expenditure of \$ 3,422 ± 159 per annum incurred by an average Australian household, the costliest item was the private health insurance for hospital, medical, and dental care. As noted previously, just over half of the households had taken out this optional insurance. A much smaller proportion of households had sickness, personal accident, or separate ambulance insurances. Nearly one-quarter of the households reported taking these insurances. They were more or less equally divided between those taking separate ambulance insurance and those taking sickness and personal accident policies. The sickness and personal accident policies generally cover costs that are not payable by Medicare or private health insurance. Such costs may involve loss of wages and compensation for trauma resulting from accidents and/or serious illnesses such as cancers and heart attacks.

The biggest out-of-pocket expense categorized by health professionals was for dental fees, closely followed by the specialist doctors' fees. At present dental care and services of allied health professionals are not covered by Medicare, and even the rebates by the private health insurance, depending upon the insurance policy, leave a sizeable gap for the patients to pay themselves. While there are many general practitioner doctors who bulk-bill, i.e., they charge only what Medicare pays, most specialists do not bulk-bill.

Medicines, pharmaceutical and therapeutic products was the third most expensive group of items, accounting for just over one-quarter of the total out-of-pocket expenditure. Prescription medicines, although subsidised through the PBS, cost about half of the non-prescription medicines and other therapeutic goods. Generally these are all paid for by the individual patients or their households, though some limited subsidies may be available through private health insurance.

As noted earlier, treatment in public hospitals is free; there is a government subsidy for private hospital stays, and the private health insurance covers a sizeable proportion of the charges. Co-payments may be required for specialist services, operating theatre time, diagnostic tests, and other treatments, and these co-payments can, in some cases, run into thousands of dollars. Care for older or disabled persons in nursing homes is heavily subsidised by the federal government, although means-testing requires those with major assets to make sizeable contributions to their care.

Table 13.5 Annual out-of-pocket expenditure on medical care and health by the type of goods and services purchased and the household types. (Household Expenditure Survey 2009–2010)

Goods and services for medical care and health	All house-hold types combined	Couple-only	Couple-with-children	Lone-person	Single-parent-with-children	Other-types
Private health insurance	*1,385±28*	*1,576±52*	*2,057±76*	*660±28*	*568±86*	*1,029±70*
Hospital, medical and dental	1,157±21	1,401±39	1,613±51	579±23	448±56	923±64
Ambulance/sickness/personal	228±16	175±28	444±45	81±12	120*	106±24
Health practitioners' fees	*991±52*	*1,051±67*	*1,366±78*	*491±70*	*1,014*****	*850±99*
GP doctors' fees	86±3	98±7	119±6	39±5	44±10	93±14
Specialist doctors' fees	325±41	394±49	383±48	184*	601**	149**
Dentists' fees	377±20	341±40	587±55	153±23	274±63	411±74
Opticians' fees	80±6	88±11	102±12	50±10	39*	83*
Physio/chiropractors' fees	68±5	73±8	99±12	34±6	27*	62*
Other health practitioners fees	54±7	57±10	75±13	31*	30*	51**
Medicine, pharmaceutical and therapeutic products	*932±147*	*911±36*	*928±40*	*540±51*	*475±51*	*2,133*****
Prescription medicines	304±14	368±21	312±22	258±43	137±24	323±33
Other pharmaceuticals	517±76	489±27	572±29	252±17	317±37	1,130**
First aid/therapeutic products	111**	54±11	45±10	30*	21±5	679**
Other medical care and health expenses	*114±121*	*88±18*	*131±23*	*123*****	*122*****	*104**
Hospital/nursing home fees	96±21	67±16	110±22	116**	120**	66*
Other health-related expenses	18±4	20*	21*	7*	2*	38**
Total out-of-pocket expenditure on medical care and health	*3,422±159*	*3,626±105*	*4,482±128*	*1,814±127*	*2,179**	*4,116**

Estimates marked with a single asterisk (*) had *RSEs* of 25 % to < 50 % and should be treated with caution, while those marked with a double asterisk (**) had *RSEs* of ≥50 % and are very unreliable. Because of rounding individual items may not add to the sub-totals

Some of the important findings relating the selected characteristics of households with various components of their out-of-pocket expenditure on medical care and health are presented below. These are based on Tables 13.5 and 13.7.

Private health insurance

Out-of-pocket expenditure on health insurance was above the national average among couple households with or without children, while the other three household types spent much less—the smallest amount spent was by the single-parent-with-children households, they spent just over 41 % of the average insurance premiums paid by all household types combined.

Expenditure on health insurance increased with age of the reference persons until they reached 65 years, after which the expenditure decreased despite the likelihood of need for medical care increasing with age. The decline may have been for general financial reasons or attributable to changes in personal circumstances; for example, 42 % each of the reference persons 65+ were either living in couple-only or lone-person households.

Households with a female reference person and those where one or more members had a healthcare card spent substantially less on health insurance. Given that about half of the female reference persons were living in lone-person or single-parent-with-children households, the sex differential in income might explain why these households spend less on health insurance. Interestingly, even among those households that had at least one member holding a healthcare card, nearly 39 % opted for private health insurance.

As noted before, income had a positive association with expenditure on private health insurance. On the other hand, relatively disadvantaged households, i.e. those with greater than 25 % of their income coming from government pensions/allowances, spent much less on private health insurance. Nevertheless, nearly one-third of such households had private health insurance.

Health practitioners' fees

Couple-only and couple-with-children households spent significantly more than other household types, while lone-person and other types of households spent substantially less.

Age showed a mixed association with the out-of-pocket expenditure on fees for doctors and other health professionals; the older households spending the least amounts on these items. This does not necessarily mean that older people consult health professionals less frequently. Older people tend to have healthcare cards entitling them to free care.

There was no substantial difference by sex of the reference person, but as expected those households possessing one or more healthcare cards had much less out-of-pocket expenses in this category.

Table 13.6 Annual out-of-pocket expenditure on medical care and health by the type of goods and services purchased and the age and sex of the household reference person. (Household Expenditure Survey 2009–2010)

Goods and services for medical care and health	Age of the reference person			Sex of the reference person	
	<35	35–64	65+	Male	Female
Private health insurance	*925±33*	*1,666±43*	*1,056±42*	*1,568±48*	*1,113±37*
Hospital, medical and dental	783±30	1,344±32	1,009±31	1,287±35	963±27
Ambulance/sickness/personal	143±14	323±25	47**	280±25	149±20
Health practitioners' fees	*956±177*	*1,089±54*	*753±56*	*1,034±56*	*927±104*
GP doctors' fees	89±7	101±5	43±5	99±5	67±5
Specialist doctors' fees	404*	310±38	289±29	314±36	342*
Dentists' fees	284±42	454±35	258±41	406±30	335±30
Opticians' fees	37±7	93±9	87±10	85±8	72±10
Physio/chiropractors' fees	74±11	80±7	26±5	73±8	59±6
Other health *practitioners'* fees	67±13	51±7	50*	56±9	51±10
Medicine, pharmaceutical and therapeutic products	*476±29*	*867±30*	*1563**	*1,030±248*	*787±42*
Prescription medicines	135±14	335±18	383±35	296±14	315±32
Other pharmaceuticals	316±24	488±19	797*	576±125	429±21
First aid/therapeutic products	26±3	44±8	383**	157**	43±8
Other medical care and health expenses	*76±17*	*92±15*	*213**	*84±11*	*159**
Hospital/nursing home fees	65±15	76±14	183*	67±10	139*
Other health-related expenses	11**	16*	30*	17*	20*
Total out-of-pocket expenditure on medical care and health	*2,434±197*	*3,714±86*	*3,585±686*	*3,715±258*	*2,985±133*

Estimates marked with a single asterisk (*) had *RSEs* between 25 % and <50 % and should be treated with caution, while those marked with a double asterisk (**) had *RSEs* of ≥50 % and are very unreliable. Because of rounding individual items may not add to the sub-totals

Table 13.7 Annual out-of-pocket expenditure on medical care and health by the type of goods and services purchased and the selected characteristics of households. (Household Expenditure Survey 2009–2010)

Goods and services for medical care and health	Healthcare card?		Quintile of disposable income			Govt. allowances as % of income	
	Yes	No	Q1	Q3	Q5	Zero %	>25 %
Private health insurance	*847 ± 37*	*1,767 ± 41*	*592 ± 33*	*1,170 ± 57*	*2,715 ± 83*	*1,741 ± 43*	*639 ± 32*
Hospital, medical and dental	768 ± 32	1,434 ± 31	545 ± 31	1,009 ± 37	2,085 ± 45	1,414 ± 31	602 ± 25
Ambulance/sickness/personal	*79**	*333 ± 25*	*47**	*161 ± 35*	*630 ± 60*	*327 ± 25*	*38**
Health practitioners' fees	*696 ± 91*	*1,201 ± 58*	*631**	*761 ± 59*	*1,785 ± 123*	*1,201 ± 59*	*592 ± 122*
GP doctors' fees	46 ± 4	115 ± 5	33 ± 4	87 ± 8	160 ± 12	115 ± 5	26 ± 3
Specialist doctors' fees	269*	365 ± 40	325**	215 ± 33	519 ± 70	376 ± 40	267*
Dentists' fees	241 ± 25	475 ± 33	177 ± 35	299 ± 30	715 ± 81	460 ± 35	190 ± 24
Opticians' fees	68 ± 7	89 ± 8	47 ± 7	67 ± 12	145 ± 24	87 ± 8	64 ± 9
Physio/chiropractors' fees	31 ± 5	94 ± 7	27*	57 ± 9	125 ± 18	94 ± 8	18 ± 3
Other health practitioners' fees	40*	64 ± 8	22 ± 5	36 ± 7	122 ± 24	69 ± 10	27*
Medicine, pharmaceutical and therapeutic products	*1,125**	*795 ± 24*	*597 ± 34*	*1,468**	*1,061 ± 50*	*828 ± 28*	*1,204**
Prescription medicines	310 ± 27	299 ± 13	261 ± 31	293 ± 29	388 ± 32	311 ± 16	304 ± 36
Other pharmaceuticals	598*	460 ± 17	297 ± 14	791*	624 ± 40	475 ± 19	627*
First aid/therapeutic products	217**	36 ± 5	39*	384**	49*	42 ± 7	273**
Other medical care and health expenses	*138**	*97 ± 12*	*144***	*91**	*179 ± 37*	*104 ± 14*	*128**
Hospital/nursing home fees	118*	81 ± 11	136**	76*	144 ± 34	88 ± 13	113*
Other health-related expenses	21*	16*	8*	15*	36*	16*	16*
Total out-of-pocket expenditure on medical care and health	*2,806 ± 373*	*3,860 ± 85*	*1,965 ± 203*	*3,941 ± 721*	*5,740 ± 183*	*3,874 ± 96*	*2,563 ± 514*

Estimates marked with a single asterisk (*) had *RSEs* between 25 % and < 50 % and should be treated with caution, while those marked with a double asterisk (**) had *RSEs* of ≥ 50 % and are very unreliable. Because of rounding individual items may not add to the sub-totals

Households in higher income quintiles spent more on the gap between the Medicare schedule and general practitioners' fees but surprisingly the same was not true for specialist doctors' fees. Doctors and other health practitioners operating in more affluent areas tend not to bulk-bill as frequently as those in less advantaged areas, so the co-payment for general practice consultations is higher in more affluent areas, where the use of private specialists is also higher. The gap in dental fees was larger for the households in higher income quintiles, though differences were not significant.

Households that received 25 % or more of their income through government pension or allowances spent substantially less, possibly as many of them had access to healthcare cards.

Medicine, pharmaceutical and therapeutic products

Lone-person and single-parent-with-children households had somewhat more out-of-pocket expenses for prescription medicines and other pharmaceuticals There was little variation in the expenditure on other pharmaceutical products among various household types. The other types of households were an exception. They spent more on prescription medicines as well as the first aid supplies, surgical dressings, and other therapeutic appliances. Because of the heterogeneity of this group, it is not possible to suggest a plausible explanation.

Households with older reference persons spent more on all type of medicines and other pharmaceutical products. There was no significant differential in terms of the sex of the reference person of household.

Households that had one or more member with a healthcare card spent substantially more on all types of medicines and other pharmaceutical products.

Households with higher incomes seemed to spend more on medicines and other pharmaceutical products. A comparison of those households that received more than 25 % of their income from government pension/allowances with those that did not receive any government subsidy showed that the former group spent much more on medicines and other pharmaceutical products than those getting no government subsidies.

Other medical care and health expenses

This category of expenditures had the largest number of estimates that were based on small numbers and were therefore subjected to large sampling variations. Considering only the statistically significant estimates it appears that couples with children, household with reference persons aged 35-64 years and those in the highest income quintile spent more than other groups.

National Estimates of the Out-of-Pocket Expenditure on Medical Care and Health

Analysis of the HES data presented in Table 13.5 shows that the average out-of-pocket expenditure on medical care and health was \$ 3,422 ± 159 per household per annum, while according to Table 13.1 the number of households was 8,399 ± 26 thousand. Multiplying these two numbers, we estimated that nationally Australian households spent \$ 28,738 ± 1,335 million as out-of-pocket expenditure on medical care and health in 2009–2010. This represents 23.7 % of the \$ 121.4 billion spent nationally on medical care and health in Australia during 2009–2010. It is substantially higher than the 17.5 % estimated by the AIHW (2011). The most probable reason for this difference is that the AIHW's estimate did not include the cost of private health insurance premiums. Moreover, it may be noted that unlike the AIHW's data—primarily based on administrative records—the estimates presented in this study represent the actual amounts spent by the Australian households.

Repeating this multiplication process for each cell in the second column of Table 13.5, we made estimates for various health-related goods and services for all households. Breaking down the total expenditure into various goods and services revealed that Australian households spent \$ 9,717 ± 176 million for hospital, medical and dental insurance premiums and \$ 1,915 ± 134 million for ambulance, sickness and personal accident insurance.

Of the remaining \$ 17.1 billion out-of-pocket expenditure by Australian households, \$ 722 ± 25 million and \$ 2,730 ± 344 million were spent on the co-payments for doctors' and specialists' fees, and, \$ 3,166 ± 168 million, \$ 672 ± 50 million, \$ 571 ± 42 million, and \$ 454 ± 59 million were paid for the fees of dentists, opticians, physiotherapists/chiropractors and other health professionals respectively.

The PBS subsidised prescription medicines cost \$ 2,553 ± 118 million, while other pharmaceuticals cost \$ 4,342 ± 638 million and \$ 932 ± 613 million for the first aid and other therapeutic products. The last figure was statistically unreliable, as it had an $RSE > 50\,\%$.

About \$ 806 ± 176 million was spent on co-payments for hospital/nursing home fees, and \$ 151 ± 34 million for other health-related expenses.

Conclusion

Payment by individuals for health goods and services is a matter of concern in policy development that seeks to ease the burden of illness and injury by distributing its cost within the community. Universal health insurance is one response to this burden, and it is a matter of judgement then as to how much of the total costs of care should be met through insurance and how much left to the individual to meet both through optional supplementary insurance and payment at the time of use. Most economically advanced nations struggle with this policy problem. Copious evidence supports the view that the expectation that healthcare costs be met, even in part, by individuals will have differential effects, and that citizens on low incomes and those who have complex and continuing problems (especially if they have more than one problem, such as diabetes and heart disease) will fare worst (Jan et al. 2012).

In terms of policy response, trends in out-of-pocket expenditure can be used to indicate where adjustments might be made to soften the impact, and indeed a complex web of safety nets and concessions already operates in Australia and many other countries with that goal in mind. The larger matter—of what it is reasonable to expect individuals to pay for their own healthcare at the point of use—would benefit from broader public debate.

Appendix

For each of the sample households, the ABS provided a weighting factor being the inverse of the probability of selection of that household and 60 replicate weighting factors derived using the "delete-a-group jackknife" method (ABS 2012; Kott 1998).

The national estimate for a particular characteristic of households, say $\hat{Y}$, was calculated as:

$$\hat{Y} = \sum_{i=1}^{i=9774} y_i * w_i$$

where y_i and w_i were the values of the characteristic and weighting factor of the ith household respectively. By definition such estimates were subject to sampling errors, having been based on a sample rather than the whole population. An indicator of this error is the standard error (*SE*) which was calculated as:

$$SE(\hat{Y}) = \sqrt{\frac{59}{60} \sum_{j=1}^{j=60} (\hat{Y}_j - \hat{Y})^2}$$

The term $\hat{Y}_j$ used in the above equation was estimated as:

$$\hat{Y}_j = \sum_{i=1}^{i=9774} y_i * r_{ij}$$

where y_i was the value of the characteristic and r_{ij} was the jth replicate weighting factor—both for the ith household.

The *RSE* of the ratio of the national estimates of two characteristics $\hat{Y}$ and $\hat{Z}$ could be estimated as:

$$RSE(\frac{\hat{Y}}{\hat{Z}}) = \sqrt{[RSE(\hat{Y})]^2 - [RSE(\hat{Z})]^2}$$

The above formulae were used for the calculation of the *SE* and *RSE* for each average expenditure reported in this paper.

References

ABS. (2010). *Year book Australia, 2009–2010. Catalogue No. 1301.0.* Canberra: Australian Bureau of Statistics. http://www.abs.gov.au/AUSSTATS/abs@.nsf/Latestproducts/4ED550A390396D70CA25773700169C8A?opendocument. Accessed Oct 2013.

ABS. (2011). *Household expenditure survey, Australia: Summary of results 2009–2010.* Canberra: Australian Bureau of Statistics. http://www.abs.gov.au/ausstats/abs@.nsf/mf/6530.0. Accessed Oct 2013.

ABS. (2012). *Household expenditure survey and survey of income and housing, user guide, Australia, 2009–2010.* Canberra: Australian Bureau of Statistics. http://www.ausstats.abs.gov.au/ausstats/subscriber.nsf/0/1D03ACBBD40275ADCA257A3900173E85/$File/65030_1.pdf. Accessed Oct 2013.

AIHW. (2011). *Health expenditure Australia 2009–2010. Catalogue No. HWE55.* Canberra: Australian Institute of Health and Welfare. http://www.aihw.gov.au/WorkArea/DownloadAsset.aspx?id=10737420254. Accessed Oct 2013.

Ang, J. B. (2010). The determinants of healthcare expenditure in Australia. *Applied Economics Letters, 17*(7–9), 639–644.

Barrett, G. F., & Conlon, R. (2003). Healthcare spending, family structure and family health. *Economic and Labour Relations Review, 14*(1), 143–152.

Butler, J. R. G., & Smith, J. P. (1992). The expenditure on health in Australia: 1960–1961 to 1988–1989. *Australian Economic Review, 99,* 43–58.

Jan, S., Essue, B. M., & Leeder, S. R. (2012). Falling through the cracks: The hidden economic burden chronic illness and disability on Australian households. *Medical Journal of Australia, 196*(1), 29–31. http://www.mja.com.au/journal/2012/196/1/falling-through-cracks-hidden-economic-burden-chronic-illness-and-disability. Accessed Dec 2013.

Jones, G., Savage, E., & van Gool, K. (2008). The distribution of household health expenditures in Australia. *The Economic Record, 84,* 99–114.

Kott, P. S. (1998). Using the delete-a-group jackknife variance estimator in practice. *Proceedings of the Annual Meeting of the American Statistical Association, Section on Survey Research Methods,* 763–768. http://www.amstat.org/sections/srms/proceedings/papers/1998_130.pdf. Accessed Oct 2013.

OECD. (undated). *What are equivalence scales?* Paris: OECD. http://www.oecd.org/LongAbstract/0,3425,en_2649_33933_35411112_119669_1_1_1,00.html. Accessed Dec 2013.

Polder, J. J., Meerding, W. J., Bonneaux, L., & van der Maas, P. J. (2005). A cross-national perspective on cost of illness: A comparison of studies from the Netherlands, Australia, Canada, Germany, United Kingdom, and Sweden. *European Journal of Health Economics, 6*(3), 223–232.

Schofield, D. (2000). Public hospital expenditure: How is it divided between lower, middle and upper income groups. *Australian Economic Review, 33*(4), 303–316.

Sharma, A., & Srivastava, P. (2011). Does disaggregation affect the relationship between healthcare expenditure and GDP? An analysis using regime shifts. *Australian Economic Papers, 50*(1), 27–39.

Smith, J. (2001). Tax expenditures and public health financing in Australia. *Economic and Labour Relations Review, 12*(2), 239–262.

Yusuf, F., & Leeder, S. R. (2013). Can't escape it: The out-of-pocket cost of healthcare in Australia. *Medical Journal of Australia,* 199(7), 475–478.

Chapter 14
Mobile Home Population Displacement: The Case of Anchorage, Alaska

Donna Shai and Kristen Eaton

Introduction

Mobile homes are an important form of affordable housing for people unable or unwilling to live in tenements and other high-density, low-income housing or who prefer the mobile home park lifestyle. This lifestyle also reflects basic values of American society such as mobility, self-reliance, and independence. Given the organization of mobile home parks, there is a "disconnect" between the park and the surrounding residential community. Parks are often segregated from other housing developments and managed by private entities, similar to gated communities at the other end of the economic scale (Dwyer 2007), contributing to the gap between lower income housing and the affluent (Dwyer 2007). This segregation is partially due to the stigma attached to mobile homes and mobile home parks (Genz 2001). While in recent years there has been increased scholarly attention to low-income housing in the United States (Briggs 2005; Lobao et al. 2007; Newburger et al. 2011), there has been little attention in these studies to mobile home parks as low-income housing.

Over the past 20 years, while the number of housing units in the United States has risen, the percentage of mobile home has decreased from 7.6 % in 2000 to 6.8 % in 2005–2009. Mobile homes can vary from high-end units to aging and deteriorating structures. According to the 2000 Census there were mobile homes in all fifty states, but these were concentrated especially in the south, the southwest, and the western states. While the largest numbers of mobile homes were in Florida, South Carolina had the highest percentage with 18.1 % of its housing classified as mobile homes. Hawaii and Connecticut, at the other end of the scale, have less than 1 % (U.S. Census Bureau, American Community Survey, 2005–2009, hereafter ACS).

D. Shai (✉)
Villanova University, Villanova, PA, USA
e-mail: donna.shai@villanova.edu

K. Eaton
Temple University, Philadelphia, PA, USA

M. N. Hoque, L. B. Potter (eds.), *Emerging Techniques in Applied Demography*, Applied Demography Series 4, DOI 10.1007/978-94-017-8990-5_14,

While this study concentrates on displacement in Anchorage, there is anecdotal evidence from newspaper accounts that displacement is taking place elsewhere in the United States as well, e.g., North Carolina (Geary 2008), Washington State (Bird 2008), Florida (Hargot 2008; Schoettler 2010), Mississippi, Georgia, Ohio, and Maryland (Hendrix 2004). One measure of displacement of mobile home populations can be found in the American Housing Survey (American Housing Survey for the United States 2007–2009), which includes "private displacements" from mobile homes due to a company or person who wanted to develop the land or build commercially. Using a national sample, that category included an estimated 25,000 cases nationwide in 2007 and 22,000 cases in 2009. It is likely that the Recession of 2008 and after resulted in decreased development in many parts of the United States, offering a reprieve of sorts to residents of mobile home parks (Corvin 2010; Friedman 2009).

Mobile homes are not well-suited to Alaska for two main reasons: the state lacks an extensive road system for the transporting of mobile homes and the poor insulation characteristic of many mobile homes is not sufficient for the cold climate. Nevertheless, mobile homes, many located off the road system, can be found in all Alaskan counties, constituting 5.5 % of all housing units in 2005–2009 (ACS). Many mobile homes were brought to Alaska, including Anchorage, during the boom years, particularly when the pipeline was being constructed, 1974–1977, because of the urgent need for housing (Cole 1997). Several large mobile home parks were built in Anchorage between the mid-1960s and the early 1980s to accommodate the increasing population attracted by job opportunities (Anchorage 2020 Comprehensive Plan 2002).

The displacement of mobile home populations can be seen in the context of the growing inequality in housing and income (Dwyer 2007). There is evidence that new housing is likely to be more expensive and much larger than older housing, further segregating the affluent from the disadvantaged (Dwyer 2007). In this study we discuss displacement of mobile home populations in Anchorage, Alaska, since 2000, within the framework of Massey's "Age of Extremes" theory described below.

Theoretical Approaches to Housing and Income

Massey (1996) has argued that during a brief period in the United States, post-World War II, there was relative equality in which the middle class "mixed residentially with both the upper and lower classes" (395). After 1970, the U.S. entered a new period of inequality in which there were increasing geographical concentrations of the affluent and the poor, leading to a "special intensification of both privilege and poverty" (395). While the poor were becoming isolated in urban neighborhoods, the middle and upper classes moved to affluent suburbs on the outskirts of the cities, creating concentrations of poverty and affluence that were spatially separated. This geographical pattern was also influenced by a post-industrial economy with high-paying jobs for the well-educated, a shrinking number of middle income jobs for the modestly educated, and a large number of poorly paying jobs for those with the least education. Massey continues that class segregation can lead to geographically isolated, poor neighborhoods with joblessness, inadequate schools, public services, increased crime, and socially destructive behavior. This process resulted in urban poor people living in neighborhoods with higher and higher densities of poverty. Meanwhile, the affluent live in an environment that is the opposite of the poor neighborhood and derive benefits from living among others who are wealthy.

Dwyer (2007) applied Massey's theory to the new housing for the affluent, which tends to be larger, equipped with "grand entryways and elaborate kitchens" (Dwyer 2007, p. 25), increasing the polarization of affluent and poor. Both Massey (1996) and Dwyer (2007) suggest that the stratification of housing will intensify during the twenty-first century, as will the growing inequality of income. While not all mobile home households are characterized by lower income, in general they represent a population that sought an affordable form of housing.

Dwyer (2010) points out that the pattern of housing segregation may differ by city, and she notes the emergence of small-scale mechanisms such as gates and zoning to enhance segregation. This is applicable to Anchorage mobile home parks, which are socially disconnected from the surrounding neighborhood by large streets and other barriers. The isolation is increased by the stigma surrounding the parks and creates a situation in which the residents have few connections that can lead to jobs and better schooling. Zoning regulations are another mechanism that can limit the park, since local zoning requires that mobile homes must have a specific distance between housing units. This leads to the argument by city planners that the parks "take up too much land" that could be used more efficiently for other purposes.

Impression Management and Stigma in a Mobile Home Park

A number of sociologists have studied the problem of stigma in mobile home parks. While mobile home parks in Alaska do not draw the same type of avoidance as the trailer parks created after the Katrina disaster of 2005 by FEMA (Lee et al. 2007), sociologists have studied identity management in trailer parks and the struggle to maintain a reputation for decency despite the suspicion and hostility of neighbors outside of the park (Salamon 2003; Kiter Edwards 2004; MacTavish and Salamon 2006; Kusenbach 2009). Compounding this is the problem that mobile home residents face in obtaining a home mortgage (Williams et al. 2005), and in Anchorage in particular, the difficulty of obtaining alternative affordable housing (Municipality of Anchorage 2007).

Anchorage and the Spatial Forms of Class Segregation

Anchorage has a large service economy, along with trade and government, oil, mining, and fishing, with tourism becoming increasingly important (Freedman 2000; Municipality of Anchorage 2007). The ten census tracts with the lowest median

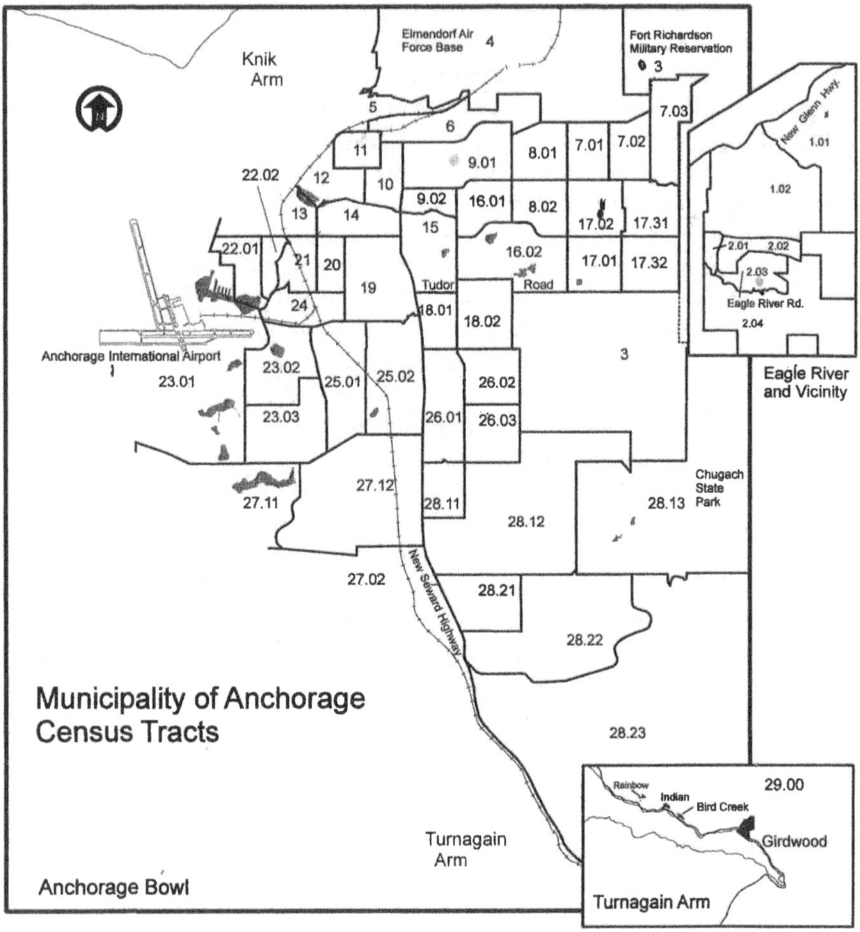

Fig. 14.1 Municipality of Anchorage census tracts

household income are in the northwest, the oldest part of the city (see Fig. 14.1), and include Government Hill, Mountain View, Downtown, Fairview, Russian Jack Park, North Star, and Spenard. The ten tracts with the highest median household income are in Eagle River, to the north, Turnagain Heights on the western coastline, and the newer areas to the southeast, including Hillside and South Anchorage.

The Perspective of the Mobile Home Resident

The displacement of mobile home residents has been a largely neglected topic of research (Kusenbach 2009), outside of local government documents, with the exception of Robinson (2009). It is an important form of housing for low-income residents who might become homeless without it. Displacing a park has social, lifestyle, financial, and practical implications, and can take place under a variety of circumstances. Sudden increases in the cost of renting or leasing can result in eviction or voluntary withdrawal or abandonment by the homeowners or renters. More common reasons are that the landowner can sell the property at a profit to developers or that the property is owned by the local government and the land is considered desirable for other purposes.

From a social perspective, the residents may have lived in the park for decades. The resulting displacement is likely to include a separation from friends and relatives, a loss of social support, and the interruption of school for children. In addition, mobile home residents value ownership without large debt, living on one floor, not sharing walls, and reasonable property taxes (Aurand 2005). Conventional low-income housing is often unacceptable to mobile home residents who say they "don't want to share walls" (Aurand 2005). They may own several dogs or have other problems that make relocation in conventional housing difficult, resulting in a hard-to-relocate population.

Financially, displacement can be devastating for the resident. Many who live in mobile homes do so by necessity. In Anchorage, apartment rents are increasing but wages have not kept up (O'Malley 2007). Minorities and single-parent families are the most vulnerable and at risk for ending up in shelters. Over time the mobile home depreciates like a car. Financially it can be devastating for the resident who may have insufficient funds for relocation. The resident may be offered a few thousand dollars for the move, but that may not be enough to cover the expenses of a move and some parks may not take older trailers (Breese 2007a, b).

Finally there are practical issues, such as the trailer may be too old to be moved, and there may be no buyers for it (Anchorage Daily News 2007). Since many bought the home on site, the owner may not know if it has the axles needed to move. The financial burden of moving includes obtaining required permits such as a certificate of code compliance. A mobile home set up permit is also required if the home is to be moved within Anchorage. Retired persons may not have the money to move and may have to walk away (Breese 2007a). Notice may even be as short as a month when a park is closed or owners sell the park to developers.

The Perspective of the Developer and Planner

Undeveloped land is growing scarce in Anchorage (Schell 2006) since the city is surrounded by large military bases and parklands (Aurand 2005). Developers and planners often operate according to the "highest and best use" principle which determines what use will bring the highest return to the owner of a property (Stephens 2010). Furthermore, planners often try to maximize density for new affordable housing, but because of required spaces between mobile home units, parks preclude the desired density (Breese 2008). Another argument for development is the public health dimension, in that the average age of units in Anchorage mobile home parks is 40 years, many built during the boom years in the 1960s and 1970s, with nearly half prior to 1976 when the major safety codes, including fire prevention, were established (Robinson 2009). Due to the above considerations, mobile home parks in Anchorage have been shut down to be rebuilt into condos, strip malls, and office buildings.

Methods and Data

This paper draws on several sources. The data for Table 14.1 are from the 2000 Census (SF3) accessed through American Factfinder, and from the American Community Survey (ACS). A map of Anchorage mobile home parks in 2008 was acquired from the Planning Division of Anchorage Municipality (see Fig. 14.2). A list of present-day mobile home parks was provided by the Municipality Assessor's Office. Google Earth was used to make counts of housing units in mobile home parks. And lastly, articles from the Anchorage Daily News from 1990 to 2010 were used for newspaper coverage. Data on the racial composition of the mobile home population in Anchorage, expressed in percentages, are from the ACS.

The 2000 Census and the ACS use different forms and different timing. The Census asks about April 1 or the past year, while the ACS data were collected over a 5-year time frame (2005–2009). The sample size of the census is larger than that of the ACS, and the ACS provides a margin of error, while the census does not. Most importantly, the census focuses on the number of persons and their characteristics, while the ACS includes details about characteristics of a population including social, economic, and housing demographics (U.S. Bureau of the Census 2011). Furthermore, because of differences in "universe, question wording, residence rules, reference periods, and the way in which the data are tabulated" (U.S. Bureau of the Census 2011a), certain variables can be compared over time, and others cannot. Among those that can be compared are "units in structure" and "income and earnings" with the caveat that the latter variable (income) has different reference periods in the two data sets. For these reasons the Census Bureau suggests using "percents, means, medians and rates" (U.S. Bureau of the Census 2011b, question 4). In this study we used percents and medians for the major findings. In regard to the income question, we consulted Posey et al. (2003), who compare median household income in the 2000 census and in the ACS by state. For Alaska, the ACS estimate was −0.7 % lower than the 2000 census, but was not statistically significant (Posey et al. 2003).

There are presently 55 census tracts in Anchorage. Measures for each of the two census years included the ten census tracts with the highest median household income, the ten tracts with the lowest median household income, and the numbers of mobile homes in the lowest and highest income tracts. The rationale for using median household income instead of the relationship of income to poverty is that

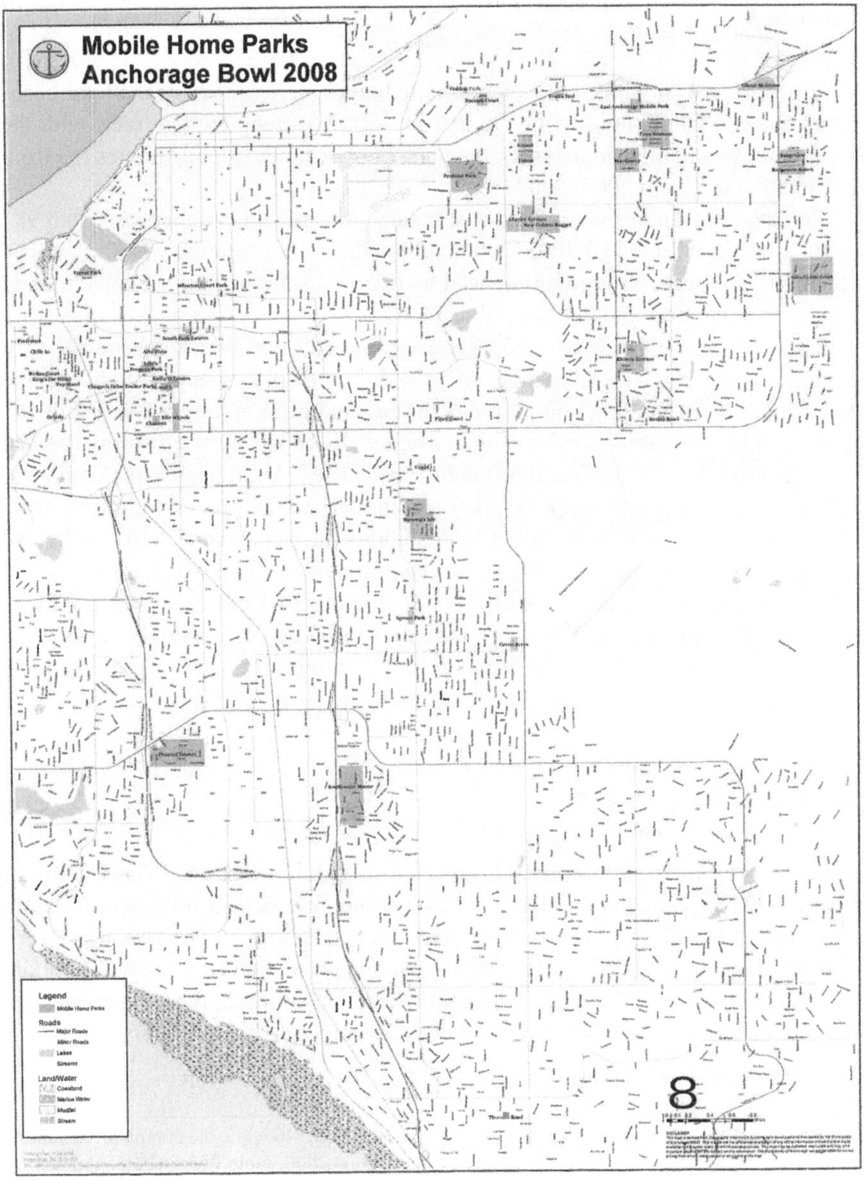

Fig. 14.2 Anchorage bowl mobile home parks, 2008

Anchorage has a higher median income and lower poverty rates than the cities on which Massey's theory was based.[1]

[1] The Anchorage population is relatively well to do, making it difficult to apply the criteria of poverty used for cities such as Philadelphia, which has a much greater extent of poverty. For example,

Findings

For Anchorage as a whole, occupied mobile homes were 5.71 % of the total occupied homes in 2000 but only 4.63 % in 2005–2009. Among the ten tracts with the highest household median incomes, the number of occupied mobile homes fell from 275 in 2000 to 238 in 2005–2009.

Among the ten tracts with the lowest median income, the number rose from 981 to 1002 between 2000 and 2005–2009. Unlike the numbers in the wealthier tracts, the differences were strongly influenced by two concentrations of occupied mobile homes, in tracts 9.01 and 20 (See Table 14.1.)

Since the census question is framed to ask about a mobile home, rather than a mobile home park, these changes may be due to displacement of mobile home parks and/or the changing opportunities to rent land for a mobile home. While the number of housing units is increasing in Anchorage, "it has been a disproportionate number of units at the high end of the housing scale" (Municipality of Anchorage 2007). In the years following the ACS, additional mobile homes were displaced. The remaining mobile home parks in Anchorage as of January 2010 number 47 with a total of 3,995 mobile homes. The smallest parks had only one or two mobile homes and the largest had 505. In 2011, one additional park closed, affecting 17 mobile homes (Municipality Assessor's Office). This count may include unoccupied mobile homes, since assessment is made for the purpose of taxation, regardless of occupancy (See Fig. 14.2 of mobile home parks below.)

Renters versus Owners

Home ownership is often used as a criterion of stability (National Association of Realtors 2012). The total number of mobile home owners in 2000 was 4,117, with 1,294 renters, totaling 5,411. In 2005–2009, the total number of owners was 3,625, with 1170 renters, totaling 4,795. The ratio of owners to renters has remained about the same with a slight increase in renters overall. In addition, there is obviously a drop in the mobile home population, especially in mobile home ownership, reflect-

---

the median household income in 1999 for Anchorage was $ 55,546 while the comparative number for Philadelphia was $ 30,746 (U.S. Bureau of the Census 2000, table P53). The 55 Anchorage census tracts have percentages of persons under the poverty line that range from under 1 % (0.93) to over 25 % (25.10) in the 2000 census. Kasarda (1993), cited in Massey (1996), defined a "poor" neighborhood as one with a poverty rate over 20 %. By this criterion, only four Anchorage tracts (6, 8.02, 10, and 11) can be described as "poor." Of these, tract 11 is in downtown Anchorage which has only a handful of mobile homes (10) and no mobile home parks. Tract 6 has only one park left with four mobile homes. Tract 10, adjacent to downtown, has no parks left. However, tract 8.02 has two mobile home parks with a total of 266 housing units combined. Anchorage does not have concentric circles with a poor center city and wealthy suburbs in outer rings. Instead, the orientation is North/South. The city started from the port in the north and was settled from there, with the newest and wealthiest areas in the southeast.

Table 14.1 Number of occupied mobile homes and the percentage of all occupied housing for the ten wealthiest tracts and the ten poorest tracts: Anchorage, 2000 (census) and 2005–2009 (American Community Survey). (Sources: 2000 census (SF 3) American Factfinder, Table H32, Tenure by units in structure: Occupied housing units; American Community Survey, 2005–2009 (American Factfinder) B25032 Tenure by units in structure: Occupied housing units. 2000 census SF 3 median household income; ACS 04-09 median household income)

Ten Wealthiest Tracks

Tract	2000 Mobile Homes # Mobile Homes	2000 Mobile Homes % Mobile Homes	2005-09 Mobile Homes # Mobile Homes	2005-09 Mobile Homes % Mobile Homes
1.01	135	8.42%	88	5.23%
2.03	17	0.59%	14	0.43%
2.04	0	0.00%	10	1.00%
13.00	55	4.41%	46	3.73%
27.11	0	0.00%	0	0.00%
28.12	30	1.53%	28	1.25%
28.13	5	0.32%	0	0.00%
28.21	6	0.40%	0	0.00%
28.22	4	0.30%	41	2.87%
28.23	23	1.95%	11	0.66%

Ten Poorest Tracks

Tract	2000 Mobile Homes # Mobile Homes	2000 Mobile Homes % Mobile Homes	2005-09 Mobile Homes # Mobile Homes	2005-09 Mobile Homes % Mobile Homes
3.00	0	0.00%	0	0.00%
5.00	0	0.00%	0	0.00%
6.00	23	1.01%	18	0.79%
9.01	385	27.29%	579	32.36%
9.02	0	0.00%	0	0.00%
10.00	6	0.35%	0	0.00%
11.00	0	0.00%	10	2.23%
14.00	33	1.36%	17	0.73%
19.00	249	14.16%	54	3.23%
20.00	285	19.43%	324	23.16%

Table 14.2 Mobile home parks remaining as of January 1, 2010, Anchorage, Alaska (N=46). (Source: Anchorage Municipality Office of Assessment. The authors would like to thank Sam Myers and Kelli Ayers of the Department of Finance, Municipality of Anchorage, for their helpful assistance)

Mobile home park	No. of mobile homes	Census tract
Wagon Wheels	1	17.01
Twin Birch	2	18.02
Michou	2	20.00[a]
Garden Estates	4	6.00[a]
King's Court	5	21.00
Hill's Court	5	21.00
Chugach Drive	7	20.00[a]
Close-In	9	22.02
Baxter Road	9	17.01
Glacier Valley	9	8.02
Cupid	13	18.02
Preferred Court	14	22.02
Trail's End	17	8.01
Wharton Court	19	14.00[a]
Miller's	20	20.00[a]
Top Hand	20	21.00
Green Acres	23	26.02
Alta Vista	24	20.00[a]
Inlet View	25	1.02
Chateau	26	20.00[a]
L&L	31	20.00[a]
Forest Park Chugiak	35	1.02
Spruce Park	38	26.01
East Anchorage	38	7.01
Nanook	39	7.01
Birchwood Loop	39	1.02
Forest Park Anch.	46	13.00[b]
Penguin Park	46	20.00[a]
Kathy 'O Estates	53	20.00[a]
South Park Estates	64	19.00[a]
Idle Wheels	68	20.00[a]
Sunset	68	8.01
Totem	69	8.01
Rangeview Annex	86	7.03
Glenn Muldoon	104	7.02
Four Seasons	105	7.01
Malaspina Park	131	8.02
Golden Nugget	135	8.02
Riviera Terrace	154	7.01
Rangeview	160	7.03
Mayflower Circle	202	7.01
Manoog's Isle	324	18.02
Penland Park	376	9.01[a]
Southwood Manor	393	28.11[b]
Glencaren	415	17.31
Dimond Estates	505	27.12[b]
Total	3978	

[a] Poorest 10 tracks
[b] Wealthiest 10 tracks

ing the diminishing number of mobile homes in Anchorage between the census years.[2]

The Mobile Home Population

While there is limited information available on the mobile home population, there are data on race of mobile home householders. We compared this mobile home population with the Anchorage population as a whole in regard to race. In Anchorage, according to the ACS, the largest group is whites who constitute almost 70 % of the population. In descending order, the next largest are Asian and Pacific Islanders at 7.56 %, Blacks or African Americans at 5.90 %, American Indians and Alaska Natives at 5.63 %, and persons of some other race or two or more races comprising 11 %. The mobile home population is also largely white at 63.52 %, American Indians and Alaskan Natives at 13.24 %, a slightly lower percent of Blacks or African Americans at 4.00 %, and nearly an identical percent of Asian and Pacific Islanders to their percentage of the Anchorage population. Therefore, while reflecting the Anchorage population in general, the mobile home population has more than double the percentage of American Indians and Alaska Natives, and slightly fewer Blacks.

While there are no data available on the income levels of mobile home residents, we can speculate about the economic standings by looking at the median family income over the last 12 months by race in Anchorage using the ACS, which shows that the Anchorage population has a median income of $ 81,384. For whites alone, in Anchorage the median household income is $ 89,324, for Blacks or African Americans the median income is $ 61,056, for American Indians and Alaska Natives $ 50,977, for Asians and Pacific Islanders $ 65,872 and $ 63,542 respectively and some other race, $ 55,669. Therefore the highest income group (whites alone) has a smaller percentage among mobile home householders while the lowest income group, American Indians and Alaska Natives, has twice the percent of householders in mobile homes than in the general Anchorage population.

Looking at the census tracts of the 46 remaining mobile home parks both in 2000 and 2005–2009, one is in the highest median household income group of ten tracts—Forest Park, Anchorage, in tract 13. Thirteen parks are in the lowest median income tracts. The remaining parks are in the intermediate median household income group. When we look at the mobile home units in the highest median income tracts, there are 46. That contrasts with 898 units in the ten lowest household median income tracts. Comparing the remaining mobile home parks with 22 recently closed parks,[3] four were located in the lowest median income tracts (tracts 6 and 10), and

[2] The sources are the 2000 Census (SF 3), American Factfinder, Table H32, Tenure by Units in Structure: Occupied Housing Unites; American Community Survey, 2005–2009 (American Factfinder) B25032 Tenure by Units in Structure: Occupied Housing Units.

[3] Due to discrepancies in data on mobile home parks between the Municipality Assessor and the Planning Department, this list eliminates Twin Birch mobile home park that appears as open in the Assessor's office, and includes Cupid mobile home park, which is considered closed by the Tax

the remaining sixteen were from the intermediate median income tracts. Therefore it would appear that parks in the tracts that are in the lowest and medium income tracts are less likely to close and those parks that are in high median income tracts are more likely to close, suggesting Massey's paradigm of the "age of extremes" (1996). There is increased separation between the residences of the wealthy and those of the poor, played out in mobile home displacement. Furthermore, in the high median income tracts with mobile homes, there appears to be a squeezing effect in which segments of a park have disappeared and the number of units has diminished in some cases to one or two (Table 14.2).

Discussion

While Anchorage does not conform to the model of a manufacturing city, the pattern of spatial segregation by class appears to be similar to that found by sociologists working from the "age of extremes" perspective. There appears to be a tendency for mobile homes, a housing alternative available to low-income individuals and families, to gravitate toward the tracts with lower median income and away from the higher median income tracts. In addition, as elsewhere in the United States, new housing is largely for the affluent and is concentrated in the suburban fringes of the far northeast and southwest Anchorage.

Eliminating mobile home parks in a city with few reasonable alternatives is a devastating event for mobile home park residents. Especially for long-term residents, the problem is not only economic but social: when a mobile home park is displaced, a community disappears. One proposed solution is to build a co-op of manufactured homes and start a co-op park (O'Malley 2007; Chester 2007), with the possibility for residents to own the land. While mobile home parks and mobile homes on rented land are very vulnerable to displacement, they remain an important form of low-income housing that cannot easily be replaced without careful planning for the residents.

References

American Housing Survey for the United States, 2007, and 2009, 2008/2011. (2007–2009). Current Housing Report, U.S. Department of Housing and Urban Development, and U.S. Department of Commerce, U.S., GPO.

Anchorage Daily News. (2007). Housing crunch: An early warning of trouble to come in Anchorage. Staff, August 9.

Anchorage Municipality Planning Division. (2002). Anchorage 2020 comprehensive plan. http://www.muni.org/Depart.emts/OCPD/Planning/Publications/Pages/Anchorage2020.aspx.

Assessor but not listed as closed by the Municipality (due to recent closing), and three others with addresses that could not be found in the Factfinder2 address locator.

Aurand, A. (2005). Trailer owners seek space—midtown: As mobile home parks close, residents find fewer places to go. *Anchorage Daily News* Feb. 6, 2005, Final ed., section Alaska, p.B. http://docs.newsbank.com/s/Infoweb/aggdocs/AWNB/10825996EA5747A7/0F877CE85BA06642. Accessed 8 Dec 2005.

Bird, F. (2008). Mobile home parks residents facing eviction: County council seeks solutions for mobile home park conversion crisis. Snohomish County Council, Washington. http://www.snoco.org. Accessed 12 Sept 2008.

Breese, D. L. (2007a). Finding a new home is difficult for mobile home owners. Alaska Star Thursday, Feb. 14, 2007. http://www.alaskastar.com/stories/021507/new_2007021507.shtml. Accessed 12 Sept 2008.

Breese, D. L. (2007b). Days numbered for Lazy Mountain residents: time running out for mobile home owners. Alaska Star, Thursday, Aug. 9, 2007. http://www.alaskastar.com/stories/080907/new_20070809002.shtml. Accessed 12 Sept 2008.

Breese, D. L. (2008). 200-plus condos planned for Lazy Mountain. Alaska Star, Thursday, April 17. http://alaskastar.com/stories/041708/new_20080417003.shtml. Accessed 12 Sept 2008.

Briggs, X. (Ed.). (2005). *The geography of opportunity: Race and housing choice in Metropolitan America*. Washington, D.C.: Brookings Institution Press.

Chester, M. (2007). Proposed solutions for mobile home displacement. http://www.mitchellchaster.com/Mobile%20home%20Discussion.htm. Accessed 19 May 2009.

Cole, D. (1997). *Amazing pipeline stories: How building the trans-Alaska pipeline transformed life in the last frontier*. Fairbanks: Epicenter Press.

Corvin, A. (2010). Weak economy slows shutdowns of mobile home parks. Business Journal (Pudget Sound, Seattle). http://seattle.bizjournals.com/seattle/stories/2010/02/15/focus4.html. Accessed 10 Dec 2010.

Dwyer, R. (2007). Expanding homes and increasing inequalities: U.S. Housing Development and the residential segregation of the affluent. *Social Problems, 54,* 23–46. Accessed 5 Jan 2008.

Dwyer, R. (2010). Poverty, prosperity, and place: the shape of class segregation in the age of extremes. *Social Problems, 57,* 114–137. Accessed 13 May 2011.

Freedman, D. (2000). *Anchorage*. John Muir Publications.

Friedman, A. (2009). In down economy, trailer parks are given second glance. *New Jersey Real-Time News*. http://www.nj.com/news/index.ssf/2009/04/in_down_economy_trailers_parks.html. Accessed 13 Aug 2010.

Geary, B. (2008). Mobile home park residents caught in Catch-22: Paradise lost. *Independent Weekly* July 9, 2008. http://www.indyweek.com/indyweek/mobile-home-park-residents-caught-in-catch-22/Cont. Accessed 12 Sept 2008.

Genz, R. (2001). Why advocates need to rethink manufactured housing. *Housing Policy Debate, 12*(2), 393–414. Accessed 7 Oct 2006.

Hargot, A. (2008). The difficulty of displacement: Hallandale Beach bought a trailer park to eliminate it, but some residents are fighting back. Miami Sun Post, Feb. 13, 2008. http//www.corallakemhp.com/txthouse/msp02132008.html. Accessed 13 Aug 2010.

Hendrix, J. (2004). Mobile homes: Amidst stigma and displacement, new hope for affordable housing emerges. Next American City Magazine, July 2004. http://americancity.org/magazine/article/mobile-homes-amidst-stigma-and-displacement-h. Accessed 17 Oct 2006.

Kasarda, J. D. (1993). Inner city concentrated poverty and neighborhood distress: 1970–1990. *Housing Policy Debate, 4,* 243–302 (cited in Massey 1996). Accessed 13 May 2006.

Kiter Edwards, M. L. (2004). We're decent people: constructing and managing family identity in rural working-class communities. *Journal of Marriage and the Family, 66,* 515–529. Accessed 12 Sept 2008.

Kusenbach, M. (2009). Salvaging decency: Mobile home residents' strategies of managing the stigma of "Trailer" living. *Qualitative Sociology, 32,* 399–428. Accessed 4 Oct 2010.

Lee, M. R., Weil, F. D., & Shihadeh, E. S. (2007). The FEMA Trailer Park: Negative perceptions and the social structure of avoidance. *Sociological Spectrum, 27,* 741–766 (Albany). Accessed Nov 2011.

Lobao, L. M., Hooks, G., & Tickamyer, A. R. (Eds.). (2007). *The sociology of spatial inequality*. New York: State University of New York Press.
MacTavish, K., & Salamon, S. (2006). Pathways of youth development in a rural trailer park. *Family Relations, 55,* 163–174. Accessed 13 Aug 2010.
Massey, D. S. (1996). The age of extremes: Concentrated affluence and poverty in the twenty-first century. *Demography, 33,* 395–412. Accessed 28 May 2010.
Municipality of Anchorage. (2007). Analysis of impediments to fair housing choice. Department of Neighborhoods, Anchorage, AK. Anchorage, Alaska. http://www.muni.org. Personal communication.
National Association of Realtors. (2012). Social benefits of home ownership and stable housing. www.realtor.ovs/sites/…/social-benefits-of-stable-housing-2012-04.pdf. Accessed 29 Dec 2012.
Newburger, H. B., Birch, E. L., & Wachter, S. M. (2011). *Neighborhood and life chances: How place matters in modern America*. Philadelphia: University of Pennsylvania Press.
O'Malley, J. (2007). No place for home—Lazy Mountain's inhabitants say they can't afford to leave Eagle river trailer park residents face eviction. *Anchorage Daily News (AK)* Sunday, July 22, 2007. http://infoweb.newsbank.com/iw/Info Web. Accessed 12 Sept 2008.
Posey, K. G., Welniak, E., & Nelson, C. (2003). *Income in the American community survey: Comparisons to Census 2000*. Paper presented at the American Statistical Association Meetings, San Francisco, CA, (August). Accessed 13 May 2009.
Robinson, T. (2009). Preservation or redevelopment options, conditions, and risks facing mobile home parks in Anchorage, and the case for affordable housing. www.conservancy.umn.edu/bitstream/53765/1/Robinson%20Tyler.pdf. Accessed 11 Aug 2010.
Salamon, S. (2003). Mobile home communities. Encyclopedia of Community. Sage. www.sage-ereference.com/community/Article_n330.html. Accessed 13 May 2009.
Schell, S. (2006). Out with the old and in with the new-Redevelopment: As land grows scarce, old buildings may give way. *Anchorage Daily News (AK)* Tuesday, April 18, 2006. http://infoweb.newsbank.com/iw-search/we/InfoWeb. Accessed 13 Aug 2010.
Schoettler, J. (2010). Jacksonville residents to lose neighborhood. The Florida Times-Union. May 6. http://jacksonville.com/news/metro/2010-05-06/story/jacksonville-neighborhood-nearing-e. Accessed 16 Nov 2011.
Stephens, C. (2010). Highest best use concept drives city development. *Anchorage Daily News*, May 2, 2010. Accessed 13 Aug 2010.
U.S. Bureau of the Census. (2000). SF3, American Factfinder. Accessed 17 Oct 2006.
U.S. Bureau of the Census. (2011a). American Community Survey, (FAQ) Frequently Asked Questions. www.census.gov. Accessed 27 Sept 2012.
U.S. Bureau of the Census. (2011b). American Community Survey, 2009 Comparison quick guide. http://www.census.gov/acs/www/guidance_for_data_users/2009_comparison_quick_guide/. Accessed 9 Oct 2012.
Williams, R., Nesiba, R., & Diaz McConnell, E. (2005). The changing face of inequality in home mortgage lending. *Social Problems, 52,* 181–208. Accessed 13 May 2009.

Chapter 15
Geography is Destiny: Spatial Correlations in Poverty and Educational Attainment in a New Mexico School District

Srini Vasan, Adélamar Alcántara, Nomalanga Nefertari, Xiaomin Ruan and Jack Baker

Introduction

A number of previous studies suggest the existence of a "geography of opportunity" that is reflected in observed spatial co-patterning of poverty and educational attainment (Galster and Killen 1995; Mayer 2001; Rupasingha and Goetz 2007; Crandall and Weber 2004; Tate 2008; Orfield and Lee 2005; Briggs 2005). This spatial stratification of income and educational achievement has been identified in small areas of geography including neighborhoods (Curley 2005; Orfield and Lee, 2005; Voss et al. 2006), where a trend toward re-segregation of minority students has been observed nationwide (Orfield 2001; Orfield and Lee 2005). Within these microgeographic settings, researchers have identified complex—and often subtle—influences of social networks (Curley 2005), constrained housing choice (Oishi and Schimmack 2010; Saegert and Evans 2003; Fack and Grenet 2008), race- and socioeconomic-status-(SES)-based differential access to educational resources (Peske and Haycock 2006; Briggs 2005; Kozol 1991; Darling-Hammond 1998), race- and SES-based differential perceptions of opportunity (Oishi and Schimmack 2010; Curley 2005), and a negatively biased perception of the potential of students of color (Pigott and Cowen 2000; Orfield 2001) as contributors to the observed spatial patterning. The neighborhood-specific co-patterning of these relationships has been argued to have a collective effect that can override school environment and individual ability in predicting educational attainment (Garner and Raudenbush 1991; Ainsworth 2002). Borman et al. (2004) has argued that these environmental factors combine to make geographically segregated and impoverished schools "institutions of concentrated disadvantage," and a number of studies have related poverty and educational attainment to job opportunity (Friedman and Lichter 1998; Crandall and Weber 2004). Rupasingha and Goetz (2007) concluded that the most resilient poverty was to be found in neighborhoods where a

S. Vasan (✉)
Department of Mathematics/Statistics, University of New Mexico, Albuquerque, NM, USA
e-mail: svasan01@unm.edu

A. Alcántara · N. Nefertari · X. Ruan · J. Baker
Geospatial and Population Studies, University of New Mexico, Albuquerque, NM, USA

M. N. Hoque, L. B. Potter (eds.), *Emerging Techniques in Applied Demography*, Applied Demography Series 4, DOI 10.1007/978-94-017-8990-5_15,

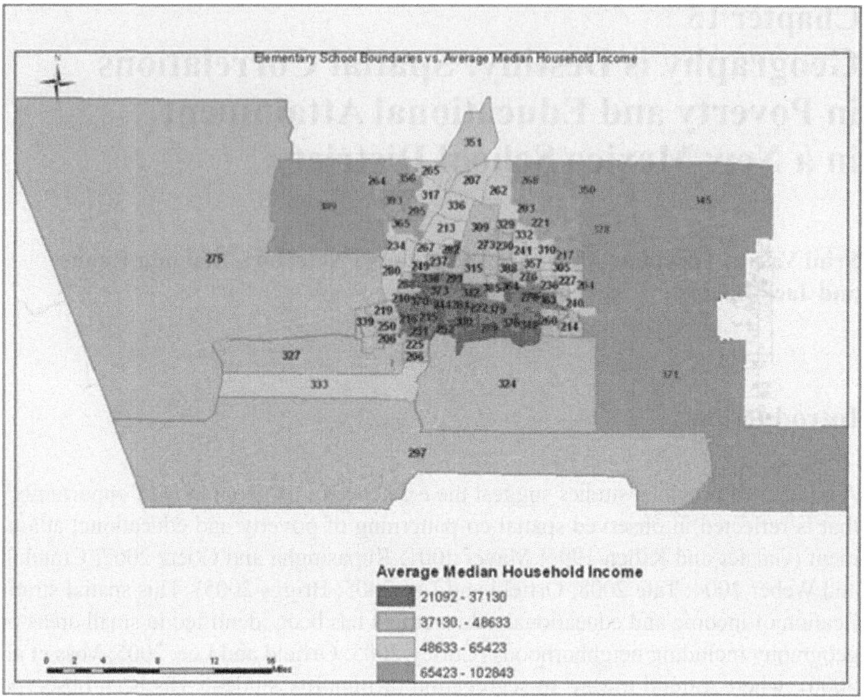

Fig. 15.1 Median household income averaged over elementary school attendance boundaries

higher proportion of permanent residents were persons of color. While it is clear from this body of research that microdeterminants underlay spatial patternings of poverty and educational attainment, these studies also suggest that geography itself may serve as a useful preliminary indicator of access to critical opportunities and resources vital to academic success (Galster and Killen 1995).

In New Mexico, as in these studies, clear spatial dependency is observable in poverty indicators such as median income or proportion of students receiving free or reduced lunches (Figs. 15.1 and 15.2). The individual elementary school attendance boundaries are shown in Fig. 15.3 along with the 2010 census tracts. Figs. 15.1 and 15.2 focus on the largest school district in New Mexico (Albuquerque Public Schools), which is home to 32% of the state's population and the largest state school district. Graduation rates within this school district reflect a nationwide trend toward higher drop-out rates for students in general, and for those of color in particular. While rates for Asian students graduating are high (84.8%), only 3 out of 4 Caucasian students (74.4%) and significantly fewer Hispanic (60.8%), African American (58.7%), and American Indian students (44.4%) graduated from high school.[1] Statewide, 25–40% of families live at

[1] 4-Year Cohort Graduation Rates, Class of 2010. New Mexico Public Education Department, 2011.

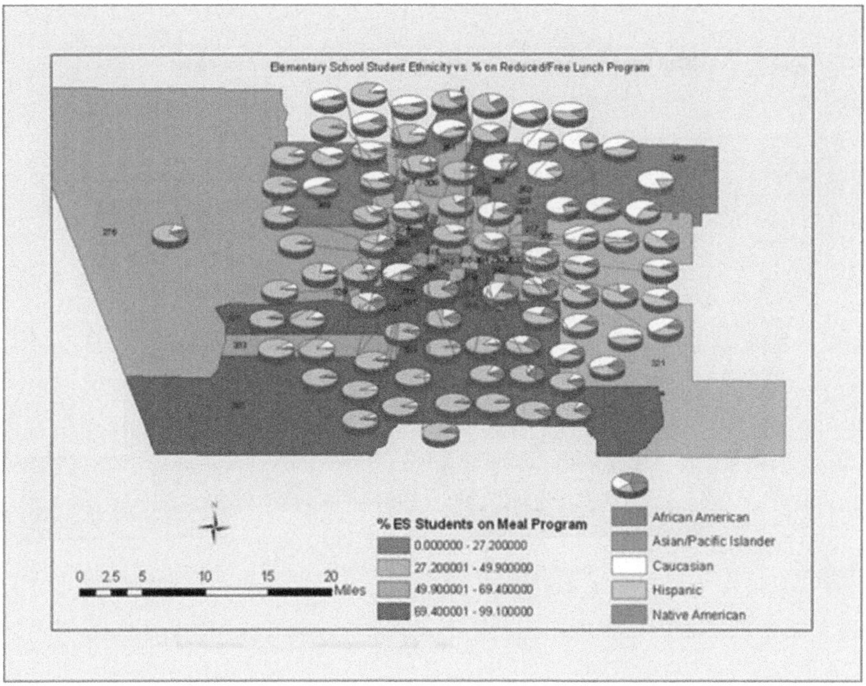

Fig. 15.2 Percentage of students in school lunch program versus elementary school student ethnicity (pie chart)

or below the poverty line, and the Albuquerque Public Schools reflect much of this variation within this single county. This variation is reflected in the elementary school attendance areas observed in Fig. 15.1, where median annual household incomes range between a low of $ 21,092 and a high of $ 102,843 in a clearly spatially-dependent manner. Lowest incomes are observed in the areas known locally as the South Valley and other highly Hispanic areas (in red) and the highest incomes are observed in the Northeast Heights and East Mountain areas. These observations fit local knowledge well, and observable conditions in terms of housing and other anecdotal indicators of income differences reflect these patterns strongly. The ethnicity breakdown by elementary school attendance boundary is depicted in the pie chart in Fig. 15.2. From Fig. 15.2, it is seen that the highest percentage of students enrolled in the meal program (a proxy of poverty level and inversely proportional to the median household income shown in Fig. 15.1) is strongly correlated to the highest proportion of students of color.

While public discourse in New Mexico in recent times has often reflected a strong concern over educational attainment, in general, to date no study has attempted to describe spatial co-patterning of poverty and educational attainment. This study attempts to fill this gap in our current knowledge by using spatial analytic methods to link indicators of poverty and socioeconomic status, including poverty rates, median household income, indicators of housing values, and ethnicity, to student

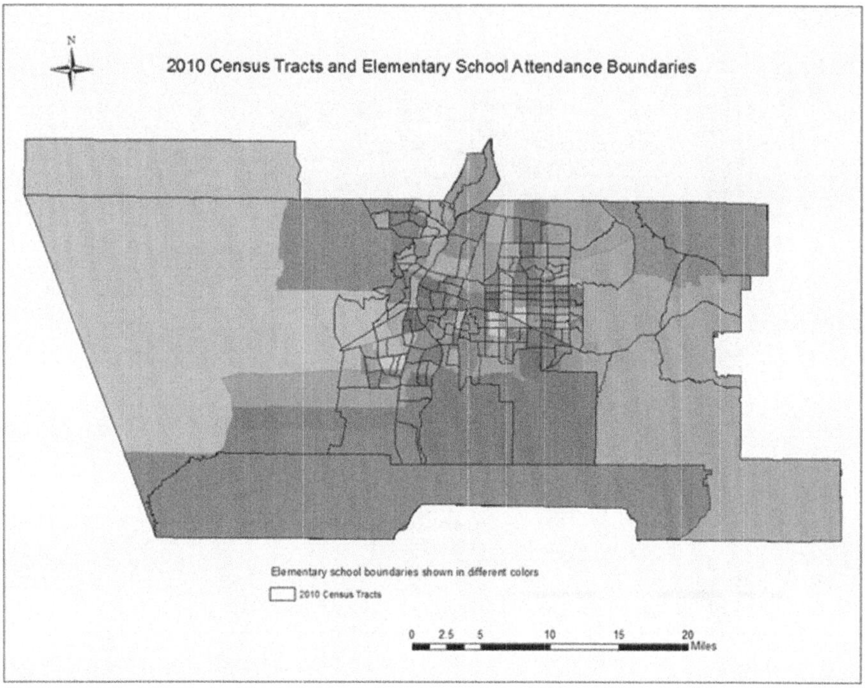

Fig. 15.3 Census tracts and elementary school attendance areas

proficiency examination scores reported at the level of school attendance boundaries as part of Adequate Yearly Progress (AYP) reporting standards set by the federal government. Specifically, the paper tests the general hypothesis that socioeconomic status and educational attainment are positively related (or, conversely, that low socioeconomic status predicts poorer educational attainment) and that these patterns reflect spatial clustering. These hypotheses are tested for school years 2004, 2005, and 2006. Next, using AYP data from 2011, this paper examines whether differences in high school graduation rates in the schools that these students eventually transfer to for a secondary education can be linked to the elementary school proficiency data; in other words, the paper seeks to ascertain whether early educational geography translates into destiny in terms of overall educational success reflected in matriculation rates. The results are discussed in light of their novel contribution to the literature on the geography of poverty and educational attainment. Limitations of the current study are reviewed and directions for future research are outlined. Last, the implications for public policy specific to New Mexico are reviewed.

Table 15.1 Variables and concepts measured in spatial regression

Study Variables	Geographic Scale	Concept Measured	Source
Independent Variables			
Student Characteristics			
Number Enrolled in Elementary School	School	Proxy for student density	New Mexico Public Education Department, Albuquerque Public Schools: Administrative Data.
School Characteristics			
% Students by School in Reduced Meal Program	School	Proxy for poverty	New Mexico Public Education Department, Albuquerque Public Schools: Administrative Data.
Population Characteristics			
Median Household Income	School (normalized)	Relative community affluence	American Community Survey, Normalized to School District Boundaries
Percent Single Family Homes		Relative community affluence	
Percent Students Foreign Born		Community cultural characteristics	
Median Age of Home		Stability of neigborhood	
Median Home Value		Neighborhood characteristics	
Median Numbers or Rooms		Neighborhood characteristics	
Dependent Variables			
Percent students proficient in Math, Reading and Science (standardized tests) in 2004, 2005 and 2006 in grades 3, 4 and 5 by school	School	Student learning outcome	New Mexico Public Education Department, Albuquerque Public Schools: Administrative Data.

Materials and Methods

Study Population: New Mexico and Albuquerque Public Schools

Albuquerque is the largest city in New Mexico, home to 32 % of the state population and the largest state school district. Albuquerque Public Schools (APS) graduation rates for 2010 reflect a nationwide trend toward higher dropout rates for students in general and students of color in particular. Student enrollments by ethnicity range from 72 to 98 % minority, with 80 % of APS students qualifying for the free (or reduced price) lunch program. Poverty is a common denominator throughout the state, with 25 to 40 % of New Mexico families living at or below the poverty line. The APS school district was chosen because it is the largest in the state, with more than 40 % of the state's population residing here. The results of this study are expected to be generalizable to other metropolitan school districts of similar size in the country.

Variables, Operationalization, and Hypotheses

The variables utilized in this study, the concepts they are designed to measure, and corresponding data sources are listed in Table 15.1 for the elementary school analysis. Socioeconomic status was operationalized to include median household income, the proportion of students enrolled in reduced price meal programs (a proxy for poverty), and characteristics of home value (age, estimated value, and number of rooms). Though an imperfect measure, total enrollment within elementary schools was included to capture the effect of student density. Outcome measures of student performance included the percent of students who were graded as "proficient" in the grades targeted by AYP guidelines for testing: 3rd, 4th, and 5th grades. The analyses conducted were performed for years 2004, 2005, and 2006. These data all represent aggregate level data within the context of an ecologic study. Data were drawn and formulated from various sources, each of which is listed in Table 15.1.

Study Design and Analytic Methods

The research reported here constitutes an ecological study with both point-in-time and lagged-effect modeling approaches. First, an identity operation was performed in ESRI's Arc-GIS 10.0 for school attendance boundaries in order to inherit the socioeconomic information. ArcGIS' ArcMap software was employed, utilizing the 88 records for the elementary schools as the input layer and the 141 records in the census tract demographic layer as the identity layer. This operation produced a new layer with 614 parcels of land. Average characteristics such as poverty level or median household income for each elementary school attendance boundary was then calculated to account for the existence of multiple census tracts within school districts (see Fig. 15.3). Next, the land layer was dissolved in ArcMap to restore the original 88 school boundaries. This final layer resulted in each elementary school attendance boundary having its own normalized characteristic of poverty rate and income. This layer was used for statistical analysis and information display.

Spatial autocorrelation of variables was conducted to assess the presence, if any, of neighborhood clustering effects. For example, does high or low average poverty rate in one school attendance boundary result in a high or low rate for its contiguous neighbor? ArcMap's local Moran's *I* (Moran 1950) procedure was performed to answer this question for poverty rate, median household income, and the proportion of students enrolled in free or reduced price school lunch program (a proxy for the local poverty rate). For example, if the poverty rate were to be randomly distributed in space over the elementary school attendance boundaries, then Moran's *I* would be zero. If the poverty rates are perfectly dispersed (i.e., uniformly distributed across the geography), then Moran's *I* would be −1. However, if one notices spatial clustering of the school zones, for example, high poverty areas in close proximity of other high poverty areas (and similarly low poverty areas in contiguity with other low poverty areas), then Moran's *I* would be closer to 1. In the foregoing, one could use median household income or proportion of students in reduced price meal program instead and evaluate Moran's *I* as well. When two variables are involved, a procedure such as bivariate LISA (Local Indicators of Spatial Association) could be run using Geo Da software (Anselin et al. 2006) to evaluate the simultaneous spatial clustering effect of two variables (e.g., student performance in Reading versus Math or Grade 3 student proficiency rate in 2004 versus 2005).

Descriptive statistics for several variables were computed for the 2004–2006 time period: proficiency percentages for grades 3, 4, or 5; proficiency percentages in Reading, Math, and Science; school enrollment size; and percentage of students

Table 15.2 Summary statistics of variables, elementary schools study

	Dependent variables					
	Grade 3, Proficient %	Grade 4, Proficient %	Grade 5, Proficient %	Reading, Proficient %	Math, Proficient %	Science, Proficient %
Mean	58.9	49.4	45.7	55.1	40.4	58.4
Standard Deviation	14.5	16.4	15.9	15.7	14.9	15.7
Minimum	27.6	14.4	14.1	22.1	10.9	23.8
Maximum	88.2	86	81	87.1	76.7	91

	Independent Variables							
	% Students in lunch program*	School Enrollment	Home size (number of rooms)	Median Home Price $	Median age of home, years	Proportion of single home units, %	Proportion under 18 years foreign born, %	Median household income $
Mean	58.3	519	5.4	173,542	35.1	72	12.3	48,792
Standard Deviation	27.3	203	0.95	76,883	16.2	20.3	44.6	15,878
Minimum	0	220	3	153,800	27	12.2	10.8	26,649
Maximum	99.1	1347	7.8	553,500	66	100	9.4	102,843

*free/reduced price lunch program; Sample size = 83; data from 2004–2006, Albuquerque Public Schools

enrolled in free or reduced price school lunch program (see Table 15.2). The student proficiencies were calculated for each grade or for each subject by averaging over the three years, 2004, 2005, and 2006. Finally, a regression model was run for each dependent variable (proficiency) as a function of the independent variables, including housing characteristics (home size, home price, single unit or not, and age of the house), student characteristics (proportion foreign born), community median household income, and school characteristics (school enrollment size and proportion of students in school lunch program). In the first stage of the elementary school analysis, the school characteristics were considered to be the primary variables, and it is hypothesized that proportion of students in the lunch program (a proxy for poverty level) (hypothesis 1) and the enrollment size (a proxy for the student/teacher ratio) (hypothesis 2) would be negatively correlated to proficiency in various grades and subjects. It is difficult to hypothesize *a priori* how the rest of the secondary variables would be correlated, if at all, to student proficiency; this aspect is investigated in the second stage of the elementary school analysis.

It is well known that student proficiency is inversely related to poverty level. What is less understood is the role housing and student acculturation characteristics (measured by proportion of foreign born students) have on student proficiency. Since the APS school performance data were not broken down by race/ethnicity, this variable could not be studied.

Spatial regression is an important analytical tool of this study. Classical methods (such as ordinary least square (OLS) regression) assume that observations are

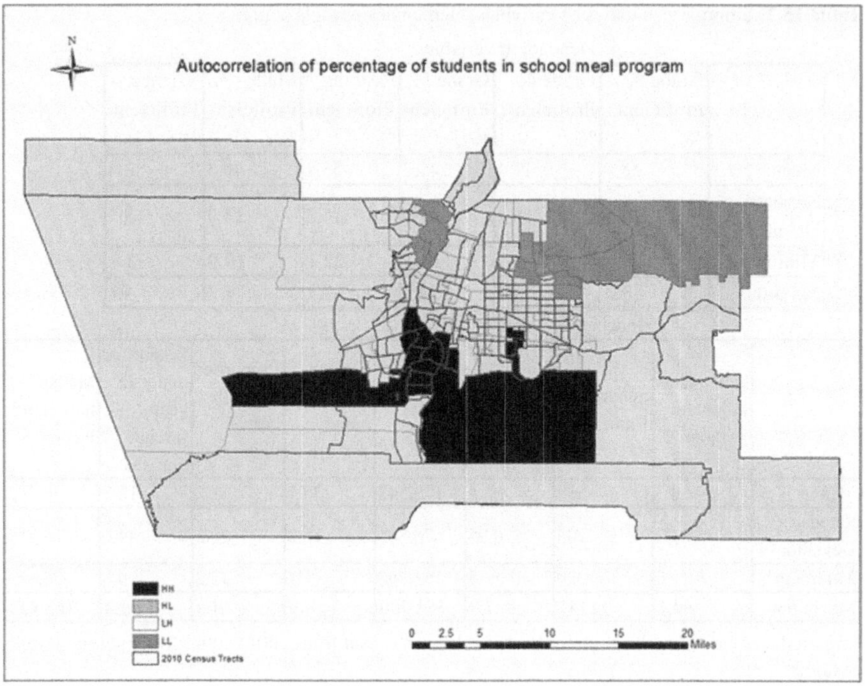

Fig. 15.4 Spatial autocorrelation of the variable percentage of students in free/reduced school meal program

independently and identically distributed and not correlated. But sociological variables such as poverty rate and income could have a strong neighborhood clustering effect (i.e., spatial autocorrelation), resulting in inaccurate estimates of the regression coefficients and research conclusions[2,3,4]. Thus, in the following analyses on elementary school student proficiency, the spatial regression effect is taken into account. Spatial regression methodology would separate out any clustering effects into a lumped quantity known as the spatial lag. Once this effect is separated out, the regression coefficients (and their corresponding statistical levels of significance) would truly reflect the effect that each of the independent variables has on the dependent variable. This enables confounding effects of geographical proximity to be separated and analyzed separately. However, prior to running a spatial regression model and presenting the results as shown in the next section, it is instructive to understand the spatial clustering effects of some of the independent and dependent variables. Figure 15.4 illustrates the spatial clustering effect observed

[2] Fowler, C.S. CDSE Statistics Workshop on Spatial Modeling, May 3, 2011. Online: http://csde.washington.edu/services/gis/workshops/Resources/SPREG_Presentation.pdf.

[3] Spatial Regression: A Brief Introduction. Business Intelligence Solutions. Online: http://www.bisolutions.us/A-Brief-Introduction-to-Spatial-Regression.php.

[4] Ward, M and Gleditsch, An Introduction to Spatial Regression Models in the Social Sciences. Online: http://www.duke.edu/web/methods/pdfs/SRMbook.pdf.

Table 15.3 Spatial autocorrelation coefficients and their significances

Variable	Global Moran's *I*	Variance	*z*-score	*p*-value
Percentage of Students in Reduced Meal Program	0.525675	0.00378	8.75457	0.000000
Performance in 2004	0.428985	0.00375	7.20699	0.000000
Performance in 2005	0.412764	0.00375	6.94199	0.000000
Performance in 2006	0.409488	0.00375	6.88921	0.000000
Performance in Reading	0.422559	0.00375	7.09706	0.000000
Performance in Math	0.368119	0.00372	6.23331	0.000000
Performance in Science	0.467475	0.00375	7.83251	0.000000
Performance in Grade 3	0.331703	0.00375	5.6132	0.000000
Performance in Grade 4	0.436442	0.00375	7.3304	0.000000
Performance in Grade 5	0.43314	0.00375	7.27704	0.000000

for the percentage of students enrolled in the school lunch program. The areas symbolized in red correspond to "High-High" (H-H in the legend), where a high poverty rate school attendance boundary is clustered among other high poverty school boundaries as in the southern portions of the city. Strong clustering effects of low performance in reading, math, and science and low performance in grades 3, 4, and 5 were also observed as evidenced by statistically significant Moran's *I* statistics (see Table 15.3). Strong bivariate spatial-temporal autocorrelation was equally noted for proficiency data for 2004 versus 2005 and 2005 versus 2006 (all grades, all subjects), with the poorly performing areas again concentrated consistently in the southern area of the city.

The strong spatial autocorrelation observed in the proportion of students in the free or reduced lunch program (Fig. 15.4) was accounted for by the regression models. Proficiency numbers obtained during 2004, 2005, and 2006 were aggregated for an average proficiency for grades 3, 4, and 5 students and in reading, math, and science. These six dependent variables were regressed over the independent variables of school enrollment, proportion of students in the school lunch program, housing characteristics (average home size, median home price, median age of the house, and proportion of single household units), student characteristics (proportion foreign born), community average median household income, and neighborhood cluster effects (spatial autocorrelation or spatial lag) in two stages. In the second phase of this research, the authors follow the elementary school students through middle and high school in a pseudo-cohort fashion to determine how high school graduation rates correlate with the elementary school performance/geography to test the following hypotheses: (1) Is a student's destiny for successful graduation from high school determined by the economic characteristics of the neighborhood in which the student attended elementary school? (2) Are there other factors such as elementary school, middle school, and high school performance measures, class size, and demographics that affect the graduation rate from high school?"

The 2011–2012 proficiency data was used for analysis of high school graduation rates in phase 2. Students from the 88 elementary schools in the Albuquerque Public Schools district completing elementary school attend one of 27 APS middle schools and then transition to one of 12 high schools. School feeder routes (elementary → middle →high school) were identified geospatially using overlay operations of school attendance boundaries. Although there are only 12 high schools with individual high school graduation percentages in the sample, the origin of these high school students, as per the assumptions of the model, is from the original 27 feeder middle schools and 88 feeder elementary schools. The implicit assumption is that there is no migration of students among schools as well as no in- or out-migration of students from the schools to outside the school attendance/county/state/country boundaries during the K-12 phase. A model was run using the dependent variable of high school graduation rate and independent variables of school enrollment and math and reading proficiency in elementary, middle, and high school, attendance rates, and demographic variables, the data corresponding to the 2011–2012 school year.

Results

In stage 1 of the elementary school performance analysis, only the primary independent variables related to the school, namely enrollment size and percentage of students in the reduced price meal program, were considered. The dependent variables were Grade 3, 4, and 5 proficiency averaged over the three years, 2004–2006, as well as reading, math, and science proficiency averaged over the same three years. Spatial weight using queen contiguity was used, i.e., the neighborhood was defined as all the school attendance boundaries that touch the particular school attendance boundary of interest on the sides and vertices. The results of the spatial regression are shown in Table 15.4.

Table 15.4 shows very strong spatial neighborhood clustering effects for math proficiency ($p=0.0173$) and weaker effects for Grade 4 proficiency ($p=0.0822$) and science proficiency ($p=0.0907$). Elementary school student performance on standardized tests is strongly and negatively correlated with the proportion of students in the free/reduced price meal program ($p=0.0000$) and school enrollment size ($p=0.0080$–0.05) depending on the grade or subject. The end result of high R-square values (0.615–0.821) is an indication that, despite aggregation, a clear relationship could be established between student performance, the percentage of students in school meal programs, and enrollment size. The inverse relationships between elementary school proficiencies and poverty and school enrollment size, as well as any spatial lag effects, have been identified.

In stage 2 of the elementary school analysis, in addition to the two primary school-related independent variables shown in Table 15.4, six other independent variables related to student and housing characteristics, namely, median household income, percentage of foreign born population under 18 years of age, median age of the home, median household value, median number of rooms in the household, and percentage of single family residents (i.e. living in a home as opposed to an apartment), were considered. The same six dependent variables of proficiencies in

Table 15.4 Spatial regression analysis results with two primary independent variables only

Variable	Coefficient	Standard Error	z_value	Probability	Model R^2 value
Dependent Variable: Grade 3 proficiency					
Spatial Lag	0.1320266	0.09250636	1.427217	0.1535	0.615
Constant	77.91945	7.583669	10.27464	0.0000	
Enrollment	-0.00977247	0.004744913	-2.059568	0.0394**	
Reduced Meal	-0.3721078	0.04127908	-9.01444	0.0000***	
Dependent Variable: Grade 4 proficiency					
Spatial Lag	0.1410607	0.08116509	1.737948	0.0822*	0.771
Constant	75.46071	6.27453	12.02651	0.0000	
Enrollment	-0.01072057	0.03945933	-11.92953	0.0000***	
Reduced Meal	-0.4707315	0.03945933	-11.92953	0.0000***	
Dependent Variable: Grade 5 proficiency					
Spatial Lag	0.1186098	0.08207464	1.445146	0.1484	0.776
Constant	72.99909	5.969793	12.22808	0.0000	
Enrollment	-0.01057688	0.003987834	-2.652286	0.0080***	
Reduced Meal	-0.4657184	0.03828291	-12.16518	0.0000***	
Dependent Variable: Reading proficiency					
Spatial Lag	0.0962956	0.07294631	1.320089	0.1868	0.799
Constant	82.15085	5.926905	13.86067	0.0000	
Enrollment	-0.008761601	0.003700134	-2.367915	0.0179***	
Reduced Meal	-0.4758448	0.03471009	-13.70912	0.0000***	
Dependent Variable: Math proficiency					
Spatial Lag	0.2441089	0.1025697	2.379932	0.0173**	0.616
Constant	55.96954	6.762024	8.27704	0.0000	
Enrollment	-0.009529536	0.004883451	-1.951394	0.0510*	
Reduced Meal	-0.3495093	0.04479889	-7.80174	0.0000***	
Dependent Variable: Science proficiency					
Spatial Lag	0.1139105	0.06734686	1.691401	0.0907*	0.821
Constant	85.7427	5.751032	14.9091	0.0000	
Enrollment	-0.01243312	0.003517584	-3.534563	0.0004***	
Reduced Meal	-0.4711527	0.0326414	-14.4342	0.0000***	

***$p<0.01$ **$p<0.05$ *$p<0.10$

grade 3, grade 4, grade 5, reading, math, and science were regressed over the eight independent variables and the results are shown in Table 15.5. As before, spatial auto-correlation effects were taken into account using a lag term.

The following are the salient observations from Table 15.5: (1) the R^2 values have improved with the inclusion of additional explanatory variables; (2) the proportion of students in the free/reduced meal program continues to be a highly significant explanatory variable in all the six cases; (3) the enrollment is significant ($p<0.05$) in five of the six cases; (4) spatial clustering effects have completely disappeared; and (5) except for science proficiency, all proficiencies are positively and significantly correlated to the proportion of foreign born under 18 years of age.

In addition, there appears to be a consistent and positive correlation (at different levels of significance) among the proficiencies and age of the home and median household income.

Table 15.5 Spatial regression analysis results with eight independent variables including student and housing characteristics

Dependent Variable: Grade 3 proficiency					
Variable	Coefficient	Standard Error	*z*-value	Probability	Model R^2 value
Spatial Lag	0.06176801	0.09473326	0.6520203	0.5143879	0.678355
Constant	76.32757	11.10972	6.87034	0.0000000	
Enrollment	-0.0111719	0.005067046	-2.204815	0.0274670**	
Reduced Meal	-0.371779	0.06158921	-6.03643	0.0000000***	
Household Income	0.000215459	0.000120856	1.78278	0.0746221*	
% Foreign Born (under 18)	0.3460303	0.1245288	2.778717	0.0054575***	
House Age	0.1059492	0.07681946	1.379197	0.1678342	
House Value	2.014123×10^{-5}	1.963735×10^{-5}	1.025659	0.3050522	
Number of Rooms	-4.140039	2.509569	-1.649701	0.0990040*	
Single Family Dwelling	0.09182715	0.0892338	1.029062	0.3034504	
Dependent Variable: Grade 4 proficiency					
Variable	Coefficient	Standard Error	*z*-value	Probability	Model R^2 value
Spatial Lag	0.1037633	0.08723885	1.189417	0.2342758	0.798284
Constant	73.22427	9.754314	7.50686	0.0000000	
Enrollment	-0.008583963	0.004535826	-1.892481	0.0584268*	
Reduced Meal	-0.5188985	0.05567736	-9.319739	0.0000000***	
Household Income	4.328329×10^{-5}	0.000110174	0.3928621	0.6944214	
% Foreign Born (under 18)	0.2221281	0.1118275	1.986347	0.0469947**	
House Age	0.139424	0.06965787	2.001554	0.0453326**	
House Value	1.743085×10^{-5}	1.75714×10^{-5}	0.9920014	0.3211968	
Number of Rooms	-1.908803	2.250405	-0.8482041	0.3963242	
Single Family Dwelling	0.04174726	0.08048587	0.5186905	0.6039766	
Dependent Variable: Grade 5 proficiency					
Variable	Coefficient	Standard Error	*z*-value	Probability	Model R^2 value
Spatial Lag	-0.01136494	0.08688769	-0.1308004	0.8959332	0.815716
Constant	61.31493	8.970219	6.835389	0.0000000	
Enrollment	-0.009697157	0.004217171	-2.299446	0.0214796**	
Reduced Meal	-0.4404241	0.05169766	-8.519226	0.0000000***	
Household Income	0.000251017	0.000103826	2.417657	0.0156208**	
% Foreign Born (under 18)	0.2453694	0.1039108	2.361345	0.0182087**	
House Age	0.1377308	0.06472695	2.127874	0.0333474**	
House Value	2.323176×10^{-5}	1.63321×10^{-5}	1.42246	0.1548928	
Number of Rooms	-0.2801833	2.095422	-0.1337121	0.8936302	
Single Family Dwelling	-0.09919975	0.07497583	-1.32309	0.1858057	

***$p<0.01$ **$p<0.05$ *$p<0.10$

In phase 2 of our analysis, several assumptions were made in order to follow the elementary school students all the way through high school graduation in a pseudo-cohort fashion. The elementary school students complete their fifth grade and attend a middle school for which their own elementary school is a feeder. Similarly, after completing grade 8, those students will attend the high school for which their own middle school is the feeder. It is assumed that in the 12 years that elapse from K through 12, there are no in- or out-migrations of students from one school attendance boundary to another or to/from a different geography altogether. These

Table 15.5 (continued)

Dependent Variable: Reading proficiency					
Variable	Coefficient	Standard Error	*z*-value	Probability	Model R^2 value
Spatial Lag	0.03816971	0.07719584	0.494453	0.6209863	0.82727
Constant	76.72348	8.662699	8.856764	0.0000000	
Enrollment	-0.008671612	0.004009196	-2.16293	0.0305464**	
Reduced Meal	-0.4864771	0.04911418	-9.905024	0.0000000***	
Household Income	0.000157372	9.750196×10^{-5}	1.614043	0.106518	
% Foreign Born (under 18)	0.2548942	0.09882861	2.579154	0.0099043***	
House Age	0.1071439	0.06143994	1.74388	0.0811798*	
House Value	8.835227×10^{-5}	1.552271×10^{-5}	0.5691808	0.5692334	
Number of Rooms	-1.022824	1.995364	-0.5126003	0.6082309	
Single Family Dwelling	-0.02089831	0.07140771	-0.2926618	0.7697808	
Dependent Variable: Math proficiency					
Variable	Coefficient	Standard Error	*z*-value	Probability	Model R^2 value
Spatial Lag	0.1155102	0.1069017	1.080527	0.2799076	0.701403
Constant	48.3737	10.70367	4.519357	0.0000062	
Enrollment	-0.009652621	0.005038416	-1.915805	0.0553898*	
Reduced Meal	-0.3800553	0.06137937	-6.191906	0.0000000***	
Household Income	0.000218046	0.000122024	1.786912	0.0739516*	
% Foreign Born (under 18)	0.4437427	0.1236211	3.589539	0.0003313***	
House Age	0.1780731	0.07658703	2.325108	0.0200662**	
House Value	2.823305×10^{-5}	1.950584×10^{-5}	1.447415	0.1477807	
Number of Rooms	-2.991815	2.489473	-1.201786	0.2294464	
Single Family Dwelling	0.04439267	0.08854103	0.5013796	0.616104	
Dependent Variable: Science proficiency					
Variable	Coefficient	Standard Error	*z*-value	Probability	Model R^2 value
Spatial Lag	0.06390375	0.07290402	0.8765463	0.380733	0.836002
Constant	85.00638	8.560515	9.930054	0.0000000	
Enrollment	-0.0108406	0.003920292	-2.765252	0.0056880**	
Reduced Meal	-0.4605867	0.04794441	-9.606682	0.0000000***	
Household Income	0.000108076	9.485045×10^{-5}	1.139432	0.2545231	
% Foreign Born (under 18)	0.1053714	0.09662269	1.090545	0.2754734	
House Age	0.08924108	0.06012743	1.484199	0.1377561	
House Value	2.130011×10^{-5}	1.520334×10^{-5}	1.401015	0.1612098	
Number of Rooms	-2.334398	1.945072	-1.20016	0.2300772	
Single Family Dwelling	0.01661664	0.06956072	0.2388796	0.811199	

***$p<0.01$ **$p<0.05$ *$p<0.10$

assumptions enable the modeling of high school graduation rate as a function of middle school and elementary school variables, as well as a few socioeconomic variables. Table 15.6 shows the results of the analysis. An adjusted R^2 value of 0.913 is obtained from the regression model. In addition to poverty rate being significantly ($p=0.005$) and negatively correlated, other parameters emerge significant to the high school graduation rate. These include reading proficiency in high school ($p=0.000$) and middle school ($p=0.043$) and middle school attendance rate ($p=0.006$), with all three variables positively correlated, and middle school enrollment ($p=0.016$), which is negatively correlated. An unexpected (and difficult to

Table 15.6 Results of high school graduation rates analysis

Dependent Variable: High School Graduation Rate

Model	Unstandardized	Coefficients	Standardized Coefficients	*t*	Significance (*p*)
Independent Variables	B	Std. Error	Beta		
Constant	-417.339	170.545		-2.447	0.017
ES_Math_Prof[a]	0.047	0.081	0.062	0.578	0.565
ES_Rdg_Prof[b]	-0.03	0.091	-0.039	-0.33	0.742
ES_Num_Enrol[c]	0.003	0.007	0.026	0.475	0.636
ES_Att_Rate[d]	0.007	0.677	0.001	0.011	0.991
Tract_Pop[e]	0.000	0.000	0.023	0.607	0.546
Median_Age[f]	0.000	0.09	0.000	-0.001	0.999
Pov09[g]	-0.219	0.075	-0.17	-2.931	0.005
Pct_Minority[h]	0.053	0.04	0.083	1.304	0.196
MedHHInc09[k]	-0.00002828	0.000	-0.045	-0.746	0.458
HS_Math_Prof[l]	0.08	0.084	0.106	0.951	0.345
HS_Rdg_Prof[m]	0.726	0.1	0.743	7.235	0.000
HS_Num_Enrol[n]	0.017	0.01	0.114	1.828	0.072
MS_Att_Rate[o]	4.456	1.577	0.187	2.825	0.006
MS_Num_Enrol[p]	-0.009	0.004	-0.167	-2.463	0.016
MS_Math_Prof[q]	-0.265	0.126	-0.329	-2.106	0.039
MS_Rdg_Prof[r]	0.198	0.096	0.252	2.067	0.043

R^2=0.930; Adjusted R^2=0.913

Explanation of variables (see Table 6 from previous page)

[a]Elementary School Math Per cent Proficient	[b]Elementary School Reading Per cent Proficient
[c]Elementary School Enrollment Size	[d]Elementary School Attendance Rate
[e]Population of Census Tract (Elementary School)	[f]Median Age of Census Tract Population
[g]Poverty Rate 2005-2009 ACS Data	[h]Per cent of population of color
[k]Median Household Income 2005-2009 ACS Data	
[l]High School Math Per cent Proficient	[m]High School Reading Per cent Proficient
[n]High School Enrollment Size	
[o]Middle School Attendance Rate	[p]Middle School Enrollment Size
[q]High School Math Per cent Proficient	[r]Middle School Reading Per cent Proficient

explain) result is the significant negative correlation between middle school math proficiency and high school graduation rate ($p=0.039$). The underlying assumptions behind this model as well as the models for elementary school performance have not been validated yet. The strength of the inverse relationship between high school graduation rate and the poverty rate averaged over the elementary school attendance boundaries feeding into high school boundaries is further illustrated in a pivot table analysis where lower graduation rates are associated with high poverty rates and *vice versa* (Table 15.7).

Table 15.7 Pivot table analysis of high school graduation rates (versus Poverty Rates)

High School Name	Graduation Rate %	Average ES Poverty%
Volcano Vista	85.20	7.0
Cibola	76.37	7.3
El Dorado	79.77	7.3
La Cueva	84.89	8.4
Del Norte	62.15	11.6
Valley	67.31	11.9
Manzano	67.83	14.0
Sandia	76.71	15.3
West Mesa	53.53	16.6
Highland	46.9	19.3
Rio Grande	49.65	22.5
Albuquerque	58.08	24.8

Discussion

This research supports the hypothesis that poverty level is a predictor of student success. Significant spatial and temporal autocorrelations are demonstrated in response to Hypothesis 1 for elementary schools. The observed spatial clustering effect of an important variable such as high poverty or low school proficiency indicates the need for a local focus on the elementary schools in high poverty and contiguous neighborhoods. We also found significant "high-high" spatial autocorrelation of poverty in the southeast, south-central, and southwestern portions of the city. The strong temporal autocorrelation of elementary school proficiencies over a 3 year period (2004–2006) suggests a chronic poverty problem in these areas. It is also seen from the second phase of our study that a high poverty level translates to lower high school graduation rates. A solution to the poverty issue is to change the makeup of the geography itself. Current unpublished studies by these authors[5] show that low income affordable housing in Albuquerque, New Mexico, is still predominantly located in higher poverty rate areas, and higher poverty areas are predominantly located in census tracts where the land use ratio of residential to commercial use is relatively low. In Albuquerque, even within the so-called "mixed use" areas, commercial parcels are segregated from residential parcels. True mixed development where there is integration of people of different incomes as well as of different zoning types in one neighborhood does not exist here.

---

[5] Work in progress, *Poverty, Zoning and Land Use: A Case Study for Albuquerque, New Mexico* and *Environmental Equity Geospatial Analysis of Albuquerque*

The other theme we have observed consistently is the role of the school enrollment size, which in effect is a surrogate for a student/teacher ratio. High student/teacher ratios could also potentially result in higher dropout rates as well as lower student proficiency. With increasing budget cuts in education, one has to come up with innovative ways of enhancing the use of technology in classrooms as well as increasing community participation via using volunteers for after-school programs such as tutoring or mentoring and thus supplementing regular academic instruction.

Conclusions

The attitudes and structural mechanisms perpetuating systemic inequities in schools have been explored, described, and analyzed in depth by social scientists for at least two decades. Researchers have also named the most favorable conditions for student learning, including positive school atmosphere and enlightened administrative leadership (Johnson and Uline 2005), collective teacher efficacy (Tschannen-Moran 2004), qualified and experienced classroom teachers (Boyd et al. 2005), racial congruence between teachers and students (Pigott and Cowen 2000; Dee 2004), and positive regard for student competencies regardless of SES (Auwarter and Aruguete 2008). Despite investigative and tactical efforts to redress race and class disparities, the achievement gap between low and high SES students prevails. Students of color experience an even higher risk of disadvantage facing race as well as class barriers. This study has identified some areas where city planners, the Public Education Department, and school officials can work together to achieve more equitable student performance across geographies.

The study limitations are as follows: (1) Microdata comprised of individual student records would enable us to track students with precision. Without individual student records, researchers are unable to isolate unique characteristics of students (including protective and risk factors) or schools that influence student performance results. Aggregate proficiency data were used instead to study APS students' performance including matriculation. (2) The study needs to be validated by replicating it in future years and/or in other similar school districts.

Federal law mandates that student data are protected from public scrutiny, limiting the ability of researchers to capture meaningful data. While the vulnerability and protection of children are important concerns, federal regulations shield educational systems from accountability that might arise from close inspection of individual records. The authors suggest that, to the degree that regulations protect opaque systems from scrutiny, public school students are at risk for systemic harm perpetuated through subtle and overt race, ethnic, and class biases.

Bibliography

Ainsworth, J. (2002). Why does it take a village? The mediation of neighborhood effects on educational achievement. *Social Forces, 81*(1), 117–152.

Anselin, L., Syabri, I., & Kho, Y. (2006). GeoDa: An introduction to spatial data analysis. *Geographical Analysis, 38,* 5–22.

Auwarter, A., & Aruguete, M. (2008). Effects of student gender and socioeconomic status on teacher perceptions. *Journal of Educational Research, 101,* 243–246.

Berube, A. (2007). *The geography of U.S. poverty and its implications.* Washington, DC: The Brookings Institution, MPP Program.

Borman, K. M., Eitle, T. M., Michael, D., Eitle, D.J., Lee, R., Johnson, L., Cobb-Roberts, D., Dorn, S., & Shircliffe, B. (2004). Accountability in a post desegregation era: The continuing significance of racial segregation in Florida's schools. *American Educational Research Journal, 3*(3), 605–631.

Boyd, D., Lankford, H., Loeb, S., & Wyckoff, J. (2005). Explaining the short careers of high-achieving teachers in schools with low-performing students. *The American Economic Review, 95,* 166–171.

Briggs, de Souza X. (ed.). (2005). More Pluribus, Less Unum? The changing geography of race and opportunity. In *The geography of opportunity. Race and housing choice in metropolitan America* (pp. 63–87). Washington, DC: The Brookings Institution.

Carr, P., & Klassen, T. (1997). Different perceptions of race in education: Racial minority and white teachers. *Canadian Journal of Education, 22,* 67–81.

Crandall, M., & Weber, B. (2004). Local social and economic conditions, spatial concentrations of poverty, and poverty dynamics. *American Journal of Agriculture Economics, 86,* 1276–1281.

Curley, A. (2005). Theories of urban poverty and implications for public housing policy. *Journal of Sociology and Social Welfare, 32,* 97–119.

Darling-Hammond, L. (1998). Unequal opportunity: Race and education. *The Brookings Review, 16,* 28–32.

Dawkins, C. (2007). Introduction-further innovations in segregation and neighborhood change research. *Urban Geography, 28,* 513–515.

Dee, T. (2004). Teachers, race, and student achievement in a randomized experiment. *The Review of Economics and Statistics, 86,* 195–210.

Dee, T. (2005) A teacher like me: Does race, ethnicity, or gender matter? *The American Economic Review, 95,* 158–165.

Dornbusch, S. M., Ritter, P. L., & Steinberg, L. (1991). Community influences on the relation of family statuses to adolescent school performance: Differences between African Americans and non-Hispanic whites. *American Journal of Education, 99*(4), 543–567. (Special issue: Development and education across adolescence).

Gould-Ellen, I., & Austin-Turner, M. (1997). Does neighborhood matter? Assessing recent evidence. *Housing Policy Debate, 8,* 4. (Fannie Mae Foundation).

Ensminger, M. E., & Slusarcick, A. L. (1992). Paths to high school dropout: A longitudinal study of a first-grade cohort. *Sociology of Education, 65*(2), 95–113.

Fack, G., & Grenet, J. (2008). *When do better schools raising housing prices? Evidence from Paris public and private schools.* Paris School of Economics, International Conference on Educational Economics, Athens. August 27–30, 2008.

Fack, G., & Grenet, J. (2010). When do better schools raise housing prices? Evidence from Paris public and private schools. *Journal of Public Economics, 94,* 59–77.

Friedman, S., & Lichter, D. (1998). Spatial inequality and poverty among American children. *Population Research and Policy Review, 17,* 91–109.

Galster, G. C., & Killen, S. P. (1995). The geography of metropolitan opportunity: A reconnaissance and conceptual framework. *Housing Policy Debate, 6*(1), 7–43.

Galster, G. C., & Mikelsons, M. (1995). The geography of metropolitan opportunity: A case study of neighborhood conditions confronting youth in Washington, DC. *Housing Policy Debate, 6*(1), 73–102.

Garner, C., & Raudenbush, S. (1991). Neighborhood effects on educational attainment: A multilevel analysis. *Sociology of Education, 64*(4), 251–262.

Gilmore, R. (2010). Fatal couplings of power and difference: Notes on racism and geography. *The Professional Geographer, 54,* 15–24.

Georgiou, S. (2002). Teacher attributions of student failure and teacher behavior toward the failing student. *Psychology in the Schools, 39,* 583–595.

Gonzales, N. A., Cauce, A. M., Friedman, R. J., & Mason, C. A. (1996). Family, peer, and neighborhood influences on academic achievement among African-American adolescents: One-year prospective effects. *American Journal of Community Psychology, 24*(3), 365–387.

Holloway, S. (2000). Identity, contingency and the urban geography of race. *Social and Cultural Geography, 1,* 197–208.

Johnson, J. F., & Uline, C. L. (2005). Preparing educational leaders to close achievement gaps. *Theory into Practice, 44*(1), 45–52.

Jud, D., & Watts, J. (1981). Schools and housing values. *Land Economies, 57*(3), 459–470. (University of Wisconsin Press).

Kozol, J. (1991). *Savage inequalities: Children in America's school.* New York: Crown Publishers.

Levin, H. (2007). *The costs and benefits of an excellent education for all of America's children* (pp. 1–24). New York: Teachers College, Columbia University.

Lloyd, D. N. (1978). Prediction of school failure from third-grade data. *Psychological Measurement, 38*(4), 1193–1200.

Mayer, S. (2001). How did the increase in economic inequality between 1970 and 1990 affect children's educational attainment? *American Journal of Sociology, 107,* 1–32.

Moran, P. A. P. (1950). Notes on continuous stochastic phenomena. *Biometrika, 3*(1), 17–23.

Oishi, G., & Schimmack, U. (2010). Residential mobility, well-being and mortality. *Journal of Personality and Social Psychology, 98,* 980–994.

Orfield, G. (2001). *Schools more separate: Consequences of a decade of resegregation.* Cambridge: The Civil Rights Project, Harvard University.

Orfield, G., & Lee, C. (2005). *Why segregation matters: Poverty and educational inequality* (pp. 1–47). Cambridge: The Civil Rights Project, Harvard University.

Parrish, T. B., Matsumoto, C. S., & Fowler ,W. J. Jr. (2005). *Disparities in public school district spending 1989–90: A multi-variate, student-weighted analysis, adjusted for differences in geographic cost of living and student need.* Washington, DC: National Center for Education Statistics, U.S. Department of Education.

Peske, H., & Haycock, K. (2006). *Teaching inequality: How poor and minority students are shortchanged on teacher quality.* A report and recommendations by the education trust, pp. 1–18.

Pigott, R., & Cowen, E. (2000). Teacher race, child race, racial congruence, and teacher ratings of children's school adjustment. *Journal of School Psychology, 38,* 177–196.

Pollack, M. (2001). How the question we ask most about race in education is the very question we most suppress. *Educational Researcher, 30,* 2–12.

Powell, M., Boyne, G., & Ashworth, R. (2001). Towards a geography of people poverty and place poverty. *Policy and Politics, 29*(3), 243–258.

Rupasingha, A., & Goetz, S. (2007). Social and political forces as determinants of poverty: A spatial analysis. *The Journal of Socio-Economics, 36,* 650–671.

Saegert, S., & Evans, G. (2003). Poverty, housing niches, and health in the United States. *Journal of Social Issues, 59,* 569–589.

Scheurich, J. (1998). Highly successful and loving, public elementary schools populated mainly by low-SES children of color: Core beliefs and cultural characteristics. *Urban Education, 33,* 451–492.

Sirin, S. (2005). Socioeconomic status and academic achievement: A meta-analytic review of research. *Review of Educational Research, 75*(3), 417–453.

Tate, W. (2008). Geography of opportunity: Poverty, place and educational outcomes. *Educational Researcher, 37,* 397–411. (Presidential Address).

Tschannen-Moran, M. (2004). Fostering student learning: The relationship of collective teacher efficacy and student achievement. *Leadership and Policy in Schools, 3,* 189–209.

Vaught, S., & Castagno, A. (2008). I don't think I'm a racist: Critical race theory, teacher attitudes, and structural racism. *Race, Ethnicity and Education, 11,* 95–113.

Voss, P., Long, D., Hammer, R., & Friedman, S. (2006). County child poverty rates in the U.S.: A spatial regression approach. *Population Research Policy Review, 25,* 369–391.

Wilson, W. J. (1996). *When work disappears: The world of the new urban poor*. New York: Alfred A. Knopf.

Part IV
GIS, Redistricting Issues, and Cohort Analysis

Chapter 16
Alternative Strategies for Mapping ACS Estimates and Error of Estimation

Joe Francis, Nij Tontisirin, Sutee Anantsuksomsri, Jan Vink and Viktor Zhong

Introduction

The beloved "long form" is dead. Long live the American Community Survey! As Eathington (2011) recently exclaimed, "Beginning in 2011, regional scientists and other socio-economic data users must finally come to terms with major changes in U.S. Census Bureau methodologies for collecting and disseminating socioeconomic data." Eathington's proclamation holds all the more true for today.

The American Community Survey (ACS) is now the primary mechanism for measuring detailed characteristics of the population at the sub-state level and especially smaller geographies like townships, places, and tracts. It is the main vehicle for disseminating information about educational attainment, occupational status, income levels (including poverty), and much more. As Sun and Wong (2010) write, "Census data have been widely used to support a variety of planning and decision making activities."

Additionally, during the past decade, there has been increasing interest among demographers, economists, planners, and regional scientists in mapping census data including the ACS. The main reason is that a map can show the spatial distribution of demographic data better than any other medium. Maps add another tool to the demographer's analytic toolbox.

Compared to the past, mapping has become an easier and more straightforward task. The widespread availability of desktop GIS systems and trained GIS professionals assures that an increasing amount of decennial, ACS, Small Area Income and Poverty Estimates (SAIPE), and other survey data will become mapped. The Census Bureau itself now routinely publishes reference maps and hosts an automated, interactive mapping service that can be invoked as part of ACS data display via the American Fact Finder. TIGERmap has been launched, for example. At the same time, mapping sample survey data like the ACS and SAIPE present significant

J. Francis (✉) · N. Tontisirin · S. Anantsuksomsri · J. Vink · V. Zhong
Program on Applied Demographics, Cornell University, Ithaca, NY, USA
e-mail: joe.francis@cornell.edu

M. N. Hoque, L. B. Potter (eds.), *Emerging Techniques in Applied Demography*, Applied Demography Series 4, DOI 10.1007/978-94-017-8990-5_16,

cartographic challenges in portraying visually both the estimates and the error of estimation on maps.

As the ACS begins its second iteration, with updated Census 2010 based geographies and new vintages of 1, 3, and 5 year ACS now available, demographers as well as geographers face quandaries about how to present such information to the intelligent public. Given that the ACS is such as a relatively small sample, particularly in the sub-county, tract. and block group geographies, it has become ever more pressing to assure the user of our research that the information is reliable. But, particularly where there is high uncertainty, to so signal that low data quality.

With the dissemination of the American Community Survey, the U.S. Census Bureau began to report forthrightly the uncertainty of its sample estimates by including not only the estimates for the various TIGER geographies, but also the accompanying error of estimation. Specifically, the ACS estimates are published with associated margins of error (MOE) representing a 90 % confidence level under an assumed Gaussian distribution. By contrast, the published 2000 Census data tables did not include this information with the estimates for data from the "long form." Today demographers increasingly recognize that this uncertainty needs to be expressed to a potential user along with the estimates. But how?

This quandary is particularly evident in mapping ACS data. Unfortunately, the most prevalent practice at present is to largely ignore the unreliability of ACS estimates when mapping these data. But this needs to change if users of our maps are to place confidence in our map making.

Because of the small sample sizes, particularly in sub-state geographies, differences between different units or percent change across time for the same unit may appear to be significant when they are not. Moreover, for GIS analysts, this becomes a problem as the apparent emergence of a spatial pattern based upon these differences of ACS estimates among areal units may not be real, but may be the result of sampling errors instead. As every spatial demographer knows, determining whether differences are significant is crucial in analyzing the spatial distribution of some characteristic before drawing any conclusion other than that of spatial randomness. On a more technical level, cartographers recognize that uncertainty, as revealed by measures of error, can also affect even the seemingly simple process of determining optimal class intervals or boundaries in a thematic classification. That is, the determination of class boundaries may be influenced by the errors of estimates.

This paper is about exploring ways to improve communication of the estimates and reliability of ACS estimates in map making and in our published map products, whether in static "printable" form (e.g. a pdf) or in web based interactive delivery format (html, JavaScript, KML). First we will summarize geo-visualization developments over the past two decades on ways to present uncertain data. Second, we will present selected works of others more directly related to the ACS situation—polygons with attributes derived from a continuous monthly sampling activity and updated periodically. Third we will present some of our own work at the Cornell Program on Applied Demographics exploring how to communicate simultaneously both the ACS estimates and margins of error for polygons at the county and sub-county levels of geography.

General Approaches to Identifying and Dealing with GIS Data Error

All GIS data have error to some degree. There are many reasons—measurement errors, interpretation errors, classification errors, interpolation errors, generalization errors—with consequences like uncertain propagations and poor decisions. Indeed one current view among GIS scientists is that both spatial (positional) and attribute information have an *inherent* associated uncertainty. Zhang and Goodchild (2002) classify uncertainty in GIS work into two broad categories—positional accuracy and attribute accuracy—and group data errors involved into three categories—error, randomness, and vagueness. Census geography has positional uncertainty issues in the TIGER files—notably boundary accuracy, missing and misaligned streets, address uncertainty for non-city style address—but considerable improvement has taken place during the last decade and work is underway to continue improvement of both TIGER and MAF accuracy, as witnessed by the Geographic Support System initiative under the direction of the Census Bureau's Geography Division (http://www.census.gov/geo/www/gss/index.html). On the other hand, the ACS, along with the SAIPE and similar surveys, has attribute uncertainty that affects the data quality we deal with as well. The latter is the main concern of this paper.

In one sense, dealing with spatial accuracy and attribute uncertainty is still a fairly new and evolving area of study in GIS and analytic cartography. A quick background search revealed that it was not until the early 1990s that GIS users as a whole begin to take notice of spatial and attribute uncertainty. One can only speculate as to the reason, but perhaps it was a special issue of *Cartography and Geographic Information Science* that served to focus and spawn a research program on the topic of 'Geo-visualization' (MacEachren and Kraak 2001). In that special issue Fairbairn et al. (2001) proposed that representation of uncertainty was a key research challenge, and even went so far as to say that attribute uncertainty could be characterized as a "new" component of data. Fairbairn et al. (2001, p. 20) for example stated, "…that a representation of uncertainty may supplement existing data or may be an item of display in its own right…" Similarly, Pang (2001, p. 12), after reviewing the visualization developments of the 1990s, expressed the viewpoint that "visualizing the uncertainty in geo-spatial data is as important as the data itself… There is a lot of opportunity to further improve the current suite of uncertainty visualization techniques to meet this challenge. Particularly, in creating new visualization techniques that treat uncertainty as an integral element with the data."

Among the early approaches taken toward mapping uncertainty was via manipulating graphic "primitives" like color, transparency, line width, and sharpness or focus. Examples that fell under this category included Yee et al. (1992) work on varying contour widths depending on certainty. Dutton (1992) explored mapping uncertainty parameters to different points in HSV (*hue*, *saturation*, and *value*) space. Monmonier (1990) experimented with using cross hatches to express the degree of unreliability. Beard et al. (1991) investigated the inclusion of "fog," where the amount of haziness corresponds to the amount of uncertainty or the decreasing amount of "focus" is represented by the amount of blurring as uncertainty increases. Pang et al. (1994) used the degree of transparency to indicate confidence in an interpolated field. Cedilnik and Rheingans (2000) utilized "perturbing" and "blurring" overlaid grid lines. Interestingly, these same kinds of approaches are being explored still today as ways to deal with ACS uncertainty in data estimates.

Meanwhile, on a related front in GIS statistics, Chrisman (1995) in discussing S. S. Steven's widely influential work on the levels of measurement expressed the belief that Steven's nominal, ordinal, interval, and ratio scales were not adequate for geography. He gave several examples where Steven's scheme, based on an implied linear measurement epistemology, falls apart for GIS data. Most convincing of his examples is the use of circular measurement in GIS where the distance from 0° to 1° is the same as from 359° to 0°, an outcome not expected under linear measurement. A second example of the inherent limitation of Steven's measurement scale system is the ability to reduce two linear orthogonal measures (the X-axis and the Y-axis) to a single scale using a radian angle measurement. Perhaps the most damning critique comes from Chrisman's pertinent illustration involving the commonly used multidimensional measurements on some spatial object in GIS analysis. He writes (1995, p. 275) "Multidimensional measurements create interactions not imagined in the simple linear world of Stevens. Since GIS is inherently multidimensional, the linear model limits our understanding concerning the interactions of measurements." Researchers who conduct spatial analyses or use spatial statistic procedures are very familiar with outcomes being a function of multidimensional interactions of measures.

One convergence of these developments in geovisualization and measurement theory was that GIS researchers began exploring the idea of using fuzzy classification as techniques for expressing uncertainty in the estimation. Burrough et al. (1997) expressed the belief that "… there is still a need for GIS methods to visually explore results of fuzzy classification." MacEachren and Kraak (1997), as well as Burrough and McDonnell (1998), advanced the notion that new visualization techniques were needed to allow users to explore uncertainty in spatial data *visually* and to investigate the effects of different decisions in the classification process. Their concern was that the common practice of presenting discrete classes of phenomenon like soils using sets of colors in a choropleth map was too constraining. They referred to this as a "double crisp" approach wherein (1) the features were drawn using sharp boundaries to delineate soil bodies and (2) crisp classes were used to classify the different types of soils. Yet they state the reality of the distribution of soils types across a landscape is that they weren't really as crisp as the choropleth map may indicate. Zhang and Goodchild (2002) also discuss the use of fuzzy classes in preference to rigidly defined classes for GIS work. The question of sharp versus fuzzy classification of values in the context of sampling and measurement uncertainty remains an issue we face today in dealing with ACS estimates in the presence of error of estimation.

Another of the new concepts advanced during this era was that of multiple membership maps, reflecting the multidimensional nature of geographic objects and how to classify them. The notion was that multiple memberships were more complex than could be adequately handled by the traditional strict classification methods used in cartography (natural breaks, quantile, equal interval, defined interval, standard deviation, etc.). Instead multiple memberships could be better handled by means of different methods. Dovetailing with the work on fuzzy classification, the notion was that memberships based on multiple attributes should be derived using some continuous classification algorithm such as fuzzy k-means (DeGruijter and McBratney 1988). For example, Hengl et al. (2002), working with digital imagery, explored the use of pixel and color mixture as techniques to deal with visual fuzziness and uncertainty. Kardos et al. (2003) explored the value of hierarchical tree structures as a geovisualisation of attribute uncertainty technique. In their paper two such structures were compared: the region quadtree and the Hexagonal or Rhombus (HoR) quadtree, both variable resolution structures. The conclusion from these explorations was that an area where attribute data is uncertain will show less resolution through the data structure, whereas an area that is more certain will show greater resolution through the quadtree structures. While this work is a bit complex for the immediate concern of the present paper, their work is instructive on alternative approaches we might take to dealing with uncertainty of sample survey data like the ACS.

Another third set of developments came from working with digital imagery, where ideas centered on the notion that when we have multiple memberships for each pixel of a map, one could make conclusions about the *ambiguity,* i.e. *indistinctness,* of a specific class and overall *confusion* among all classes. Operationally, these researchers used what they called a confusion index to inspect confusion or fuzziness among multiple membership maps (Burrough and Frank 1997). Hengl's work along with Hootsmans (1996) was focused on color confusion as the means to create and detect fuzziness, but the idea of fuzzy boundaries isn't that far afield from Xiao's concerns with robustness in classification, which will be discussed later (Xiao et al. 2007)

In the early 2000s, analytic cartographers developed some of the new interactive data exploration techniques such as the use of slide bars, point and click events, blinking and animations as ways to give impressions of the amount of data uncertainty in estimates. The research on these techniques will be discussed in the next section of this paper because they relate more directly to handling uncertainty in ACS data.

While there has been considerable attention to issues surrounding attribute uncertainty over the past 20 years, a couple of general conclusions can be drawn from the review. One is that previous research provides a number of platforms on which to build in our efforts to portray estimate unreliability via maps of ACS data. Secondly, it is currently safe to say that uncertainty in spatial information is still an evolving field of GIS and analytic cartography. Evidence of this is the current dilemma we are facing in how to deal with errors of estimation in the ACS and related surveys.

Error of Estimation in the ACS

As mentioned, this paper is focused primarily on attribute accuracy or uncertainty in the ACS. Unfortunately, for the most part, communicating the data quality of ACS estimates have been either ignored or underplayed in maps of ACS data. Torrieri et al. (2011) present several examples of this pattern from the news media, governmental agencies, and academic research. One possible reason for this may be that, while guidelines for use of ACS data indicate the importance of indicating the measures of error along with the estimates, there is no consensus yet evolved as to a standard (or set of standards) for reporting the measures of error. Sun and Wong (2010, p. 287) note there have been various national committees that have deliberated on how to present this information but no standardization has emerged. Hence, this seems to signal the need for further exploration of alternative approaches, and this is the motivation for the discussion of various considerations that follow on how to handle error of estimation from survey data like the ACS and SAIPE. A number and a mixture of issues are involved.

While not an exhaustive classification, there seem to be at least nine major issues. One issue revolves around what to use as a measure of error, whether to use the traditional 90, 95 or 99 % statistical confidence interval under an assumed Gaussian theoretical distribution, or to employ a relative measure of error like the coefficient of variation. (A closely related issue should be whether a Gaussian distribution is always the most appropriate theoretical distribution to benchmark against, but given the generally large sample size and plethora of variables being estimated, this concern seems to have been conveniently either underplayed or ignored.) A second major issue surrounds the question of whether to present error of estimation in a separate map beside the map of estimates (the adjacency technique), or overlay them on the same map (the integrative technique) and use a "bivariate" legend to aid interpretation of patterns. A third major issue surrounds the rigidity of crisp classes for categorization of estimates in our choropleth maps given the errors of estimation and the likelihood that the "true" value of the variable placed arbitrarily in a given class may actually land in an adjacent class. Falling into the latter discussion is the more basic question of whether to present ACS data via classed or unclassed (unique values) thematic maps. A fourth major issue is the number of classes to employ for categorizing estimates in the face of uncertainty. A fifth concern is classification methodology. Symbolization of uncertainty is the sixth major concern. We will show various approaches to symbolization based on the principles espoused above plus use of cartograms. A seventh issue is whether it is better to present this combination of information via static maps (pdf's, jpeg's, eps, etc.) or through web based interactive maps (html, JavaScript, KML), which have more flexibility. Each of these issues is addressed below. Torrieri et al. (2011) identify an eighth issue specific to mapping ACS data for many geographic areas simultaneously. Ninth, there is the issue of map complexity and viewing audience.

Absolute vs. Relative Error

Regarding what to use as a measure of error as well as Li and Zhao (2005) argue for the using a relative error. Like other researchers, they recognize that absolute error measures are sensitive to the scale of the estimate. That is, the larger the estimate, X, the larger the value of an absolute error measure like the standard error (X). Wong and Sun's concern is that, because larger estimates have larger standard errors of estimates, researchers will draw inappropriate conclusions in comparing two or more estimates due to possible misinterpretations about the size of error–namely that attributes with large absolute error will draw the researcher/user to conclude, somewhat mindlessly, that the attribute has greater unreliability (and therefore shouldn't be used) rather than interpreting that error relative to the size of the estimate. On the other hand those who advocate for the uses of relative error measures assert that relative measures of error don't present this confusion and that the coefficient of variation is independent of the estimate scale. Li and Zhao (2005, pp. 2–3), using the definition that relative error is one that is simply relative to some referent, develop this idea further and propose three possibilities: the coefficient of variation, the estimate relative to measurement error, and a third class of relative errors where the estimation error of one estimator is relative to that of another estimator. We will concern ourselves in this paper only with the question of whether to use (1) an absolute measure of error like the traditional $\sigma(X)$ and a 90 % confidence interval, or (2) a relative error like the coefficient of variation (CV).

Our work at the Program on Applied Demographics leads us to conclude that the choice of whether to use a traditional confidence interval as the MOE or a relative one depends on the format of the variable being estimated. Specifically, while presenting information about counts like totals (e.g. number of housing units) and frequencies (occupied, vacant) or medians (e.g. median household income) and mean averages, then use of relative measures of error like the coefficient of variation (CV) seems more appropriate. But when representing information about proportions or percentages (e.g. percent Hispanic), or information about a ratio like the sex ratio, the standard confidence interval seems the more appropriate measure to employ. Likewise, when examining changes over time like the percent change in median housing costs, it may be better to use an "absolute" confidence interval rather than a relative measure of error. In short, one shouldn't mindlessly employ a relative error measure either.

Because these estimates are bounded by 0 to 1 in the case of proportions, or 0 to 100 in the case of percentages, the CV presents misinterpretation problems that are avoided when the traditional confidence interval is employed instead. To illustrate, consider a variable like percent foreign born. Let's say we estimate for a given geographic unit that 10 % of the population in a minor civil division is foreign born and is reported to have a MOE of ±8 %. Here we have an estimate, p, with a certain standard error. On the other side of the dichotomy, we have an estimate of 1-p or 90 % native born with the same MOE of ±8 %. These two facts are structurally

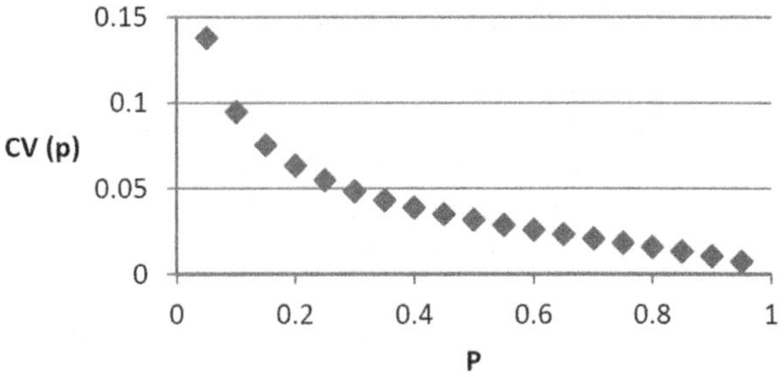

Fig. 16.1 Distribution of CV against percentage value (P)

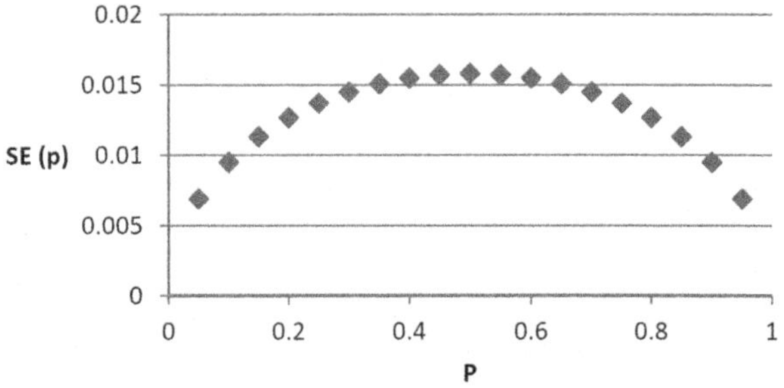

Fig. 16.2 Distribution of standard error of P against percentage value (P)

equivalent estimates, at least on the face of it, but when you calculate the CVs, the CV for the 10 % foreign born is 48 % (very unreliable), while the CV for the 90 % native born is 5 % (very reliable). Does this make sense?

The reason for this anomaly is the nature of the distribution of the CV as shown in the nearby plot (Fig. 16.1), which shows the declining, nonlinear relationship between the estimate and the CV. As the plot indicates, the smaller the estimated p value, the larger the coefficient of variation, while the larger the estimate, the smaller the coefficient of variation. Hence, even though the above two possible estimates of foreign born are equivalent structurally because they are two sides of a dichotomy, their certainty appears to be very different.

On the other hand, for variables like this, the confidence interval performs as one would expect. See Fig. 16.2. For both the estimate of $p = 10\,\%$ foreign born and $q = 90\,\%$ native born, the standard error of estimate is the same, approximately 0.01 when $n = 1{,}000$. This symmetry for placing a confidence bound on the estimate makes more sense both intuitively and statistically to us compared to a nonlinear relative error measure like the CV.

For our work, when presenting information like totals or frequencies, or summary statistics like medians and mean averages, we prefer to use relative measures of error like the coefficient of variation (CV). See Fig. 16.3, where the first map reflects Sun and Wong's cross-hatching approach with three data-driven categories, and the second is one showing our exploratory work at PAD on developing legends where category limits are set manually to values more meaningful to researchers and policy workers—0–15, 15.1–30, 30.1–60, and more than 60 %.

However, when presenting information like proportions or percentages, we prefer to use absolute measures of error like the traditional standard error of estimate

Fig. 16.3 Comparison of data driven category legends vs. researcher developed category legends

and confidence interval. See Fig. 16.4, where the first map represents the Sun and Wong crosshatching approach and the second shows some of our exploratory work with legends at the Program on Applied Demographics, here using cross hatching and color hue to differentiate

Side-by-Side Maps vs. Overlay Maps

A second major issue faced by spatial demographers and GIS analysts is whether to present error of estimation in a separate map beside the map of estimates (two map, side-by-side technique), or overlay them on the same map and use a "bivariate" legend to aid interpretation of patterns (single, integrated map technique). Compare the map layout in Fig. 16.5 for a side-by-side arrangement and Fig. 16.6 for an example of an overlay map.

MacEachren and colleagues have probably conducted the most extensive exploration of this question and have concluded that the single integrated map approach, wherein estimates are presented via color coding on a choropleth map and uncertainty of these estimates symbolized by cross-hatching, works better. Sun and Wong (2010, pp. 290–291) build on these results and present illustrations of both approaches, using New Jersey counties. In our own work, we found that both approaches were taxing to absorb for the general educated public viewer. However, for those more experienced with maps, the single integrated map was preferred.

We will address the issue of symbolization for these maps below in a later section, but in our work we find that viewers do not prefer (even dislike) the use of cross-hatching to portray uncertainty because they felt it obstructed viewing and understanding the classification of the estimate for the county or sub-county unit of geography. Compare for example the clarity of the maps in Fig. 16.7, which uses a less obstructive symbolization of error, with those in Fig. 16.6.

This judgment of cross-hatching producing an obstructed view was particularly true for maps with lots of geographic units being displayed simultaneously, like the 1,000-plus minor civil divisions (towns, cities, reservations) in New York.

Crisp vs. Modified Classes

A third major issue surrounds the structure of classes used to group estimates. For continuous attributes cartographers typically group values, for purposes of display on a choropleth map, into 4–6 classes using a classification methodology like natural breaks, equal interval, equal size (quantile), standard deviation, or some similar scheme. Doing so always raises the question of arbitrariness and rigidity of crisp class boundaries. Are these the optimal boundaries? How much alike are the spatial objects falling into a given class compared to those in an adjacent class? The latter question is of particularly high valence for spatial features "at the boundaries of the class." These questions take on an extraordinary relevance for categorization

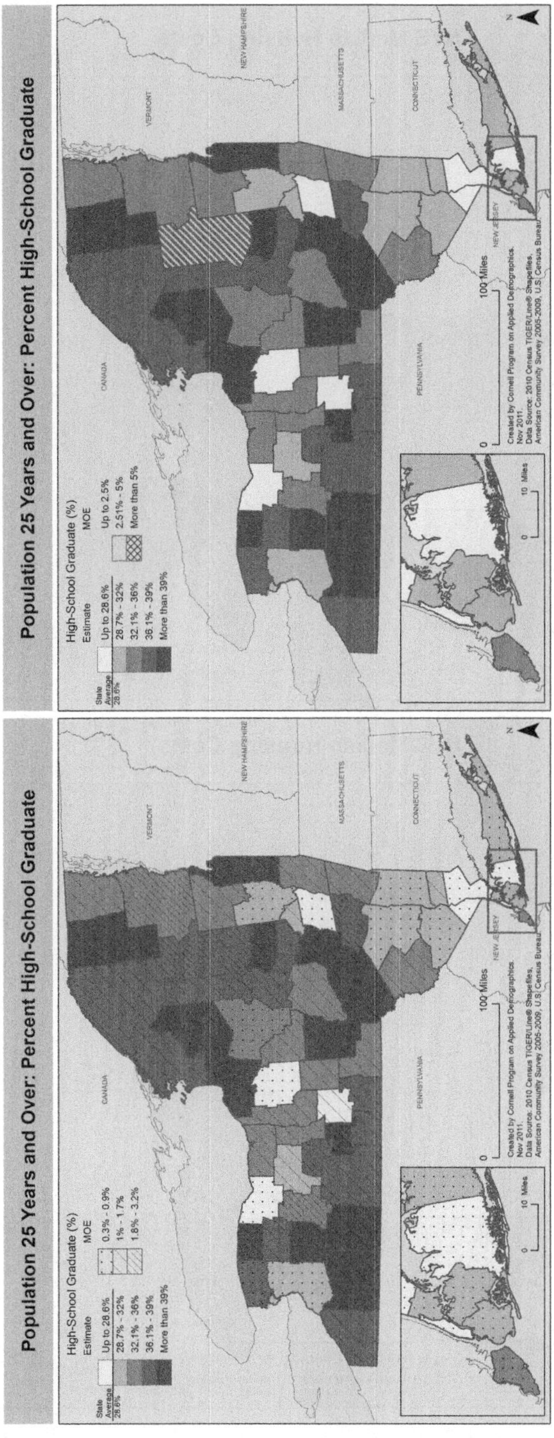

Fig. 16.4 Percent high-school graduates estimates with different MOE legend styles

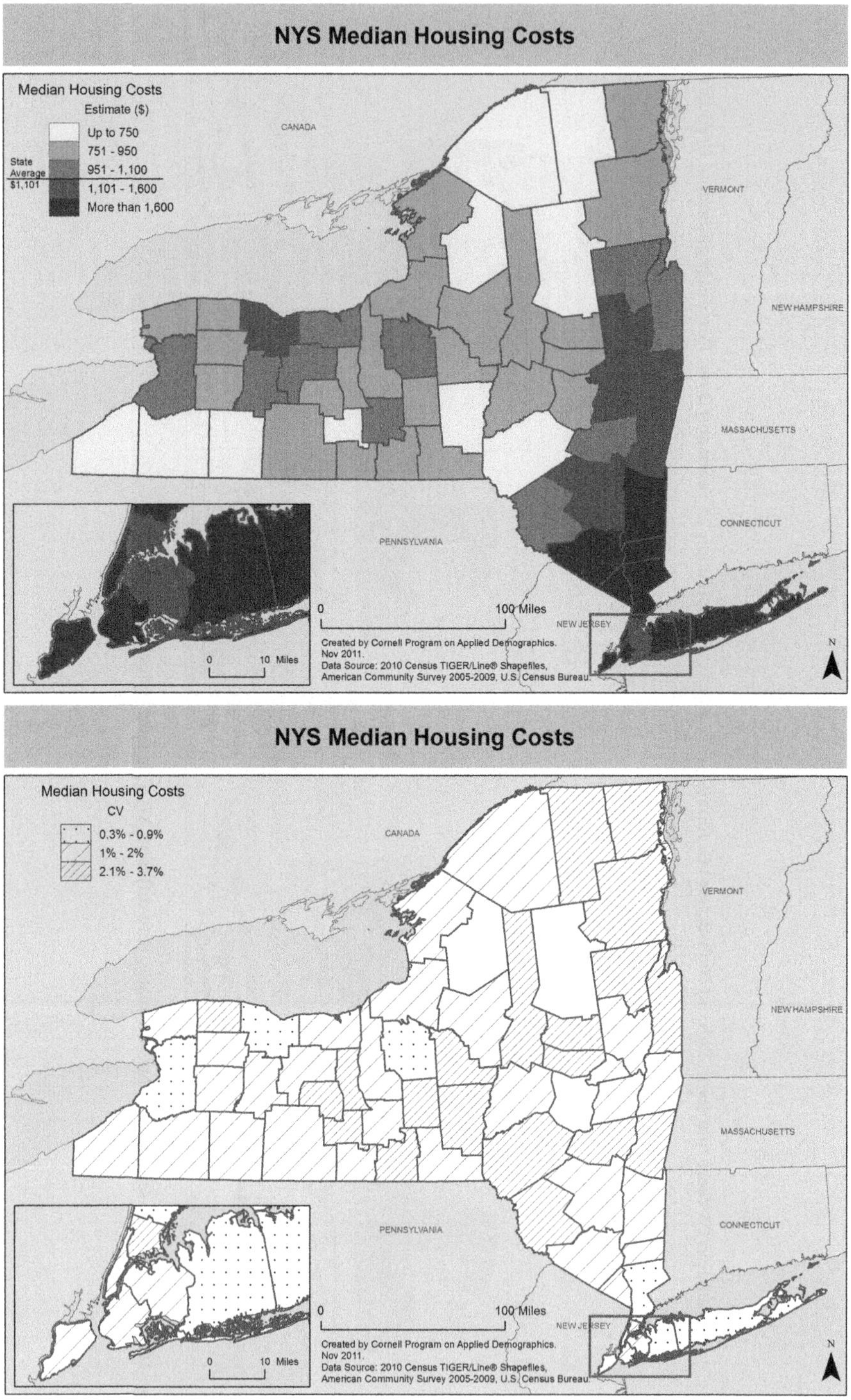

Fig. 16.5 Side by side maps, *left* showing estimates of median housing costs and *right* the MOEs

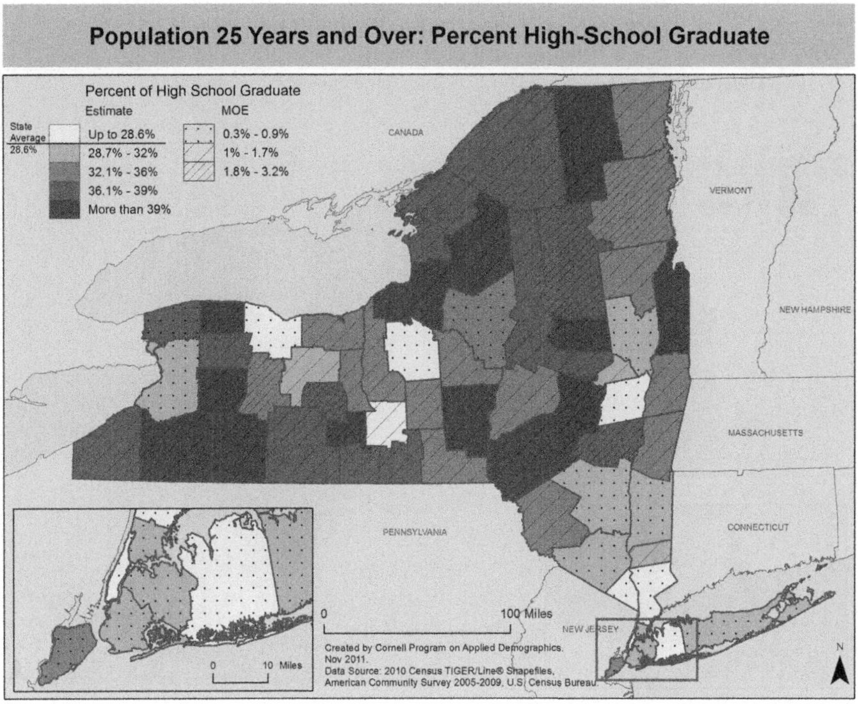

Fig. 16.6 Overlay map with one legend for estimates and the other for MOE

of estimates in our maps in the face of the errors of estimation and the likelihood that the "true" value of the variable placed arbitrarily in a given class may actually belong in an adjacent class. Xiao et al. (2007) investigated this issue and note, "the probability that an estimate is significantly different from values in other classes is a function of a number of factors, among them being the classification scheme and the size of the confidence interval."

Due to the uncertainty of estimation, settling on the number of classes, the class interval, and the class boundaries is more complex than when either (1) there is complete attribute certainty or (2) the error is small. As Xiao et al. (2007, p. 123) write, "When producing a choropleth map, it is important to realize that, owing to data uncertainty, each enumeration unit has a chance to fall into more than one class." In mapping ACS estimates, because the error is often large, margins of error need to be considered in setting the class boundaries and class interval such that when an estimate falls into a given class, the class boundaries are broad enough that they can include the confidence limits of the estimate as well.

Crisp classification of values in GIS follows the same principles as statistics—values assigned to a given class belong to that class and only that class. That is, there is no overlap of values of a given class into another class. However, because of the uncertainty of ACS estimates, unless error is taken into account in setting

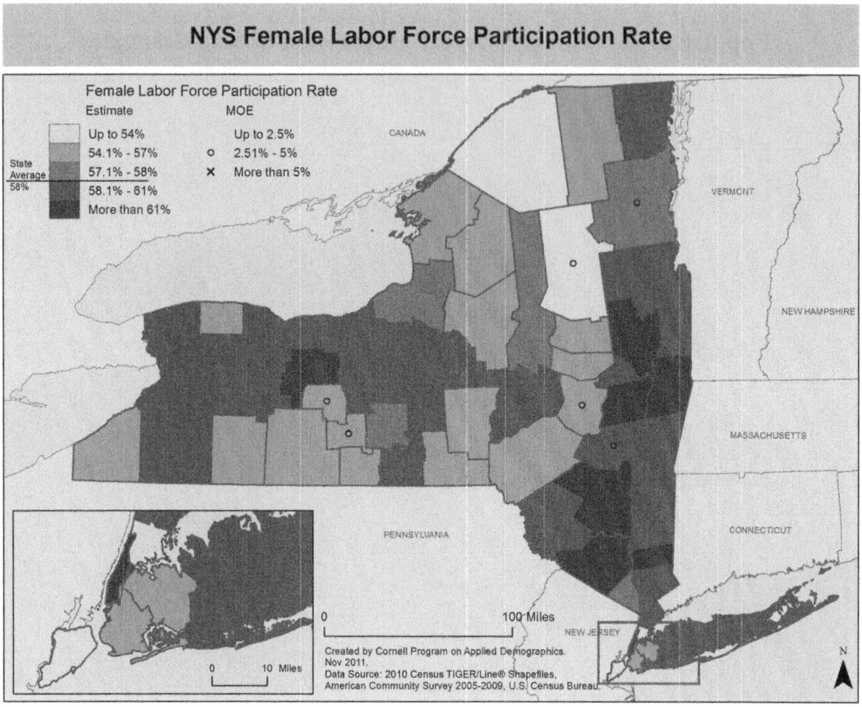

Fig. 16.7 Map of female labor force participation rate showing less obstructive MOE overlay

the class boundaries for a map legend, when the estimate is assigned to a class in the choropleth map, the confidence bounds may extend into other classes rather that coincide with the class boundaries specified (arbitrarily) for the legend. One consequence of uncertainty here is that the true value, represented by the estimate (we hope), may not be significantly different from values in those lower or upper classes in the map legend. In terms of symbology, the problem can be framed as one in which areas (e.g. townships) with different colors could have estimates that are not significantly different from each other, and areas with the same colors could have significantly different estimates. An alternative approach to dealing with this issue is to employ fuzzy classification as discussed earlier.

Sun and Wong (2010, p. 293) illustrate the issue of accommodative class interval width and boundary demarcations in the face of estimate unreliability with the following Figures (see Fig. 16.8, adapted from their Fig. 5), where the triangles represent the estimates, the class breaks (blue lines) are established at 20 and 30, and the confidence limits are represented by the error bars with round tips.

Notice in Fig. 16.8 that only for scenario one are both the estimate and the confidence limits of the estimate within the class limits. In only that situation can we be assured that the estimate is significantly different from estimates assigned to the classes above and below it. For the other scenarios, at least one of the confidence limits reaches into another class, meaning that we cannot be assured that estimates

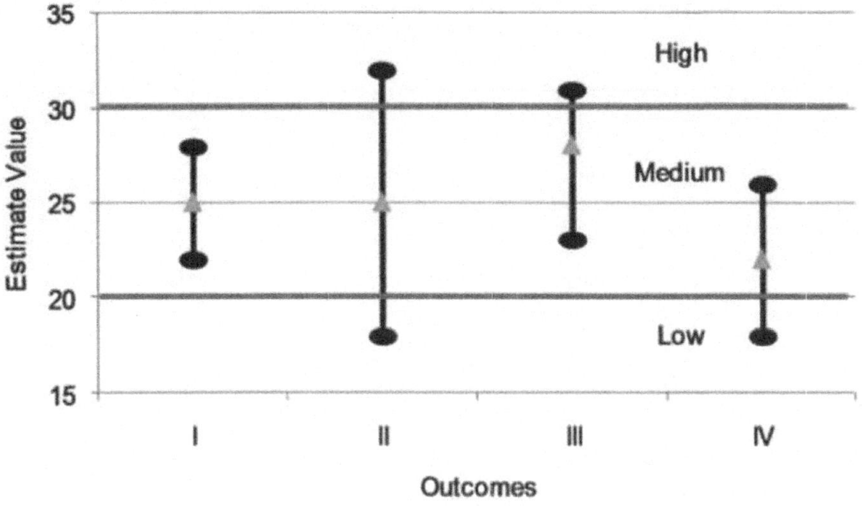

Fig. 16.8 Chart illustrating problem of establishing clear-cut category boundaries in face of measurement uncertainty

assigned to the focal class are significantly different from those assigned to the other classes.

Xiao et al. (2007) present the issue in a slightly different way. They use the term "robustness" to measure how well a classification works and define robustness of classification this way: "A classed choropleth map is robust if each enumeration unit has little chance of falling into a class other than the one to which it is assigned." To illustrate the application of their robustness concept, they ask the reader to consider two distinct enumeration units that have observation values *x* and *y*. See Fig. 16.9 (adapted from their Fig. 1).

The distributions of *x* and *y* are unknown, but with uncertainty we need to recognize that those x and y values could fall into any of the various classes depending on which of four classification schema are used. To illustrate the issue for at least two variables with uncertainty, Fig. 16.9 shows four possible classifications (A, B, C, or D), each using five classes, that the researcher may want to employ for classification and a map legend. In this illustration the class boundaries are represented by the vertical bars and the class interval represented by the width of the line between these bars.

Notice if classification scheme A is used, observations *x* and *y* will fall into classes 2 and 4, respectively. Xiao et al. (2007) indicate that under classification scheme A the classification of observation *x* is robust because all other possible values that could have occurred for ***x*** would have also fallen into class 2, since the interval of this class covers most of the distribution of ***x***. On the other hand scheme A is not robust for observation ***y*** since many of its other possible values would likely fall into class 3 or 5, instead of class 4. The reverse would be true for classification B, where the class limits for ***y*** are robust but are much too narrow for other plausible values

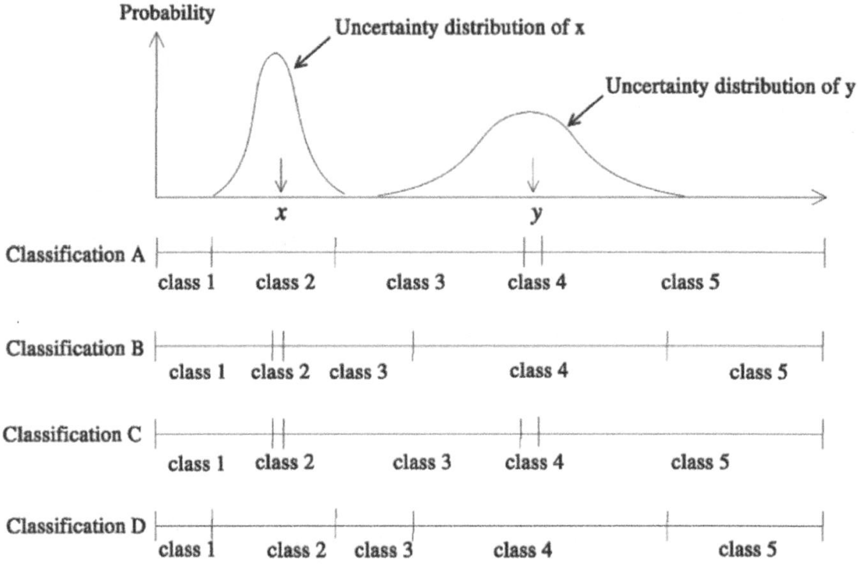

Fig. 16.9 Illustration of robustness of classification under estimate uncertainty

that ***x*** could assume. Classification scheme C is the least robust overall scheme as there is low probability that all or most of the possible values of ***x*** will fall into class 2 and likewise into class 4 for ***y***. By contrast classification D would best satisfy their criteria of overall robustness. The general point that Xiao et al. are making is that the uncertainty in attribute data makes it almost impossible to produce a perfectly robust choropleth map unless we somehow include robustness information as an element in the classification. But how do this?

Sun and Wong (2010, p. 294) suggest that one way around the problem is to first sort the estimates according to their value. Second, attach the corresponding confidence bounds to the estimates. Third, starting with some estimate, say the highest, compare it to nearby estimates to determine whether their confidence bounds overlay. If so, then group them into the same class. Fourth, proceeding onward, consecutive estimates whose confidence intervals do not overlap should be put into a different class. Their feeling is that this approach, which they call the "class comparison" approach, assures us that the estimates in a given class are significantly different from estimates in another class. On the other hand, a problem of this approach is that estimates within the same class may also be significantly different.

Xiao et al. (2007) have a much more elaborate approach that involves computing the probability of each observation x_i falling into each class j = 1…k, which they designate as p_{ij}. Letting p_{ij} be the probability that unit i belong in class j (1<j<k), they calculate p_{ij} as follows:

$$\Pr(x_i \in I_j) = \int_{I_j} \pi_i(x)dx \tag{16.1}$$

where Ij is the interval of class j. Next they introduce the idea of a robustness measure q_α for the entire choropleth map such that when the robustness values for all enumeration units are obtained, one has a set $\{p_i|1 \leq i \leq n\}$. Using q_α as their map robustness measure, where α is the tolerance level the researcher is willing to accept for complete classification accuracy, they require that $(1\text{-}q_\alpha)$% of its enumeration units have a p_i value greater than or equal to q_α.

With this conceptual development in place, Xiao et al. (2007, p. 125) state: "The key to obtaining p_i, and consequently q_α (which is the αth quantile of {pi}), is to compute p_{ij} based on the uncertainty distribution of each unit. For many circumstances, the cumulative uncertainty distribution function can be analytically expressed (i.e. p_i can be written in closed form) so that for each class the exact p_{ij} values can be directly computed using equation (1)." Otherwise, they claim to be able to estimate the p_{ij} values via Monte Carlo approaches.

Xiao et al. (2007) also conducted a number of "experiments" of how well their robustness measures perform for various tolerances. They ran analyses on various combinations of five factors: type of data, type of uncertainty distribution, level of uncertainty, number of classes, and method of classification. Data consisted of four contrived datasets represented as polygons formatted into a regular lattice of size 33 by 33. The attributes for these polygons were invented continuous values that were scaled to range between 0 and 1, and then arranged to form four statistical surfaces: (1) uniformly distributed linear, (2) multimodal linear, (3) linear with a skewed data distribution, and (4) fractal. Regarding the level of uncertainty, they indicate that for a given polygon, two different uncertainty probability distributions were tested: a uniform and a Gaussian distribution. The number of classes used for classifying the data ranged from 5–100 with an increment of 5; hence 5, 10, 15…100. However, in reporting their results, they only focus on the "5 class" and "10 class" results. Equal-intervals, quantiles, and Jenks were the classifications schemes used. Their most general finding is that indeed the robustness of classification is a function of the level of uncertainty in the data. That is, as uncertainty increases, the probability of getting the polygon values into their most likely class decreases—regardless of the distribution of the values, the number of classes used, or the classification method employed. As Xiao et al. write (2007, p. 128), "This observation suggests that uncertainty effects must be considered as part of the classification process and, more importantly, that such effects should be revealed to map readers."

In our work at the Program on Applied Demographics we explored the idea of portraying the probability that the estimate belonged to the class to which we assign it. For static maps we tried the use of pie charts, where each slice of the pie represented the cumulative probabilities for a Gaussian distribution that the estimate belonged in the class to which it had been assigned by the Jenks method. See Fig. 16.10.

We also experimented with classifying and displaying the lower bound or the upper bound of the confidence intervals. This adds much complexity to the legend and interpretation of the map, but has the advantage that standard crisp classification methods can be applied. See Fig. 16.11.

For dynamic, internet mapping one can provide this information about the probability of the estimate belonging to the class to which it was assigned as a feedback when the user clicks or enters a polygon on the screen. We will illustrate this later in

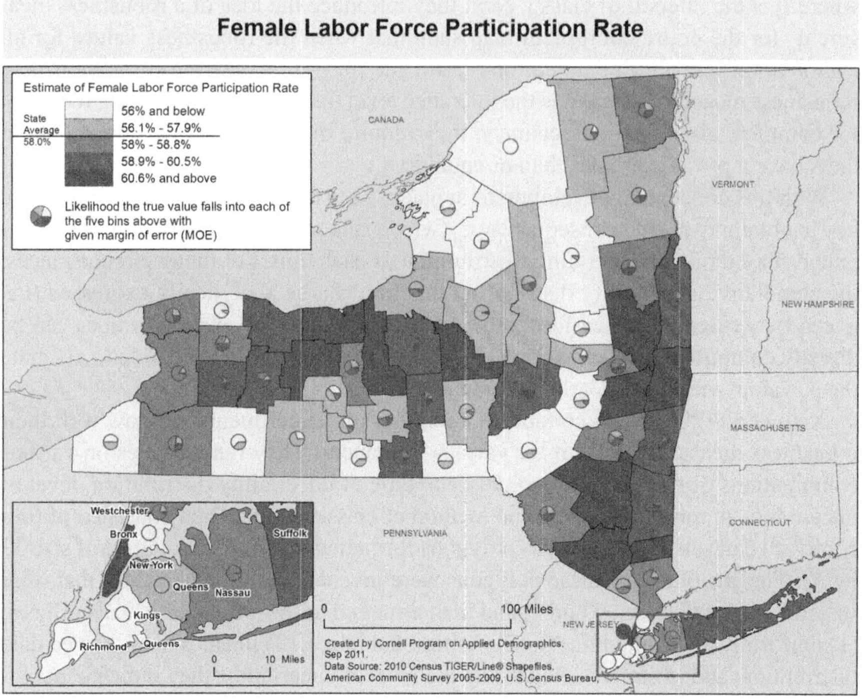

Fig. 16.10 Use of pie charts to symbolize cumulative probabilities of the estimate being what is shown for the geography

the section of this paper under the topic of static versus dynamic mapping. We have not explored fuzzy classification. This is a possible area for further work.

Number of Classes

One of the concerns we have in mapping ACS data with uncertainty is how many classes to use. Should one use more classes to achieve more certainty in classification or are fewer classes with wider class intervals better? The work of Xiao et al. is instructive here. They found that a small number of classes should be used if map robustness is a significant concern. As they state (2007, p. 131), "In general, an increase in the number of classes will induce a corresponding increase in the number of enumeration units with uncertainty distributions that overlap multiple intervals. Consequently, map robustness is reduced." Hence, when the data have high uncertainty, one can only create a robust classification map by keeping the number of classes low.

In our work, we have mostly kept the number of classes to five, sometimes using four. However, we haven't really explored the interaction of uncertainty and modification of class boundaries resulting in fewer classes with wider class intervals. This seems a useful area for additional research.

Fig. 16.11 Two approaches to estimating unemployment rate being significantly higher or lower than category boundaries

Method of Classification

One might expect that the Jenks method would provide the best classification of the attribute values under most circumstances, as it tries to minimize within-class variance while maximizing between-class variance to the extent possible. However, Xiao et al. (2007) found that among the four types of distributions they examined—linear, multimodial, skewed, and fractal—the difference between the three classification methods (equal-intervals, quantiles, and Jenks) was small under conditions of high uncertainty (low robustness). On the other hand, the Jenks method did outperform the others under conditions of (1) low uncertainty (high map robustness) and (2) use of only a few classes (i.e. less than 6). In general Xiao and colleagues found that for a dataset with a distribution similar to that of the multimodal or fractal data used in their paper, the Jenks optimal classification method appeared to be a superior choice, especially when a small number of classes was used.

In our own work we employed the Jenks classification method for "binning" the estimates and found that it seems to work well. We also experimented with the use of equal intervals for proportions, which allows one to express the corresponding MOE's in terms of the interval width.

Symbolizing Uncertainty

One aspect of research on spatially referenced attribute uncertainty during the past decade is in the area of geovisualization. As Kardos et al. (2003, p. 2) write, "Most research in attribute uncertainty has been focused on generating an uncertainty measure and then using visualization techniques to show uncertain areas." They further note that different attribute data uncertainty models are used for different spatial data. In GIS and analytic cartography, some models are ideal when using soil data, like fuzzy set theory, to express vagueness in soil type boundaries (Goodchild 1994). Other models like Monte Carlo can be used sequentially to express propagation of error and are good when dealing with random inaccuracies (Longley et al. 2001). Sun and Wong (2010), building on the work of MacEachren and Kraak (1997, 2001) for symbolizing errors of estimation for polygons, use metaphors (models) involving color and cross-hatching. But this isn't the complete extent of the work that has been done in the area and it is instructive to review some of the work of others at this point.

Lots of models or metaphors have been tried to improve the user's viewing of spatial information. Dent (1993) discusses using metaphors in representation through geometric shapes such as circles, squares, and triangles. In our own work on ACS data, we explored the use of circles, triangles, and squares as an abstraction to represent attribute uncertainty (Fig. 16.12).

MacEachren (1992) demonstrates the use of visual metaphors that included fog cover to hide the uncertain map parts and the blurring of uncertain areas. Kardos et al. (2003, p. 815) provide a very informative summary of things that have been

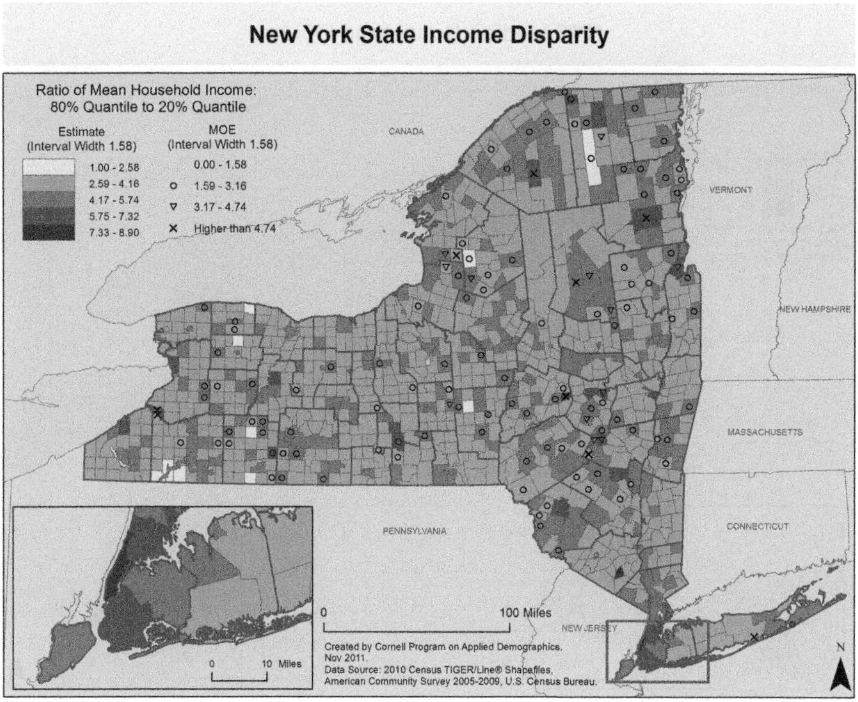

Fig. 16.12 Illustration of use of hollow geometric shapes to symbolize MOE overlaying estimates of income disparity

Technique Metaphor of:	Fog – Detail	Blur – Focus	Blinking Pixels – Stability	Colour Mix – Clarity	Pixel Mix – Fuzziness
Certain Data Metaphor of:	Clear – Revealing detail	Sharp Focus – Focused	No Blinking – No Movement, therefore more stable	High Saturation – High clarity, less recessive	Single Hue – Low fuzziness
Uncertain Data Metaphor of:	Foggy – Hiding Detail	Blurry – Unfocused and merging	Blinking over areas – Less stable, more unsettling	Low Saturation – Low clarity, more recessive	Multiple Hues – High fuzziness

Fig. 16.13 Suggested visual metaphors to signal estimate uncertainty

tried, particularly the effects being sought through the symbolization metaphors that various researchers have either proposed or used. See Fig. 16.13 (adapted from their Table 1).

Kardos, et al. (2003) have summarized also the details of research that GIS scientists and analytic cartographers have either proposed or used in the symbolization metaphors over the past decade. See their Table 1).

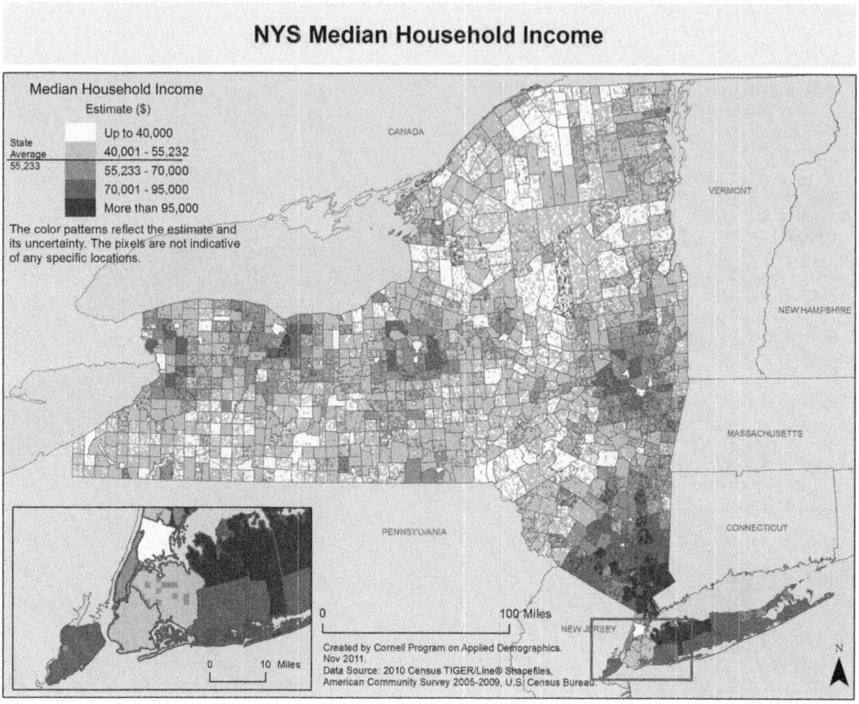

Fig. 16.14 Illustration of the use of pixel mixture to symbolize amount of estimate uncertainty overlying the estimate

Since examples of adjacent and overlay maps have already been presented, of interest here might be examples of a pixel mixture (pixelated) map (Fig. 16.14) and a saturated color map (Fig. 16.15).

In this pixel mixture map, pixels values were assigned proportional to their value under the Gaussian distribution. Hence, the greater the number of pixels having the same category value as an estimate value (low mixture), the greater the certainty of the estimate. On the other hand, when the polygon contains a lot of "spottiness" (high mixture), the lower is the certainty of the estimate.

Another alternative approach to expressing uncertainty along with an estimate value on the same map mentioned by Kardos et al. (2003) above is a map using color saturation. Figure 16.15 gives an illustration of one using a combination of saturation and intensity to symbolize both the value of the estimate and the uncertainty of the estimate. Here darker color symbolizes polygons with estimates of higher median household income while simultaneously intensity (dark to light) symbolizes the degree of uncertainty of the estimate (from 0–100 %). So subcounty units just north of New York City, as well as parts of Long Island, have high median household income and the coefficient of variation is low. By contrast, areas further north up the Hudson River have low estimated median household income and the

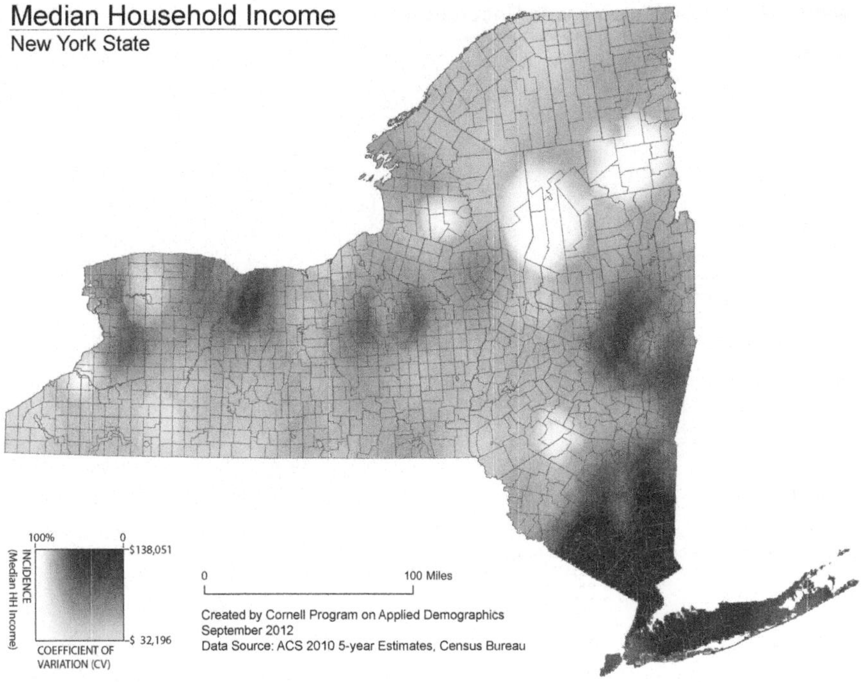

Fig. 16.15 Illustration of the use of color saturation and intensity to symbolize estimate uncertainty in combination with the estimate

coefficient of variation is large, reflecting the uncertainty that comes with smaller sized samples for those areas.

Kardos et al. (2003) also conducted a bit of research on how users perceived and utilized various symbolization (geovisualization) techniques designed to communicate data uncertainty. Their research is especially pertinent to the ACS estimate and error of estimation context. The data used was from the New Zealand 2001 census. They derived an uncertainty value for each feature using data from the 2001 post enumeration survey. Their survey was conducted via the internet and was designed to provide answers to three aspects of various symbolizations: (1) the visual appeal, (2) speed of comprehension of the information, and (3) overall effectiveness of the symbolizations. The respondents were all experienced GIS users.

The maps presented to the respondents to evaluate in terms of visual appeal, speed of comprehension, and symbology effectiveness consisted of the following "treatments." Nine different techniques were assessed and rated—adjacent maps, overlays, blurring, fog, pixel mix, saturation of color, sound, blinking pixels, and animation–using a five-point assessment scale (excellent, good, moderate, limited, and ineffective), along with the option of stating that the metaphor was "not useful." After examining the performance of their nine techniques on the usefulness, visual appeal, and speed of comprehension criteria, Kardos et al. (2003) drew the conclusion that the blinking of areas metaphor/technique outperformed the other

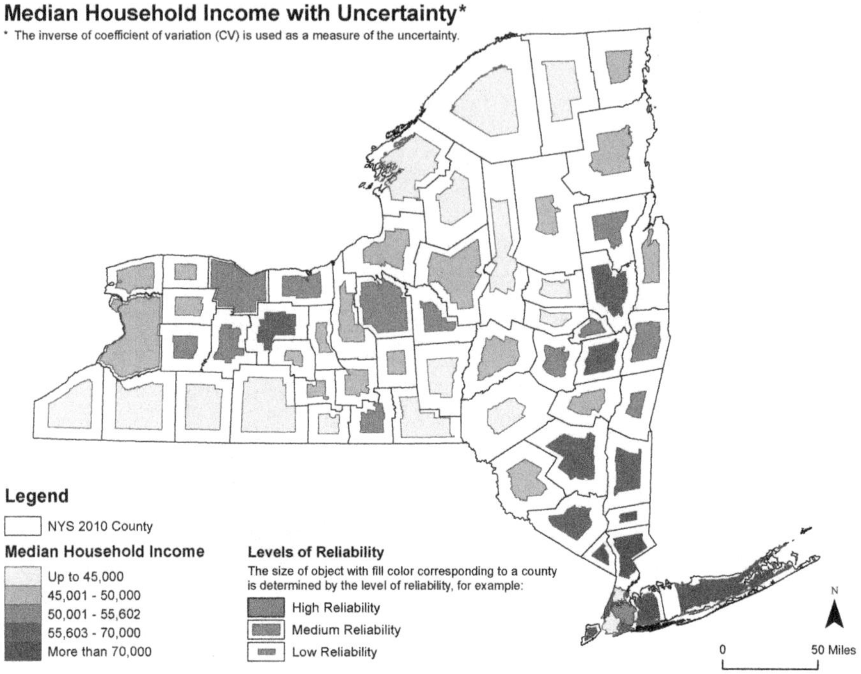

Fig. 16.16 Illustration of use of cartograms to symbolize uncertainty in combination with estimates of median household income

techniques. Overlay was found to be useful by 84 % of the respondents, while 78 % found adjacent maps (one for the estimate and one for uncertainty) were useful, with "fogging" and "blurring" next most useful.

The reason the respondents stated for preferring the blinking technique over others is that it didn't obstruct their viewing of the original information values. While they found the overlay technique useful, the felt it interfered with their understanding of the values symbolized by color. These are very useful finding.

In our own work, we found the same problem of confusion when presenting both the estimate and uncertainty information overlay. Side-by-side maps were just too awkward. So, we explored a modification of a "blinking" technique. For our static (pdf) maps, we first present the estimate for the geographic areas of interest) and then, with one mouse click, the viewer overlays the error of estimation information.

A final example of a map overlaying both ACS estimate and error of estimation is the Cartogram. This approach was suggested by Jerzy Wieczorek (2012, http://civilstat.com/?p=50), who provided an illustration that spurred the development of the cartogram approach in Fig. 16.16.

In this cartogram approach, the polygons (counties of NY) were kept in accurate size but the internal polygons were distorted in size to reflect the degree of uncertainty in three classes—high, medium, and low. Hence, the more the internal polygons are shrunk relative to the county boundaries, the lower the reliability of the estimate.

Static vs. Dynamic Interactive Maps

Dynamic interactive maps permit much more flexibility in presenting information compared to static maps. As Torrieri et al. (2011, p. 11) state, "Digital maps that include options for concealing or displaying information relating to the quality of the data displayed offer greater flexibility to the map designer." For one thing, you can program the application that serves out the information to "blink" those areas with high uncertainty as well as having MOEs displayed when the user passes a mouse cursor over the area. With the increasing availability of APIs for implementing these techniques, this is an area that should be explored by the Census Bureau and others. Jan Vink has done this for ACS data and New York geographies). Nicholas Nagel has built a version for SAIPE data and Tennessee geographies). For these interactive, internet maps the user has only to move the mouse over a geographic unit of interest and the error of estimation is displayed.

A slightly different approach to an internet-based map containing a layer of estimates and a layer of measures of error of estimation is one in which each of the layers of information can be toggled on or off, as can various boundaries.

While we think these approaches will improve the effectiveness of presenting both the estimates and their error, there are limitations to these techniques as well. For one, they require the user to make that mouse movement. Secondly, digital display techniques are generally outside the training of most spatial demographers, so this portends slow adoption of this approach.

ESRI has experimented with presenting maps of ACS estimates and error of estimation in the ESRI Business Analyst Online. It is served out via the internet but is only available via subscription. Moreover, unlike the Vink and the Nagel dynamic maps, the Business Analysts Online maps are served one at a time and are not overlain. Hence, they are really akin to the side-by-side maps discussed earlier.

Research is needed comparing these internet served interactive maps with static maps to see what users find more useful, understandable, and appealing.

Number of Geographic Units on Map

Lastly, Torrieri et al. (2011, p. 10) have noted that the overlay approach to communicating error of estimation via an integrated map has limitations when the number of geographic units in the map display is numerous. They illustrate this by asking the reader to imagine presenting both kinds of information (estimate and MOE) on a map for all 3,143 counties in the United States. For this situation they suggest that the map maker present only selected regions of the entire geographic coverage at time.

In our work at the Program on Applied Demographics, we explored the idea of using unfilled symbols of different shapes overlaid on a choropleth map of approximately 1,000 sub-county geographies (towns, cities, and reservations) in New York State.

References

Beard, M. K., & Buttenfield, B. P. (1991). *NCGIA Research Initiative 7: Visualization of Spatial Data Quality*. NCGIA, Technical Paper, pp. 91–26.

Burrough, P. A., & Frank, A. U. (1997). Geographic objects with indeterminate boundaries. *Transactions in GIS,* 2(4), 377–378.

Burrough, P. A., & McDonald, R. A. (1998). Principles of geographical information systems. Oxford: Oxford University Press.

Cedilnik, A., & Rheingans, P. (2000). *Procedural Annotation of Uncertain Information*. Proceedings of visualization 00, pp. 77–84. IEEE Computer Society Press, 2000.

Chrisman, N. (1995). *Beyond Stevens: A revised approach to measurement for geographic information*. http://mapcontext.com/autocarto/proceedings/auto…/pages281–290.

Dent, B. D. (1993). *Cartography: Thematic map design*. Dubuque: William C. Brown Publishers

Dutton, G. (1992). *Handling Positional Uncertainty in Spatial Databases*. Proceedings 5th international symposium on spatial data handling, pp. 460–469. University of South Carolina, August 1992.

De Gruijter, J. J., & McBratney, A. B. (1988). A modified fuzzy k-means method for predictive classification. In H. H. Bock (Ed.), *Classification and related methods of data analysis* (pp. 97–104). Amsterdam: Elsevier.

Eathington, L. (2011). *Holy MOE! Don't Marginalize the Error in the American Community Survey*. Paper was prepared for presentation at the 2011 annual meeting of the Southern Regional Science Association in New Orleans, LA.

Fairbairn, D., Andrienko, G., Andrienko, N., Buziek, G., & Dykes, J. (2001). Representation and its relationship with cartographic visualization. *Cartography and Geographic Information Science, 28*(1), 13–28.

Goodchild, M. F. (1994). *Spatial Accuracy*. Proceedings, 22nd annual conference, Australasian Urban and Regional Information Systems Association, Sydney, addendum. [216].

Hengl, T., Walvoort, D. J. J., & Brown, A. (2002). *Pixel and Colour Mixture: GIS Techniques for Visualisation of Fuzzyness and Uncertainty of Natural Resource Inventories*. In G. Hunter (ed), Proceedings: International symposium on spatial accuracy in natural resources and environmental science10–12 July 2002, Melbourne, Australia.

Hootsmans, R. M. (1996). *Fuzzy sets and series analysis for visual decision support in spatial data exploration*. PhD Thesis, University of Utrecht, Utrecht, 167 pp.

Kardos, J. D., Moore, J. A., & Benwell, G. L. (2003). *The Visualization of Uncertainty in Spatially-Referenced Attribute Data Using Trustworthy Data Structures*. Proceeding of 15th annual colloquium of the Spatial Information Research Centre (SIRC 2003: Land, Place and Space).

Li, X. R., & Zhao, Z. (2005). *Relative Error Measures for Evaluation of Estimation Algorithms*. Paper presented at IEEE conference, 2005.

Longley, P. A., Goodchild, M. F., Maguire, D. J., & Rhind, D. W. (2001). *Geographic information systems and science*. New York: Wiley.

MacEachren, A. M. (1992). Visualizing uncertain information. *Cartographic Perspective, 13*(Fall), 10–19.

MacEachren, A. M., & Kraak, M. J. (1997). Exploratory cartographic visualization: Advancing the agenda. *Computers & Geosciences, 23*(4), 335–343.

MacEachren, A. M., & Kraak, M. J. (2001). Visualization in modern Cartography. *Cartography and Geographic Information Science, 28*(1), 3–12.

Monmonier, M. (1990). *Strategies for the Interactive Exploration of Geographic Correlation*. Proceedings of the 4th international symposium on spatial data handling, Vol. 1, pp. 512–521. IGU, July 1990.

Pang, A. (2001). *Visualizing Uncertainty in Geo-Spatial Data*. Paper prepared for a committee of the computer science and telecommunications board.

Pang, A., Furman, J., & Nuss, W. (February 1994). Data quality issues in visualization. In J. Robert, I. I. Moorhead, D. E. Silver, & S. P. Uselton (Eds.), *SPIE Vol. 2178 Visual data exploration and analysis* (pp. 12–23). Bellingham: SPIE.

Sun, M., & Wong, D. S. (2010). Incorporating data quality information in mapping American community survey data. *Cartography and Geographic Information Science, 37*(4), 285–300.

Torrieri, N., Wong, D., & Ratcliffe, M. (2011). *Mapping American Community Survey Data.* Paper dated September 2011.

Wieczorek, J. (2012). (http://civilstat.com/?p=50) in his March 9, 2012 posting.

Xiao, N., Calder, C. A., & Armstrong, M. P. (2007). Assessing the effect of attribute uncertainty on the robustness of choropleth map classification. *International Journal of Geographical Information Science, 21*(2), 121–144.

Yee, L., Goodchild, M., & Lin, C.-C. (1992). *Visualization of Fuzzy Scenes and Probability Fields.* Proceedings 5th international symposium on spatial data handling, pp. 480–490. University of South Carolina, August 1992.

Zhang, J. X., & Goodchild, M. F. (2002). *Uncertainty in geographic information.* New York: Taylor and Francis.

Chapter 17
Older Moms Deliver: How Increased Births to Older Mothers Can Impact School Enrollment

Richard Lycan and Charles Rynerson

Introduction

This paper is an outgrowth of demographic support provided to Portland Public Schools (PPS) by the Center for Population Research at Portland State University. The District's enrollment began to decline in the mid 1990's but in the mid 2000's some of the elementary schools in established middle class neighborhoods began to show modest increases in enrollment. We noted that there also was a shift in numbers of births from younger to older mothers in the District that outpaced national and regional trends.

We mapped the spatial trends in births by age of mother using grid mapping tools. Our mapping revealed that the younger to older shift was most prominent in the same general areas where elementary enrollment had turned around. To pursue this issue in more depth we created analytical regions based on the proportion of births to older (age 30 and over) mothers. Key areas of interest were three *older moms areas* where over 75 % of the births in recent years were to older mothers. We were fortunate to have access to geo-coded data including the assessor's tax-lot data, birth records, and student records. We linked the student record and birth data to the tax-lot data based on common tax-lot location and tabulated these data for the six analytical regions.

We explored the relationships between the characteristics of the birth mothers and their housing context, as they varied across six classes of *older moms areas*. This revealed that the older moms were a special group. Ninety percent of those older moms living in the *older moms areas* had a baccalaureate degree or higher and nearly 45 % had post baccalaureate educations. Data from the American Community Survey showed that most of the age 25–44 households in this area were married couple households and that their annual household incomes were over $ 100,000. Tax-lot data showed that the housing occupied by the "older moms" was among

R. Lycan (✉) · C. Rynerson
Portland State University, Portland, Oregon, USA
e-mail: lycand@pdx.edu

M. N. Hoque, L. B. Potter (eds.), *Emerging Techniques in Applied Demography*,
Applied Demography Series 4, DOI 10.1007/978-94-017-8990-5_17,

the most rapidly appreciating in the metropolitan area. The in-migration of the affluent young households was facilitated by the out-migration of seniors, perhaps accelerated by the escalation in housing prices. We made use of David Ley's operational definitions of gentrification, based on growth in the share of highly educated persons employed in the managerial, technical, and professional occupations, and found the mapping of these coincided well with the *older moms areas*.

We attempted to explain how the younger to older shift in the age of birth mothers was linked to the turnaround in elementary school enrollment. It was important for us to do this to better deploy our forecasting models and to have an explanation of the enrollment turnaround for parents and school administrators. One simple explanation was that an increase in births in the *older moms areas* resulted in more students when the newborn became kindergarten age and this was true to a limited degree. However more of the increase could be attributed to increased retention over the 5 years from birth to kindergarten. We attempt to quantify the relative impacts of changes in the numbers of older mothers, shifts in birth rates, net migration, and the public school capture rate on school enrollment.

We hope that this paper will provide the reader with a view of the borderlands between applied demographic research and more thematically focused academic research.

School enrollment forecasting is a specialty of a small number of consulting firms, turn-key software developers, and academic programs. In order to provide this service on a cost effective basis, the research efforts need to be sharply focused on the end product. This study was carried out in an academic setting by the Population Research Center at Portland State University and offered the opportunity to explore the roots of school enrollment changes in the broader context of metropolitan housing and demographic changes.

The paper attempts to provide the back-story for a turnaround in enrollment that occurred in Portland Public Schools, Oregon (PPS). Some of the factors involved in telling this story include:

- The increasing number of births to older mothers, defined for this study as mothers age 30 plus
- The concentration of the older mothers in regions of the city that were gentrifying or experiencing turnover of older households
- The uptick in enrollment that began in the elementary grades in 2004 after a decade of declines
- The filtering effect of housing stock in determining the location of households
- The use of Geographic Information Systems (GIS) tools to study changes for small customized geographies

How all of these factors come together to account for the shift in school enrollment is complicated and we do not claim to understand all of the reasons. We will start by looking at what happened with births.

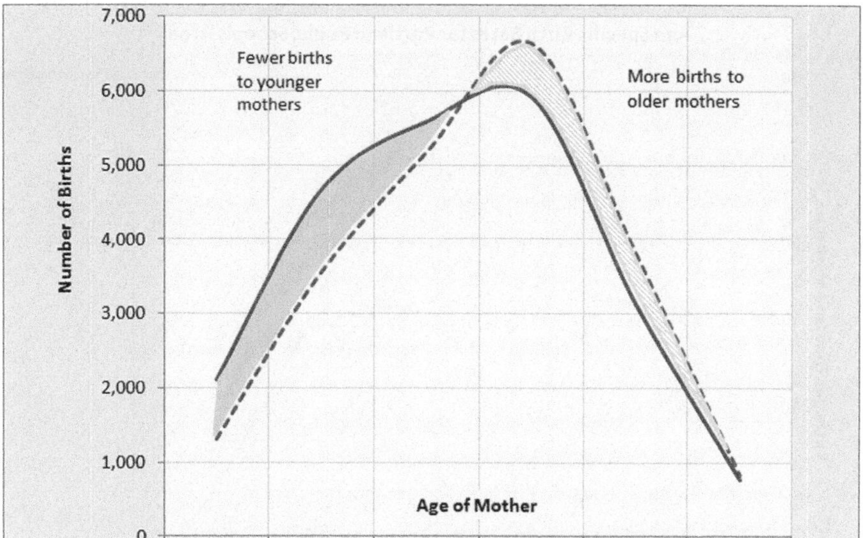

	15-19	20-24	25-29	30-34	35-39	40+
—— 1998-2001	2,111	4,662	5,584	5,929	3,149	770
- - - 2002-2005	1,312	3,553	5,172	6,649	3,831	831

Fig. 17.1 Births by age of mother. (Source: Oregon Health Authority)

The Shift in Births from Younger to Older Mothers

Beginning in 2002 the number of births to mothers age 30 and over exceeded the number of births to mothers age 29 and under within the PPS District (Fig. 17.1). The increase was due to the growth of the 30 and over population in the District, but also to the decline in the birthrate to younger mothers and the increase in the birthrate to older mothers (Fig. 17.2).

Analysis Regions Based on Age of Mother

In order to be able to visualize the geography of births to older mothers, the proportion of births to mothers age 30 plus was calculated from geocoded birth record data and mapped using GIS grid density tools (ESRI Spatial Anlyst Extension, Environmental Systems Research Institute, 2012, Kernel Density; Silverman 1986). The analysis and mapping of the birth data resulted in the District being divided into six regions based on when the births to older mothers (age 30 plus) rose to 50 or 75% of all births (Fig. 17.3).

1. *East OMA*. This area, the *east older moms area*, is the main focus of this paper because the geographic extent within which most of the births were to older mothers grew significantly from 1990 to 2008 and the growth of births to older

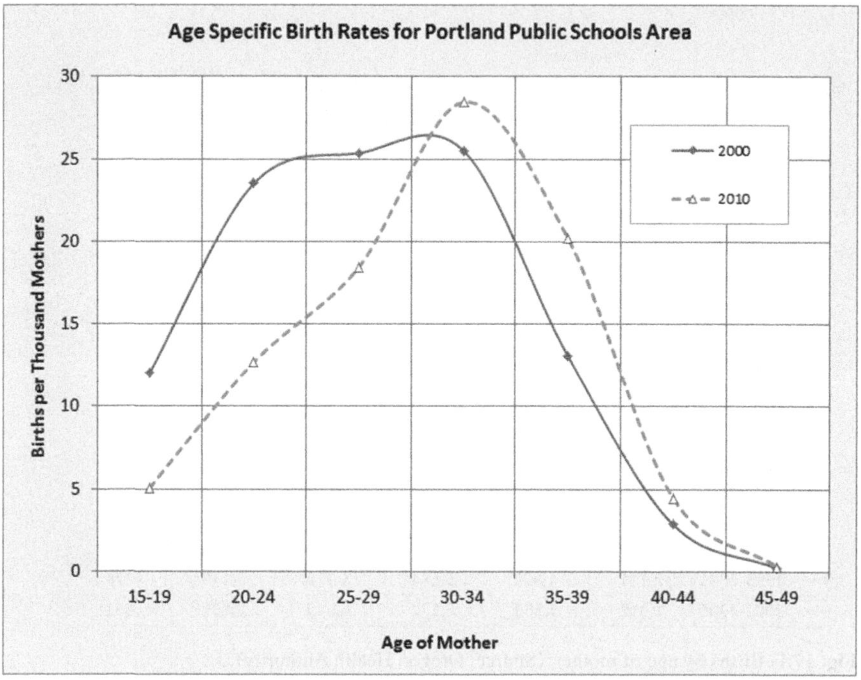

Fig. 17.2 Age specific birth rates for Portland Public Schools area. (Sources: Population from 2000 and 2010 Census of Population, births from Oregon Health Authority)

mothers made the largest contribution to enrollment growth relative to the other five areas. This is an area of primarily early twentieth century, high value housing, with many larger homes. The *East OMA* is divided into three areas, based on when the 75 % level was reached, for some analyses.

2. *East Surround.* This area, which surrounds the *East OMA* and within which 50 % of births were to older mothers, is a secondary interest for this paper. It houses a large proportion of the district's students. Demographic trends in this area have a large impact on school enrollment.
3. *South OMA.* This is a smaller area with a concentration of births to older mothers. Houses in this area are less spacious and less expensive on average. Enrollment in the lower grades in this area began to increase recently.
4. *West OMA.* This is an area of post-World War II housing where most of the births have been to older mothers, but the area of births to older mothers has not grown in the way that it did in the *East OMA*.
5. *West Surround.* This area within which 50 % of the births were to older mothers is characterized by less expensive smaller housing units and houses fewer students than the *East Surround* area.
6. *Remainder of the SD.* In this area, less than 50 % of the births were to older mothers. It is characterized by having more rental housing and smaller houses, and it contains much of the District's Hispanic population. Like the *East Surround* area, this region contains a large share of the District's students.

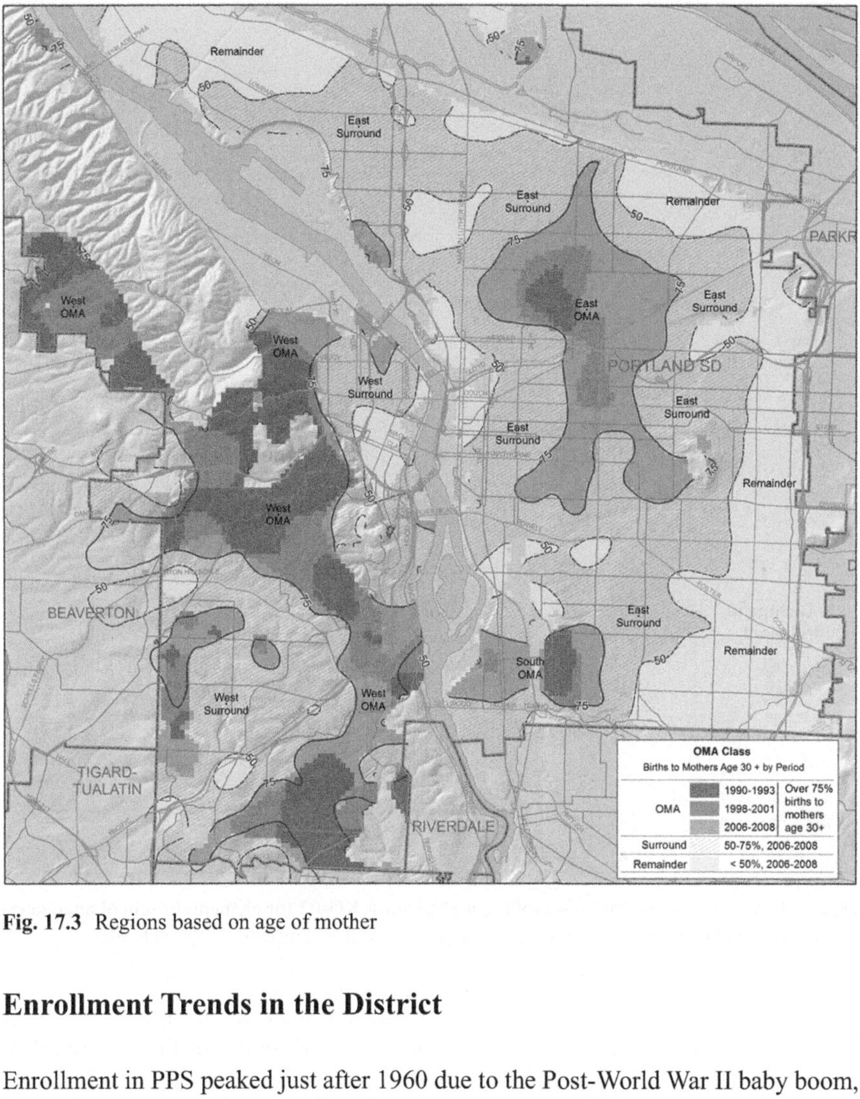

Fig. 17.3 Regions based on age of mother

Enrollment Trends in the District

Enrollment in PPS peaked just after 1960 due to the Post-World War II baby boom, at nearly 80,000 students, and again 35 years later with the baby boom echo, at about 58,000 students. After 1996 the District's enrollment declined for 12 consecutive years, reaching a low of 45,000 in 2008. There were a number of reasons for the post-1996 enrollment declines, but major causes were declining birthrates, fewer households with children, and more non-family and one person households. The District experienced loss of white students for a number of years, but this loss was offset by the growth of Hispanic enrollment and, until 2000, black enrollment. From 2000 to 2010 the black population under age 18 residing in the District declined by 17%. However, by 2006 white enrollment began to stabilize and then increased, and some elementary schools began showing increasing enrollments.

The recent turnaround in enrollment for the District was due in part to growth in enrollment in *East OMA* (Fig. 17.4, *East OMA* marked with dotted ellipse). The

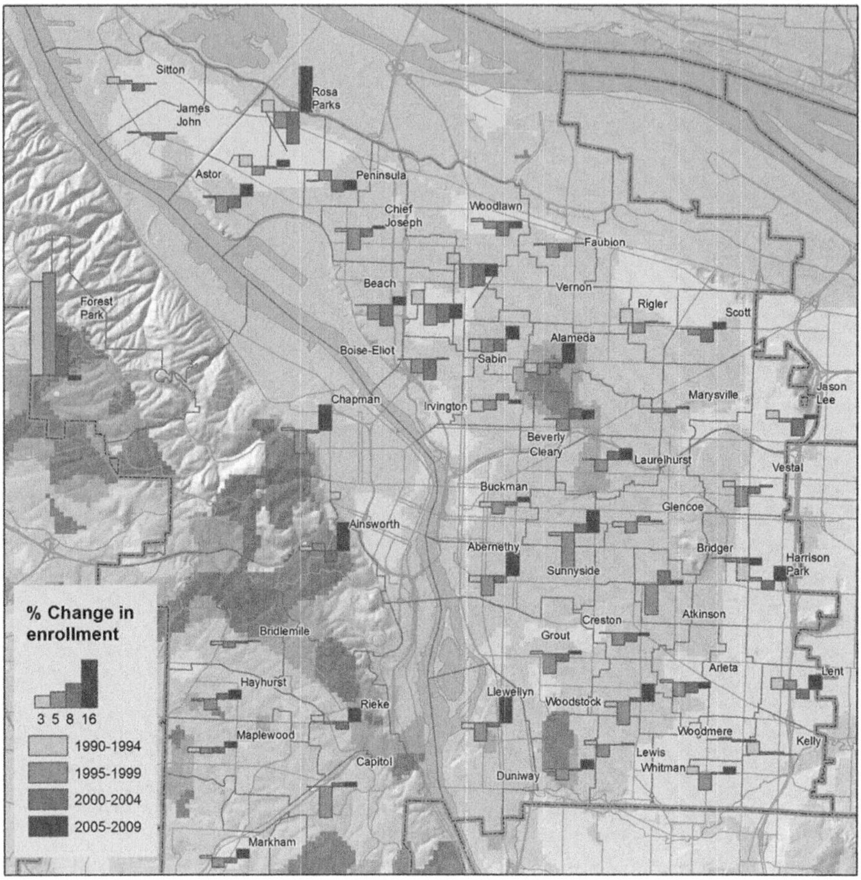

Fig. 17.4 Annual percent rate of enrollment change for KG-02 for elementary school attendance areas (*bars*) and *Older Moms* areas (*shaded colors*). (Source: Portland Public Schools)

maps in Fig. 17.4 show the periods of enrollment growth and decline for the lower elementary grades, kindergarten through grade two (KG-02), for the current attendance areas of the District's elementary schools.

In the 1990–1996 period KG-02 enrollments in many of the attendance areas experienced modest growth, but by the 1996–2000 period nearly all areas experienced enrollment declines. In the 2000–2005 period KG-02 enrollments grew in a few attendance areas, particularly in the *East OMA*. By the 2005–2010 period the pace of growth had increased in many parts of the District but particularly in the *East, South*, and *West older moms areas*. We will attempt to show that this enrollment growth was due in part to a rebound in the number of births but also to the higher retention rate of the 30-something older moms households. In some areas, this rebound in enrollment was reflected in the enrollment forecasts made in the mid-2000s when the steep declines in early grades enrollment had ended. The use of geo-coded birth data ensured that growth due to increased births was reflected in those forecasts, but the effects of increased retention were only partly reflected in the forecasts.

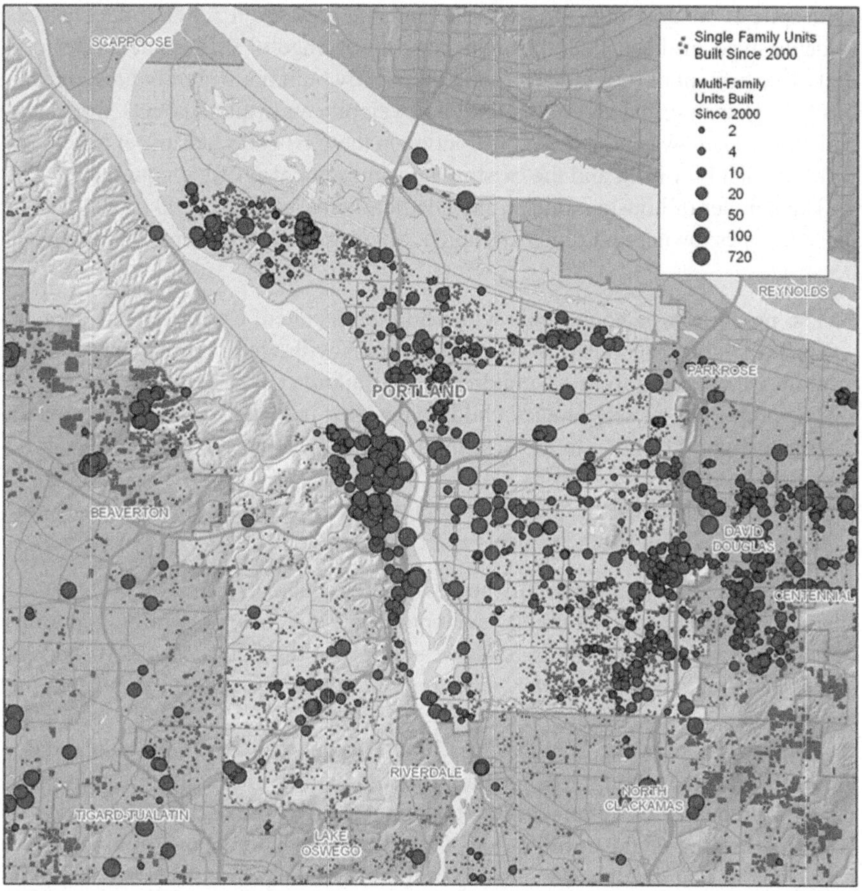

Fig. 17.5 Housing constructed in the District from 2000–2011. (Source: Portland Metro Regional Land Information System)

Housing and School Enrollment in the District

Before beginning the analysis of the birth and enrollment data it may help the reader to learn about some of the relationships between housing and school enrollment within the PPS area as reported in the School Districts Demographic System (National Center for Educational Statistics 2012).

The District is a largely built-out part of the Portland Metropolitan Area and is surrounded by suburban school districts. With much of the new single family housing built outside of the District in recent decades, the dynamics of school enrollment are dependent on city-suburb choices by householders. There was some infill and build-out of lands in the district, but from 2000 to 2011 there were only 8,044 single family units built in the District, compared to 49,846 units in the three surrounding Oregon counties outside of the District. By contrast there were 17,328 multi-family units built within the District and 14,845 outside during the same time period (Fig. 17.5).

In spite of the growth in multi-family housing, only about 2,400 of the District's students lived in these recently built units, an average of 0.14 students per unit. Sixty five percent of the students living in recently built multi-family housing were black or Hispanic, but in condominium developments white students were more numerous. There was little new construction in the *East OMA* because it is built-out with little land for infill and the existing housing stock was of high quality.

The number of housing units in the District increased from 2000 to 2010 for all housing types, owner and renter occupied, but in spite of this, enrollment declined because:

- The proportion of households with children declined, especially in renter occupied households. Also, in those households with children, there were fewer children, dropping from 1.2 children to 1.1 children per household.
- The proportion of school aged children enrolled in Portland Public Schools declined slightly from 87 to 84 %, with the greatest declines in areas of owner occupied housing.
- Much of the increase in housing was in types that tend not to house many children, such as high rise apartments and condominiums.

In 2000, high quality single family homes were available in the *East OMA* at lower costs than in some new suburban developments (Fig. 17.6), presenting opportunities for upwardly mobile households headed by young adults. By 2010 housing values had escalated in the *older moms area* but opportunities still existed around the margins.

Housing values in the *East OMA* in 2000 were among the highest compared to the Portland three county area median. As competition for quality housing in the *East OMA* grew, housing prices more than doubled over the decade (Fig. 17.7).

One constraint on the in-migration of families with children, or planning to have children, was that much of the housing built in Portland prior to World War II consisted of two bedroom homes, which by present standards may not offer enough space for families with children. The county tax assessor's office stopped maintaining bedroom counts a few years ago in part because officials felt that the concept of what counted as a bedroom was unclear. Many affluent families want room for a home office or hobbies and a two bedroom home does not offer enough space for this purpose and even a single child. The *older moms area* does contain many larger housing units averaging 2,000 sq feet or more but the growth of the *older moms area* beyond this contour expanded into areas of smaller and less expensive housing.

Gentrification or Simply Housing Turnover?

Was this growth in the *East OMA* a result of *gentrification* or was it simply due to *turnover* of households as empty nesters and others moved away? David Ley describes gentrification in the context of changing inner-city housing markets but

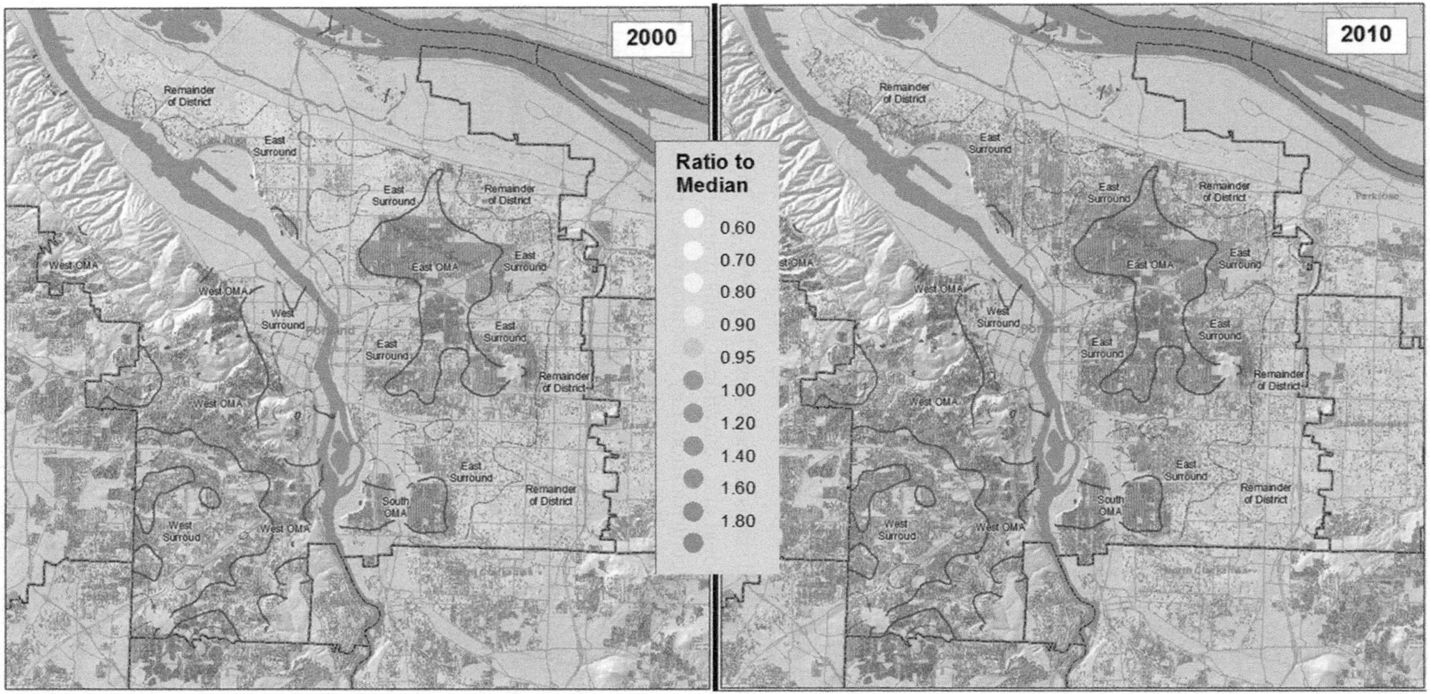

Fig. 17.6 Housing values for single family housing as proportion of median housing value for three county area. (Source: Portland Metro Regional Land Information System)

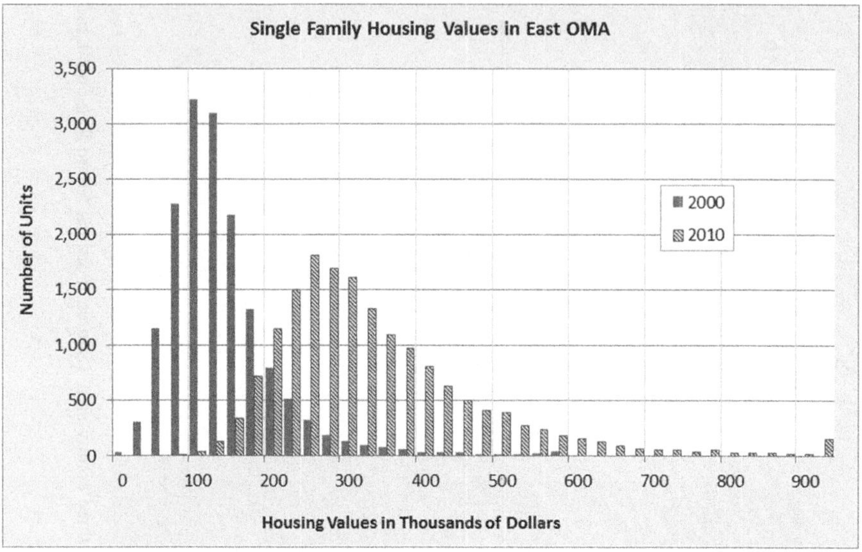

Fig. 17.7 Housing values in the *east older moms* area in 2000 and 2010. (Source: Portland Metro Regional Land Information System)

also attributes class and status connotations (Ley 1996, pp. 35–36). He also suggests that changing occupational and educational status of inner city residents is a good marker for identifying gentrification. Ley's method was applied to the Portland situation based on changes in the proportion of residents with baccalaureate degrees or higher education and in the proportion of persons employed in managerial, technical, and professional occupations (Fig. 17.8).

Data from the 1990 and 2000 censuses and the 2010 American Community Survey were used to compute the two proportions that were then averaged and the top 20% of the tracts mapped[1]. What it shows is that the *East OMA* and the *East Surround* area experienced growth in the gentrification indices from 1990 to 2000 and that the measure of gentrification spread out from the *East OMA*. Since the housing in the *East OMA* was spacious, high value housing, it may not be accurate to describe this process as gentrification. The gentrification taking place in the region surrounding the *East OMA* better fits the concept of gentrification as it occurred in areas of lower value housing, involved a younger population, and was accompanied by out-migration of much of the black population.

Insights into the demographic changes can be gained by examining net migration by age group for the *East OMA* and *East Surround areas* (Fig. 17.9).

[1] We chose to represent the 2006–2010 ACS data as representing 2008, the middle year for the 5 year sample. We think the in-migration of the young and educated was a relatively constant from 2006–2010. The difference between the 10 year period from 1990 to 2000 and 8 year period from 2000 to 2008 is accounted for by mapping by decile units. Ley considers those the tracts in the top 20% to be gentrifying. Both the data from the 2000 census and the 2010 ACS have considerable sampling variation at the census tract level, but it is highly unlikely that the geographical patterns arose through sampling error.

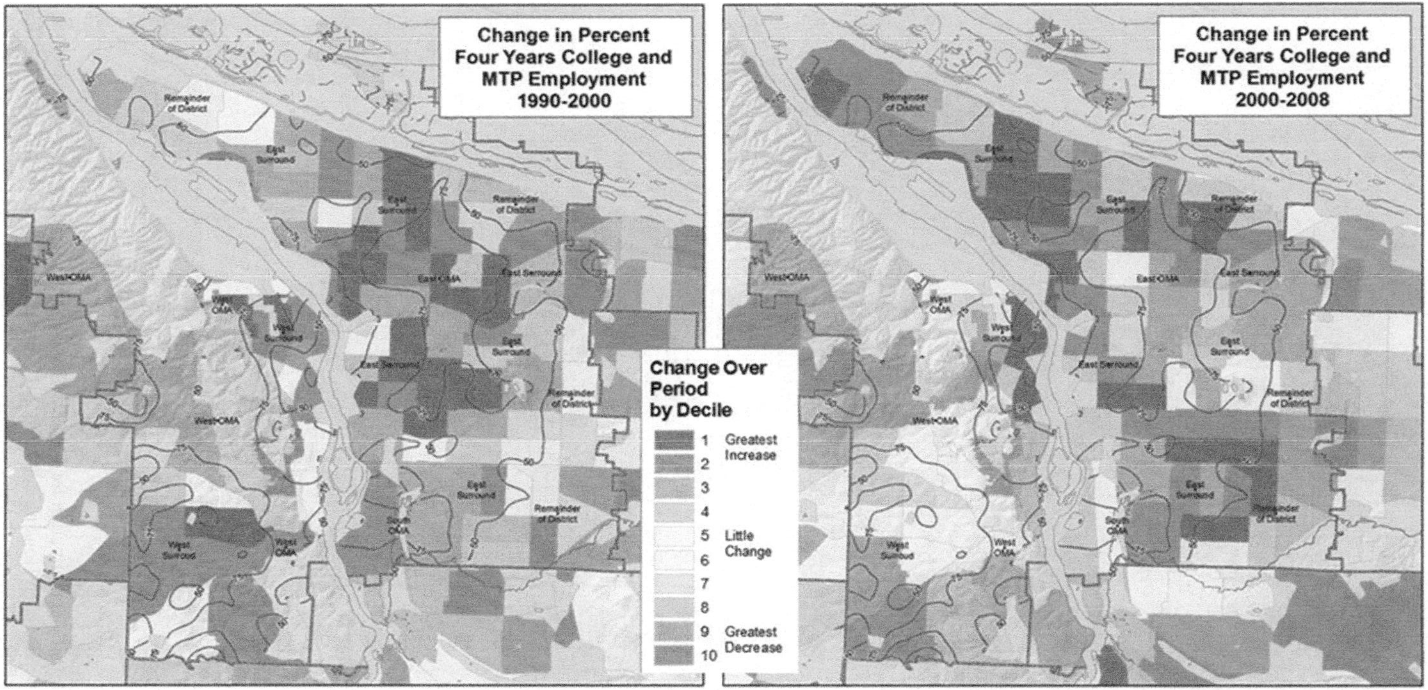

Fig. 17.8 Census tracts by decile ranking classified by growth of managerial, technical, and professional occupations and baccalaureate and higher level educations. (Sources: U.S. Census of Population and Housing 1990 and 2000, American Community Survey 2006–2010, 5 year estimates)

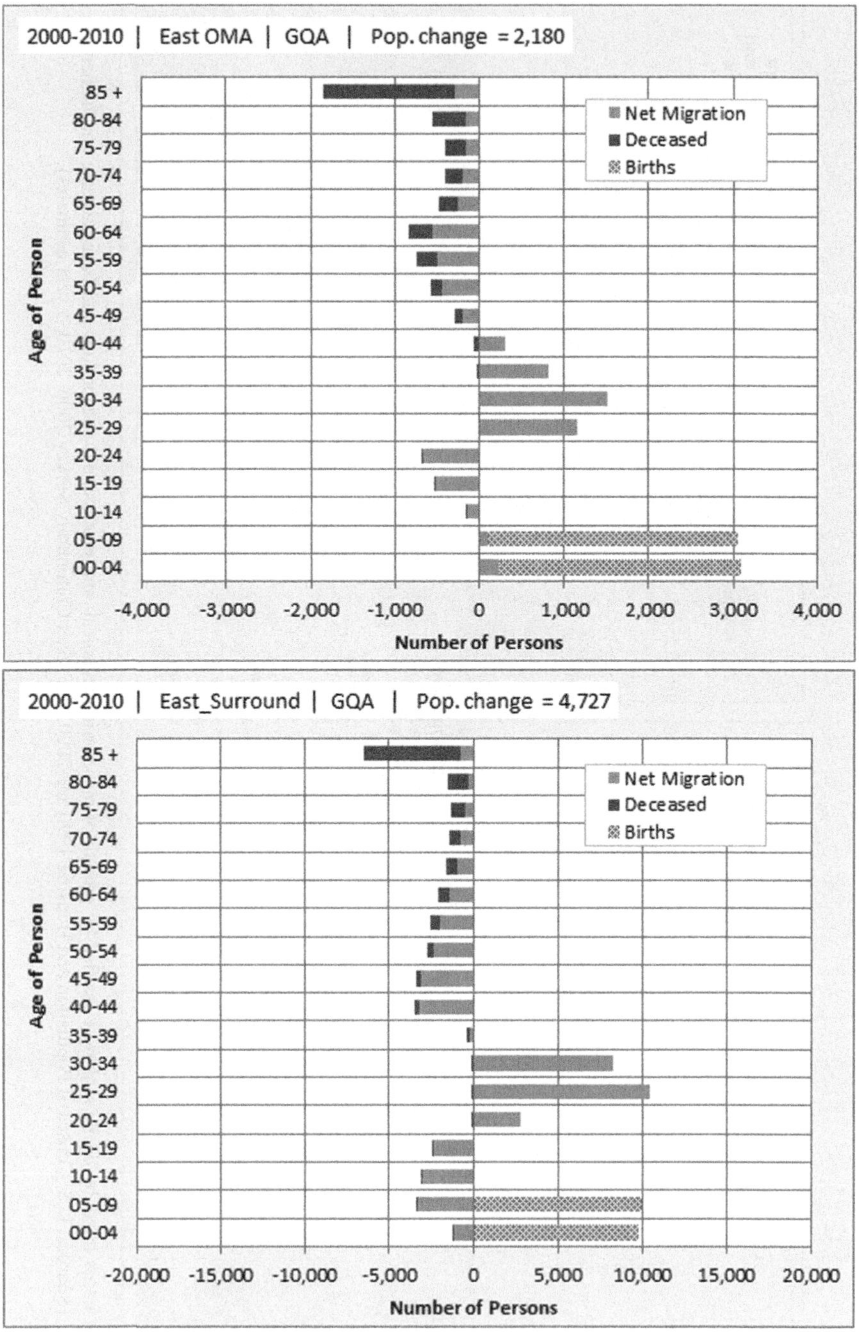

Fig. 17.9 Estimated net migration for *East OMA* and *East Surround* areas. (Sources: U.S. Census of Population and Housing 2000 and 2010, mortality from National Center for Health Statistics, births from Oregon Health Authority)

Net migration was calculated by comparing cohort change with an estimate of the numbers of deaths based on age and sex specific mortality. The data also were adjusted to better reflect numbers residing in households by removing the group quarters population.

The modal age group for net migrants for the *East OMA* is 30–34 while that for the *East Surround* is 25–29. Housing vacancies in both areas are created by the out-migration of older households but the *East OMA* experienced more out-migration of the age 20–24 population who for the most part cannot find suitable or affordable housing in the more expensive *East OMA*. In the *East OMA* more of the loss of older households was due to outmigration than in the *East Surround* area.

The definition of gentrification is somewhat slippery, but the growth of the older moms population in the *East OMA* perhaps is better viewed as turnover resulting from the out-migration of affluent older owners rather than as gentrification. The growth of the older mothers population in the surrounding areas of less expensive and less spacious housing perhaps can better be seen as gentrification and (as will be shown later) was related to the out-migration of the District's black population to the outer parts of the District and the surrounding communities.

Who are the Older Mothers?

The older mothers in Portland are a remarkable group. They have grown in numbers in Portland, as they have nationally, but they also have concentrated in areas of older high quality housing in the central city and are a key group in the return of population to the central city. We have data from a variety of sources describing these older mothers. One key source is the collection of geo-coded birth records from 1990 to 2010, which are in turn linked to the residence where they reside through the assessor's tax-lot database.

Educational Levels

The older mothers living in single family owner occupied housing in the older mother areas are highly educated, with nearly 90 % having a baccalaureate level education and nearly 45 % having completed more than 16 years of schooling (Fig. 17.10).

The educational levels drop substantially in the *East Surround* area, and drop further in the *Remainder of the SD*, where fewer than 50 % of the births are to older mothers, and a large share are to mothers with a high school education or less. Data for mothers living in owner occupied single family housing show higher educational levels for older mothers. The combination of high educational levels, small families, and ownership of moderately expensive housing fits the picture of mothers who have likely taken advantage of their educations, worked for a number of years, postponed having children, and have accumulated resources to be able to move into this area of high quality housing.

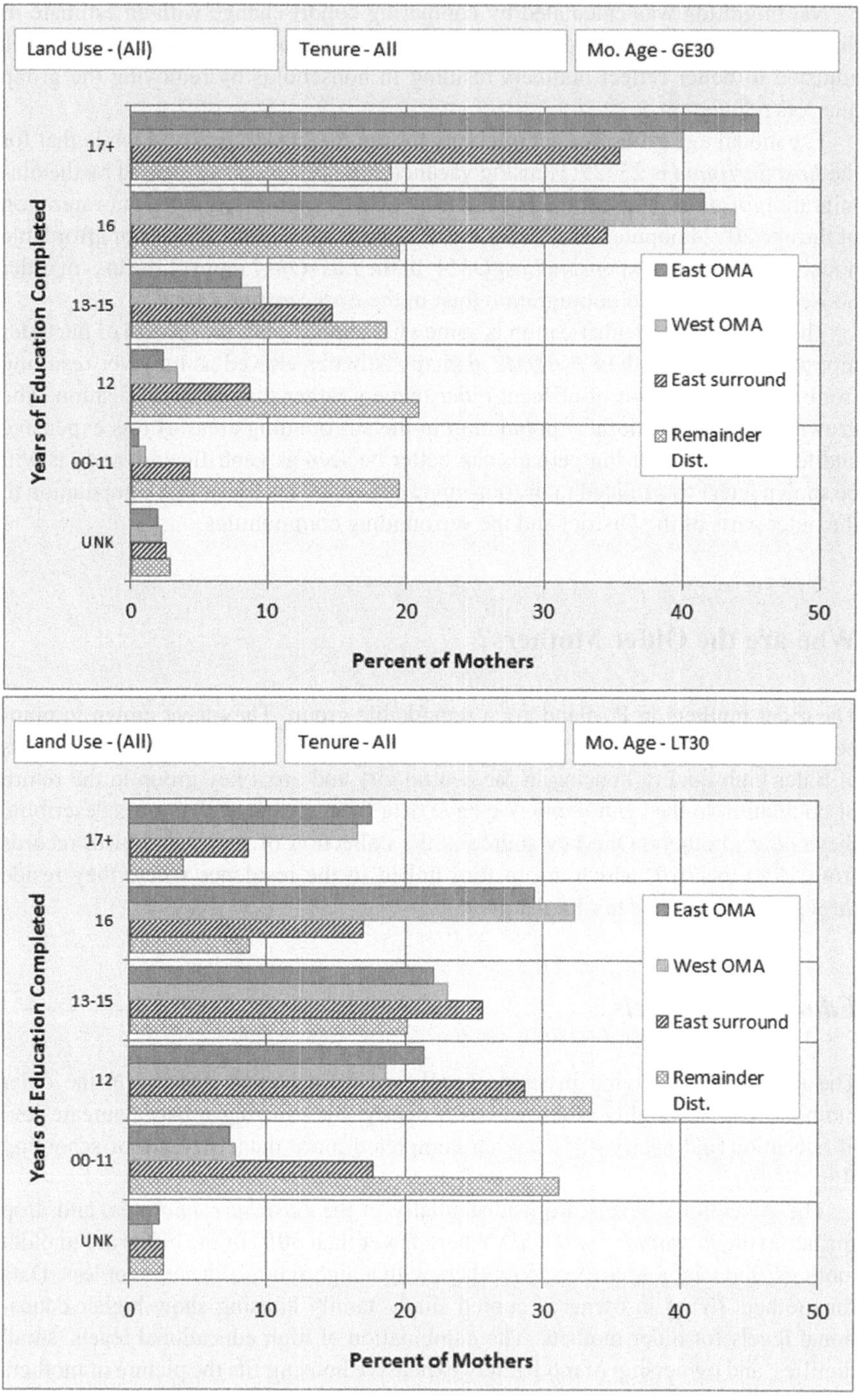

Fig. 17.10 Educational levels of mothers over and under age 30 at time of birth. (Source: Oregon Health Authority)

Length of Residence

In the *East OMA* the modal period of residence for first births was 5 years and for second births tied at 5 or 6 years[2]. About half of the births for all birth orders were to mothers who resided there for 5 years or less. This implies that for the current crop of students entering kindergarten in 2009 approximately half in-migrated in about 1999, counting back 5 years from the date the mother moved in and adding five more years from the year of birth to entry into kindergarten. Thus the beginnings of the enrollment turnaround likely began in the mid 1990's. In addition to children born at the *East OMA* location, about 52 % of the mothers brought children with them, based on birth order for each recorded birth.

Housing Type, Value, and Tenure

The *East OMA* stands out because nearly all of the older mothers reside in single family, owner occupied housing. In the *East Surround* there are older mothers but more of them reside in rental single family housing or multiple family units. The *East OMA* has a higher proportion of older mothers residing in owner occupied single family housing than in the *South OMA* or the *West OMA*. Younger mothers are most numerous in the *East Surround* area and in the *Remainder of the District* where they are housed in approximately equal parts owner occupied single family housing, renter occupied single family housing, and multifamily housing.

Within the PPS District older mothers live in housing that ranges in value from under $ 200,000 to over $ 750,000, with older mothers occupying more of the housing valued over $ 250,000 than younger mothers. Most older mothers living in the *East OMA* live in housing valued in the $ 300,000 to $ 400,000 price range, somewhat more expensive than housing for older mothers district-wide.

Did the Births to Older Mothers Reverse the Decline in Enrollments?

Until 2006 there was a significant drop in white enrollment in PPS, averaging 1,200 students per year over a 10 year period. The loss of black enrollment that began after 2000 has continued to the present, mainly due to the out-migration of black households from PPS to the inner suburbs, but also to a decline in birthrates of young women. The loss of black students was greatest in the *East Surround* area, which contained Portland's historic black neighborhoods.

[2] Length of residence was determined from the linked tax-lot and birth record data. The date that the birth mother in-migrated was calculated to be the last date of sale for the property, but only for owner occupied units. Most of the housing units in the East OMA were owner occupied.

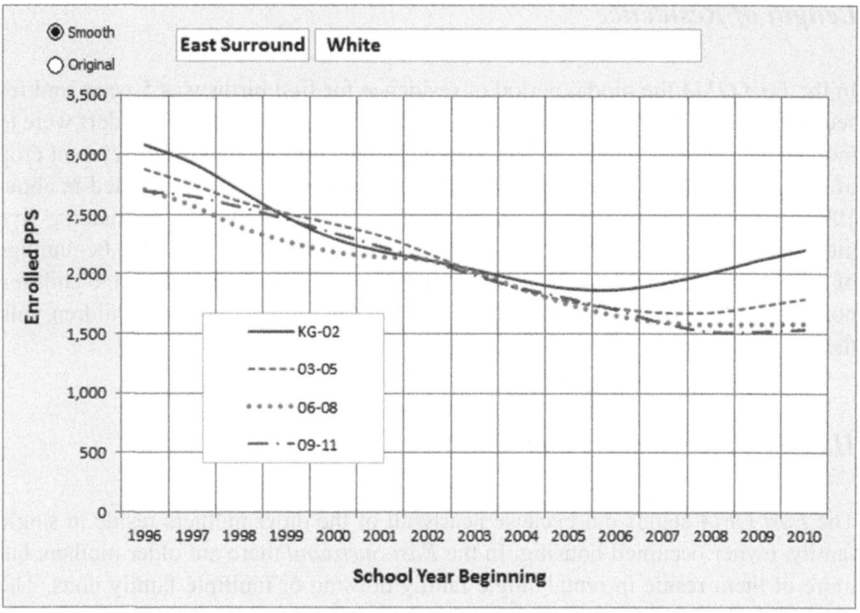

Fig. 17.11 White enrollment by grade level for *East Surround* area. (Source: Portland Public Schools)

In the three *older moms areas* (East, South, and West) enrollment stopped declining in the lower elementary grades (KG-02) in about 2000 and began to grow in about 2004. Most of the growth in the OMA areas has been among white students. There were few black and Hispanic students added but a modest number of Asian origin.

By 2007 enrollment growth began to filter upward into the upper elementary levels (03–05) and by 2009 into the middle school levels (06–08). As the gentrification process spread outwards into the *East Surround* area there was a similar pattern of increased enrollment of white students in KG-02 beginning in about 2006 and stabilization or small increases in the upper grades (Fig. 17.11).

Was the growth in enrollment in the gentrifying areas sufficient to turn around the District's downward enrollment trend? The answer is a qualified yes. The District's resident K-12 enrollment bottomed out at 44,061 in 2008 and rose to 44,727 in 2010 (Fig. 17.12). By 2012, resident K-12 enrollment rose to 45,511, 3.3 % above its 2008 level.

Enrollment in the lower elementary grades (KG-02) began to rise in 2004 followed in 2007 by growth in the upper elementary grades (03–05). Of the 1,071 increase in KG-02 enrollment from 2005–2010, 470 was from growth in the *OMA areas* and 134 from the *East Surround* area. White KG-02 enrollment in the *East Surround* area grew by 389 students, but there was a loss of 255 non-white KG-02 students.

Enrollment in the elementary grades (KG-05) began to grow and enrollment in middle school stabilized. However, high school enrollment continued to decline,

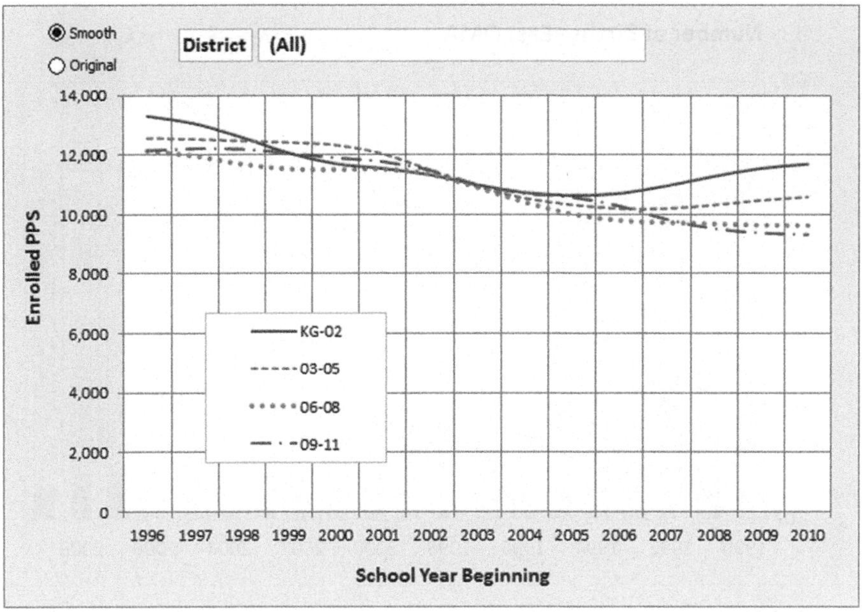

Fig. 17.12 Overall enrollment by grade level for PPS. (Source: Portland Public Schools)

perhaps due in part to increases in private school enrollment and uncertainty about school choice policies and potential school closures.

If the reader will assume for now that the gentrification process did in part turn around the District's slump in enrollment, what was it about the gentrification process that resulted in the change?

Age Structure and Birth Rates

A simple explanation would be that the increase in births to older mothers created a larger pool of potential kindergarteners. It appears that this was the case to a limited degree, but as we will explain later not the main factor. We will examine these issues for the *East OMA* and *East Surround* areas where most of the effects of gentrification occurred.

East OMA

From 1996 to 2002 there was an increase in births in this area from 531 to 621 (Fig. 17.13).

If these children remained in the District and enrolled in kindergarten, these births should have generated enrollment 5 years later, from 2001 to 2007. Was this

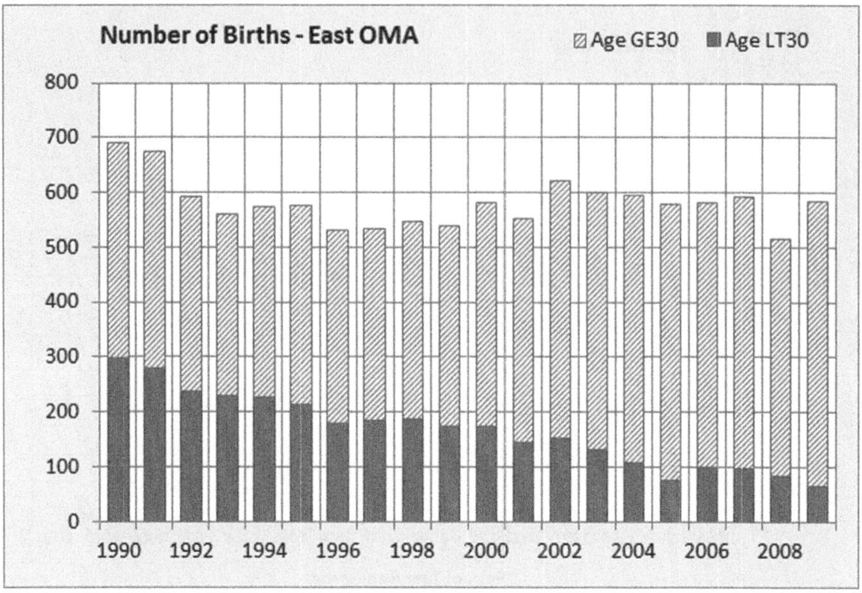

Fig. 17.13 Births in the *East OMA* areas by age of mother. (Source: Oregon Health Authority)

increase in births due to net in-migration of birth age mothers or due to an increase in birth rates? From 2000 to 2010 there was a small increase in the numbers of women age 35–39 and a small decrease in the numbers under age 30 (Fig. 17.14).

For this same period there was a relatively large increase in the birth rate for women over age 35 (Fig. 17.15).

We can not accurately calculate the numbers of women by age or the age specific birthrates for the years between 2000 and 2010, but it appears likely to us that the increase in births during this time frame was due to a combination of growth in the older female cohorts and the increase in the birth rate for these cohorts.

The East Surround Area

The number of births in the *East Surround* area generally declined from 1990 until about 2005 when births began to increase. The number of women in the age groups from 25 to 39 increased in the *East Surround* area. This is due in part to net in-migration of older households in this transtion area but also to infill housing growth. Birth rates in this area declined dramatically for women age 29 and under and increased substantially for women age 30 and older. The growth in births after 2004 is a result of both higher birth rates to older mothers and larger cohorts of older mothers.

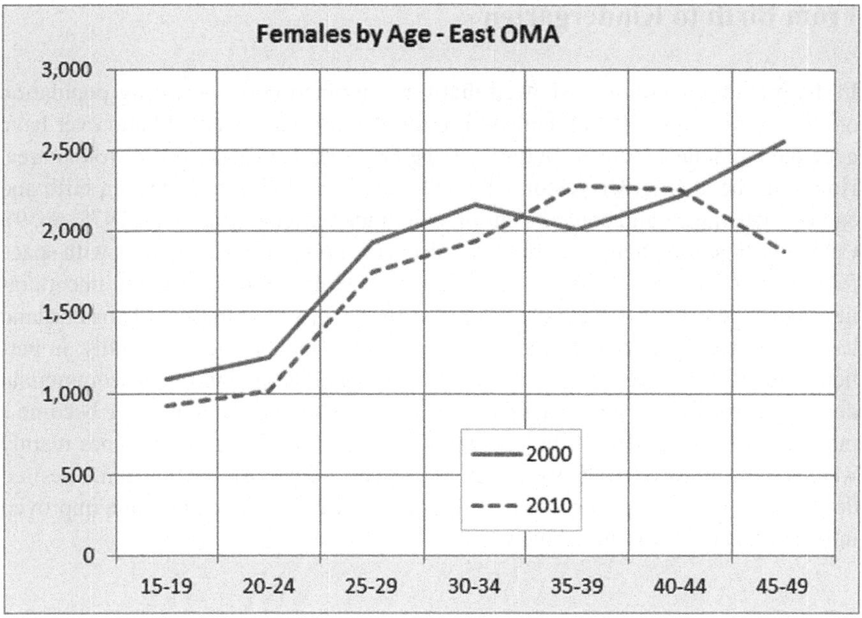

Fig. 17.14 Number of women by age for *East OMA*. (Source: U.S. Census of Population and Housing 2000 and 2010)

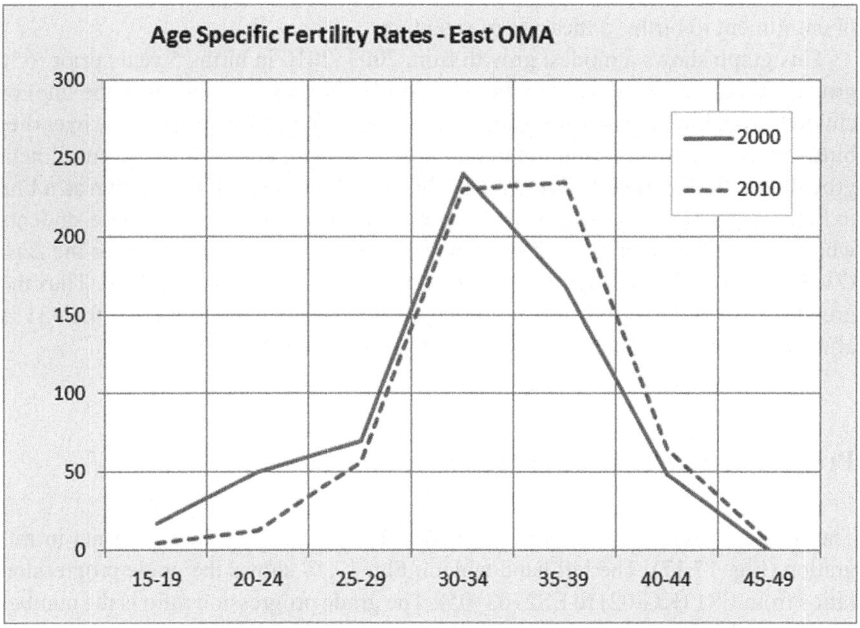

Fig. 17.15 Age specific birth rates per thousand women for *East OMA*. (Sources: Population from U.S. Census of Population and Housing 2000 and 2010, births from Oregon Health Authority)

From Birth to Kindergarten

In the previous section we showed that the combination of increasing population of women age 25 to 39 and increased birth rates for women age 30 and over have generated a modest increase in births in the *East OMA* and the *East Surround* area. However, the District has historically had a net loss of children between birth and age five when the child could be enrolled in kindergarten (Lycan et al. 1978, pp. 9). Causes of this trend may have been: insufficient supply of housing units with space for growing families, better housing values in suburban locations, and uncertainties about the quality of schools. However in recent years households in Portland have exhibited some of the same housing preferences observed nationally, in particular to live in close-in urban housing near walkable neighborhood commercial districts. Portland's east side neighborhoods of quality older homes have become a magnet for this segment of the population. At one time these older homes mainly were sought by local residents, but in recent years they also have become desired destinations for in-migrants to the metropolitan area, due in part to much improved information about housing choices.

Oregon Health Authority

Figure 17.16 shows enrollment, the number of births 5 years previous, and the ratio of enrollment to births, a measure of retention.

This graph shows a modest growth from 2003–2010 in births 5 years prior (6 % growth) and a major increase in the retention (31 % increase, shown as the line) of children from birth to entry into kindergarten. In combination, the increase in earlier births made a small contribution to enrollment growth, but most of the enrollment growth was due to increased retention. The cohort progression rate shown as a line in Fig. 17.16 combines the effects of net migration with the share of these students who enroll in the District's schools, the capture rate. The capture rate for the *East OMA* for grades KG-02 declined from 82.5 % in 2000 to 80.4 % in 2010. Thus the growth attributable to the shift in migration trends was slightly greater than 31 % after accounting for the increasing losses to private schools.

Progression after Kindergarten

The passage from grades KG-02 to grades 03–05 also benefited from net in-migration (Fig. 17.17). The left hand table in Fig. 17.17 shows the grade progression ratios from ES1 (KG-02) to ES2 (03–05). The grade progression ratio is the number in grades 03–05 as a proportion of the number in grades KG-02 3 years prior. This

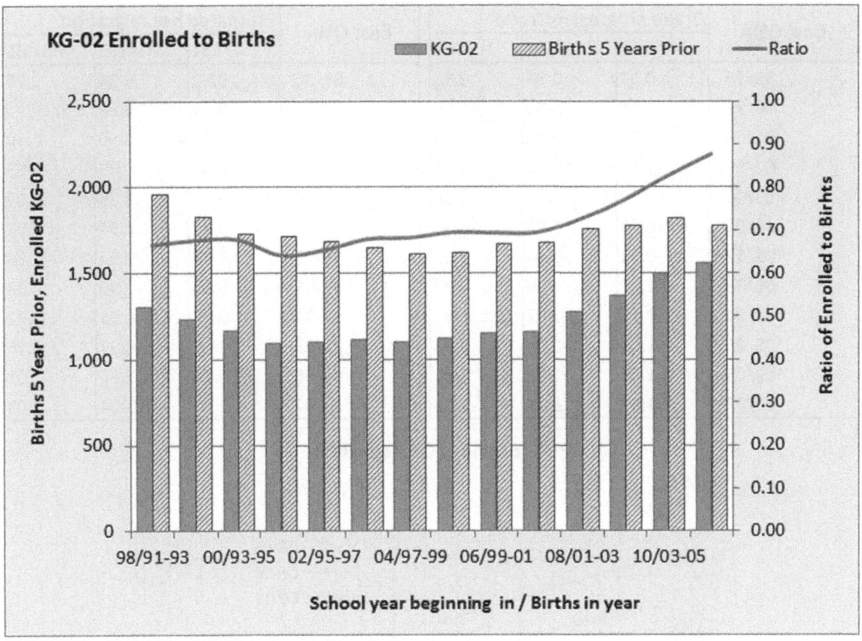

Fig. 17.16 Comparison of enrollment in KG-02 with births 5 years prior for *East OMA*. (Sources: Enrollment from Portland Public Schools, births from Oregon Health Authority)

ratio also combines the effects of net migration with changes in the public school capture rate. Factoring in the downward trend in public school capture rates from 2000 to 2010, the grade progression ratios isolating the effects of net migration are in the rightmost table in Fig. 17.17.

Values over 1.00 in the progression rates indicate that enrollment in the cohort is growing. Generally the progression ratios in tables in Fig. 17.17 increase over time indicating that a greater share of the cohort is remaining within the area, or that the cohort is augmented through in-migration. The progression ratios rise first for the transition from grades KG-02 to 03–05 and later for the middle school and high school levels. But for enrollment to grow, net in-migration of the relatively affluent 30-somethings must overcome the likelyhood that they will privately school their children. The decline in the public school capture rate is consistent with an observed positive relationship between household income and enrollment in private schools, however for the *East OMA* area the proportion of children in public schools is high compared to other affluent parts of the Portland metropolitan area.

East OMA	Grade progression ratio		
School Years	ES2/ES1	MS/ES2	HS/MS
99/96	0.90	0.96	0.95
00/97	0.96	0.91	0.90
01/98	0.95	0.92	0.89
02/99	0.95	0.95	0.88
03/00	0.97	0.90	0.86
04/01	0.98	0.96	0.90
05/02	0.98	0.94	0.93
06/03	1.00	0.96	0.99
07/04	0.99	0.97	0.91
08/05	1.03	0.98	0.95
09/06	1.09	1.01	1.01
10/07	1.08	1.05	1.03

East OMA	Estimated net migration		
School Years	ES2/ES1	MS/ES2	HS/MS
99/96	0.92	0.94	0.96
00/97	0.97	0.89	0.91
01/98	0.96	0.90	0.90
02/99	0.95	0.93	0.89
03/00	0.97	0.89	0.87
04/01	0.97	0.94	0.91
05/02	0.98	0.92	0.94
06/03	0.99	0.95	0.99
07/04	0.97	0.95	0.92
08/05	1.01	0.97	0.96
09/06	1.06	1.00	1.01
10/07	1.05	1.04	1.03

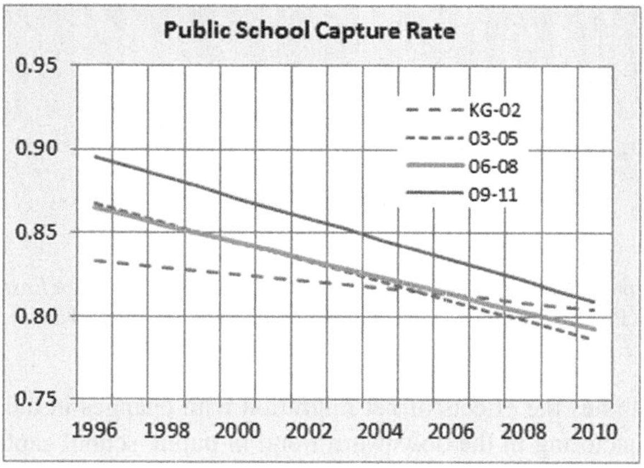

Fig. 17.17 Grade progression ratios, capture rates, and net migration for East OMA. (Sources: Enrollment from Portland Public Schools, age data from U.S. Census of Population and Housing 2000 and 2010)

Measuring the Effects of Births and Retention

An analysis similar to that for the *East OMA* was carried out for each of the study areas. Rather than repeating these analyses in detail, an overall assessment of the impacts of the number of births, changes in the public school capture rate, and net-migration will be presented[3]. A simple model is used to assess the effects.

Prior enrolled * net migration ratio * capture rate = Subsequent enrollment

Each of the three factors was held constant at the observed value in 2,000 and the impact on enrollment was recorded.

[3] The net migration ratio is calculated by dividing the grade progression ratio by the public school capture rate. The grade progression ratio is the number in a particular cohort divided by the number in the previous time period. It is the product of the net migration rate and the public school capture rate.

East OMA

The effect of births grows after 2000 (the year) vs 2,000 (a value) to a high value of 56 additional students in 2010. The impact of the net migration ratio (NMR) from births to grades KG-02 is much greater, growing to 447 additional students in 2010, an effect nearly 8 times greater than the increase in number of births (Table 17.1, left).

The public school capture rate (PSCR) has a downward impact by 2010 of -40 students, small compared to the effects of net in-migration. Finally, a small interaction term is shown to account for the difference between the sum of the individual factors and their compounded effect.

A similar analysis was done for the transition from grades KG-02 to grades 03–05 (Table 17.1, right). The impact of the number of KG-02 students 3 years previous vs 5 years prior is negative, but the negative impact declines somewhat after 2004. The effects of net migration (NMR) grow slowly after 2000 then accelerated to an increase of 151 students in 2010. The public school capture rate (PSCR) has a small negative effect.

East Surround

The impacts of births, net migration, and the public school capture rate on the *East Surround* area are somewhat similar to those on the *East OMA*, but their impact is felt later (Table 17.2, left).

After 2000 declining births tended to drive KG-02 enrollment down, reaching a maximum loss of -745 students in 2010. The net migration ratio (NMR) from birth to KG-02 also has a negative impact on enrollment until 2008, after which it begins to lift enrollment. A decline in the public school capture rate (PSCR) from 2000 to 2010 also has a negative impact on enrollment. For the progression from grades KG-02 to 03–05 earlier declines in KG-02 enrollment continue to drag down enrollment in grades 03–05 (Table 17.2, right). The negative impact of the net migration ratio (NMR) grows from 2000 to 2006 and then falls until it turns slightly positive in 2010. The declining public school capture rate (PSCR) has a considerable negative impact on enrollment, but is less negative in 2010 than in earlier years. The modest turnaround in the net migration ratio and the public school capture rate was not sufficient to overcome the decline in the number of KG-02 students. However, recall that there was an enrollment turnaround in the lower grades for white students but this was countered by declines in the number of minority students.

Conclusions

The research on which this paper is based was a practical effort to provide the Portland Public School District with information on which to base its planning. The funding and time frame for this type of research limited the amount of back-

Births to KG-02

Year	Births 5 Yrs Prev	Effects Births	NMR	PSCR	INT
1997	1,955	162	38	10	-6
1998	1,827	78	58	6	-4
1999	1,726	10	60	3	-1
2000	1,711	0	0	0	0
2001	1,681	-20	23	-3	0
2002	1,643	-46	67	-6	3
2003	1,612	-67	73	-8	5
2004	1,620	-63	97	-11	6
2005	1,667	-30	100	-15	4
2006	1,673	-26	105	-18	4
2007	1,755	32	171	-23	-1
2008	1,773	48	254	-28	-3
2009	1,817	88	364	-34	-11
2010	1,775	56	447	-40	-4

KG-02 to 03-05

Year	KG-02	Effects KG-02	NMR	PSCR	INT
1997	1,301				
1998	1,235				
1999	1,169	0	-74	6	0
2000	1,097	-67	0	1	0
2001	1,098	-129	-12	-5	-2
2002	1,115	-192	-9	-9	-3
2003	1,099	-264	10	-14	-1
2004	1,125	-265	21	-19	1
2005	1,155	-249	32	-24	3
2006	1,162	-269	53	-30	7
2007	1,277	-239	38	-35	2
2008	1,368	-216	80	-43	10
2009	1,503	-220	147	-51	24
2010	1,557	-97	151	-62	14

Table 17.1 Assessment of births, ratios, and capture rates, for *East OMA*. (Sources: Enrollment from Portland Public Schools, age data from U.S. Census of Population and Housing 2000 and 2010)

Births to KG-02

Year	Births 5 Yrs Prev	Effects Births	NMR	PSCR	INT
1997	7,627	471	284	45	-34
1998	7,452	347	154	29	-14
1999	7,216	192	8	13	-1
2000	6,900	0	0	0	0
2001	6,718	-110	10	-12	0
2002	6,575	-196	21	-25	0
2003	6,477	-248	-79	-35	-8
2004	6,381	-294	-198	-45	-22
2005	6,371	-300	-183	-56	-23
2006	6,217	-388	-163	-66	-29
2007	6,031	-511	-28	-78	-16
2008	5,923	-587	60	-89	-3
2009	5,893	-613	119	-102	7
2010	5,756	-745	371	-118	64

KG-02 to 03-05

Year	KG-02	Effects KG-02	NMR	PSCR	INT
1997	4,941				
1998	4,691				
1999	4,388	0	-115	-216	-6
2000	4,175	-112	0	-210	-5
2001	4,062	-343	113	-198	-1
2002	3,975	-612	55	-177	-16
2003	3,804	-786	-39	-158	-44
2004	3,616	-865	-125	-145	-73
2005	3,613	-915	-221	-132	-108
2006	3,530	-1069	-182	-123	-111
2007	3,543	-1269	-76	-115	-81
2008	3,556	-1291	-33	-112	-60
2009	3,586	-1380	-2	-105	-47
2010	3,747	-1378	14	-101	-37

Table 17.2 Assessment of births, ratios, and capture rates, for *East Surround.* (Sources: Enrollment from Portland Public Schools, age data from U.S. Census of Population and Housing 2000 and 2010)

ground research that could be done. However, forecasts based blindly on numbers and trends can go awry and are improved by digging into causes and background. This search for causes can branch out in many directions, in this case including changes in birth rates, gentrification, turnover of senior households, and retention of students. Pursuing a wide range of topics takes the researcher into unfamiliar territory. But it helps in the design and implementation of the forecasting models and hopefully limits the likelihood of forecasting blunders. It also provides the background and anecdotal information needed to make credible presentations at public meetings of locally knowledgeable parents and school administrators.

Did the paper succeed in explaning how the shift in births from younger mothers to older mothers resulted in the turn around in school enrollment in PPS? We think that it did, but the answer was more complex that we first thought. Our initial observation was the geographical coincidence of enrollment growth in the lower grades and the concentration of older mothers who bore the children who later enrolled in the District's schools. Viewing these concentrations as a manifestation of gentrification that linked a highly educated group of older mothers to nationally observed trends to reside in the central city suggested that the concentrations of the older moms was a matter of housing choices by this group. Whereas younger couples living in these same areas 20 or 30 years ago might have fled to the suburbs when their first or second child was born, these *older moms* came for a purpose and stayed. We were able to quantify this in the cohort progression ratios and show that it was increased retention more than increased births that drove the District's turn around in school enrollment.

It it reasonable to characterize the movement of the highly educated mothers into Portland's east housing as gentrification? The literature on gentrification is rather fragmented and lacking in a common definition of what constitutes gentrification. Some authors, such as Ehrenhalt (2012) simply see an "inversion" in which people are moving back into the central city, with differing manifestations in different locations. We used Ley's (1996) measures to examine the situation in Portland and found that it seemed to fit his definition of gentrification well. The vacancies that facilitated the in-migration of the older moms resulted mainly from the death and out-migration of seniors, suggesting that normal housing turnover was involved. However the in-migrating older moms were better educated and considerably more affluent than the older families departing. We also were able to show where there was accelerated out-migration of seniors, perhaps due to the very rapid escalation of house prices in the affected areas.

We were fortunate to have access to highly detailed geo-coded administrative data: birth records, student records, and tax-lot data as well as the usual data from the Census and the American Community Survey. Linking birth record and student record data to the housing data from the tax assessor's files multiplied the value of these data. Working with geo-coded data also freed us from the sometimes arbitrary aggregations of data into units such as census tracts and allowed us to create our own regions for tabulation of our data. The use of GIS tools provided efficient ways to manage and relate large data sources that would have been impossible 20 years ago. The GIS tools also facilititated mapping of the data as an aid to visualization and hypotheses generation. There are limitations to the use of administrative data collected by others for their own purposes. For example, the tax assessor in our county of interest stopped maintaining bedroom counts for houses, because of budget concerns and lack of a requirement for its business operations.

Finally, we hope this paper will be of some interest to you in providing a view of work in the niche area referred to as *school demography* and a view of the borderlands between applied demographic research and topically focused research of a more scholarly nature.

References

Ehrenhalt, A. (2012). The great inversion. New York: Alfred A. Knopf.

Environmental Systems Research Institute. (2012). ArcGIS for desktop. http://www.esri.com/software/arcgis/arcgis-for-desktop/index.html. Accessed 14 May 2012.

Kirmeyer, S. E., & Hamilton, B. E. (2011). Childbearing differences among three generations of U.S. women. NCHS Data Brief No. 68, August 2011.

Ley, D. (1996). *The new middle class and the remaking of the central city*. New York: Oxford University Press.

Lycan, R., Pendleton, P., & Weiss, J. (1978). Residential mobility study for Portland, Oregon, City of Portland Office of Planning and Development.

Lycan, D. R. (2008). Linking tax-lot and student record data: Applications in school planning. In H. M. Steve & A. S. David, *Applied demography in the twenty first century*. Dordrecht: Springer Science+Business B.V.

National Center for Educational Statistics. (2012). School district demographics system. http://nces.ed.gov/surveys/sdds/index.aspx. Accessed 14 May 2012.

Silverman, B. W. (1986). *Density estimation for statistics and data analysis*. New York: Chapman and Hall.

Chapter 18
Who Must Elect by District in California?

A Demographer's Perspective on Methods for Assessing Racially Polarized Voting

Jeanne Gobalet and Shelley Lapkoff

The California Voting Rights Act

The California Voting Rights Act (CVRA) was signed into law on July 9, 2002. It applies to jurisdictions that elect boards and councils at-large (all voters in the jurisdiction may vote for all members of the governing board or council). The CVRA disallows the use of the at-large type of election if it "impairs the ability of a protected class to elect candidates of its choice or its ability to influence the outcome of an election." The law was intended to enable members of protected groups (Hispanics, African Americans, Asian Americans, other non-White groups) to elect or to influence the election of representatives of their choice by requiring the election of board and council members from single-member districts (rather than at-large).

The CVRA expands on the Federal Voting Rights Act of 1965, making it simpler for California's minority groups to compel jurisdictions to change their election methods. Unlike the Federal Voting Rights Act, the CVRA does not require plaintiffs to demonstrate that a specific minority-majority single-member district or districts can be configured.

A major concern for potential defendants in CVRA litigation is that the law requires the defendant to pay the plaintiff's legal fees if the plaintiff's lawsuit is successful. The City of Modesto reportedly paid $3 million to attorneys for the plaintiff who sued them (Leoni and Skinnell 2009). Madera Unified School District is said to have paid $162,500 in plaintiff attorney fees (reduced from an original claim for $1.8 million). These awards have prompted many California jurisdictions to change their method of election rather than to risk litigation. However, some cities, school districts, and special districts, as well as a county, have undertaken the technical analyses needed to determine their exposure to litigation under the CVRA. The

J. Gobalet (✉)
Lapkoff & Gobalet Demographic Research, Inc., Saratoga, CA, USA
e-mail: gobalet@demographers.com

S. Lapkoff
Lapkoff & Gobalet Demographic Research, Inc., Berkeley, CA, USA

M. N. Hoque, L. B. Potter (eds.), *Emerging Techniques in Applied Demography*, Applied Demography Series 4, DOI 10.1007/978-94-017-8990-5_18,

necessary information concerns whether there is evidence of racially polarized voting (also called "racial bloc voting" and "minority vote dilution").[1]

Statistical Methods Currently Used to Identify Racially Polarized Voting

Questions about whether voting is racially polarized arise whenever a jurisdiction's population includes a significant number of members of protected groups. Two methods for establishing the existence of racially polarized voting have been accepted by courts: homogeneous precincts and ecological regression. A third method, ecological inference, has been used, as well, but it has not yet been widely accepted.

Homogeneous Precinct Analysis

Homogeneous precinct analysis is appropriate in jurisdictions where there is substantial residential segregation that concentrates different racial/ethnic groups in different precincts. The standard for determining the level of concentration of an ethnic group is the group's share of the voting age population (persons of voting age) in each precinct. A precinct is generally considered highly concentrated (homogeneous) if over 90 percent of its voting age population is of the same racial/ethnic group. Homogeneous precinct analysis is used when a jurisdiction has multiple precincts with these concentration levels. Typically, decennial census data are used to identify these precincts.

Table 18.1 provides a hypothetical example in which the voters in Black precincts overwhelmingly preferred Candidate 1, while voters in the White precincts overwhelmingly voted for Candidate 2. Although there is some "crossover voting" (Whites voting for the African American-preferred candidate and African Americans voting for the White-preferred candidate), this case would be interpreted as showing racially polarized voting; that is, that voters' choices are highly associated with their race.[2]

---

[1] California Elections Code, Section 14026:

"As used in this chapter:

(e) "Racially polarized voting" means voting in which there is a difference, as defined in case law regarding enforcement of the federal Voting Rights Act (42 U.S.C. Section 1973 et seq.), in the choice of candidates or other electoral choices that are preferred by voters in a protected class, and in the choice of candidates and electoral choices that are preferred by voters in the rest of the electorate. The methodologies for estimating group voting behavior as approved in applicable federal cases to enforce the federal Voting Rights Act (42 U.S.C. Section 1973 et seq.) to establish racially polarized voting may be used for purposes of this section to prove that elections are characterized by racially polarized voting".

[2] One could conduct a Chi-Square or Fisher's Exact test to suggest the probability that the observed pattern might occur by random chance.

Table 18.1 Illustration summarizing voting, by candidate, in homogeneous voting precincts

Precinct type	Candidate 1, favored by African American voters	Candidate 2, favored by White voters
95% of precinct's voting age population is African American	85%	15%
90% of precinct's voting age population is White	20%	80%

In homogeneous precinct analysis, the first step is to identify the homogeneous precincts in which the minority (or majority) share of the voting age population is 90 percent or more. The identification is generally based on data from the most recent decennial census. The second step is to accumulate the voting shares for each candidate in each precinct. A simple comparison, perhaps a scattergram or scatter plot, shows whether the different ethnic groups favor different candidates. Note that the "candidate of choice" need not be of the same ethnicity as the precincts' ethnic group. That is, African Americans might prefer a candidate even though the candidate himself is not African American. Thus, for this analysis, it is not necessary to identify the race of the candidates (which can sometimes be challenging, especially for past elections).

In California, racial/ethnic populations are seldom completely segregated, and homogeneous precincts are rare, in our experience. Even when we find them, there are not enough of them for a homogeneous precinct analysis—usually only one, or at most a handful, in a particular jurisdiction.

Ecological Regression Analysis

Ecological regression (ER) analysis was developed to analyze voting data in non-homogeneous precincts. In this method, information about voting behavior in all precincts, not just homogeneous precincts, is analyzed. This type of analysis produces *estimates* of voting patterns by race/ethnicity. It is called *ecological* because aggregated data (the combination of all voters in a precinct) rather than individual-level data are analyzed. It is *regression analysis* because it relies on the statistical procedure of summarizing the relationship between the two variables by assuming a linear relationship between them and calculating the line that best fits the data.

This method is most straightforward when there are just two major groups in a jurisdiction (Whites and Hispanics, or Whites and African Americans), rather than multiple racial/ethnic groups. For the analysis, one assembles a database of precincts. For each precinct, we need to know the share (proportion or percentage)

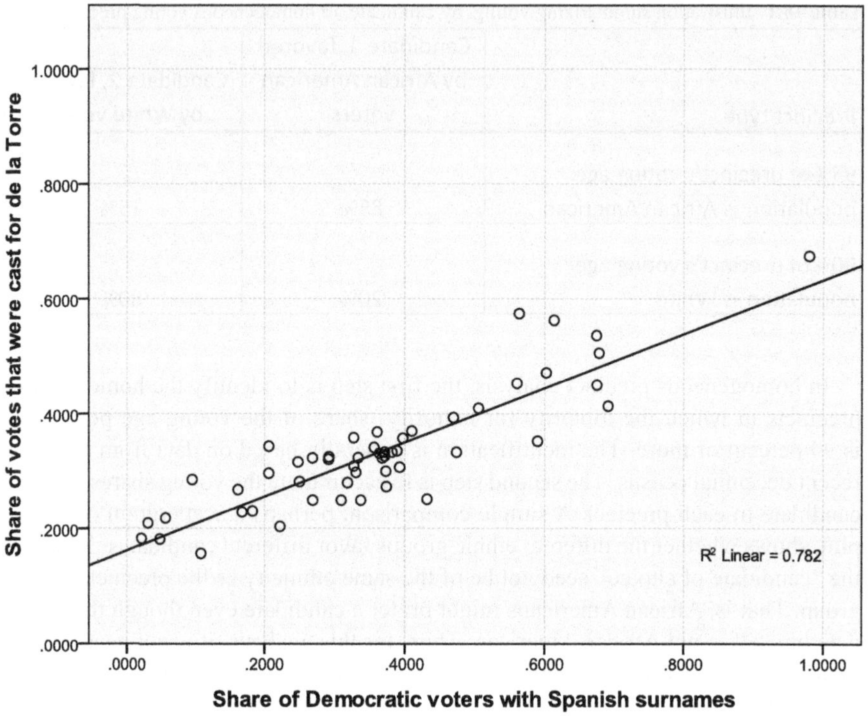

Fig. 18.1 Sample scattergram (in a party's primary election)

of the population that belongs to the groups of interest.[3] We also need to know the share of the votes received by each candidate in the elections of interest.

We derive the percentage of the voting age population in each group of interest from the decennial census (by aggregating census blocks to the precinct level), as described above in the discussion of homogeneous precinct analysis. However, for California jurisdictions, we perform Spanish surname analyses of a list of actual voters in each precinct in the elections of interest. The data gathered are: (1) share of voters with Spanish surnames in each precinct; and (2) the share of voters in each precinct who voted for each candidate.

Once we have performed the surname analysis, a scatterplot graph can be drawn that illustrates the relationship between the percentage of voters with Spanish surnames and the percentage of votes for a particular candidate. The graph in Fig. 18.1 illustrates such a relationship. The estimated percentage of voters with Spanish surnames in each precinct (the independent variable) is shown on the X axis, while the percentage of voters casting ballots for the candidate of interest (the dependent variable) is shown on the Y axis. A bivariate regression analysis is run, with the voter

[3] Measures of the population used in ER include voting age population, citizen voting age population, registered voters, and actual voters in each group of interest.

Table 18.2 Part of database used for ecological regression analysis (note single homogeneous precinct, in which 93 percent of the voters had Spanish surnames)—some precincts omitted

Precinct	*Weight analysis by number of voters in election* Voted_03	SSvoted_03	Bustamante	Schwarzenegger	all others	*Independent variable* SS_pct	nonSS_pct	*Dependent variable* Pct_Bustamante
22370	43	40	38	2	3	93%	7%	88%
22358	1057	562	383	152	178	53%	47%	36%
16934	504	64	119	151	107	13%	87%	24%
19324	614	76	110	184	128	12%	88%	18%
19618	787	93	133	228	139	12%	88%	17%
22728	254	29	50	78	53	11%	89%	20%
22338	323	34	56	107	81	11%	89%	17%
22342	519	52	74	192	101	10%	90%	14%
24240	281	27	44	98	60	10%	90%	16%
21608	553	51	106	192	108	9%	91%	19%
16606	598	53	91	172	135	9%	91%	15%
22742	769	62	123	237	154	8%	92%	16%
22320	498	39	67	168	80	8%	92%	13%
22310	358	27	46	158	72	8%	92%	13%
22736	393	29	67	138	71	7%	93%	17%
22146	685	43	69	283	125	6%	94%	10%
21620	566	33	89	180	97	6%	94%	16%
22716	1076	60	169	364	201	6%	94%	16%
22330	544	25	64	194	137	5%	95%	12%
22366	453	15	54	176	91	3%	97%	12%
6247902	155	2	10	100	47	1%	99%	6%
21728	2	0	0	2	0	0%	100%	0%

"SS" = Spanish surname

share as the dependent variable and the share of voters with Spanish surnames (or other ethnic group) as the independent variable. The precincts should be weighted by the number of voters for the analysis.

The resulting R-squared coefficient (R^2, or coefficient of determination) is used to judge the extent of racially polarized voting. This measure indicates the proportion of the variation in the dependent variable that is explained by the independent variable. Although the courts have not provided guidance on the degree/size of the correlation coefficient necessary to be considered racially polarized, in our experience, coefficients less than 0.2 typically are interpreted to mean that the community does not have significant levels of racially polarized voting. R-squared coefficients of 0.4 and above are considered evidence of severely racially polarized voting. R-squared values between 0.2 and 0.4 are said to indicate moderate polarization. We believe these levels are used because, on a scattergram, one cannot see a relationship between the two variables with an R-squared coefficient less than 0.2, whereas with an R-squared of 0.4 or higher, one can almost draw the regression line manually.

Figure 18.1 is a scattergram showing the relationship between the share of the voters who had Spanish surnames and the share of votes received by Hector de la Torre (losing candidate for California Insurance Commissioner in the June 2010 Democratic primary) in a jurisdiction for which we performed a CVRA risk assessment study. Each small circle on the scattergram represents one precinct. The R-squared statistic for this analysis was 0.782, which would be interpreted as indicating a high degree of racial polarization in the voting.

Table 18.2 provides a partial database used to analyze voting patterns in one jurisdiction's precincts in the California special 2003 gubernatorial election (the

Table 18.3 Results of ecological regression analysis

Model Summary

Model	R	R Square	Adjusted R Square	Std. Error of the Estimate
1	.766[a]	.587	.587	.0603444

a. Predictors: (Constant), pct_SSvoted

Coefficients[a]

Model		Unstandardized Coefficients		Standardized Coefficients	t	Sig.
		B	Std. Error	Beta		
1	(Constant)	.149	.001		282.138	.000
	pct_SSvoted	.910	.004	.766	235.770	.000

a. Dependent Variable: Pct_Bustamante

Table 18.4 Summary table

Election	Office	Candidate	R-squared	Estimated Share of group's vote (weighted ER*)			Share of voters with Spanish surnames
				estimated % of Spanish surname vote	estimated % of non-Spanish surname vote	Share of total vote received in jurisdiction	
2003 special recall election	Governor	Cruz Bustamante	0.587	101%	15%	25%	11%

* ER (ecological regression) analysis was weighted by the number of poll voters in each precinct in the election.

incumbent governor was recalled in that election). In this election, Cruz Bustamante (the Democratic candidate, who is Hispanic) lost to Arnold Schwarzenegger (the Republican candidate). Our ecological regression analysis showed rather pronounced racially polarized voting in this race and jurisdiction, with an R-squared value of 0.587 (Table 18.3).

The results of this analysis suggested that, if 100 percent of a precinct's voters had non-Spanish surnames, an estimated 15 percent of the votes would have been for Bustamante. The results also suggested (impossibly) that if all of a precinct's voters had Spanish surnames, Bustamante would have received 101 percent of the votes. Table 18.4 shows how we reported the results of this ER analysis.

Criticisms of Ecological Regression

There are some important and common criticisms of the ecological regression method. First, the method is not appropriate when the precincts in a jurisdiction have racially/ethnically diverse populations. In the extreme case, imagine a jurisdiction in which all precincts had the same ethnic distribution. In this case, there would be no information available for the independent variable, because there was no variation by precinct. Ecological regression was developed to take advantage of voting data when the precincts were not homogeneous. But if the opposite were the case and all precincts had the same ethnic distribution, no results would be possible. When there is little variation in the ethnic distributions of a jurisdiction's precincts, ecological regression results become subject to random variations and the influences of other factors, including party affiliation, incumbency, candidates' reputations, socioeconomic influences on political preferences, and so forth. Of course, these other factors may have important effects on voting patterns in all types of jurisdictions, both those that have homogeneous precincts and those that are completely heterogeneous.

A second criticism of ecological regression is its reliance on the "constancy assumption." The method is based on the assumption that an Hispanic voter's likelihood of voting for a candidate is the same in all precincts (and a non-Hispanic's likelihood of voting for a candidate also is the same across all precincts). This assumption might be reasonable when analyzing voting behavior of African Americans, who tend to have the same party affiliation regardless of income and education. However, this is less likely to be the case for Hispanics and Asians. There is some evidence that Hispanics or Asians who are college-educated Republicans will not vote the same way as Hispanics or Asians who are low-income, less educated Democrats. Moreover, since higher income Hispanics and Asians are likely to live in different neighborhoods than lower-income Hispanics and Asians, voting behavior is likely to vary by precinct. In communities with relatively few African Americans and relatively more Asians and Hispanics, the constancy assumption is suspect.

A third criticism of the ecological regression method is that it is only *bivariate,* examining the relationship between just two variables: the racial/ethnic composition of the precinct and the votes cast within the precinct for a given candidate. Obviously, voting behavior is influenced by many factors, not just race/ethnicity, so multivariate analysis would assess the relative importance of all the different factors, including gender (of candidates as well as of voters), political party affiliation, educational attainment, income, and other socioeconomic variables. Note that even with multivariate analysis, the same constancy assumption is required: that members of a particular racial/ethnic group vote alike, no matter where they live or what their other characteristics are.

A fourth, and somewhat embarrassing, problem with this technique is that it can produce estimates that fall outside the bounds of possibility. Fairly often, bivariate regression analysis produces results that suggest that a negative share of voters preferred a candidate, or that more than 100 percent of a group voted for a candidate. These are called "out-of-bounds" estimates.

Ecological Inference (EI)

This method was developed by Harvard Professor Gary King (King et al. 2004), in part to address the problem of the out-of-bounds estimates that are possible with bivariate ecological regression analysis. Although this methodology has been used in some court cases regarding the presence or absence of racially polarized voting, it has not been specifically embraced by the U.S. Supreme Court as have the other two statistical techniques (in *Thornburg v. Gingles*, 478 U.S. 30 (1986).

The ecological inference method (method of bounds) is used in combination with maximum likelihood statistics to produce estimates of voting patterns by race. The estimates are the result of a simulation procedure. One difficulty associated with explaining this method is that the estimates can change slightly each time the simulation is run (i.e., the estimates may not necessarily be duplicated precisely on subsequent runs).

The merits of this method have been disputed (Greiner 2007; Freedman et al. 1998). Furthermore, it is particularly challenging to explain to courts.

Conclusion

There is much work for demographers in sorting out which jurisdictions need to change their method of election. For years the work has resulted from analyses required under Section "Statistical Methods Currently Used to Identify Racially Polarized Voting" of the Federal Voting Rights Act. During the last 10 years, in California, increased attention has been paid to changing election methods as a result of passage of the California Voting Rights Act. Demographers who elect to analyze whether a jurisdiction needs to change its method of electing must understand the methods accepted in the courts for identifying the presence of racially polarized voting.

References

Freedman, D. A., Klein, S. P., Ostland, M., & Roberts, M. (1998). *On "solutions" to the ecological inference problem*. Technical Report No. 515, Statistics Department University of California, Berkeley, 10 June 1998. http://emlab.berkeley.edu/pub/users/cle/Archive/e250c_s10/freedman-ecological.pdf.

Greiner, D. J. (2007). Ecological inference in voting rights act disputes: Where are we now, and where do we want to be? *Jurimetrics, 47,* 115–167.

King, G. (1997). *A Solution to the Ecological Inference Problem: Reconstructing Individual Behavior from Aggregate Data*. Princeton: Princeton University Press. http://j.mp/kpuI5R.

King, G., Rosen, O., & Tanner, M. (2004). Information in ecological inference: An introduction. In G. King, O. Rosen, & M. Tanner (Eds.), *Ecological inference: New methodological strategies*. New York: Cambridge University Press. (http://j.mp/ln9wgx and http://gking.harvard.edu/gking/files/eiintro.pdf).

Leoni, M., & Skinnell, C. (Spring 2009). The California Voting Rights Act. *The Public Law Journal, 32*(2). (www.calbar.ca.gov/publiclaw).

Part V
Health Disparities

Chapter 19
Individuals' Perceptions of Belonging to an Age Cohort and Consequential Cohort-Based Decision-Making

Alison Yacyshyn and Kwame Boadu

Introduction

Individuals are raised in contemporary Western society to know that those who are born in similar years are part of a group, experiencing life events together. This grouping, or divisions in the population, can be based merely on age alone. For example, baby boomers, Generation X, Gen X, baby bust, Generation Y, Gen Y, and Millennials are commonly used terms to describe individuals belonging to a particular age cohort. Although the aforementioned terms are commonly used to categorize the population, whether individuals know which group they actually belong to, or how connected they feel in contemporary society, is uncertain. One can question then, whether the perception of belonging to a cohort is the same for everyone. As well, if cohorts suggest that individuals are experiencing different "stages-of-life," with individuals who belong to a specific cohort in a certain life stage, is a life-course approach viewed as being appropriate for policies to be based upon? These questions provide direction for this exploratory paper to address cohorts, perceptions of belonging, and the life-course approach as they are used in applied demographic analysis. The more theoretical discussion of cohorts, perceptions of belonging, and the life-course approach are discussed first, followed by data analysis of a sample from a relevant survey.

Cohorts

In general, an age cohort can be seen as an ascription and "age ascription is the cross-sectional counterpart of cohort differentiation. Similarities of experience within and differentiation of experience between age groups are observable in every culture"

A. Yacyshyn (✉)
Alberta School of Business, University of Alberta, Edmonton, AB T6G 2R6, Canada
e-mail: Alison.Yacyshyn@ualberta.ca

K. Boadu
Office of Statistics and Information, Government of Alberta, Edmonton, AB T5K 0G5, Canada

M. N. Hoque, L. B. Potter (eds.), *Emerging Techniques in Applied Demography*, Applied Demography Series 4, DOI 10.1007/978-94-017-8990-5_19,

(Ryder 1965, p. 846). Important years, which commonly define the boundaries for a cohort, can thus vary according to events experienced by country. For example, in comparing cohort terminology for Canada and the United States, years defining select cohorts can vary. The baby bust (echo boom, Generation X, or Gen X) in Canada is commonly referred to as people born between 1966 and 1974, whereas in the United States the years are 1965 and 1976 (Yacyshyn 2012). So, the year in which an individual is born is an approximation of individuals' lives according to a cohort and their developmental trajectories (Elder 1995). By focusing on generalizable cohort characteristics, researchers can analyze data to "reveal something not revealed by ordinary period analysis; in other words, members of a cohort prove to have something in common beyond the defining property" (Carlsson and Karlsson 1970, p. 710). Similarly, our population is ever changing, and Mannheim (1952) provided insight to population evolution, noting that:

> the continuous emergence of new human beings in our society acts as compensation for the restrictive and partial nature of individual consciousness; it facilitates re-evaluation of our inventory and teaches us both to forget that which is no longer useful and to covet that which has yet to be won. (Mannheim 1952, p. 294)

As individuals travel through life together, they may share a common cohort, and communal socialization and cohort solidarity is often an outcome (Ryder 1965). So, to identify those who belong to a particular cohort, "determining boundaries and cut-off points is another issue in generational politics research" (Braungart and Braungart 1986, p. 218). Since life experiences are not definitive for everyone, the idea of a peer-group phenomenon (Ryder 1965) is not easily adopted. Yet, "age-related research is often discussed in terms of age, period and cohort effects" (Smets 2008 p. 6), particularly as the life experiences of individuals in society are "always conditioned by their historical context" (Rindfuss et al. 1987, p. 785). From an historical standpoint, addressing the experiences of a segment of the population at certain stages of the life course can be quite meaningful (Braungart and Braungart 1986) and allude to differences in individuals' beliefs and behaviors. As cohorts experience different historical events, generation gaps can exist. Researchers like Franz Kolland (1994, p. 321) have commented that, "it is nevertheless still worth evaluating the *structural segregation of age-groups* in present-day society where social relationships shift and regroup themselves"; therefore, the time period and context are important dimensions of demographic analysis to consider in cohort analysis. Similarly, "the study of age-group differences in politics becomes especially important from a political standpoint when political attitudes divide along age-group lines, indicating that a political generation may be taking form" (Braungart and Braungart 1986, p. 217). Perception of belonging is important to cohort analysis, as belonging is more than just being born at a certain time.

Perceptions of Belonging

Given that an individual is born into a specific cohort, the examination of individuals according to a specific life stage can occur at any time. As there is increased migration throughout the world, issues of culture and identity are important, particularly for younger cohorts who experience migration at a young age. For example,

> … children of immigrants also may begin the process of ethnic identity development at a younger age as a result of the pressure they feel from the majority culture in which they live. This idea has not been investigated thoroughly with emerging adolescents, illustrating the need for examination of early adolescents' unique perspective, particularly the perceptions of belonging within multiple groups (e.g., cultural and minority) and the effectiveness with which they navigate between cultures. Investigation of the understanding and adherence to the values of one's ethnic or cultural background (i.e., a measure of ethnic identity) along with generation and/or immigration status appears to be the most appropriate method of measuring this dimension of acculturation for this young population. (Klein 2001, p. 8)

Given that an individual may have a diverse number of identities, focusing on certain basic demographic characteristics can be enlightening when comparing and contrasting cohort groups. "The community of date equips each cohort with its own expanse of time, its own style and its own truth" (Ryder 1965, p. 855). Again, dates and historical events are most important and this is re-iterated by several researchers. For example,

> dramatic historical events, such as economic depression, war, immigration, technological innovation, and cultural change affect all members of society but are considered to have an especially strong impact on the political attitudes of youth who are in their formative stage of political learning. When society changes rapidly and cohorts come of age under different conditions, the members of each cohort are likely to develop their own perception and style of politics which, if substantially different from the experiences of others, may provoke generational conflict. (Braungart and Braungart 1986, p. 215)

One cohort may experience an historical event that will affect the individuals in the age group forever; those not experiencing the event may hear reports and accounts of the event but will never actually experience the same event first-hand. So, "understanding the nature and importance of sequencing in the life course requires analyzing what the roles themselves mean and how they are causally linked" (Rindfuss et al. 1987, p. 799). With linked lives, individuals "are typically embedded in social relationships with kin and friends across the life span" (Elder 1994, p. 6). Social relationships are often identified in one's expressions of belonging and this belonging often includes kin ties and social networks (Irwin 2005). It is recognized that over one's life, social relationships (kin and friendship) and individuals come and go.

Life-Course Approach

The life-course approach has been used in many disciplines (Elder 1994; Featherman 1983) to demonstrate "the interplay of lived experience and socio-historical context, and the intertwining of subjective and shared meanings that shape lives over developmental and historical time" (Cohler and Hostetler 2003, p. 555). Elder (1994) identified four life-course approach themes (where research has typically focused), including: the interplay of human lives and historical times, the timing of lives, linked or interdependent lives, and human agency in choice making.

Political engagement is one example of how the life-course approach can be used to explain varying cohort behaviors. Young adults may vote less than other age groups, "because they are faced with 'start-up' problems: pre-occupations outside the political sphere that lead to low attachment to civic life" (Smets 2008, p. 1). This does not mean that all young adults are not politically engaged, but suggests that on average, young adults are less politically engaged compared to individuals in older age groups. As priorities in an individual's life change over the life course, political engagement varies. The life-course approach can enlighten policy makers not just in terms of which policies are important, but also in terms of how politically engaged constituents are throughout their lives. It is suggested that:

> the life-course approach to explaining political behavior is based largely on life-cycle interpretations of human behavior. The assumptions of the life-course approach are that as individuals grow older, they undergo certain qualitative changes in physiology, cognitive functioning, emotional patterns, and needs. These biopsychological changes occur over the life span and are considered to be sequential, irreversible, and for the most part universal. The maturational unfolding process occurs as individuals of similar age levels move in a sequential direction toward certain characteristic growth patterns. Because each stage of life is associated with its own orientations, needs, and interests, relations between age groups are not likely to be smooth, and this sets the stage for generational conflict. (Braungart and Braungart 1986, p. 208)

As time does not stand still, every year, an individual grows one year older and follows predictable social trajectories (Elder 1994, p. 5). In some groupings, such as "older age," researchers must consider that those who are 65 vary from those who are in their 90 s (Wister and Wanless 2007), and although there may be an interconnectedness of the various eras of the life course (Zollinger and Elder 1998), individuals who have lived a longer life vary from those who are younger in age and have lived fewer years. In contemporary society, technological advancements seem to have differentiated younger cohorts from older. Populations that are experiencing rapid change warrant specific examination. In fact,

> historical effects on the life course take the form of a cohort effect in which social change differentiates the life patterns of successive cohorts, such as older and younger women before World War II. History also takes the form of a period effect when the effect of change is relatively uniform across successive birth cohorts. (Elder 1994, p. 5)

The changes in household structures and living arrangements (Kolland 1994, p. 323) are also indicative of historical changes. Households with a single dweller (one-person household) are increasingly common in contemporary Canadian society (Statistics Canada 2007), as elsewhere in the world (Klinenberg 2012). A Canadian survey, with a representative sample, asking respondents about their demographic characteristics and perceptions can be enlightening to assess contemporary cohort issues.

Methodology

The Alberta Survey is a random-sample telephone survey of 1,200 adults (18 years of age and older) residing in Alberta, Canada, using a 25–30 minute questionnaire administered on the computer-assisted telephone interviewing system (Population Research Laboratory 2010). The telephone survey includes an equal balance

Table 19.1 Subject areas included in the 2010 Alberta Survey

1.	Socio-demographic characteristics: household composition, age, gender, marital status, highest level of education, household income, individual income, religion, ethnicity, country of birth, employment status, occupation, industry, home ownership, political party support and perceptions of financial status
2.	Participation in physical activity
3.	Opinions regarding cancer prevention, tobacco use, healthy eating, and excessive alcohol use
4.	Thoughts on traffic safety in Alberta
5.	Opinions about access to H1N1 information and the extent of understanding about issues surrounding H1N1
6.	Targeted marketing approaches and use of the internet by demographic cohorts
7.	Opinions regarding the prevalence of mental health issues among children and youth
8.	Death and dying, living wills, and end of life issues

of urban and rural participants, and respondents are representative of the adult population. The survey contains three sub-samples: the City of Edmonton metro area (N=400), the City of Calgary metro area (N=400), and the remainder of Alberta, which includes both smaller urban (non-metropolitan) and rural defined areas (Other Alberta, N=400).

Each year, researchers and other stake-holders buy in to the annually conducted survey and so, besides the regular questions, the focus of the survey can change from year to year. The subject areas of the 2010 Alberta Survey include socio-demographic and background characteristics as well as other substantive topics. Table 19.1 indentifies the diverse research topics included in the 2010 Alberta Survey. Targeted marketing approaches and use of the Internet by demographic cohorts is one of the subject areas included in the survey that directly apply to this research.

As the Alberta Survey is an annual telephone survey conducted throughout the province of Alberta, Canada, it provides an adequate sample for this contemporary research. The sample only includes those individuals who completed the entire interview. Those interviews that were incomplete and those in which respondents had language problems or refused to be interviewed are also represented in Table 19.2. The overall response rate of the survey in 2010 was 21.2%, and this percentage varies year by year.

In comparing the sample of the Alberta Survey to the population as counted by Statistics Canada, Table 19.3 allows for comparison between the population and the sample. The 2010 Alberta Survey slightly under surveys individuals in the 18–44 age groups and slightly over surveys individuals 45 years of age and older. The Index of Dissimilarity allows one to measure the degree to which the population characteristics are distributed differently between the respondents in the Alberta Survey and those people counted by Statistics Canada. The Index of Dissimilarity can be calculated using the formula $\frac{1}{2}\sum|x-y|$ and is 17.2. Overall, the Index of Dissimilarity suggests that the 2010 Alberta Survey appropriately captures the diversity of the population and is an appropriate data set for analytic purposes.

Although the number of refusals to participate in the survey (Table 19.2) is high (N=4,283), the number of completed interviews and the similarity of the surveyed

Table 19.2 2010 Alberta Survey sample breakdown

	Number (N)	Percentage (%)
Completed interviews	1203	21.2
Incomplete interviews	46	0.8
Refusals	4283	75.6
Language problems	135	2.4
Total	5,667	100.0

Table 19.3 Age distribution of Alberta in 2010

Age group	Statistics Canada[a] 2010	Alberta survey
2010		
18–24	13.3	5.8
25–34	20.9	12.6
35–44	18.7	17.2
45–54	19.6	22.9
55–64	13.9	22.4
65+	13.7	19.0
Total	100.0	100.0

[a] Source: Statistics Canada 2010

respondents to the population as a whole indicate that the data are appropriate for exploratory research purposes. The representativeness of the sample, responses, and analysis are presented and discussed in the next section.

Results

As the Alberta Survey sample is a representative sample of the Alberta population, the two major municipalities (Edmonton and Calgary) and Other Alberta (which includes smaller urban areas and rural Alberta) are analyzed separately to determine whether geographic differences occur. Table 19.4 presents the basic demographic characteristics of the survey respondents. The average age is roughly 49 years and the percentage of males and females is approximately equal (at approximately 50 %). A high percentage of the respondents are married (61.1 % for Edmonton, 64.0 % for Calgary, and 69.4 % for Other Alberta). The educational attainment levels of the three geographic areas in the Alberta Survey vary, with Calgary having a greater percentage having completed high school or more (83.3 %). Respondents located in Other Alberta (rural and small municipalities) have a lower educational attainment, at 62.2 %, than in the larger municipalities (Edmonton and Calgary). Analyzing basic demographic characteristics of Alberta Survey respondents, such as marital status and education attainment levels, demonstrates that unique geographic differences between urban and rural areas exist.

Table 19.4 Demographic profile of respondents

Geographic area			
	Edmonton	Calgary	Other Alberta
Mean age (y)	48.5	49.4	49.2
Sex (%)			
Male	49.9	49.8	49.5
Female	50.1	50.3	50.5
Marital status (%)			
Never married (single)	17.2	14.5	10.9
Married	61.1	64.0	69.4
Common-law relationship/live-in partner	6.2	5.3	7.2
Divorced	6.2	7.8	3.7
Separated	2.2	2.0	2.7
Widowed	7.0	6.0	5.2
No response	0.0	0.5	0.7
Education (years of schooling) (%)			
Less than high school	22.2	12.8	24.9
High school complete	70.1	82.5	61.7
Post secondary	0.7	0.8	0.5
No response	7.0	4.0	12.9

Given the disparities between the Edmonton, Calgary, and Other Alberta respondents, it is important to retain (where feasible) the geographic separations and/or the respondent's cohort affiliation in the analysis. As cohort affiliation is the focus of this research, knowing which age cohort to which an individual belongs is instrumental in assessing the individual's perceptions of different cohorts, and geographic location is a secondary level of analysis.

As Table 19.5 demonstrates, most individuals in this telephone survey feel that the age group to which they belong is not ignored in marketing campaigns (77.2% of respondents). Of those who do feel that the cohort they belong to is ignored by marketing campaigns, the largest group is the baby boomers (individuals born between 1946 and 1965). That some baby boomers feel they are ignored is rather surprising, as this cohort currently represents a large number of individuals in the Canadian population. In 2010, Alberta exhibited a median age of 35.8 years and the Canadian population as a whole had a median age of 39.7 years (Statistics Canada 2011). Clearly, Alberta is a province in Canada with a "younger" population and those who are older (and reside in Alberta) feel as though marketers are focusing on those who are "younger." Given that respondents to the survey only reside in Alberta, other provincial comparisons cannot be made.

Broadly, respondents were subsequently asked: "Which of the following age cohorts do you feel receives the most media attention?" The majority of individuals, in this survey, feel that the baby boomers (37.0%) and Generation Y (38.5%) cohorts receive the most media attention. It is no surprise that individuals would think that the baby boomer cohort, which makes up a large segment of the Canadian population, receives the most media attention. Similarly, individuals in Generation Y, who at the time of the survey are between the ages of 15 and 35 years of age,

Table 19.5 Perceptions of marketing campaigns by age cohort

	Do you feel that the age cohort you belong to is ignored by marketing campaigns?		
Would you say you were born...	Yes	No	Total
Pre-baby boomer (<1946)	78 (30.2 %)	135 (15.4 %)	213
Baby boomer (1946–1965)	106 (41.1 %)	405 (46.3 %)	511
Generation X (1966–1974)	46 (17.8 %)	134 (15.3 %)	180
Generation Y (1975–1995)	28 (10.9 %)	200 (22.9 %)	228
Total	258 (22.8 %)	874 (77.2 %)	1,132

Note: 71 individuals in the sample responded "Don't know" or had "No response" to this question and are not included. Pearson chi-square (12) = 125.9359, Pr = 0.000

are experiencing such life-course events as buying a home, getting married, having children, etc., and these major life-course events are often focused on by marketers (Table 19.6).

Given the different cohort sizes, no matter the size of the cohort to which an individual belongs, the majority of individuals agree that it is appropriate for governments to shape policy based on the size of age groups in the population. When respondents were asked "is it appropriate for government to shape policy based on the size of age groups," of those who responded yes, the majority belong to the baby boomer group (N = 344 out of 723, or 47.6 % of the Yes respondents) (Table 19.7).

The relationship between whether it is appropriate for government to shape policy based on the size of age groups and when the respondent was born had a P-value > 0.05 indicating a non-statistically significant relationship. The overall percentage distribution of the one variable, however, indicates that it is appropriate for government to shape policy based on the size of age groups. This is also suggestive that individuals understand the importance of cohorts and the life-course approach in policy-making. Additional analysis is recommended given that this relationship is not statistically significant, and this is addressed in the limitations section of the paper. The analysis does lead to discussion of cohorts in terms of marketing and public policy and a discussion of this follows.

Discussion

For years, marketers have identified consumers according to demographic characteristics that include: age, sex, marital status, education, income, etc. Segmentation has also included grouping consumers by cohorts. It has been noted that "marketing to specific cohorts is especially effective… for those selling food, music, clothing, cars, financial services, insurance, and entertainment products" (Bidwell 2009, p 2). The validity and utility of using cohorts as a segmentation technique has been analyzed by several marketing researchers, as an example, Schewe and Noble (2010). Their in-depth analysis of market segmentation by cohorts concluded that:

Table 19.6 Perceptions of media attention by age cohort

	Which of the following age cohorts do you feel receives the most media attention?				
	Pre-baby boomer (<1946)	Baby boomer (1946–1965)	Generation X (1966–1974)	Generation Y (1975–1995)	Total
Would you say you were born...					
Pre-baby boomer (<1946)	15 (18.5%)	80 (21.1%)	29 (17.1%)	62 (15.7%)	186
Baby boomer (1946–1965)	42 (51.9%)	183 (48.3%)	83 (48.8%)	149 (37.8%)	457
Generation X (1966–1974)	16 (19.8%)	58 (15.3%)	23 (13.5%)	67 (17.0%)	164
Generation Y (1975–1995)	8 (9.9%)	58 (15.3%)	35 (20.6%)	116 (29.4%)	217
Total	81 (7.9%)	379 (37.0%)	170 (16.6%)	394 (38.5%)	1,024

Note: 179 individuals in the sample responded "Don't know" or had "No response" to these questions and are not included in the table. Pearson chi-square (20)=70.8254, Pr=0.000

> one potential benefit to managers is that segmenting consumers by cohorts may be a more effective segmentation technique than presently employed. Consumers are more savvy than ever before, demanding personal attention and products that suit their lifestyle. They do not want to be encumbered with mistargeted or misguided products and promotions. A cohort analysis can provide a sense of familiarity and personal appeal to these savvy consumers, bringing them one step closer to making a purchase and providing the groundwork for building long-term relationships. (Schewe and Noble 2010, p. 140)

Although segmentation is regarded as a useful marketing strategy, "segmentation needs to be regarded as a dynamic process, which accounts for behavioral change together with the various factors that combine to determine what consumers prefer" (Gurau 2012, p 113). As the data in this paper indicated (Table 19.5), the majority of respondents do not feel ignored by marketing campaigns. When marketers are aware of population dynamics, they can modify their campaigns to best suit consumer groups. Similarly, governments are also able to adjust governmental policies based on population dynamics.

In 2003, a "Canada Pension Plan Actuarial Adjustment Factors Study" recommended that:

> in the context of an aging (Canadian) population, where life expectancy at age 65 is expected to continue to increase and projected labour force shortages could induce older workers to stay at work longer, policymakers will have to determine whether the current actuarial adjustments should be changed or certain Plan provisions modified to restore neutrality. (Office of the Chief Actuary 2003, p. 6)

Recently, in the 2012 Budget of Canada, the Government of Canada proposed "to gradually increase the age of eligibility for the Old Age Security (OAS) pension and the Guaranteed Income Supplement (GIS) between the years 2023 and 2029, from 65–67" (Service Canada 2012). Similarly, "the Government of Canada also proposes to gradually increase the ages at which the Allowance and the Allowance for the Survivor are provided, from 6064 today to 62–66" (Service Canada 2012).

Table 19.7 Perceptions of government policy making by age cohort

	Is it appropriate for government to shape policy based on the size of age groups?		
Would you say you were born...	Yes	No	Total
Pre-baby boomer (< 1946)	132 (18.3 %)	84 (21.5 %)	216
Baby boomer (1946–1965)	344 (47.6 %)	158 (40.5 %)	502
Generation X (1966–1974)	115 (15.9 %)	63 (16.2 %)	178
Generation Y (1975–1995)	132 (18.3 %)	85 (21.8 %)	217
Total	723 (65.0 %)	390 (35.0 %)	1,113

Note: 90 individuals in the sample responded "Don't know" or had "No response" to these questions and are not included in the table. Pearson chi-square (12) = 10.5442, Pr = 0.568.

Rationale for the policy change was budget sustainability, given that Old Age Security Program is a major cost to the federal government. With population ageing, the Canadian government's proactive policy-making will take years to implement and for the public to adjust. In many ways, "the formulation of public policy helps to produce the conditions that affirm the public policies" (Aleinikoff and Rumbaut 1998). Using basic frequencies of responses, in the 2010 Alberta Survey, more respondents felt that it was appropriate for governments to shape policy based on the size of their age group. In accordance with the survey responses, the Canadian government's pension plan rationale would most likely be supported by the majority of Canadians.

Overall, the analysis in this paper confirms (as with previous studies) that addressing demographic characteristics and cohort-based analysis is essential in both marketing and governmental policy strategies. Cohort segmentation is an important dimension in both marketing and policy making; however, this paper is limited by several factors and these are noted and discussed in the next section.

Limitations

Indeed, the data and analysis in this paper is limited by several factors. First, the sample that is used is small ($N = 1{,}200$), although it is deemed statistically representative of the more general population. Similarly, the population consists of Alberta and not of Canada as a whole. Alberta could be considered a unique province in Canada given that it has a younger median age than other Canadian provinces. Similarly, the urban and rural differences within the Alberta sample could be addressed by creation of a dummy geography variable so that geographic differences are minimized.

Second, the survey is cross-sectional, limiting the cohort and life-course analytical approach to a select year. The line that separates individuals into a cohort is often blurred. Researchers respect that cohorts are not fixed and have fluid boundaries. In fact,

> adjacent cohorts tend to permeate one another as the pattern of life chances works itself out. Definitions of age become pre-dominantly social rather than biological categories; they change with time, and with the groups one joins and leaves. (Ryder 1965, p. 858)

Researchers know, for example, that an individual who falls in to a specific age cohort may feel more connected to an adjacent cohort given his/her life experiences. In this analysis one's cohort is determined by the year of birth.

Third, the survey is a random digit dialed telephone interview and individuals are trusted to provide reliable and valid information. There is evidence in the literature that older people tend to exaggerate their age on both censuses and surveys (Wister and Wanless 2007; Jeune and Vaupel 1999; Thatcher 1999). The information provided by the respondent is in no way verifiable. As with all social surveys, it is assumed that the respondents have provided accurate information and that the results allow valuable insights to the topic at hand. Taken with a grain of salt (and a certain amount of acceptable statistical error), the results of this analysis are nonetheless important to understanding cohorts and the perceptions individuals have about belonging to a cohort.

Given the limitations of this study, future studies should consider a larger sample, a larger geographic area (i.e., Canada as a whole, rather than a single province like Alberta), longitudinal analysis (i.e., where individuals are asked their perceptions over their life course), and focus groups/additional questions related to cohorts and perceptions of belonging to an age cohort. The aforementioned considerations will provide for additional insight to cohort analysis.

Conclusions

Although one may belong to a specific age cohort due to being born in a specific year, one's perceptions of belonging are individualistic. This paper attempted to address individuals' feelings of belonging to their respective cohort. It is inherent that individuals are socialized into the society they belong. Yet,

> socialization need not mean rigidification. Normative postures are often acquired imperfectly, incompletely and tentatively. Perhaps it is simpler to indoctrinate entrants with a set of immutable recipes for action in prescribed situations, but room is almost always left for interpretation. (Ryder 1965, p 859).

It is the subjective and individual interpretations of belonging to a cohort that provide perpetual pondering.

Cohort analysis can be viewed as technical tool for both marketers and government policy makers. Similarly, as the life-course approach has been used in many disciplines, this approach can also demonstrate how individuals at various stages of life collectively comprise a population. In the end, the results of this paper suggest that addressing demographic characteristics and cohort-based analysis are essential in both marketing and governmental policy strategies; however, additional research is required. Moreover, individuals' perception of belonging to a group is an important area for future applied demographic analysis. As additional cohorts are added to a population, and others die out, cohorts will continuously provide interesting demographic research opportunities.

Acknowledgements Thank you to the Society of Edmonton Demographers for providing financial support for this research to be conducted and disseminated. The Population Research Laboratory (http://www.prl.ualberta.ca/) at the University of Alberta is thanked for annually conducting the Alberta Survey.

References

Aleinikoff, T. A., & R. umbaut, Rubén G. (1998). Terms of belonging: Are models of membership self-fulfilling prophecies? *Georgetown Immigration Law Journal, 13*. Available at SSRN: http://ssrn.com/abstract=1898486.

Bidwell, I. D. (2009). Cohorts: Age-based marketing, strategic marketing and branding. http://freedownload.is/pdf/cohorts-age-based-marketing-9592973.html. Accessed 13 May 2012.

Braungart, R. G., & Braungart, M. M. (1986). Life-course and generational politics. *Annual Review of Sociology, 12,* 205–231.

Carlsson, G., & Karlsson, K. (1970). Age, cohorts and the generation of generations. *American Sociological Review, 35*(4), 710–718.

Cohler, B. J., & Hostetler, A. (2003). Linking life course and life story: Social change and the narrative study of lives over time, handbook of the life course. *Handbooks of Sociology and Social Research, VI*(A), 555–576.

Elder, G. H. (1994). Time, human agency, and social change: Perspectives on the life course. *Social Psychology Quarterly, 57*(1), 4–15.

Elder, G. H. (1995). The life course paradigm: Social change and individual development. In P. Moen, G. Elder, & K. Lüscher (Eds.), *Examining lives in context: Perspectives on the ecology of human development* (pp. 101–139). Washington, DC: American Psychological Association.

Featherman, D. L. (1983). The life-span perspectives in social science research. In P. B. Baltes & O. G. Brim, Jr. (Eds.), *Life-span development and behavior* (pp. 1–57). New York: Academic.

Gurau, C. (2012). A life-stage analysis of consumer loyalty profile: Comparing Generation X and Millennial consumers. *Journal of Consumer Marketing, 29*(2), 103–113.

Irwin, S. (2005). *Reshaping social life*. New York: Routledge Taylor and Francis Group.

Jeune, B., & Vaupel, J. W. (Eds.). (1999). *Validation of exceptional longevity*. Odense: Odense University Press.

Klein, J. L. (2001). *Acculturation, social acceptance, and adjustment of early adolescents*. A thesis submitted in partial fulfillment of the requirements for the degree of master of science in the department of psychology in the college of arts and sciences at the University of Central Florida, Orlando, Florida.

Klinenberg, E. (2012). I want to be alone: The rise and rise of solo living. *The Guardian*. http://www.guardian.co.uk/lifeandstyle/2012/mar/30/the-rise-of-solo-living. Accessed 13 May 2012.

Kolland, F. (1994). Contrasting cultural profiles between generations: Interests and common activities in three intrafamilial generations. *Ageing and Society, 14*(3), 319–340.

Mannheim, K. (1952). The sociological problem of generations. In P. Kecskemeti (Ed.), *Essays on the sociology of knowledge* (pp. 276–322). New York: Oxford University Press.

Office of the Chief Actuary. (2003). Canada pension plan actuarial adjustment factors study. Actuarial study no. 2 (March). http://www.osfi-bsif.gc.ca/app/DocRepository/1/eng/oca/studies/CPP_ActuarialStudy2_e.pdf. Accessed 13 May 2012.

Population Research Laboratory. (2010). Population Research Laboratory, Department of Sociology at the University of Alberta. http://www.ualberta.ca/~prl/easdata/as2010methodsreport.pdf. Accessed 13 May 2012.

Rindfuss, R. R., Swicegood, C. G., &Rosenfeld, R. A. (1987). Disorder in the life course: How common and does it matter? *American Sociological Review, 52*(6), 785–801.

Ryder, N. (1965). The cohort as a concept in the study of social change. *American Sociological Review, 30*(6), 843–861.

Schewe, C. D., & Noble, S. M. (2000). Market segmentation by cohorts: The value and validity of cohorts in America and abroad. *Journal of Marketing Management, 16,* 129–142.

Service Canada. (2012). Changes to old age security. Old age security (OAS) program. http://www.servicecanada.gc.ca/eng/isp/oas/changes/index.shtml. Accessed 13 May 2012.

Smets, K. (2008). *In need of an update or overdue? Re-evaluating the political life-cycle model.* 'Youth and politics: Strange bedfellows? Conference: Comparative perspectives on political socialization', July 3–4, 2008, Bruges.

Statistics Canada. (2007). *Family portrait: Continuity and change in Canadian families and households in 2006.* 2006 Census. Cat. No. 97–553-XWE2006001. Ottawa.

Statistics Canada. (2010). *CANSIM using CHASS.* Table 510001: Estimates of population, by age group and sex for July 1, Canada, provinces and territories, annually. Ottawa.

Statistics Canada. (2011). Table 3: Population estimates, age distribution and media age as of July 1, 2010, Canada, provinces and territories. Canada's population estimates. *The Daily*, Wed, 29 September 2010.

Thatcher, R. (1999). The demography of centenarians in England and Wales. *Population Trends, 96,* 5–12.

Wister, A., & Wanless, D. (2007). A health profile of community-living nonagenarians in Canada. *Canadian Journal on Aging, 26*(1), 1–18.

Yacyshyn, A. (2012). Demographic cohorts and marketing research In N. Hoque & D. A. Swanson (Eds.), *Opportunities and challenges for applied demography in the 21st century. Applied Demography Series* (Vol. 2). New York: Springer.

Zollinger, J., & Elder, G. H. (1998). *Methods of life course research: Qualitative and quantitative approaches*. Thousand Oaks: Sage.

Chapter 20
Access to Health Care on the International Border of Texas

Stephanie L. McFall and David W. Smith

Introduction

Access to health care is a topic of policy interest in the United States. Barriers to access indicate lack of equity in relation to health and health care and also contribute to adverse health outcomes (McWilliams 2009). At least some shortfalls in access will be addressed by the Affordable Care Act (ACA). The ACA will address access through enhanced ability of persons without employment-based insurance to purchase coverage, with subsidy for lower income persons, and by expansion of Medicaid coverage (Cline and Murdock 2012; Hofer et al. 2011).

Applied demography includes a major focus on demographic patterns in small areas as well as population health. We compare access in the 32 county Border Region, i.e., counties within 100 km. (approximately 60 miles) of the international border with Mexico, to the rest of the state. This border definition was first established by the La Paz Agreement between Mexico and the United States in 1983. The La Paz Agreement is available from the web site of the Joint Advisory Committee for the Improvement of Air Quality (1995). The 32 counties are listed in the Appendix.

The Texas Border Region has distinct demographic and socioeconomic characteristics. Eighty-seven percent of the border population is Hispanic, compared to 37% for the state of Texas, and the population is also somewhat younger (Center for Health Statistics 2012). The per capita personal income is about $ 23,000 compared to the statewide figure of more than $ 37,000, and the rate of employment is lower (Texas Department of State Health Services 2012). Texas has the third largest foreign born population of all states. One survey of border residents found that 55% were Hispanics born outside the United States and 28% were U.S.-born Hispanics (Su et al. 2011).

S. L. McFall (✉)
Institute for Social and Economic Research, University of Essex, Colchester, UK
e-mail: slmcfall@gmail.com

D. W. Smith
Colchester, UK

M. N. Hoque, L. B. Potter (eds.), *Emerging Techniques in Applied Demography,* Applied Demography Series 4, DOI 10.1007/978-94-017-8990-5_20,

Border regions are influenced by the economies in each country (Bastida et al. 2008). Public health issues are frequently related to the large transfers of persons and goods across the borders. Organized public health efforts have traditionally emphasized the control of infectious diseases such as tuberculosis, sexually transmitted infections, HIV/AIDS, and rabies, as well as environmental issues, such as food-borne disease and air or water pollution (Warner and Jahnke 2003). There is also concern about conditions common in low-income individuals, for example poor oral health, and chronic conditions of high prevalence in the region like diabetes (Rodriguez-Saldana 2005). Public health also is concerned about the impact of lack of health care access. For example, almost all counties on the Texas-Mexico border are Health Professions Shortage Areas for primary care (Health Resource Service Agency 2013).

Some health related issues faced in the Border Region will be influenced by the high proportion of the population that is Hispanic. Hispanics are more likely to be uninsured than non-Hispanic white Americans and are also more likely to lack a usual source of care, even when controlling for health coverage (Weinick et al. 2000). Hispanics experience disparities in relation to use of preventive services, in the prevalence of some chronic conditions, and in the adequacy of treatment of chronic diseases (Ortega et al. 2007; Short et al. 1990).

There is also interest in disentangling the effects of ethnic category and social disadvantage measured by education level and income (McWilliams 2009; Schachter et al. 2012; Short et al. 1990). The effects of immigration status and acculturation on health access and health status (Derose et al. 2009; Pourat et al. 2010; Siddiqi et al. 2009) have also been explored.

While much research on access had used national surveys, some studies have been able to examine variation among or within states. A study of access and use of preventive services during the period 1991–2004 showed that there was a gap between Hispanics and non-Hispanic whites throughout this interval, with wide variation among states (Kang-Kim et al. 2008; Waidmann and Rajan 2000). Texas has a large immigrant population and also serious problems related to health care access. Texas has the highest proportion of uninsured adults in the United States: 27.4% of non-elderly adults lack health insurance (Kaiser Commission on Medicaid and the Uninsured 2010). A study of states participating in the National Survey of America's Families found that ethnic disparities in access in Texas were higher than the national average and the highest among the states studied on lack of insurance coverage and of a usual source of care (Waidman and Rajan 2000). There is a particularly low level of health insurance in the Border Region of Texas (Cline and Murdock 2012).

Multiple measures of access are necessary to assess a person's ability to use health services when needed. Having health insurance is the most frequently examined indicator of access, and probably rightly so, since insurance removes barriers to the use of care and shapes whether a person will establish a usual source of care. Having a usual source of care, particularly of primary health care, removes barriers to service use and, at its best, provides continuity of care and a greater degree of responsiveness to the needs of the individual. The failure to use services, when need is perceived, for financial reasons occurs among those with health problems. Healthy people should not report this type of access barrier.

This study uses the 2007 Texas Behavioral Risk Factor Surveillance System (BRFSS). The data collected in that year featured a major over-sample of the border population and a state-added module on access. We examine three indicators of access: having health insurance, having a usual source of care, and being unable to obtain care because of cost. Our purpose is to describe and compare access in border and non-border regions. Given the major differences in population characteristics in the Border Region, we will be examining the role of a large Hispanic population and other factors influencing access. We will also augment the flexible framework of the Behavioral Model of Care with indicators related to ethnicity and migration (Andersen 1995). Controlling for factors associated with ethnicity, e.g., immigration status or education level, will help identify pathways through which ethnicity contributes to differences in access.

The Behavioral Model of Care is a highly flexible framework to support analysis of health care access and utilization (Andersen 1995). It has been used as a guide to the selection of variables since the 1970s to analyze a wide variety of outcomes. Most often it has addressed individual- or family-level attributes, but it has been expanded to incorporate indicators of regions or societies. (As an example, we have noted that much of the Border Region is classified as a health professional shortage area.) The individual-level attributes can be seen as operating roughly in a sequence. There are first variables designated as predisposing characteristics, influencing the propensity to use services while not being directly related to service use. Predisposing variables include demographic characteristics that are associated with use of health care, such as sex. Other predisposing variables include knowledge and attitudes relating to care that encourage or discourage utilization. Enabling variables influence the person's ability to obtain services. These might include variables like income. Given the propensity and ability to obtain services, a person has to perceive illness to seek care. These variables are labelled "need characteristics" and include diagnoses and symptoms.

Methods

The BRFSS is a system of annual, random-digit-dialed telephone surveys of the non-institutionalized civilian population aged 18 years and older. The surveys are conducted by state health agencies with support from the Centers of Disease Control and Prevention (CDC). The BRFSS questionnaire consists of a core component, used by all states, as well as optional modules, and state added questions.

In 2007, the Texas BRFSS sampled a total of 17,248 respondents. The cooperation rate, or the percentage of households contacted where the selected respondent completed an interview, was 72.1 % for all states in 2007 and 62.5 % for Texas. The Council of American Survey Research Organizations (CASRO) response rate, the percentage of possible phone numbers that complete or partially complete an interview, had a median of 50.6 % for all states and 39.0 % for Texas. The CASRO response rate calculation assumes that the unresolved telephone numbers that were sampled have the same percentage of eligible households as the records for which eligibility or ineligibility was determined (CDC 2007).

Dependent Variable

There are three measures of access to care that have been used by the BRFSS for several years. Insurance coverage is assessed with the question, "Do you have any kind of health care coverage, including health insurance, prepaid plans such as HMOs, or government plans such as Medicare?" Usual source of care is measured as, "Do you have one person you think of as your personal doctor or health care provider?" If the answer is no, respondents are also asked, "Is there more than one, or is there no person who you think of as your personal doctor or health care provider?" Responses to these questions are coded as a single item with categories of "more than one, one, or none." In analysis, we contrasted persons with no personal provider with those who reported one or more providers. Not being able to afford care is assessed with the item, "Was there a time in the past 12 months when you needed to see a doctor but could not because of cost?"

Independent Variable

Border Region is based on a classification of counties located within 100 km. of the border, (32 counties, described earlier). Predisposing variables are personal characteristics that influence the use of services. We used age category, sex, marital status, race/ethnicity, and two indicators of acculturation, whether born in the U.S. or elsewhere and primary language. The six age categories are 18–24, 25–34, 35–44, 45–54, 55–64, and 65 or older. Marital status is classified as married or part of an unmarried couple, and all other marital classifications (never married, widowed, divorced, or separated) were categorized as unmarried. We used four categories of race and ethnicity in analyses: Hispanic, non-Hispanic white, non-Hispanic black, and all others. The measure of language is a state-added question, which asked, "What language would you say you speak most of the time?" Responses were English, Spanish, and other. We recoded it as English and all others for analysis. The Texas BRFSS also asked, "What country were you born in?" A large number of countries were reported. We recoded responses in three categories: the United States, Mexico, and all others, using U.S. and all others in analyses.

Enabling characteristics included employment status, income, education, and, for some analyses, having insurance coverage. Employment status contrasts those employed full or part-time with all other categories. Education was categorized as not completed high school, graduated from high school, some education beyond high school, and graduated from college. Income was grouped into the following brackets: under $ 15,000, 15,000–24,999, 25,000–34,999, 35,000–49,999, and over 50,000.

Need characteristics are assessed with a single indicator, general health. General health is categorized as excellent/very good, good, and fair/poor.

Statistical Analysis

All estimates incorporated the complex sample design structure and unequal survey weights used by the BRFSS. Analysis procedures in Stata 10.0 and 12.0 were used to take the design into account and make proper estimates of parameters and their standard errors. Logistic regression was used to assess the association of the independent variables with access. These results are presented as adjusted odds ratios and 95 % confidence intervals. Reported p-values were based on two sided tests of the coefficients.

Results

Estimates of the characteristics of Texans, total and by region, are shown in Table 20.1. Border residents are somewhat younger than residents outside the border. There is a much higher proportion of Hispanics in the Border Region, 76 % compared with 21 % elsewhere. A higher proportion of border residents were born in Mexico and more speak primarily Spanish. The achieved education levels are lower in the Border Region, which has a smaller proportion who completed high school and that graduated from college. Income is substantially lower in the Border Region. The proportion male and female and married is similar in the two regions.

Border residents rated their health worse than residents elsewhere in Texas. They rated their health as excellent or very good 41.4 % (se: 1.3 %) of the time compared with 50.3 % (se: 0.7 %) in the rest of the state. Border residents rated their health as fair or poor 25.6 % (se: 1.0 %) of the time compared with 17.0 % (se: 0.5 %) elsewhere.

Health care coverage was 59.6 % (se: 1.2 %) in the Border Region, substantially below the 77.2 % (se: 0.7 %) in the rest of Texas. Unmet need was also higher in the Border Region: 28.5 % (se: 1.3 %) of border residents needed to see a doctor but could not because of costs, compared with 18.4 % (se: 0.6 %) in the rest of the state. Substantially more border residents did not have a regular source of health care, 39.8 % (se: 1.3 %), compared with 27.2 % (se: 0.8 %) in the rest of Texas.

In summary then, the Border Region has a higher proportion of Hispanics, fewer resources to obtain health care, both in terms of insurance and income, and poorer self-rated health than the rest of Texas.

To illustrate the importance of population composition in the large differences in access, we show the three access variables by Border Region and ethnicity in Fig. 20.1. We include only non-Hispanic whites and Hispanics. There are minor

Table 20.1 Estimates of population characteristics in Texas and in the border region and the non-border region with standard errors in parentheses. The border region includes 32 counties that are within 100 kilometers of the international border of Texas with Mexico. The non-border region includes the rest of Texas

Predisposing characteristics	Texas	Border region	Non-border region
	Est. (se)	Est. (se)	Est. (se)
Age group (years)			
18–24	12.2 (0.6)	13.9 (1.1)	12.1 (0.7)
25–34	21.9 (0.6)	24.5 (1.4)	21.3 (0.7)
35–44	21.5 (0.5)	20.6 (0.9)	21.7 (0.6)
45–54	17.9 (0.4)	15.7 (0.7)	18.2 (0.5)
55–64	12.9 (0.3)	11.8 (0.6)	13.1 (0.3)
65 and over	13.6 (0.3)	13.5 (0.6)	13.6 (0.3)
Sex			
Male	50.3 (0.7)	51.2 (1.3)	50.4 (0.7)
Female	49.7 (0.7)	48.8 (1.3)	49.6 (0.7)
Race/ethnicity			
Hispanic (all)	26.8 (0.6)	75.6 (1.2)	20.7 (0.7)
White-non hispanic	58.8 (0.7)	20.1 (0.9)	63.7 (0.7)
Black-non hispanic	9.3 (0.4)	2.4 (1.0)	10.1 (0.5)
Other	5.2 (0.3)	1.9 (0.3)	5.5 (0.4)
Place of birth			
United States	71.7 (0.6)	57.9 (1.2)	74.3 (0.7)
Mexico	8.2 (0.3)	26.2 (1.0)	5.6 (0.3)
Another place	20.0 (0.6)	16.0 (0.9)	20.1 (0.6)
Primary language			
English	86.3 (0.6)	58.0 (1.3)	90.3 (0.6)
Spanish	12.0 (0.5)	39.1 (1.2)	8.2 (0.6)
Other	1.7 (0.2)	2.9 (0.4)	1.6 (0.2)
Married or couple	63.0 (0.7)	59.9 (1.2)	63.5 (0.7)
Enabling characteristics			
Achieved education			
Not a high school graduate	14.0 (0.4)	23.6 (1.0)	12.1 (0.5)
High school graduate	27.4 (0.6)	28.5 (1.1)	27.4 (0.7)
Some college	26.7 (0.6)	26.1 (1.1)	27.0 (0.6)
College graduate	31.9 (0.6)	21.8 (1.2)	33.5 (0.7)
Employed	60.2 (0.6)	55.8 (1.2)	60.8 (0.7)
Income (per year)			
Under $ 15,000	10.3 (0.4)	19.8 (0.9)	8.9 (0.4)
$ 15,000–25,000	18.0 (0.6)	25.4 (1.1)	16.7 (0.6)
$ 25,000–35,000	11.1 (0.4)	12.0 (0.8)	10.9 (0.5)
$ 35,000–50,000	15.0 (0.5)	13.8 (0.9)	15.4 (0.6)
$ 50,000 or more	45.7 (0.7)	29.1 (1.4)	48.2 (0.8)
Need characteristics			
General health			
Excellent or very good	49.2 (0.7)	41.4 (1.3)	50.3 (0.7)
Good	32.7 (0.6)	33.0 (1.1)	32.7 (0.7)
Fair or poor	18.1 (0.5)	25.6 (1.0)	17.0 (0.5)

Table 20.1 (continued)

Predisposing characteristics	Texas	Border region	Non-border region
	Est. (se)	Est. (se)	Est. (se)
Access			
Health care coverage	74.9 (0.6)	59.6 (1.2)	77.2 (0.7)
Needed to see a doctor in the last 12 months but could not due to cost	19.6 (0.6)	28.5 (1.3)	18.4 (0.6)
Regular provider of health care			
One provider	64.1 (0.7)	54.1 (1.3)	65.6 (0.8)
More than one	7.0 (0.3)	6.1 (0.4)	7.2 (0.3)
None	28.9 (0.7)	39.8 (1.3)	27.2 (0.8)
Sample size[a]	17,248	4,527	12,068

[a] There were 653 missing values for region

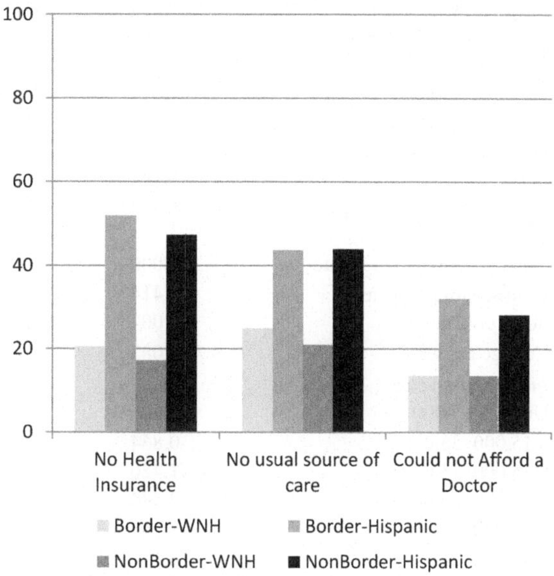

Fig. 20.1 Access by border region and Hispanic ethnicity

differences by border location, with Hispanics having lower access on all access variables, irrespective of region of residence.

Table 20.2 presents the regression results for having health insurance. It excludes persons aged 65 or older because nearly all persons over age 65 had insurance coverage. In persons aged 64 or less, border residents were less likely to have health insurance than the rest of Texas. Among predisposing variables, having insurance increased with age, particularly for those over age 45. In addition, those who primarily speak English were more likely to be insured. Enabling characteristics of employment, education, and income were associated with health insurance with a gradient for level of education and household income. General health was not associated with insurance.

Table 20.2 Logistic regression for health care coverage, ages 18–64

	Odds ratio	95 % ci	*P*-value
Variable			
Resides in border region	0.733	0.580–0.926	0.009
General health			
Excellent or very good	1.000		0.081
Good	0.782	0.630–0.972	0.027
Fair or poor	0.900	0.674–1.202	0.476
Age group (years)			
18–24	1.000		<0.001
25–34	1.031	0.709–1.498	0.875
35–44	1.413	0.977–2.045	0.067
45–54	1.715	1.198–2.457	0.003
55–64	2.806	1.948–4.043	<0.001
65 and over			
Sex (Male)	0.832	0.677–1.022	0.079
Married or couple	1.069	0.854–1.339	0.558
Born outside the US	1.221	0.914–1.629	0.176
English is primary language	1.686	1.177–2.414	0.004
Race/ethnicity			
Hispanic (all)	1.000		0.282
White-non hispanic	0.857	0.592–1.241	0.415
Black-non hispanic	0.861	0.643–1.155	0.319
Other	1.448	0.855–2.452	0.168
Employed full time or part time	1.384	1.086–1.765	0.009
Achieved education			
Not a high school graduate	1.000		<0.001
High school graduate	1.414	1.055–1.896	0.020
Some college	2.007	1.490–2.704	<0.001
College graduate	3.083	2.137–4.449	<0.001
Income (per year)			
Under $ 15,000	1.000	<0.001	
$ 15,000–25,000	0.864	0.642–1.163	0.334
$ 25,000–35,000	1.420	1.000–2.018	0.050
$ 35,000–50,000	2.484	1.741–3.544	<0.001
$ 50,000 or more	6.267	4.197–9.357	<0.001
Constant	0.275	0.161–0.470	<0.001

Number of observations 9,161, *ci* confidence interval

Border residents were somewhat less likely to have a regular provider (see Table 20.3). Several of the predisposing variables increased the likelihood of having a usual source of care. In addition to the increase with age, women, those part of a couple, and U.S.-born persons were more likely to have a regular health care provider. With the exception of having health insurance, which is strongly associated with a usual source of care, the enabling variables were less strongly associated with usual source than with having insurance. For example, there is not a clear gradient for education, and income is largely influential through contrasts between

Table 20.3 Logistic regression of unmet need for care, all ages

	Odds ratio	95% ci	*P*-Value
Variable			
Resides in border region	1.276	0.913–1.784	0.153
General health			
Excellent or very good	1.000		<0.001
Good	1.425	1.137–1.787	0.002
Fair or poor	3.030	2.368–3.876	<0.001
Age group (years)			
18–24	1.000		<0.001
25–34	0.942	0.623–1.424	0.777
35–44	1.007	0.679–1.496	0.971
45–54	0.811	0.550–1.196	0.291
55–64	0.559	0.377–0.829	0.004
65 and over	0.166	0.108–0.256	<0.001
Sex	0.595	0.482–0.735	<0.001
Married or couple	1.212	0.976–1.506	0.082
Born outside the US	1.270	0.940–1.714	0.119
English is primary language	1.456	0.975–2.175	0.066
Race/ethnicity			
Hispanic (all)	1.000		0.030
White-nonhispanic	1.412	0.945–2.112	0.093
Black-nonhispanic	1.017	0.747–1.385	0.913
Other	1.780	1.139–2.781	0.011
Employed full time or part time	0.847	0.671–1.068	0.161
Achieved education			
Not a high school graduate	1.000		0.701
High school graduate	0.842	0.625–1.135	0.260
Some college	0.887	0.651–1.209	0.449
College graduate	0.836	0.584–1.197	0.328
Income (per year)			
Under $ 15,000	1.000		<0.001
$ 15,000–25,000	0.871	0.657–1.155	0.337
$ 25,000–35,000	0.612	0.439–0.855	0.004
$ 35,000–50,000	0.559	0.396–0.789	0.001
$ 50,000 or more	0.248	0.164–0.373	<0.001
Has health insurance	0.234	0.184–0.297	<0.001
Constant	0.878	0.524–1.472	0.622

Number of observations = 12,104, *ci* confidence interval

highest and lowest categories. General health was not associated with having a usual source of care.

The indicator of not seeking care (see Table 20.4) because of cost should be influenced both by the propensity to use services, that is, by illness behaviour, and by financial resources. Controlling for other variables, living on the border was not associated with being unable to afford care. Among predisposing variables, older

Table 20.4 Logistic regression of usual source of care, all ages

	Odds ratio	95% ci	*P*-value
Variable			
Resides in border region	0.771	0.606–0.982	0.035
General health			
Excellent or very good	1.000		0.198
Good	0.949	0.782–1.152	0.597
Fair or poor	1.190	0.924–1.534	0.178
Age group (years)			
18–24	1.000		<0.001
25–34	1.089	0.752–1.577	0.653
35–44	1.834	1.269–2.650	0.001
45–54	2.700	1.869–3.899	<0.001
55–64	4.122	2.833–5.999	<0.001
65 and over	5.894	3.967–8.758	<0.001
Sex	0.379	0.320–0.450	<0.001
Married or couple	1.300	1.068–1.584	0.009
Born outside the US	1.317	1.010–1.718	0.042
English is primary language	1.309	0.950–1.802	0.099
Race/ethnicity			
Hispanic (all)	1.000		0.236
White-nonhispanic	0.830	0.594–1.160	0.275
Black-nonhispanic	1.054	0.808–1.375	0.697
Other	1.432	0.933–2.196	0.100
Employed full time or part time	0.881	0.713–1.089	0.241
Achieved education			
Not a high school graduate	1.000		0.011
High school graduate	1.315	0.987–1.752	0.061
Some college	1.615	1.196–2.180	0.002
College graduate	1.279	0.937–1.747	0.121
Income (per year)			
Under $ 15,000	1.000		0.001
$ 15,000–25,000	1.108	0.842–1.457	0.465
$ 25,000–35,000	1.238	0.882–1.736	0.217
$ 35,000–50,000	1.403	0.983–2.003	0.062
$ 50,000 or more	1.989	1.382–2.864	<0.001
Has health insurance	4.414	3.578–5.446	<0.001
Constant	0.243	0.144–0.411	<0.001

Number of observations = 12,104, *ci* confidence interval

persons and males were less likely to forego care for reasons of cost. Only income and health insurance coverage were associated with this access outcome. General health was not related to not seeking care because of costs when controlling for insurance coverage, but when health insurance was not in the model, those with poorer health were more likely to report not seeking care because of costs.

Discussion

The Border Region has lower access on all three indicators. However because population characteristics are so different from the rest of the state, we apply the Behavioral Model of Care (Andersen 1995) to examine the role of predisposing, enabling, and need-related variables on access to care.

Not surprisingly there are strong relationships between enabling variables and access, most clearly shown for health insurance. For example, there is the gradient in the association of both education and income with having health insurance. The relationships of enabling variables with usual source and not being able to afford care are somewhat less striking than the relationship of enabling variables with health insurance. Income was associated with forgoing care for cost, but education was not. However, having insurance is a particularly important enabling variable for both usual source of care and being able to afford needed care.

Age is the most important of the variables classified as predisposing. Older persons were more likely to have insurance and a usual source of care but also were more likely to not seek care because of expenses, perhaps because they have more ongoing health problems. With greater health problems, older persons were more likely to have selected a regular provider but also were more likely to not get care because of the expense. Having a usual source of care was more common for women and members of couples. Sociologists have described differences in illness behaviour related to gender and family relationships. Illness behaviour differences are also seen in the link between general health and cost for care.

The set of predisposing variables also included indicators of acculturation, i.e., immigrant status and primary language. When controlling for other variables, persons who primarily speak Spanish were less likely to have health insurance and immigrants were less likely to have a usual source of care.

Race/ethnicity was not associated with access when controlling for variables tapping social resources and acculturation. Hispanics and other ethnic minorities have decidedly lower education and incomes on average. Differential resources in education, income, and health insurance are a major source of ethnic disparities in health care access, with acculturation factors contributing to some degree.

The investment by the Texas BRFSS in the oversampling of border residents provides important information for the planning of public health interventions. This examination of access describes the factors influencing the ability of Texas residents to enter the health system. Subsequent research should explore the potential differentials associated with use of preventive services and the role played by access in disparities in treatment and health status.

While we appreciate the importance of the BRFSS data, there are inevitably shortcomings. Those tied to the design of the BRFSS concern the declining rates of response and potential differential telephone coverage. Shortcomings related specifically to this study concern the selection of a single indicator of health status. While general health is regarded as a good summary measure and is correlated with health outcomes ranging from mortality to various morbidity measures, it may not do as good a job of assessing demand for health services. We note, however, that it was associated, as expected, with not seeking care because of costs when we did not control for health insurance.

Border residents were less likely to have health insurance or a usual source of care, even when controlling for multiple variables. It is clear that policy initiatives to address gaps in insurance coverage are important, particularly in Texas, a state that has among the lowest rates of coverage in the United States. As mechanisms to increase coverage are implemented, it will be important to assess their effects on the U.S.–Mexican border since eligibility restrictions may limit their impact. The ACA is expected to have strong positive effects on access to health insurance in the Texas Border Region. However, its mechanisms will not directly benefit undocumented immigrants.

Policy initiatives should also address shortfalls resulting from the organization of services. Almost all Mexican border counties are designated Health Professions Shortage Areas (Health Resource Service Agency 2013), so mechanisms like community health centers could reduce barriers to access, particularly having a usual source of care. Outreach efforts will also be important to reduce barriers to seeking and making use of services.

Acknowledgments We thank Michelle Cook, former BRFSS coordinator, Texas Department of State Health Services, for access to the 2007 Texas BRFSS data.

Appendix

List of Texas counties classified in the Border Region:

1. Brewster
2. Brooks
3. Cameron
4. Crockett
5. Culberson
6. Dimmit
7. Duval
8. Edwards
9. El Paso
10. Frio
11. Hidalgo
12. Hudspeth
13. Jeff Davis
14. Jim Hogg
15. Kenedy
16. Kinney
17. La Salle
18. Maverick
19. McMullen

20. Pecos
21. Presidio
22. Real
23. Reeves
24. Starr
25. Sutton
26. Terrell
27. Uvalde
28. Val Verde
29. Webb
30. Willacy
31. Zapata

References

Andersen, R. M. (1995). Revisiting the behavioral model and access to medical care: Does it matter? *Journal of Health and Social Behavior, 36*(1), 1–10.

Bastida, E., Brown, H. S. 3rd, Pagan, J. A. (2008). Persistent disparities in the use of health care along the US-Mexico border: An ecological perspective. *American Journal of Public Health, 98*(11), 1987–1995.

Center for Health Statistics. (2012). Health facts profile 2009—border areas (32). http://www.dshs.state.tx.us/chs. The dates are 4/16/13.

Centers for Disease Control and Prevention. (2007). 2007 Summary data quality report. http://www.cdc.gov/brfss/annual_data/annual_2007.htm.

Cline, M. E., & Murdock, S. H. (2012). *Estimates of the impact of the Affordable Care Act on Texas Counties*. San Antonio: Methodist Health Ministries.

Derose, K. P., Bahney, B. W., Lurie, N., & Escarce, J. J. (2009). Review: Immigrants and health care access, quality, and cost. *Medical Care Research and Review, 66*(4), 355–408.

Health Resource Service Agency. (2013). Shortage designation: health professional shortage areas and medically underserved areas/populations. http://www.hrsa.gov/shortage/.

Hofer, A. N., Abraham, J. M., & Moscovice, I. (2011). Expansion of coverage under the Patient Protection and Affordable Care Act and primary care utilization. *Milbank Quarterly, 89*(1), 69–89.

Joint Advisory Committee for the Improvement of Air Quality. (1995). La Paz agreement: Agreement between the United States of America and the United Mexican States on cooperation for the protection and improvement of the environment in the border area. http://www.jac-ccc.org/agreement.htm.

Kaiser Commission on Medicaid and the Uninsured. (2010). The uninsured: A primer. http://www.kff.org/uninsured/7451.cfm

Kang-Kim, M., Betancourt, J. R., Ayanian, J. Z., Zaslavsky, A. M., Yucel, R. M., & Weissman, J. S. (2008). Access to care and use of preventive services by Hispanics: State-based variations from 1991 to 2004. *Medical Care, 46*(5), 507–515.

McWilliams, J. W. (2009). Health consequences of uninsurance among adults in the United States: Recent evidence and implications. *Milbank Quarterly, 87*(2), 443–494.

Ortega, A. N., Fang, H., Perez, V. H., Rizzo, J. A., Carter-Pokras, O., Wallace, S. P., et al. (2007). Health care access, use of services, and experiences among undocumented Mexicans and other Latinos. *Archives of Internal Medicine, 167*(21), 2354–2360.

Pourat, N., Kagawa-Singer, M., Breen, N., & Sripipatana, A. (2010). Access versus acculturation: Identifying modifiable factors to promote cancer screening among Asian American women. *Medical Care, 48*(12), 1088–1096.

Rodriguez-Saldana, J. (2005). Challenges and opportunities in border health. *Preventing Chronic Disease, 2*(1), A03.

Schachter, A., Kimbro, R. T., & Gorman, B. K. (2012). Language proficiency and health status: Are bilingual immigrants healthier? *Journal of Health and Social Behavior, 53*(1), 124–145.

Short, P. F., Cornelius, L. J., & Goldstone, D. E. (1990). Health insurance of minorities in the United States. *Journal of Health Care for the Poor and Underserved, 1*(1), 9–24 (discussion 28–30).

Siddiqi, A., Zuberi, D., & Nguyen, Q. C. (2009). The role of health insurance in explaining immigrant versus non-immigrant disparities in access to health care: Comparing the United States to Canada. *Social Science and Medicine, 69*(10), 1452–1459.

Su, D., Richardson, C., Wen, M., & Pagan, J. A. (2011). Cross-border utilization of health care: Evidence from a population-based study in south Texas. *Health Services Research, 46*(3), 859–876.

Waidmann, T. A., & Rajan, S. (2000). Race and ethnic disparities in health care access and utilization: an examination of state variation. *Medical Care Research and Review, 57*(Suppl 1), 55–84.

Warner, D. C., & Jahnke, L. R. (2003). *U.S./Mexico border health issues: The Texas Rio Grande Valley*. San Antonio: The University of Texas Health Science Center-San Antonio.

Weinick, R. M., Zuvekas, S. H., & Cohen, J. W. (2000). Racial and ethnic differences in access to and use of health care services, 1977 to 1996. *Medical Care Research and Review, 57*(Suppl 1), 36–54.

Chapter 21
Factors Influencing Differentials in Rural-Urban Living Arrangements, Health Status, and Abuse of the Elderly in Rajshahi District of Bangladesh

Md. Ismail Tareque, M. Nazrul Hoque, Towfiqua Mahfuza Islam, Kazuo Kawahara and Makiko Sugawa

Introduction

Population ageing is a global phenomenon, a process by which the elderly population (60 years and above) of a nation becomes a proportionately greater share of the total population. Like other countries of the Asia-Pacific region, Bangladesh has experienced a steady decline in mortality accompanied by a modest decline in fertility. The outcome of these decreases constitutes the framework within which the implication of population ageing and the extension of life are considered (Tareque 2007). In Bangladesh, people aged 60 and above years were about 5.8% of the total population during 1950 to 2000, but after year 2000, the proportion has been increasing dramatically (United Nations 2010). Bangladesh will soon enter into an ageing society, i.e. persons aged 60 and above years will account for about 10% of the total population in 2025 to 2030 (having between 9.8 and 11.9% aged), and the percentage is projected to increase to 22.4 and 35.6% by the years 2050 and 2100, respectively. So, there is time to think about the elderly in Bangladesh. Considering the huge number (9.9 million elderly in 2010), it is the right time to work on the overall status of the elderly, as Bangladesh has right now the third largest number of poor elderly people, after India and China (Help Age International 2006).

M. I. Tareque (✉)
Department of Population Science and Human Resource Development,
University of Rajshahi, Rajshahi, Bangladesh
e-mail: tareque_pshd@yahoo.com

M. N. Hoque
Hobby Center for Public Policy, University of Houston, Houston, TX, USA
e-mail: mnhoque@uh.edu

T. M. Islam · K. Kawahara · M. Sugawa
Department of Health Care Management and Planning, Tokyo Medical
and Dental University, Tokyo, Japan

M. N. Hoque, L. B. Potter (eds.), *Emerging Techniques in Applied Demography*,
Applied Demography Series 4, DOI 10.1007/978-94-017-8990-5_21,

The problems of old age dependency, being single, and having physical and functional disabilities are becoming significant issues of public health importance (Swami et al. 2003). In Bangladesh many older people spend their lives in poverty and ill health. After a lifetime of deprivation, old age is likely to mean ill health, social isolation, and poverty. Poverty and exclusion are threats to the wellbeing of older people. This is especially true for older women (Munsur et al. 2010) who suffer from multiple disadvantages resulting from biases to gender, widowhood, and old age. Women, particularly widows who are without living sons or who live alone, are particularly at risk of economic destitution, social isolation, poor health and death, (Abedin 2003; Kabir et al. 2005) and depressive symptoms (Hsu 2011; de Beurs et al. 2001; Kessing et al. 2003). Some studies pointed out that a majority of elderly people in Bangladesh can be seen as having problems in meeting their basic needs due to lack of social security, loss of income, and physical disability (Ahmed et al. 2002; Mostafa and van Ginneken 2000). Though socio-economic development for all citizens is the cornerstone of Bangladesh's constitution (Ministry of Health and Family Welfare 2004), it is difficult to provide support to the elderly in this country (Bangladesh Institute of Labour Studies 2003).In traditional Bangladesh, family had been the primary source of support for elderly people, and especially the sons are expected to support their elderly parents (Kabir et al. 2002; Ghuman and Ofstedal 2004). The support patterns shows the patrilineal family system in Bangladesh, which stresses the importance of sons in caring for and providing assistance to parents in old age (Ghuman and Ofstedal 2004). Exceptionally in urban areas, most of the families are nuclear. The traditional extended family structure in rural Bangladesh is breaking down due to poverty, attitudes of self-interest, quarrels, maladjustment, and so on. Extended families are gradually being replaced by nuclear families (UNESCO 1992)

Elder abuse is a global social issue that affects the health and human rights of millions of older persons around the world and an issue that deserves the attention of the international community (United Nations 2013). It is a problem that exists in both developing and developed countries yet is typically underreported globally (World Health Organization 2013). It is reported to be more frequent in situations where a trust relationship exists, for example, relatives, neighbors, and friends (Block and Sinnott 1979; Lau and Kosberg 1979; Papadopoulos and La Fontaine 2000; Cohen et al. 2006). In particular children, adults, and spouses are, with more frequency, probably responsible for elder abuse (National Center on Elder Abuse 1998; Schiamberg and Gans 2000). In an extensive study by the National Center on Elder Abuse (NCEA 1998), neglect was found to be the most common form of abuse, followed by psychological abuse, financial exploitation, physical abuse, abandonment, and sexual abuse. Rahman et al. (2010) pointed out that the elderly who were unhealthy, economically dependent, and illiterate are more likely to face abuse, and Tareque et al. (2008) concluded that though most of the elder abuse remains unreported because people are too frightened, ashamed, or embarrassed, young old and the females who are widows and illiterate are more likely to face abusive behaviour.

Based on the above discussion, in view of the size of the population, scarcity of resources, existing poverty, insufficient health facilities, and absence of social security system, ageing is going to be a major problem in Bangladesh. Therefore, special attention should be placed on the elderly as well as elderly-oriented research in Bangladesh, however, very little and fragmented research has been done in this field (Tareque 2007; Munsur et al. 2010; Kabir et al. 2002; Rahman et al. 2010; Tareque et al. 2008; Hosain and Begum 2003; Rahman et al. 2008). The current study is thus an attempt to examine the overall status and the factors influencing differentials in rural-urban living arrangements, health status, and abuse of the elderly, particularly how the elderly live, what their present health status is, whether the family as well as society is aged-friendly, or in other words, whether the elderly face abusive behaviour in Bangladesh. The present study contributes by enriching the existing literatures on the overall status of the elderly and identifying the main problems regarding living arrangements, health status, and abuse of the elderly to make society and the environment aged friendly in the future.

Methods

Sample

Data came from a promotional research project titled, "Socio-demographic status of the aged population and elderly abuse: a study on rural-urban differentials in Rajshahi district, Bangladesh," sponsored by the social science research council (SSRC), planning division, ministry of planning, the Government of Bangladesh. The objectives, sampling design, and methodologies are described elsewhere in detail (Tareque 2009). In brief, the project was the socio-economic and demographic study of the aged (60 years old and over) population of Rajshahi district, Bangladesh. Rajshahi is situated in the northern part of Bangladesh; it has a total area of 2,407.01 km^2 and is one of the least developed divisional districts in Bangladesh. Two Mouzas of Yusufpur Union (namely, Baduria and Sahapur) from rural areas and Ward number 5 from the urban areas of Rajshahi district were selected as study areas, with probability proportional to size (in terms of households). All households in the selected Mouzas and Ward were enumerated and all elderly residing in the households were interviewed during April 2009. Eight hundred and ninty-six individuals constituted the total sample size, out of which 477 came from rural areas and the rest from urban areas.

A questionnaire was prepared and pre-tested by a pilot survey. Then necessary corrections were made to the final version of the questionnaire. Finally, field investigators went to each house where they found an eligible person and asked the questions of the respondents and answers were recorded on paper forms. To reach a full response rate, repeated visits were made. A structural interview schedule containing closed questions except income information was used to collect information on the following: (1) identification of respondents, (2) details about family members, (3) health conditions, (4) daily activities, (5) economic activities, (6) living arrangements and conditions, and (7) abuse, etc. A Bengali version of the questionnaire was prepared for field use, then it was translated into English for data entry and analysis.

Measures

Living Arrangement

Elders' living arrangement was measured based on responses to the individual question regarding whom do you live with? Five options were (a) alone; (b) spouse; (c) unmarried son/daughter; (d) married son/daughter; (e) others. To obtain two categories for multivariate analysis, living alone was kept same with a value of 1, while those who mentioned living with someone (options b-e) were combined and assigned a value of 0.

Health Status

Self-perceived health is the most informative, unique, and valuable indicator of human health status (Jylhä 2009). Here, self-perceived health status was measured based on a 5-point Likert scale regarding how would you describe your state of health these days? Would you say it is (a) very good; (b) good; (c) fair; (d) poor; or (e) very poor. This variable serves as the dependent variable of a multivariate analysis where a value of 1 was assigned if the response was (a) or (b), and 0 for (c), (d) or (e).

Abuse

Our study used the definition and types of elder abuse declared by the National Center on Elder Abuse (NCEA 2008), viz. elder abuse is a term referring to any knowing, intentional, or negligent act by a caregiver or any other person that causes harm or a serious risk of harm to a vulnerable adult. In a broad sense, abuse may be: (1) physical abuse—inflicting, or threatening to inflict, physical pain or injury on a vulnerable elder, or depriving them of a basic need, (2) emotional abuse—inflicting mental pain, anguish, or distress on an elder person through verbal or nonverbal acts, (3) sexual abuse—non-consensual sexual contact of any kind, (4) exploitation—illegal taking, misuse, or concealment of funds, property, or assets of a vulnerable elder, (5) neglect—refusal or failure by those responsible to provide food, shelter, health care, or protection for a vulnerable elder, or (6) abandonment—the desertion of a vulnerable elder by anyone who has assumed the responsibility for care or custody of that person. Adopting the above definition and types, the question "Have you ever been abused?" was asked to the elderly to uncover the actual situation of elderly abuse in the study area. The response "yes" was coded 1 and "no" as 0 for estimating the multiple logistic models.

Statistical Analysis

Univariate analysis was done to find percentages of self-reported occurrences of the background characteristics. Finally, three logistic regression models by residence for each living arrangement, health status, and abuse were fitted for determining factors that are more influential to living arrangements, health status, and abuse of elderly population.

The most significant explanatory factors were considered in Model I first. Extensions to Model II and Model III were done in steps including less significant and theoretically relevant variables. In all, we constructed 18 multivariate models. The entire analysis of the study was conducted using SPSS version 15.0 for windows (SPSS, Inc., Chicago, IL).

Results

Sample Characteristics

Table 21.1 displays the mean or percentage distribution of the basic characteristics of the study respondents with rural-urban differentials. On average, the study sample has almost the same age and clear differences in their individual as well as family monthly income in rural and in urban areas. Overwhelmingly, the majority (97 %) are Muslim, with more females in rural areas compared to urban areas. Four-fifths of the rural elderly have no formal education, while about one-third in urban areas have no formal education. Urban respondents have been found to have more monthly income, more family income, bank accounts in their names, and daily expenditure than their rural counterparts.

Table 21.2 displays the percentage distribution of household characteristics and living arrangements with rural-urban differentials. Dominantly, male-headed household were about 90 % in the study areas. More than three-fourths of urban elderly live in Pucca dwellings—better conditioned houses—while less than one-sixth in the rural areas live in Pucca dwellings. Urban elderly were also found to have better toilet facilities and more access to TV and radio. Though electric facility is universal in urban areas, 25 % of the rural households were without electricity. More urban elderly than rural elderly were found to remain married and live with married children.

Table 21.1 Basic characteristics of the respondents by residence

Background characteristics	Rural (N=477)	Urban (N=419)
	Mean (SD)	Mean (SD)
Average age	68.26 (9.04)	68.50 (8.85)
Average monthly income	974.00 (1441.14)	3210.95 (4310.38)
Average monthly family income	3356.39 (2286.40)	8589.50 (5077.80)
	Percentage	*Percentage*
Age groups		
60–69	57.4	58.5
70–79	28.7	28.2
80+	13.8	13.4
Sex		
Male	43.2	48.9
Female	56.8	51.1
Religion		
Muslim	96.9	96.9
Hindu	3.1	1.2
Others	–	1.9
Educational level		
No formal education	80.3	34.8
Primary	10.5	23.9
Secondary and above	9.2	41.3
Occupation		
Housewife	38.6	25.5
Farmer	17.6	3.1
Service	1.5	7.6
Business	5.0	6.0
Others	11.5	6.9
Do not work	25.8	50.8
Respondent's monthly income		
up to 2999	87.6	56.6
3000–5999	11.1	26.0
6000+	1.3	17.4
Monthly family income		
up to 2999	44.0	6.0
3000–5999	43.0	25.1
6000+	13.0	69.0
Having bank account in respondent's name		
No	98.3	68.0
Yes	1.7	32.0
Having daily family expenditure to the respondent		
No	54.7	40.3
Yes	45.3	59.7

Income is in Bangladeshi currency—Taka (BDT)

Table 21.2 Household characteristics and living arrangements of the respondents by residence

Characteristics	Rural (N=477)	Urban (N=419)
	Percentage	Percentage
Household head		
Male	88.9	90.5
Female	11.1	9.5
Condition of houses		
Pucca	16.1	75.9
Kancha	57.0	1.7
Half pucca	13.2	8.1
Tin	1.9	12.4
Others	11.7	1.9
Access to		
Television	29.4	88.8
Radio	1.7	8.1
Electricity	75.3	99.8
Source of drinking water		
Tube well	99.6	98.3
Tap	0.2	1.7
Others	0.2	–
Types of toilet		
Sanitary	18.4	7.6
Pucca	11.1	89.5
Kancha	39.6	2.6
Open	0.4	0.2
Others	30.4	
Marital status		
Single	0.2	0.7
Married	56.6	63.2
Widow/widower	41.5	36.0
Others	1.7	–
Living arrangements		
Living alone	10.3	3.6
Living with spouse	20.8	10.3
Living with unmarried son/daughter	17.8	10.7
Living with married son/daughter	50.3	74.2
Living with others	0.8	1.2

Pucca house is made up of brick, cement, and iron, etc.
Kancha house is made up of mud or hay stack or tin roof

Table 21.3 displays the distribution of health status, illness, treatment source, and abuse of the study respondents with rural-urban differentials. More urban elderly are in fair and good health than rural elderly. Almost all respondents can do their regular activities without major difficulty and help the family members by supplying food, keeping house, and taking care of the children in the absence of

Table 21.3 Elderly responses to health status and the abuse-related questions by residence

Characteristics	Rural (N=477)	Urban (N=419)
	Percentage	Percentage
Current health status		
Very poor	23.5	10.5
Poor	42.3	39.6
Fair	28.3	38.4
Good	5.9	10.7
Very good	–	0.7
Ability to do regular work		
No	2.1	3.3
Yes	97.9	96.7
Support to family members, e.g. food supply, house keeping and child care		
No	2.7	5.0
Yes	97.3	95.0
Types of illness		
Arthritis	64.4	38.4
Gastric	71.5	60.9
Eye problem	51.2	32.2
Hearing problem	13.4	7.2
Asthma	5.9	5.5
Cough	3.6	2.1
Diabetes	4.0	18.6
Tuberculosis	0.4	0.5
Blood pressure problem	19.7	50.1
Paralysis	3.6	2.6
Heart problem	4.8	14.1
Others	31.0	15.0
Sources of treatment		
Government hospital	41.5	88.8
Clinic	1.0	43.0
Homeopathic	1.5	–
Village doctors	88.9	–
Others	2.5	5.0
Having physical exercise during last six months preceding the survey		
No	41.3	42.0
Yes	58.7	58.0
Having intoxication habits		
No	34.8	37.0
Yes	65.2	63.0
Ever abused		
No	47.6	85.7
Yes	52.4	14.3
Types of abuse		
Physical	2.3	1.4
Emotional	4.8	5.5
Sexual	–	–
Exploitation	0.8	0.5
Neglect	50.5	12.2
Abandonment	4.6	1.7

Table 21.3 (continued)

Characteristics	Rural (N=477)	Urban (N=419)
	Percentage	Percentage
Reasons for abuse		
Poverty	50.7	11.9
Inability	4.8	3.3
Dependency	1.0	0.7
Property distribution	1.0	1.2
Illness	2.9	1.0
Others	6.9	w3.8

Intoxication habits include consumption of tobacco such as bidi/cigarette, betel leaf, ganja, tari- a kind of house made wine;
Bidi consists of sun-dried and cured tobacco flakes hand-rolled in a rectangular piece of paper or tobacco leaf

the other family members. More rural elderly were found to have multiple diseases such as arthritis, gastric issues, eye problems, and hearing problems compared to urban elderly. More urban elderly reported diabetes, blood pressure problems, and heart problems compared to rural elderly. Village doctors are found to be the major sources of treatment in rural areas whereas the government hospitals followed by clinics were found to provide health services for the urban residents. A few more rural elderly reported having some physical exercises during the six months preceding the survey and having addiction to bad habits such as bidi/cigarette, betel leaf, ganja, tari—a kind of house made wine—etc. than urban elderly. More than half the rural elderly were found to be abused, whereas only about 14 % in urban areas reported abuse. In both the areas, neglect was found to be the main type and poverty was the main reason, according to the respondents.

Multivariate Analyses

Table 21.4 shows the net effects of some selected socio-demographic variables on the living arrangements with rural-urban differentials. Marital status, working status, and ever being abused were found as the most significant explanatory variables in Model I. Addition of some control variables, viz. age, sex, and owner of the houses, was done in Model II, followed by inclusion of educational status, individual income, family income, and physical condition in Model III. Those who were currently working were 6 times in rural areas and 14 times in urban areas more likely to live alone than those who were not working. Those who had ever been abused were 45 times more likely to live in rural areas and 22 times more likely to live alone than reference categories in urban areas. The married elderly were less likely to live alone than others in both the areas. Controlling for the effects of age, sex, and owner of the houses in Model II shows the same direction but higher odds ratios for the marital status, working status, and being abused compared with Model I. In the final Model III, some differentials such as in rural areas those who are old

Table 21.4 Results of logistic regression analysis concerning living arrangements of the study respondents

Explanatory variables	Odds ratios					
	Rural			Urban		
	Model I	Model II	Model III	Model I	Model II	Model III
Marital status						
Others (ref.)	1	1	1	1	1	1
Married	0.006*	0.01*	0.002*	0.021*	0.03*	0.04**
Work status						
Not working (ref.)	1	1	1	1	1	1
Working	6.007*	10.42*	13.89*	14.38*	14.58*	4.78
Abused						
No (ref.)	1	1	1	1	1	1
Yes	44.65*	51.54*	38.37*	21.66*	23.07*	6.78***
Age groups						
60–69 (ref.)		1	1		1	1
70–79		0.66	1.01		0.42	0.49
80+		4.83**	7.38**		2.31	1.43
Sex						
Male		0.97	0.55		0.41	0.52
Female (ref.)		1	1 ·		1	1
Owner of the houses						
Own		2.10***	2.95**		2.52	5.60***
Others (ref.)		1	1		1	1
Educational level						
No education (ref.)			1			1
Primary			6.52			0.69
Secondary and above			5.55			0.21
Respondent's monthly income (in BDT)						
up to 2999 (ref.)			1			1
3000–5999			6E+008			0.001
6000+			4E+008			15.88***
Family's monthly income (in BDT)						
up to 2999 (ref.)			1			1
3000–5999			0.001			0.03**
6000+			0.001			0.06**
Present physical condition						
Poor (ref.)			1			1
Good			0.885			1.23

ref. reference category, *BDT* Bangladesh currency—Taka
$*p<0.01$; $**p<0.05$; $***p<0.10$

Table 21.5 Results of logistic regression analysis concerning health status of the study respondents

Explanatory variables	Odds ratios					
	Rural			Urban		
	Model I	Model II	Model III	Model I	Model II	Model III
Having physical exercise during last six months preceding the survey						
No (ref.)	1	1	1	1	1	1
Yes	4.78*	4.45*	4.11*	7.01*	5.55*	6.06*
Age groups		1				
60–69 (ref.)			1		1	1
70–79		0.87	0.88		0.63***	0.62***
80+		0.59	0.73		0.28*	0.26*
Sex						
Male		1.42	1.39		1.19	1.10
Female (ref.)		1	1		1	1
Marital status						
Others (ref.)		1	1		1	1
Married		1.11	1.04		1.21	1.23
Educational level						
No education (ref.)			1			1
Primary			0.89			0.61
Secondary and above			1.36			0.79
Family's monthly income (in BDT)						
up to 2999 (ref.)			1			1
3000–5999			2.11*			2.19
6000+			2.32**			2.30
Work status						
Not working (ref.)			1			1
Working			1.77**			0.75
Having intoxication habit						
No (ref.)			1			1
Yes			1.26			1.45
Having safe toilet facilities						
No (ref.)			1			1
Yes			1.26			1.76

ref. reference category, *BDT* Bangladesh currency—Taka
Level of significance: $*p<0.01$; $**p<0.05$; $***p<0.10$

aged (80+) and in urban areas those who have more individual income (6000+ BDT) are significantly more likely to live alone. But in both the areas, the elderly with higher family incomes are less likely to live alone than the elderly with lower family incomes, and the odds ratios are especially significant in urban areas.

Table 21.5 shows the odds ratios for some selected variables on the health status of the elderly in both the rural and urban areas. Model I shows the most positive significant single predictor, viz. doing some physical exercises during the six months preceding the survey, for health status of the elderly population. Without controlling for other variables, Model I shows that those who did some physical exercises during the last six months preceding the survey were 4.78 times in rural areas and 7.01 times in urban areas more likely to be in good health than the elderly who did not do so. Though addition of some controls lowered the odds ratios of having physical exercise in Model II and Model III, it was the most highly significant single independent variable among all other explanatory variables affecting the health of the elderly positively in the study area. Those who were married, have more family income, and have safe toilet facilities are more likely to have good health than the reference category. Those who were working are more likely to be healthy in rural areas, but the reverse picture is shown in urban areas. The middle and old aged (70–79 and 80+ years) elderly are less like to have good health than the young old (60–69 years) elderly in both areas. Unexpectedly, those having an intoxication habit are more likely to have good health than those who do not have an intoxication habit in both rural and urban areas.

Table 21.6 shows results of logistic regression on the abuse of the elderly. Those who live alone are significantly more likely to be abused than those who live with a spouse or unmarried son/daughter or married son/daughter in both rural and urban areas. Persons who are living with others have a higher likelihood of being abused than persons living alone. In both the areas, elderly with higher family income and with higher education are less likely to be abused than the elderly with less income and with no education. Differentials in sex and marital status were found in rural and urban areas.

Discussion

The findings of this study revealed that more rural elderly have no formal education and less income. Patriarchal family is pervasive in the study areas. Urban elderly have better facilities—better houses, better toilets, electricity, and television and more often live with married children. One thing should be noted here that though almost all urban households and three-fourths of the rural households have electricity, in every summer they face an enormous load shedding problem, and eventually they face one of the worst power crises in the world (Ehsan et al. 2012).

More rural elderly were found to live alone than the urban counterparts. The possible reasons include internal migration and widowhood. The young members of a rural family usually go to urban areas for the purpose of study or work, making the older alone in the households.

This study also finds more urban elderly in good health conditions, though a prevalence for diabetes, blood pressure problems, and heart problems is comparatively much higher in urban areas. This may be the due to the availability of modern health technologies in urban areas. Urban residents were found to have treatments from government hospitals and/or clinics, thus more cases with such diseases were found

Table 21.6 Results of logistic regression analysis concerning the abuse of the study respondents

Explanatory variables	Odds ratios					
	Rural			Urban		
	Model I	Model II	Model III	Model I	Model II	Model III
Living arrangements						
Living alone (ref.)	1	1	1	1	1	1
Living with spouse	0.70	0.70	0.38	0.34	0.39	0.45
Living with unmarried son/daughter	0.11*	0.13*	0.09*	0.09**	0.10**	0.09**
Living with married son/daughter	0.03*	0.03*	0.02*	0.13*	0.14*	0.13*
Living with others	1E+008	9E+007	9E+007	3.88	3.26	2.27
Family's monthly income (in BDT)						
up to 2999 (ref.)		1	1	1	1	1
3000–5999	0.45*	0.48*	0.49*	0.32***	0.33***	0.34***
6000+	0.03*	0.04*	0.04*	0.05*	0.06*	0.06*
Educational level						
No education (ref.)		1	1		1	1
Primary		0.73	0.63		0.90	0.79
Secondary and above		0.36**	0.30**		0.62	0.46
Age groups						
60–69 (ref.)			1			1
70–79			1.02			0.99
80+			0.69			0.89
Sex						
Male			0.82			2.53**
Female (ref.)			1			1
Marital status						
Others (ref.)			1			1
Married			1.99**			0.61
Present physical condition						
Poor (ref.)			1			1
Good			0.81			0.62

ref. reference category, *BDT* Bangladesh currency—Taka
Level of significance: $*p<0.01$; $**p<0.05$; $***p<0.10$

in the urban areas compared to rural areas, where the patients usually have their treatments from village doctors. There might be a possibility of getting more rural elderly than in this study with diabetes, blood pressure problems, and heart problems if they are treated in government hospitals and/or clinics. The reasons for rural elderly not going to hospitals/clinics may be distance between residence and government hospitals/clinics, education, and income. A decrease in the utilization of medical services was observed for patients living longer distances from the medical services (Gregory et al. 2000; Piette and Moos 1996; Meden et al. 2002; Engelman et al. 2002; Goodman et al. 1997; Mooney et al. 2000). With very little/no education, the rural elderly usually ignore such life threatening diseases and fear bearing the costs of recovering health as well. Gazmararian et al. (2003) found health literacy is important for dealing with a range of chronic diseases and independently influences the knowledge of disease. Participants with inadequate health literacy compared to those with adequate health literacy knew much less about their chronic diseases.

Bangladesh has a long tradition of tobacco consumption, either by smoking or through other means, such as cigarette, bidi, hookah, and betel quid with areca nut, dried tobacco leaves, called shada pata, lime, and gul (processed tobacco powder) (Kamal et al. 2011). A considerable number of people are still living in extreme poverty and nearly half of them are addicted to smoking. Our study supports the study of Hanifi et al. (2011) that smoking is more prevalent among the poor compared with the better off, among men compared with women, and among the illiterate compared with the literate. The current study also uncovers elderly abuse, which is invisible because of many reasons, particularly lack of awareness, lack of a universal definition (Hansberry et al. 2005), and many barriers about this topic. Elderly abuse prevails in both areas, especially with a higher prevalence in rural areas. Poverty is reported as the main problem contributing to being neglected in both areas.

Findings of percentage distributions elucidate that the relevance of some sociodemographic measures (age, sex, educational status, work status, house ownership, monthly income, etc.) in living arrangement, health, and abuse status must not be underestimated. And in multivariate analyses, work status, ever abused, and house ownership are found to have significant influences on living arrangements. Physical exercise during the six months preceding the survey is found to be the most significant independent variable shaping the health status of the elderly in the study areas. And living arrangements and family income are found to have significant influence on elderly abuse. The results of these raise concerns about elderly education, their income, their physical exercise, and abusive behaviours toward them. A direct relation between education and health outcomes has been reported in several studies (Mostafa and van Genneken 2000; Ahmed et al. 2002). A recent study in Bangladesh found that socioeconomic status, and education in particular, has a strong influence on adult mortality in rural areas. Both men and women with education had lower mortality compared with those without education (Hurt et al. 2004). Our study suggests that providing education and involving elderly in income generation activities to alleviate their financial problems in old age might not only help the elderly to lead good lives in later life but also keep them away from neglect and abusive behaviour. Furthermore, family cohesiveness, awareness about health, physical exercise, education of the younger starting in childhood to respect the older, and providing urban facilities in rural areas should be given consideration.

Limitations

The study has a few limitations. The sample size is limited and collected from one district, Rajshahi of Bangladesh. Some priority questions concerning abuse, namely, who abused the elderly? and why did the abuser do so? have not been addressed here. Inclusion of these issues in future research is vital for removing the problems to make society and the environment aged-friendly.

Conclusions

In conclusion, the overall situation of the aged is not satisfactory. The results indicate an urgent need for developing suitable programs to address the needs and welfare of the elderly, not only in the Rajshahi district but also across Bangladesh in general. We should keep in mind, 'Ageing developing countries are slated to face a heavy double burden of infectious and non-communicable diseases; yet they often lack sufficient resources, including comprehensive ageing policies, to cope,' as stated by the World Health Organization (2012), and work to solve the existing problems of elderly in order to create an aged-friendly society in the future. Further public health research addressing the limitations of this study also warrants immediate attention to fill the gap of the present study that was conducted in a small area in Bangladesh.

Acknowledgements An earlier version of this paper was presented at the 2012 Applied Demography Conference (2012ADC), San Antonio, TX, USA. Thanks are due to the participants of 2012ADC for valuable comments on the earlier version. Finally, the authors are grateful to the interviewees and the field investigators, without whom the study was impossible.

References

Abedin, S. (2003). Living and care arrangements of the elderly in Bangladesh. In M. Kabir (Ed.), *The elderly-contemporary issues* (pp. 100–107). Dhaka: Dhaka Presidency Press.

Ahmed, S. M., Rana, A. K., Chowdhury, M., & Bhuiya, A. (2002). Measuring perceived health outcomes in non-western culture: Does SF-36 have a place? *Journal of Health, Population, and Nutrition, 20*(4), 334–342.

Bangladesh Institute of Labour Studies (BILS). (2003). Overview of current economic condition in Bangladesh. Global Policy Network. http://www.gpn.org/data/bangladesh/bangladesh-analysis.pdf. Accessed 4 Dec 2009.

Block, M. R., & Sinnott, J. D. (Eds.). (1979). *The battered elder syndrome: An exploratory study*. College Park: University of Maryland, Center on Aging.

Cohen, M., Halevi-Levin, S., Gagin, R., & Friedman, G. (2006). Development of a screening tool for identifying elderly people at risk of abuse by their caregivers. *Journal of Aging and Health, 10,* 660–685.

de Beurs, E., Beekman, A., Geerlings, S., Deeg, D., van Dyck, R., & van Tilburg, W. (2001). On becoming depressed or anxious in later life: Similar vulnerability factors but different effects of stressful life events. *The British Journal of Psychiatry: The Journal of Mental Science, 179,* 426–431.

Ehsan, M., Ovy, E., Shariar, K. F., & Ferdous, S. M. (2012). A novel approach of electrification of the high rise buildings at Dhaka city during load shedding hours. *International Journal of Renewable Energy Research, 2*(1), 455–462.

Engelman, K. K., Hawley, D. B., Gazaway, R., Mosier, M. C., Ahluwalia, J. S., & Ellerbeck, E. F. (2002). Impact of geographic barriers on the utilization of mammograms by older rural women. *Journal of American Geriatrics Society, 50,* 62–68.

Gazmararian, J. A., Williams, M. V., Peel, J., & Baker, D. W. (2003). Health literacy and knowledge of chronic disease. *Patient Education and Counseling, 51,* 267–275.

Ghuman, S., & Ofstedal, M. B. (2004). *Gender and family support for older adults in Bangladesh*. PSC Research Report. No. 04-563. University of Michigan, USA.

Goodman, D. C., Fisher, E., Stukel, T. A., & Chang, C. (1997). The distance to community medical care and the likelihood of hospitalization: Is closer always better? *American Journal of Public Health, 87*(7), 1144–1150.

Gregory, P. M., Malka, E. S., Kostis, J. B., Wilson, A. C., Arora, J. K., & Rhoads, G. G. (2000). Impact of geographic proximity to cardiac revascularization services on service utilization. *Medical Care, 38,* 45–57.

Hanifi, S. M. A., Mahmood, S. S., & Bhuiya, A. (2011). Smoking has declined but not for all: Findings from a study in a rural area of Bangladesh. *Asia-Pacific Journal of Public Health/ Asia-Pacific Academic Consortium for Public Health, 23*(5), 662–671.

Hansberry, M. R., Chen, E., & Gorbien, M. J. (2005). Dementia and elder abuse. *Clinics in Geriatric Medicine, 21,* 315–332.

Help Age International (HAI). (2006). Social pensions in Bangladesh. http://www.helpage.org/Researchandpolicy/PensionWatch/Bangladesh. Accessed 7 Nov 2009.

Hosain, G. M. M., & Begum, A. (2003). Health needs and health status of the elderly in rural Bangladesh. *Asia-Pacific Journal of Public Health/Asia-Pacific Academic Consortium for Public Health, 15*(1), 3–9.

Hsu, H. C. (2011). Impact of morbidity and life events on successful aging. *Asia-Pacific Journal of Public Health/Asia-Pacific Academic Consortium for Public Health, 23*(4), 458–469.

Hurt, L. S., Ronsmans, C., & Saha, S. (2004). Effects of education and other socioeconomic factors on middle age mortality in rural Bangladesh. *Journal of Epidemiology and Community Health, 58,* 315–320.

Jylhä, M. (2009). What is self-rated health and why does it predict mortality? Towards a unified conceptual model. *Social Science & Medicine (1982), 69,* 307–316.

Kabir, M., Haque, M., & Chaklader, H. (2005). *Mainstreaming ageing in health: Will it be possible.* Paper presented in the International conference on mainstreaming ageing in health system and rural development, held in Dhaka, November 2005, pp. 28–30.

Kabir, Z. N., Szebehely, M., & Tishelman, C. (2002). Support in old age in the changing society of Bangladesh. *Ageing and Society, 22*(5), 615–636.

Kamal, S. M. M., Islam, M. A., & Raihan, M. A. (2011). Differentials of tobacco consumption and its effect on illicit drug use in rural men in Bangladesh. *Asia-Pacific Journal of Public Health/ Asia-Pacific Academic Consortium for Public Health, 23*(3), 349–362.

Kessing, L. V., Agerbo, E., & Mortensen, P. B. (2003). Does the impact of major stressful life events on the risk of developing depression change throughout life? *Psychological Medicine, 33,* 1177–1184.

Lau, E. E., & Kosberg, J. I. (1979). Abuse of the elderly by informal care providers. *Aging (Albany NY), 299,* 10–15.

Meden, T., St. John-Larkin, C., Hermes, D., Sommerschield, S. (2002). Relationship between travel distance and utilization of breast cancer treatment in rural Northern Michigan. *JAMA: The Journal of the American Medical Association, 287,* 111.

Ministry of Health and Family Welfare (MHFW). (2004) *Bangladesh population policy.* Dhaka: Ministry of Health and Family Welfare, Government of the People's Republic of Bangladesh.

Mooney, C., Zwanziger, J., Phibbs, C. S., & Schmitt, S. (2000). Is travel distance a barrier to veterans' use of VA hospitals for medical surgical care? *Social Science & Medicine (1982), 50,* 1743–1755.

Mostafa, G., & van Ginneken, J. K. (2000). Trends in and determinants of mortality in the elderly population of Matlab, Bangladesh. *Social Science & Medicine (1982), 50,* 763–771.

Munsur, A. M., Tareque, M. I., & Rahman, K. M. M. (2010). Determinants of living arrangements, health status and abuse among elderly women: A study of rural Naogaon district, Bangladesh. *Journal of International Women's Study, 11*(4), 162–176.

National Center on Elder Abuse (NCEA). (1998). The national elder abuse incidence study: Final report. http://www.aoa.gov/AoARoot/AoA_Programs/Elder_Rights/Elder_Abuse/docs/ABuseReport_Full.pdf. Accessed 5 Dec 2008.

National Center on Elder Abuse (NCEA). (2008). Frequently asked questions. National Center on elder abuse. http://www.ncea.aoa.gov/NCEAroot/Main_Site/FAQ/Questions.aspx. Accessed 24 March 2008.

Papadopoulos, A., & La Fontaine, J. (Eds.). (2000). *Elder abuse: Therapeutic perspectives in practice*. Oxon: Winslow.

Piette, J. D., & Moos, R. H. (1996). The influence of distance on ambulatory care use, death, and reassessment following a myocardial infarction. *Health Services Research, 31,* 573–591.

Rahman, K. M. M., Tareque, M. I., & Rahman, M. M. (2008). Gender differences in economic support, well-being and satisfaction of the rural elderly in Naogaon district, Bangladesh. *Journal of Indian Academy of Geriatrics, 4,* 98–105.

Rahman, K. M. M., Tareque, M. I., Munsur, A. M., & Rahman, M. M. (2010). Elderly abuse: Causes and determinants in rural Naogaon district of Bangladesh. *Journal of Population and Social Studies, 19*(1), 25–36.

Schiamberg, L. B., & Gans, D. M. (2000). Elder abuse by adult children: An applied ecological framework for understanding contextual risk factors and the intergenerational character of quality of life. *International Journal of Aging and Human Development, 50*(4), 329–359.

Swami, H. M., Bhatia, V., Parashar, A., & Bhatia, S. P. S. (2003). Social and functional status of older persons in a north Indian community. *Asia-Pacific journal of public health/Asia-Pacific Academic Consortium for Public Health, 15*(1), 10–16.

Tareque, M. I. (2007). Future appeal of geriatrics in Bangladesh. *Middle East Journal of Age and Ageing, 4*(4), 14–16.

Tareque, M. I. (2009). *Socio-demographic status of the aged population and elderly abuse: A study on rural-urban differentials in Rajshahi district, Bangladesh*. Dhaka: Social Science Research Council (SSRC), Planning Division, Ministry of Planning, the Government of Bangladesh.

Tareque, M. I., Islam, T. M., & Rahman, M. M. (2008). Determinants of elder abuse in Rajshahi city corporation, Bangladesh: Evidence from a micro-level survey. *Indian Journal of Gerontology, 22*(3 & 4), 411–421.

UNESCO. (1992). *The changing family in ASIA*. Social and Human Sciences in Asia and the Pacific. RUSHSAP Series on Monographs and Occasional Papers 35. Bangkok.

United Nations. (2010). World population prospects: The 2010 Revision. United Nations Population Division. http://esa.un.org/unpd/wpp/unpp/p2k0data.asp. Accessed 3 Dec 2011.

United Nations. (2013). World elder abuse awareness day- 15 June. http://www.un.org/en/events/elderabuse/. Accessed 19 June 2013.

World Health Organization. (2012). Healthy ageing is vital for development. http://www.who.int/mediacentre/news/releases/release24/en/. Accessed 4 April 2012.

World Health Organization. (2013). Ageing and life-course: Elder abuse. http://www.who.int/ageing/projects/elder_abuse/en/. Accessed 19 June 2013.

Chapter 22
The Conceptualization and Measurement of the Homosexual, Heterosexual, and Bisexual Populations in the United States

Dudley L. Poston and Yu-Ting Chang

Introduction

In this chapter we use sexuality data from the 2006–2008 Survey of Family Growth (NSFG) to conceptualize and measure sexuality and sexual orientation. We first discuss the two main approaches used by social scientists to conceptualize sexual orientation, namely, essentialism and social constructionism. Next we review some of the prior empirical literature that has endeavored to measure sexual orientation. We next specify three different dimensions of sexuality, namely, sexual behavior in one's lifetime, sexual self-identification, and sexual preference. We use the 2006–2008 NSFG data to explore the multiple dimensions of sexuality, in contrast to using only a single dimension, say, only behavior or only self-identification or only desire. We examine the consistency in the dimensions for heterosexual persons, homosexual persons, and bisexual persons. We show that an essentialist view works in a fairly consistent manner for heterosexual persons but is not at all consistent for homosexual and bisexual persons. This is so because heterosexuality is more pervasive, with less room for differences. We then develop several percentages of the U.S. adult population who according to various definitions may be classified as heterosexual, homosexual, or bisexual. Finally we discuss some of the implications of the findings of our research for demographic analyses of sexuality.

Conceptualizing Sexuality

Most of the social science literature on sexual orientation conceptualizes the phenomenon using two basic perspectives or approaches, or a combination thereof. These two views are known as *essentialism* and *social constructionism* (Laumann et al. 1994, p. 284; Baumle et al. 2009, pp. 19–21). Founded in biology, the

D. L. Poston (✉) · Y.-T. Chang
Department of Sociology, Texas A&M University, College Station, TX, USA
e-mail: d-poston@tamu.edu

M. N. Hoque, L. B. Potter (eds.), *Emerging Techniques in Applied Demography*, Applied Demography Series 4, DOI 10.1007/978-94-017-8990-5_22,

essentialist view is one of dimorphism; it states that there is an "essential" biological or psychological characteristic or attribute that is common to all persons and that distinguishes them as either of one sexuality or not of that sexuality. This common characteristic, or essence, is thought to be a fundamental drive or trait that establishes a person's inclusion into, or not into, one of the sexual categories of heterosexual, homosexual, or bisexual (Laumann et al. 1994, p. 285; Baumle et al. 2009, pp. 19–20). The essentialist view states that a person is classified, or is not classified, as homosexual or as heterosexual or as bisexual; a binary distinction is made between one who is in that category and one who is not. Thus, sexual orientation is determined by the definition of the sexually distinct categories.

The social constructionist view of homosexuality on the other hand counters and critiques the essentialist perspective. Social constructionism argues against the notion of binary categories, that is, that one either is or is not in a specific sexual category (Foucault 1978; Butler 1990; Seidman 1996; Baumle et al. 2009, pp. 20–21). Instead, this approach argues for a continuum with varying degrees of the categories of sexuality. For example, social constructionists point out that the degree of homosexual and bisexual prevalence and visibility tends to vary across time and settings and that the concepts, definitions, and practices of homosexuality and bisexuality are often not the same across context and cultures (Laumann et al. 1994, p. 285). To illustrate, what in one culture may be defined as "homosexual" may not be so defined in another culture. For example, an individual may engage in same-sex sexual behavior but not identify himself/herself as homosexual. Likewise, one might identify as homosexual but never have experienced same-sex sex. Also, the sexuality definitions and labels attached to individuals by other persons and by the larger society may be incongruent with how individuals self-identify (Baumle et al. 2009, pp. 19–21). Social constructionists would make similar statements with regard to heterosexuality and bisexuality. Or as Hanne Blank (2012, p. xviii) writes in her intriguing book about the history of heterosexuality, "despite the fact that most of us use the term 'heterosexual' with enormous and cavalier certainty, there seems to be no aspect of 'heterosexual' for which a truly iron-clad definition has been established." And the same may be stated about "homosexual" and "bisexual."

Until the sexuality research conducted in the 1940s and 1950s by Alfred Kinsey and his colleagues (Kinsey et al. 1948; Kinsey et al. 1953), most sexuality researchers used an essentialist orientation. It was Kinsey who moved sexuality research away from a position of essentialism. He argued that the sexuality of humans is a lot more varied than was originally thought. The range of expression he created has become known as the "Kinsey scale," which is a 7-point scale that ranks overall sexuality from completely heterosexual (scored 0) to completely homosexual (scored 6) and everything in-between. When he introduced his 7-point scale, he wrote the following:

> Males do not represent two discrete populations, heterosexual and homosexual. The world is not to be divided into sheep and goats. It is a fundamental of taxonomy that nature rarely deals with discrete categories... The living world is a continuum in each and every one of its aspects ... While emphasizing the continuity of the gradations between exclusively heterosexual and exclusively homosexual histories, it has seemed desirable to develop some

> sort of classification which could be based on the relative amounts of heterosexual and homosexual experience or response in each history… An individual may be assigned a position on this scale, for each period in his life… A seven-point scale comes nearer to showing the many gradations that actually exist (Kinsey et al. 1948, pp. 639, 656).

In demographic and social science research on sexuality, the manner in which sexuality and sexual orientation is conceptualized tends to vary. This is largely due to the different ways sexual orientation has been defined in surveys and conceptualized by the researchers (Saewyc et al. 2004). Sexuality may be defined in terms of sexual behavior, sexual desire (including fantasy), and self-identification (Laumann et al. 1994; Saewyc et al. 2004). In analyses based on data from national surveys, social scientists have used one or more of the above concepts of sexuality but particularly those based on self-identification and behavior.

For instance, analyses of homosexuality using data from the General Social Survey (GSS) usually employ a behavioral definition of homosexuality, such as whether a person's sex partners within a particular timeframe (such as over the past 12 months, or the past 5 years, or in one's lifetime) have or have not been entirely or predominantly of the same sex as the respondent (Badgett 1995; Berg and Lien 2002; Black et al. 2003). The GSS does not include a question on the self-identification of the respondent's sexual orientation.

Researchers using data from other surveys sometimes use questions tapping different definitions or dimensions of homosexuality. For instance, the NSFG includes questions dealing with sexual behavior, sexual orientation, and sexual desire; these are the survey data we use in this chapter. Another source is the National Health and Social Life Survey (NHSLS) conducted by Laumann and his associates in 1992 (see *The Social Organization of Sexuality: Sexual Practices in the United States* [1994]). Because these surveys allow researchers to define sexuality in various ways, it is possible for their analyses to be more closely attuned to a social constructionist, rather than to an essentialist, view of sexuality in general and homosexuality in particular (Baumle et al. 2009, p. 20).

In contrast, when demographers and other social scientists use census data to analyze sexuality, they almost always take an essentialist view owing to the type of data available. Employing the so-called "unmarried partner" census data, for instance, involves, by definition, a clear-cut and straightforward definition of a partnered same-sex individual, a partnered opposite-sex person, and a married person.

Overall, a review of the literature about the conceptualization of sexuality shows some basic methodological critiques, namely, the lack of common and consistent definitions across the various surveys, samples not sufficiently representative of the subpopulations under investigation, and a reliance on only one or two sexuality-related questions. These issues may well be associated with social stigma attached to sexualities other than heterosexuality, thus affecting not only the way the questionnaires are designed, but also the ways in which the respondents answer the questions. For example, a person may be reluctant to identify as a homosexual or as a bisexual and/or to report homosexual or bisexual behavior (Laumann et al. 1994, p. 284; Baumle et al. 2009, p. 21).

No doubt there are problems with data on sexuality no matter how the phenomenon is conceptualized and quantified. There are likely methodological limitations and problems inherent in gathering and analyzing any data about sexuality, particularly the sexually stigmatized minorities. Nonetheless, we find that the survey data from the National Survey of Family Growth are particularly useful for researchers following a social constructionist approach.

Empirical Analyses of Sexuality

In our opinion, perhaps the very best and most comprehensive analysis of sexuality in the United States is *The Social Organization of Sexuality: Sexual Practices in the United States* by Edward O. Laumann, John H. Gagnon, Robert T. Michael, and Stuart Michaels, published in 1994. The authors began their chapter on "Homosexuality" with the following sentence: "Perhaps no other single number in this study will attract greater public interest than our estimate of the prevalence of homosexuality" (Laumann et al. 1994, p. 283). They then reviewed some of the prior research on this topic and addressed what they referred to as the "myth of 10 %," i.e., the belief that "there is a single prevalence rate of homosexuality and a single estimate of 10 %," and that both come from the same source, namely, the sexuality research conducted by Alfred Kinsey and his associates in the 1940s and 1950 (Kinsey et al. 1948; Kinsey et al. 1953).

In their research, Laumann et al. (1994) showed that there is not a single prevalence rate of homosexuality, and, moreover, that the 10 % figure did not come from the work of Kinsey and his colleagues. The prevalence of homosexuality depends on the way that homosexuality is defined. If one defines as homosexual a person who self-identifies as homosexual, Laumann and his associates (1994) showed that the percentage of persons who are homosexual is about 1.4 % for women and 2.8 % for men. If the definition of homosexuality depends on same-sex desire and attraction, then they showed that the levels for males and females vary around 5 %. If one uses same-sex behavior as the criterion, then the percentages for females range from 1.3 to 4.1 %, depending on how the behavior is defined, and from 2.7 to 4.1 % for males. An important contribution of the research by Laumann and his colleagues is that the prevalence of homosexuality, and also of heterosexuality and of bisexuality by implication, varies according to the dimension of sexuality employed by the researcher. If one chooses to focus on self-identification, then the prevalence of homosexuality (and heterosexuality and bisexuality) in the population will likely differ from the prevalence level obtained were one to use behavior or desire as the principal criterion.

In a more recent analysis, Gates (2011) combined five population-based surveys containing data on sexuality that were conducted between 2004 and 2009. He estimated that on average for the adult populations enumerated in the surveys, 3.4 % of females and 3.6 % of males in the United States identified themselves as lesbian, gay, or bisexual. More interestingly, within the several surveys, he found that women were more likely than men to identify as bisexual, with more than half of the men who engage in gay and/or bisexual sex identifying themselves as gay men.

Self-identification, however, as we have shown above, is not the only criterion used for measuring sexual orientation. Different dimensions for approaching sexual orientation often result in different estimates of homosexual and bisexual prevalence. Considering the dimensions of same-sex attraction and behavior, Gates (2011, p. 5) reported that "adults are two to three times more likely to say that they are attracted to individuals of the same sex or have had same-sex sexual experiences than they are to self-identify" as lesbian, gay, or bisexual. He showed that over 8 % of adults stated that they have ever engaged in same-sex sexual behaviors and about 11 % have at least some same-sex sexual attraction.

In a much older study, Fay et al. (1989) used data from a national survey conducted in the late 1970s to estimate that about one of five American men had ever had same-sex sexual contacts in their lifetimes. They also indicated that about half of men who had ever had same-sex sexual contacts were currently or previously married. Smith (1991) used data from an adult household sample surveyed in 1989 to show that there were no sex differences in same-sex behavior prevalence; also he reported that 5.6 % of American adults had been bisexual and only 0.7 % were exclusively homosexual. Analyses of more recent data by Chandra et al. (2011) showed that twice as many women than men reported having any same-sex sex behavior in their lifetimes.

In all the above analyses, a common finding seems to be the fluidity of sexual orientation. All the analyses show that the estimated prevalence rates of homosexuality, heterosexuality, and bisexuality vary, often considerably, according to the particular dimension of sexuality (behavior, attraction/desire, or self-identification) used. We find similar results in our analyses of the 2006–2008 NSFG data. Accordingly, in this chapter we examine sexuality from a social constructionist perspective, using one or more of the three dimensions of sexuality. We hold that heterosexuality, homosexuality, and bisexuality are complex phenomena, without universal definitions. By following a social constructionist approach and using data on all three dimensions of sexuality, we hope to show empirically the multi-faceted nature and the fluidity of sexuality.

With respect to the three dimensions, strictly speaking, identification is a straightforward question and, thus, should be a simple matter to measure. Were persons to self-identify themselves as homosexual or heterosexual or bisexual, they would be so identified in the research. But this does not necessarily mean that they would respond in a similar manner to questions dealing with other dimensions of sexuality, i.e., behavior or desire. Indeed a person could self-identify as homosexual, but state that he or she has engaged in sexual activity with both males and females.

Alternately, sexual desire or attraction is a variable that is not as straightforward as personal identification in the construction of a sexual category. Desire has to do with individual feelings and wants regardless of behavior or identification. If a respondent were to declare to desire sexual relations with someone of the same sex, he or she would be defined as homosexual according to this dimension of sexuality.

Like desire, behavior is only one aspect of a constructed view of sexuality. For instance, a person may engage in same-sex sexual behavior but not self-identify as homosexual.

The 2006–2008 NSFG includes questions enabling us to directly assess each of the above dimensions of sexuality. We discuss next these issues in more detail.

The NSFG Data

The data in this chapter are from the 2006–2008 National Survey of Family Growth (NSFG). The data were generated from 7,356 interviews with women and 6,139 interviews with men; the respondents were 15–44 years of age, and the interviews were conducted from about July 1, 2006, through December 2008. Also, in some parts of our chapter, data are drawn from comparable samples of women and men interviewed in the 2002 NSFG. The "interviewing and data processing for the 2006–2008 NSFG were conducted by the University of Michigan's Institute for Social Research, under a contract with the National Center for Health Statistics (NCHS). In-person interviews were conducted by trained professional interviewers in the homes of a national sample of households. Interviewers entered respondents' answers directly into laptop computers. Interviews averaged about 80 min in length. The interview was voluntary; participants were provided information about the survey before being asked for signed informed consent. The survey was reviewed and approved by the NCHS and University of Michigan Institutional Review Boards. The overall response rate was 75%.... The sample is a nationally representative multistage area probability sample drawn from 85 areas across the country" (Mosher 2010, pp. 2–3).

The 2006–2008 NSFG questions we used to obtain respondent data on the behavioral dimension of sexuality are two. For females, the two questions are:

- Counting all your male sexual partners, even those you had intercourse with only once, how many men have you had sexual intercourse with in your life?
- Thinking about your entire life, how many female sex partners have you had?

For males, the two questions are:

- How many different females have you ever had intercourse with? This includes any female you had intercourse with, even if it was only once or if you did not know her well.
- Thinking about your entire life, how many male sex partners have you had?

A respondent answering having only opposite-sex partners and no same-sex partners is defined as heterosexual on the behavior dimension of sexuality. A respondent answering having both opposite-sex partners and same-sex partners is defined as bisexual, and a respondent answering having only same-sex partners and no opposite-sex partners is defined as homosexual. It is important to note that this behavioral measurement is limited to assessing behaviors in one's lifetime.

With respect to the self-identification of sexual orientation, the 2006–2008 NSFG asked each respondent the following question:

- Do you think of yourself as heterosexual or straight; as homosexual, gay or lesbian; as bisexual; or as something else?

One's sexuality status according to the self-identification dimension is based on the person's answer to the above question.

With respect to sexual desire and attraction, the 2006–2008 NSFG asked males the following question, and a similar question was asked of females:

- People are different in their sexual attraction to other people. Which best describes your feelings? Are you…Only attracted to females; Mostly attracted to females; Equally attracted to females and males; Mostly attracted to males; Only attracted to males; Not sure.

We specified the sexuality of males on the desire dimension as follows. Males who are only attracted or mostly attracted to females are heterosexual; males who are only attracted or mostly attracted to males are homosexual; males who are equally attracted to females and males are bisexual. We specified the sexuality of females on the desire dimension in a similar way.

In our chapter, we report estimates of the U.S. male and female population aged 15–44 who provide the "heterosexual response," the "homosexual response," and the "bisexual response" to at least one of the above questions on behavior, self-identification, and desire. We also use a social constructionist approach and combine the responses to the above three questions and provide estimates of the percentages of persons who give one of the three "sexual responses" according to one or more of the above three questions. We first examine empirically the dimensions of sexuality, i.e., self-identification, behavior, and desire, with regard specifically to homosexuality, heterosexuality, and bisexuality.

Our Empirical Analyses of Sexuality

The Empirical Interrelations of the Dimensions of Sexuality

We now examine empirically the intersection of the three dimensions of sexuality. We use data from the 2006–2008 NSFG and combine the sexuality responses to the above three NSFG questions into seven possible outcomes as follows: providing a homosexual (or a heterosexual or a bisexual) response (1) only to identification, (2) only to desire, (3) only to behavior, (4) to both identification and desire, (5) to both identification and behavior, (6) to both desire and behavior, and (7) to identification, desire, and behavior. Unweighted percentages for U.S. females and males aged 15–44 are shown in the Venn diagrams in Figs. 22.1, 22.2, 22.3, 22.4, 22.5, 22.6.

Figure 22.1 refers to the intersection of the sexuality dimensions for heterosexuality for females. The Venn diagram shows the degree of overlap among the conceptually

Interrelations of Components of Heterosexuality, females ,U.S., 2006-2008

Categories	(%)
Behavior	0.43
Desire	1.44
Identity	0.56
Behave & Desire	0.50
Behave & ID	0.88
Desire & ID	21.22
Beh. & Des. & ID	74.96
Sample Size	6,878
% of total sample (unweighted)	93.50

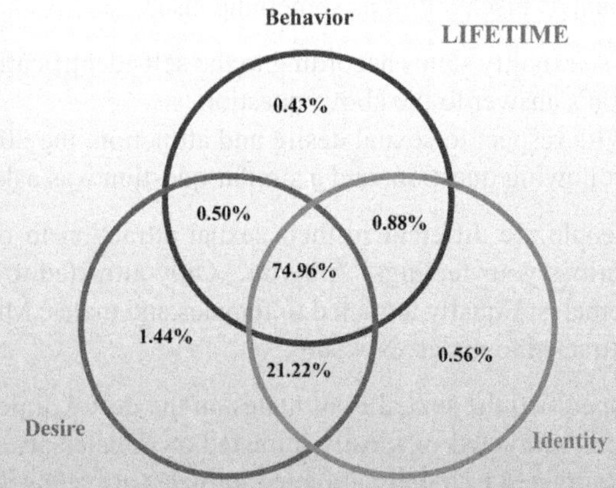

Fig. 22.1 Heterosexual females

Interrelations of Components of Heterosexuality, males ,U.S., 2006-2008

Categories	(%)
Behavior	0.11
Desire	0.41
Identity	0.22
Behave & Desire	0.28
Behave & ID	0.23
Desire & ID	16.16
Beh. & Des. & ID	82.59
Sample Size	5,768
% of total sample (unweighted)	93.96

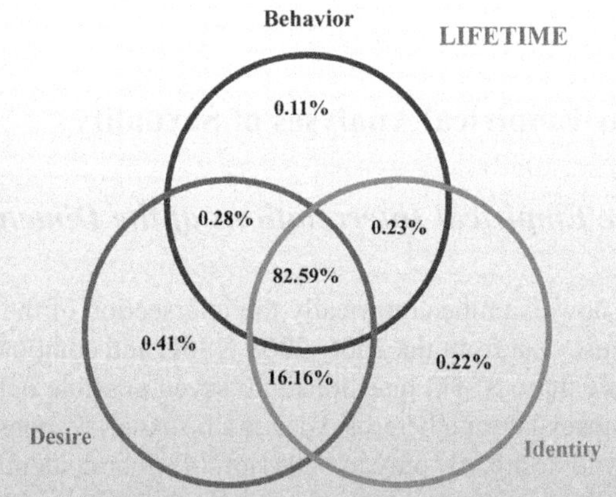

Fig. 22.2 Heterosexual males

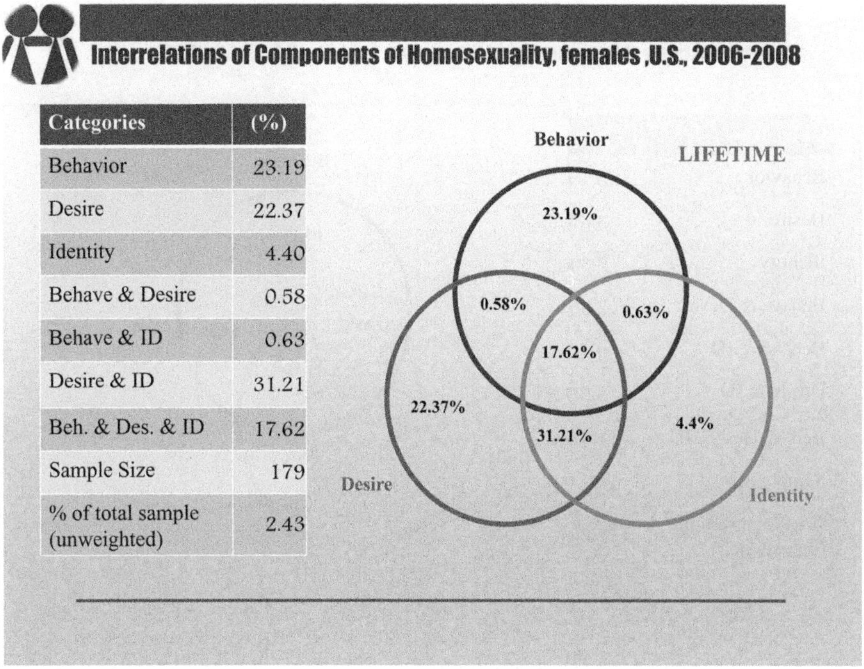

Categories	(%)
Behavior	23.19
Desire	22.37
Identity	4.40
Behave & Desire	0.58
Behave & ID	0.63
Desire & ID	31.21
Beh. & Des. & ID	17.62
Sample Size	179
% of total sample (unweighted)	2.43

Fig. 22.3 Homosexual females

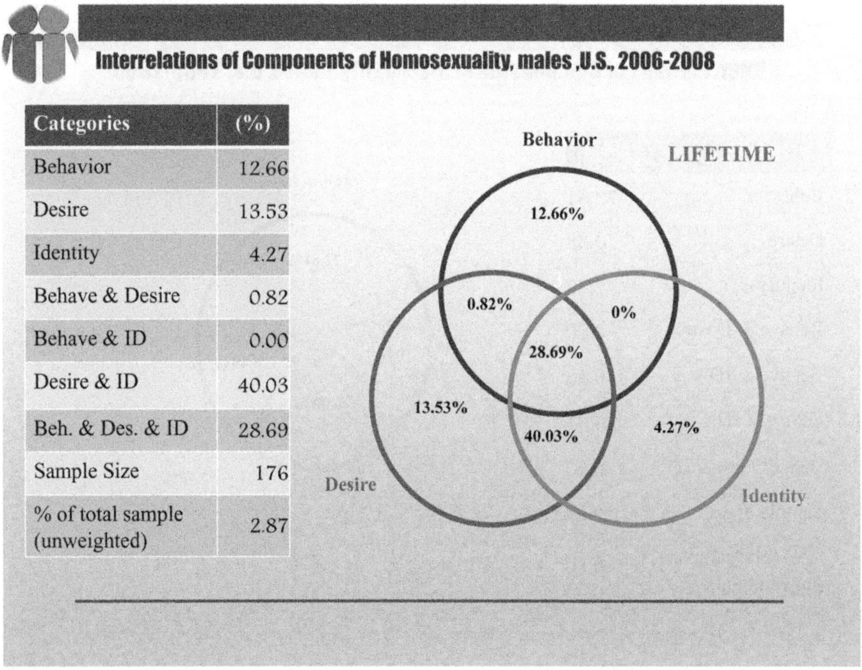

Categories	(%)
Behavior	12.66
Desire	13.53
Identity	4.27
Behave & Desire	0.82
Behave & ID	0.00
Desire & ID	40.03
Beh. & Des. & ID	28.69
Sample Size	176
% of total sample (unweighted)	2.87

Fig. 22.4 Homosexual males

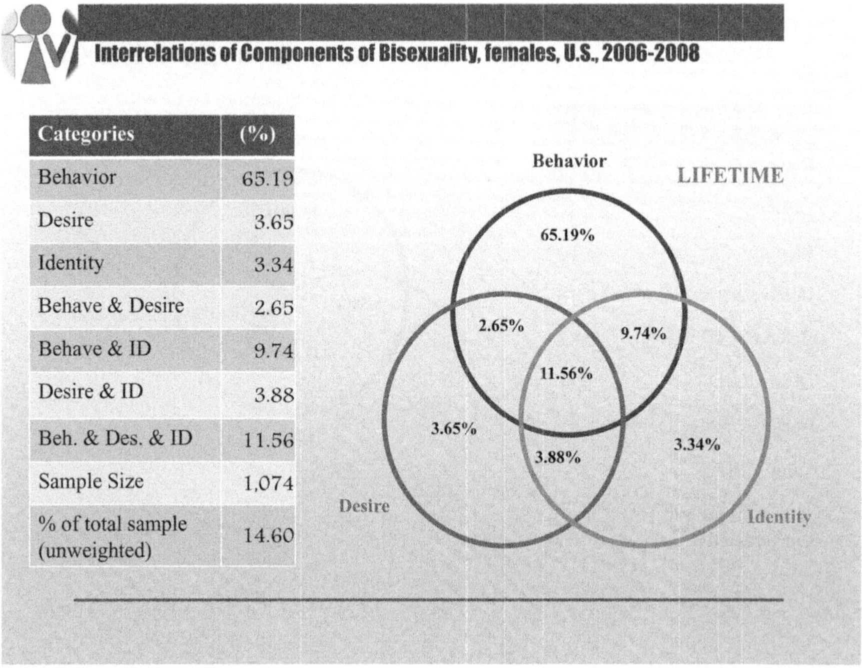

Categories	(%)
Behavior	65.19
Desire	3.65
Identity	3.34
Behave & Desire	2.65
Behave & ID	9.74
Desire & ID	3.88
Beh. & Des. & ID	11.56
Sample Size	1,074
% of total sample (unweighted)	14.60

Fig. 22.5 Bisexual females

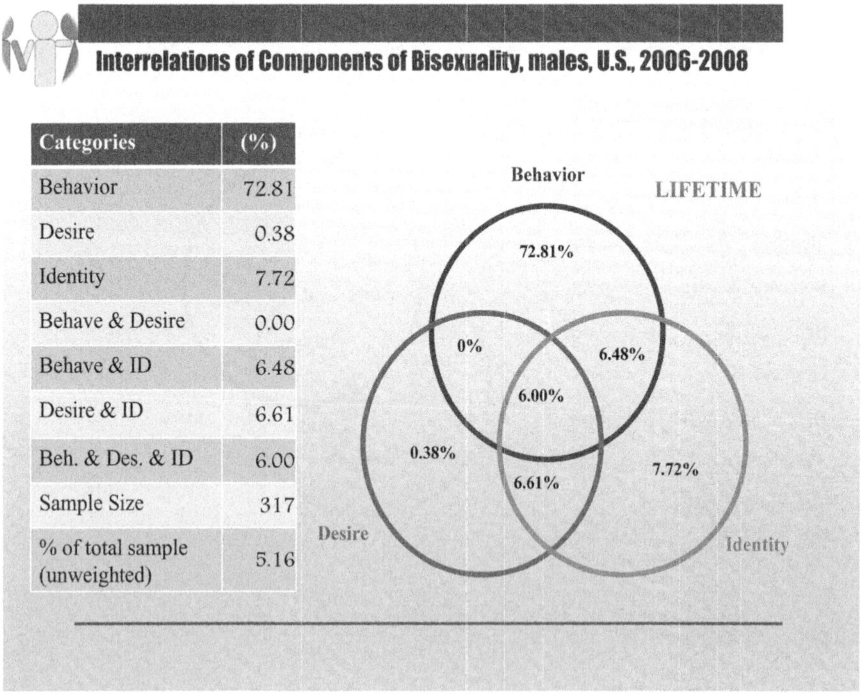

Categories	(%)
Behavior	72.81
Desire	0.38
Identity	7.72
Behave & Desire	0.00
Behave & ID	6.48
Desire & ID	6.61
Beh. & Des. & ID	6.00
Sample Size	317
% of total sample (unweighted)	5.16

Fig. 22.6 Bisexual males

distinct dimensions of sexuality applied to female heterosexuality. As Laumann et al. (1994, p. 298) have written in a similar presentation, "these (Venn) diagrams make use of overlapping circles to display all the logically possible intersections among different categories (of sexuality)." Whereas the diagrams in this chapter show all possible combinations, they do not scale the areas of each circle; instead the percentages attached to each area are shown in the figures. Each circle represents a dimension of sexuality. We show in Fig. 22.1 how exactly the 6,878 women who reported any heterosexual behavior, desire, or identity are actually distributed across the seven mutually exclusive combinations of the three sexuality dimensions.

The data and diagram in Fig. 22.1 indicate that 93.5 % of all the female respondents in the 2006–2008 NSFG, that is, 6,878 women of the total NSFG sample of 7,356 women, gave a "heterosexual" response to at least one of the three questions pertaining to sexual behavior, self-identification, and desire. Specifically, for purposes of illustration, the part of the "Desire" circle in Fig. 22.1 that does not overlap with the "Behavior" or "Identity" circles indicates that just under 1.5 % of the women giving a heterosexual response to any one or more of the three questions reported a desire for persons of the opposite sex, but did not identify themselves as heterosexual and did not report having only heterosexual sex in their lifetimes. However, nearly 75 % of the women giving a heterosexual response to at least one of the three questions gave a heterosexual response to all three questions (see the overlapping component of all three circles in the center of the Venn diagram). That is, almost three-fourths of the females reported self-identifying as heterosexual, having only opposite-sex sex behavior in their lifetimes, and being only or mostly attracted to males.

Fig. 22.2 shows corresponding data for male heterosexuality. Nearly 94 % of the males in the 2006–2008 NSFG gave a heterosexuality response to at least one of the three questions dealing with self-identification, behavior, and desire. Importantly, over 82.5 % of those males giving a heterosexual response to at least one of the three questions gave a heterosexual response to all three questions.

For males and females, there is a tremendous amount of consistency with respect to heterosexuality. Almost 75 % of females and over 82 % of males who indicate a heterosexual response to at least one of the three sexuality questions gave a heterosexual response to all three questions. As we will see when we turn next to analyses of homosexuality and of bisexuality, there is not nearly as much agreement. Whereas one could argue that an essentialist approach works fairly well for female and male heterosexuality, we show below that it does not work well at all with regard to homosexuality and bisexuality.

Figures 22.3 and 22.4 show Venn diagrams and data for female (Fig. 22.3) and male (Fig. 22.4) homosexuality. Unlike the situation with regard to female and male heterosexuality (Figs. 22.1 and 22.2), the data tables in the two figures indicate that very small percentages of females and males gave a homosexual response to at least one of the three sexuality questions dealing with self-identification, behavior, and desire. Just over 2.4 % of the females and almost 2.9 % of the males stated that they only had had same-sex sex in their lifetimes, and/or that they desired or were attracted to same-sex persons, and/or that they self-identified as homosexuals. Also, unlike the situation with heterosexuals, the Venn diagrams show that only 17.6 % (see the middle overlapping area in the diagram of Fig. 22.3) of the females giving a homosexual response to at least one of the three sexuality questions gave the homosexual response to all three questions, and the corresponding percentage for homosexual males is 28.7 % (Fig. 22.4). Whereas an essentialist approach works well for male and female heterosexuals (there is overwhelming support for treating heterosexuals as binary, that is, 75 % of females and 83 % of males are heterosexual on all three questions), the essentialist approach does not work well at all for homosexuals. Much smaller percentages of homosexuals are consistent in their homosexual categorization.

We note that a companion analysis of homosexuality in China (Farris et al. 2013) shows much lower levels of agreement and consistency among the Chinese respondents. The Venn diagram data in the China analysis indicate that only 4 % of the females giving a homosexual response to at least one of the three sexuality questions gave the homosexual response to all three questions; and the corresponding percentage for males is 3 %.

The data and diagrams for bisexuals are reported in Figs. 22.5 and 22.6, and they are similar to those for homosexuals. First, the bisexual data show that almost 15 % of all the females in the NSFG, and 5 % of all the males in the NSFG, gave a bisexual response to at least one of the three sexuality questions. Also, there is very little consistency in the categorization of bisexuals. Only 12 % of the women giving a bisexual response to at least one of the sexuality questions gave a bisexual response to all three questions (Fig. 22.5); and the corresponding percentage for males is even smaller, at 6 % (Fig. 22.6).

If one subscribes to an essentialist view of homosexuality and bisexuality (that is, persons either are or are not homosexuals or either are or are not bisexuals), we show that according to the 2006–2008 NSFG data there are very small percentages of males and females consistently categorized as homosexual or as bisexual. An essentialist strategy clearly does not work well at all with regard to conceptualizing and measuring homosexuality and bisexuality. Taking a social constructionist approach, on the other hand, permits a more flexible understanding of homosexuality and bisexuality. For example, according to this approach, homosexuals can be defined based solely on the behavioral dimension or on a combination of two or more of the dimensions of sexuality.

Our empirical analyses demonstrate the importance of a social constructionist perspective in developing an understanding of sexuality. Although some individuals provided the same sexual response (e.g., heterosexual or homosexual or bisexual) on all three dimensions, most of the respondents gave one sexual response (e.g., homosexual) to the NSFG question on one dimension and another sexual response (e.g., bisexual or heterosexual) to the NSFG question on another dimension. Using a social constructionist orientation in our analysis of sexuality provides us with a much more encompassing understanding of sexuality.

Prevalence Rates of Sexuality

Having examined the interrelations of the dimensions of sexuality for males and females with respect to heterosexuality, homosexuality, and bisexuality, we turn now to a presentation of estimates of the percentages of persons who give one of the three "sexual responses" according to one or more of the above three questions. We are endeavoring here to answer the question, what are the percentages of the U.S. population aged 15–44 who are heterosexual, who are homosexual, and who are bisexual.

We first need to attend to an important methodological issue. We noted earlier that the 2006–2008 NSFG consists of data for 7,356 women and 6,139 men, aged 15–44, in households in the United States. Mosher (2010, p. 33) has written that the 2006–2008 NSFG sample "is a nationally representative multistage area probability sample drawn from 85 areas across the country…Persons were selected for the NSFG in five major steps: Large areas (counties and cities) were chosen first. Within each large area or "Primary Sampling Unit," groups of adjacent blocks … were chosen at random. Within segments, addresses were listed and some addresses were selected at random. The selected addresses were visited in person … [If it was determined that a person 15–44 lived at the address, then] … one person was chosen at random for the interview and was offered a chance to participate."

Since the 2006–2008 NSFG is based on multistage probability sampling, one cannot use these data to make inferences to the larger population of U.S. adults from which the sample was drawn without first taking into account the sampling design. Otherwise, the data will be treated by the statistical software as based on a simple random sample. This will tend "to understate the true extent of sampling error in the data … [because] when observations are clustered [i.e., drawn from a few selected sampling points as is the case with the 2006–2008 NSFG], for many variables the within-cluster variance tends to be smaller than the variance across the population as a whole. This in turn implies that the between-cluster variance, i.e., the variance of the cluster means, which gives the standard error for clustered samples, is inflated relative to the variance of the same variable computed from a simple random sample drawn from the same population. Reduced within-cluster variance, especially with respect to sociodemographic variables, is typical within the small areas that make up … [a] stage of multistage probability samples: areas of a few blocks tend to be more homogeneous with respect to education, age, race, and so on than the population of the entire country. The result is that when we use statistical procedures based on the assumption of simple random sampling, our computed standard errors typically are too small. What we need to do is to take account not only of the variance among individuals within a cluster, but of the variance between clusters" (Treiman 2009, pp. 207–208).

Thus in the empirical analyses reported this section of our paper, we use the "svy" suite of statistical sample adjustment methods available in the Stata 12 statistical package (StataCorp 2011) that introduce survey adjustment estimators. We are thus able to adjust our analyses according to the various population and strata weights available in the 2006–2008 NSFG.

We show in Tables 22.1, 22.2, and 22.3 weighted (adjusted) percentage estimates for the period of 2006–2008 of the prevalence of female and male heterosexuality (Table 22.1), bisexuality (Table 22.2), and homosexuality (Table 22.3); we also show the 95 % confidence intervals for each estimate (reported in the tables as "margin of error"); also shown in the tables are adjusted percentage estimates for 2002 using data from the 2002 NSFG.

In the very bottom row of the tables, we provide a weighted percentage of persons selecting the respective sexuality response to any one or more of the questions pertaining to identification, behavior, and desire/attraction. For instance, the figure of 95.43 for 2008 in the female heterosexuality table (Table 22.1) means that in 2006–2008, 95.4 % of U.S. females aged 15–44 gave a heterosexual answer to at least one of the three questions dealing with the three dimensions of sexuality; an estimated 72 % of U.S. women gave the heterosexual response to all three questions. In 2002, the percentages were 96 and 78 %, respectively. For males, the corresponding percentages were 96 and 79 %, respectively, in the 2006–2008 period, and 95 and 81 % in 2002.

So what is the prevalence level of heterosexuality in the United States for females and males in 2006–2008 and in 2002? There is no one answer because it depends on how one defines heterosexuality. To repeat Blank's (2012, p. xviii) statement that we quoted earlier in this chapter, "despite the fact that most of us use the term 'heterosexual' with enormous and cavalier certainty, there seems to be no aspect of 'heterosexual' for which a truly iron-clad definition has been established."

So if we define a heterosexual as a person who identifies as a heterosexual, and engages in sexual behavior exclusively as a heterosexual, and desires or is attracted only to heterosexuals, then the answer for females is around 72 % and for males 79 %. But if we invoke a social constructionist approach and define a heterosexual as a person who identifies as a heterosexual, and/or engages in sexual behavior exclusively as a heterosexual, and/or desires or is attracted to heterosexuals, then the percentages are 95 % for females and 96 % for males.

In Table 22.2, we present similar information for female and male bisexuality. What are the percentages of bisexuality in the United States in 2006–2008 for females and males aged 15–44? Again, it depends on how we define bisexuality. If we hold that a bisexual self-identifies as a bisexual, and engages in sexual behavior with both males and females, and is attracted to persons of both sexes, then the answer for females is 1.5 % and for males 0.3 %, and the corresponding percentages for 2002 are about the same. But if we do not insist on this all-inclusive definition, and allow a bisexual to either identify herself/himself as a bisexual, and/or to engage in sex with both same sex and opposite sex persons, and/or to be attracted to both males and females, then the percentages are 13 % for females and 5 % for males, with similar percentages for 2002.

Finally, we show in in Table 22.3 similar information for female and male homosexuality. What are the percentage levels of homosexuality in the United States in 2006–2008 for female and males? Again, it depends on the definition. If we hold that a homosexual is one who self-identifies as a homosexual, and engages in sexual behavior only with persons of the same sex, and is attracted to persons of the same sex, then the answer for females is 0.3 % and for males is 0.6 %, and the corresponding percentages for 2002 are around the same. But if we do not insist on such a comprehensive definition, and if we hence define a homosexual in a broader way as one who identifies as a homosexual, and/or engages in sex only with same

Table 22.1 Percentage estimates of female and male heterosexuality, United States, 2006–2008 and 2002

	Female				Male			
	2008		2002		2008		2002	
Heterosexuality	Within sample		Within sample		Within sample		Within sample	
	%	Margin of error	%	Margin of error	%	Margin of error	%	Margin of error
Behavior	0.41	±0.17	0.60	±0.23	0.11	±0.11	0.33	±0.14
Desire	1.38	±0.41	1.43	±0.39	0.39	±0.18	0.86	±0.38
Identity	0.54	±0.25	0.17	±0.10	0.21	±0.16	0.22	±0.13
Behave & desire	0.48	±0.21	3.29	±0.54	0.27	±0.15	4.09	±0.93
Behave & ID	0.84	±0.31	0.56	±0.19	0.22	±0.14	0.58	±0.31
Desire & ID	20.25	±2.53	12.61	±1.13	15.47	±2.48	8.35	±1.09
Beh. & des. & ID	71.54	±2.33	77.82	±1.41	79.09	±2.45	80.82	±1.70
Sample (n)	6,878		6,602		5,768		4,014	
Total sample (N)	7,356		6,864		6,139		4,295	
Svy sample%	*95.43*	±0.83	*96.48*	±0.52	*95.77*	±0.88	*95.24*	±0.80

Table 22.2 Percentage estimates of female and male bisexuality, United States, 2006–2008 and 2002

	Female				Male			
	2008		2002				2008	
Bisexuality	Within sample		Within sample		Within sample		Within sample	
	%	Margin of error	%	Margin of error	%	Margin of error	%	Margin of error
Behavior	8.48	±1.32	8.53	±0.92	3.60	±0.83	4.07	±0.93
Desire	0.47	±0.29	0.29	±0.14	0.02	±0.03	0.24	±0.16
Identity	0.43	±0.22	0.26	±0.13	0.38	±0.22	0.69	±0.40
Behave & desire	0.34	±0.20	0.20	±0.12	0.00	N/A	0.17	±0.13
Behave & ID	1.27	±0.33	1.15	±0.34	0.32	±0.20	0.54	±0.32
Desire & ID	0.50	±0.18	0.29	±0.19	0.33	±0.19	0.18	±0.12
Beh. & des. & ID	1.50	±0.33	1.15	±0.24	0.30	±0.24	0.40	±0.16
Sample (n)	1,074		840		317		335	
Total sample (N)	7,356		6,864		6,139		4,295	
Svy sample %	*13.00*	±1.56	*11.86*	±1.08	*4.95*	±0.94	*6.28*	±1.07

Table 22.3 Percentage estimates of female and male homosexuality, United States, 2006–2008 and 2002

	Female				Male			
	2008		2002		2008		2002	
Homosexuality	Within sample		Within sample		Within sample		Within sample	
	%	Margin of error	%	Margin of error	%	Margin of error	%	Margin of error
Behavior	0.43	±0.18	0.17	±0.13	0.28	±0.20	0.16	±0.16
Desire	0.42	±0.19	0.52	±0.19	0.30	±0.22	0.41	±0.18
Identity	0.08	±0.09	0.50	±0.19	0.10	±0.09	0.58	±0.41
Behave & Desire	0.01	±0.02	0.05	±0.05	0.02	±0.02	0.09	±0.08
Behave & ID	0.01	±0.02	0.00	N/A	0.00	N/A	0.02	±0.03
Desire & ID	0.58	±0.24	0.56	±0.25	0.89	±0.29	0.99	±0.36
Beh. & Des. & ID	0.33	±0.16	0.26	±0.14	0.64	±0.22	0.69	±0.33
Sample (n)	179		162		176		174	
Total sample (N)	7,356		6,864		6,139		4,295	
Svy sample %	*1.86*	±0.45	*2.06*	±0.42	*2.24*	±0.48	*2.94*	±0.78

wsex persons,wand/or desires or is attracted to persons of the same sex, that is, if we use a social constructionist approach in our definition of a homosexual, then the percentages are 1.9 % for females and 2.2 % for males, with roughly similar percentages for 2002.

Since we are subscribing to a social constructionist approach and not an essentialist one, we will define each of the sexualities in a more inclusive manner. Thus we would state that a homosexual is one who gives a homosexual response to any one or more of the three questions dealing with the dimensions of sexuality, and we would define heterosexuals and bisexuals in a similar way. Hence in the 2006–2008 period, we would estimate, based on the 2006–2008 NSFG data, that among female adults (aged 15–44), 95 % are heterosexual, 13 % are bisexual, and 2 % are homosexual. The corresponding percentages for males are 96, 5, and 2 %. It is important to recognize that the percentages for females, and for males, sum to more than 100 % because of the fluid nature of our definitions. In the next section of this chapter we explore some of the implications of our analyses.

Summary and Discussion

In this chapter we used data from the 2006–2008 National Survey of Family Growth (NSFG) to conceptualize and measure various aspects of sexuality and sexual orientation. We first discussed the two main approaches used by social scientists to conceptualize sexual orientation, namely, essentialism and social constructionism and then reviewed some of the empirical literature measuring sexual orientation. We next specified three different dimensions of sexuality, namely, sexual behavior in one's lifetime, sexual self-identification, and sexual preference/attraction. We then used the 2006–2008 NSFG data to first examine the degree of consistency in the three dimensions for heterosexual persons, for homosexual persons, and for bisexual persons. We showed that an essentialist view works fairly well for heterosexual persons, but not at all for homosexuals and for bisexuals. We then calculated several percentages of the U.S. adult population who according to the different definitions would be classified as heterosexual, homosexual, and bisexual. We found that conclusions about the prevalence of homosexuality, heterosexuality, and bisexuality in the U.S. adult population depend significantly on the way we define the three sexualities.

The percentages of heterosexuality, bisexuality, and homosexuality among U.S. adults are at their highest when we use a broader definition. That is, if we follow a social constructionist approach and define, for example, a homosexual as one who gives a "homosexual" response to at least one of the three NSFG questions dealing with the three dimensions of sexuality (self-identification, behavior, and attraction), and if we define heterosexuals and if we define bisexuals in similar ways, then 95 % of the U.S. female population is heterosexual, 13 % is bisexual, and 2 % is homosexual; the corresponding figures for males are 96, 5, and 2 %. The percentages sum to more than 100 % because we used a broad definition. On the other hand, if we insist that a person's sexuality must reflect a consistency across the three dimensions, that is, for example, a homosexual must give the homosexual response to each of the three survey questions on the sexuality dimensions, then the percentages are considerably lower, at 72 and 79 % for female and male heterosexuals, 1.5 and 0.3 % for female and male bisexuals, and 0.3 and 0.6 % for female and male homosexuals. Empirical estimates of the prevalence among U.S. adults of the three sexualities certainly depend on how sexualities are conceptualized.

As Blank has written, "sexual expectations and behaviors, like all other social expectations and behaviors, change over time … [if] we speak … of interactions of males and females, these relationships have simply not always been the same, nor have the people participating in them been expected to do, think, feel, or experience the same sorts of things" (2012, p. xvii). In our opinion it is much more realistic and appropriate to view sexuality with a social constructionist eye.

Certainly, an important implication of our research is the need to use a social constructionist approach in analyses of sexuality instead of an essentialist approach. Persons in one sexual category, say, homosexuals, may be distinguished from persons in another sexual category, say, heterosexuals, in many different ways. Given the limited empirical research on sexuality and sexual orientation and the lack of agreement regarding the meaning of the sexualities, it would appear best to use as broad a purview as possible. It would be a mistake, we believe, to use an essentialist view that assumes that there is an essential biological or psychological characteristic common to all persons in a sexual category that is distinct and separate from persons in another sexual category. An essentialist approach is excessively narrow and necessarily results in the identification of very small percentages of homosexuals and bisexuals.

Our empirical results about the lack of a consistency with regard to the three dimensions of sexuality, particularly for homosexuals and for bisexuals, replicate earlier research focusing on homosexuals by Laumann and his colleagues (1994, pp. 300–301). Their research pointed to the "high degree of variability in the way that differing elements of homosexuality are distributed in the population. This variability relates to the way that homosexuality is both organized as a set of behaviors and practices and experienced subjectively. It raised quite provocative questions about the definition of homosexuality."

Overall, our findings indicate that future research should continue to refine the understanding of what it means to be heterosexual, homosexual, and bisexual, and how these meanings vary among populations and over time. There exists a real need for broad-based scholarship on the existence of the various sexualities, their components, and their defining characteristics.

We end our chapter with a pithy observation from Blank in the first pages of her book on heterosexuality. She writes the following: "every time I go to the doctor, I end up questioning my sexual orientation … The clinic I visit (has a form that) includes … little boxes, a small matter of demographic bookkeeping. Next to the boxes are the options, 'gay,' 'lesbian,' 'bisexual,' 'transgender,' or 'heterosexual.' You're supposed to check one. You might not think this would pose a difficulty" (Blank 2012, p. ix). In the balance of her very insightful book, she argues that indeed it is a difficulty; what you are depends on the definitions and the approach followed.

References

Badgett, M. V. L. (1995). The wage effects of sexual orientation discrimination. *Industrial and Labor Relations Review, 48,* 726–739.

Baumle, A. K., Compton, D., & Poston, D. L. Jr. (2009). *Same-sex partners: The social demography of sexual orientation.* New York: SUNY.

Berg, N., & Lien, D. (2002). Measuring the effect of sexual orientation on income: Evidence of discrimination? *Contemporary Economic Policy, 20,* 394–414.

Black, D. A., Makar, H. R., Sanders, S. G., Taylor, L. J. (2003). The earnings effects of sexual orientation. *Industrial and Labor Relation Review, 56,* 449–469.

Blank, H. (2012). *Straight: The surprisingly short history of heterosexuality.* Boston: Beacon.

Butler, J. (1990). *Gender trouble.* New York: Routledge.

Chandra, A., Mosher, W. D., Copen, C. (2011). *Sexual behavior, sexual attraction, and sexual identity in the United States: Data from the 2006–2008 national survey of family growth.* National vital statistics report: 36. Hyattsville, MD: National Center for Health Statistics. http://www.cdc.gov/nchs/data/nhsr/nhsr036.pdf. Accessed 15 June 2012.

Farris, D. N., He, L., Poston, D. L. Jr., Walther, C. S., Russell, C., Kincannon, H. (2013). Sexuality in China. In A. K. Baumle (Ed.), *International handbook on the demography of sexuality,* pp. 107–127. New York: Springer.

Fay, R. E., Turner, C. F., Klassen, A. D., Gagnon, J. H. (1989). Prevalence and patterns of same-gender sexual contact among men.. *Science, 243,* 338–348.

Foucault, M. (1978). *The history of sexuality: An introduction,* Vol. 1. New York: Vintage Books.

Gates, G. J. (2011). *How many people are lesbian, gay, bisexual and transgender.* Research brief, The Williams Institute (April): http://williamsinstitute.law.ucla.edu/wp-content/uploads/Gates-How-Many-People-LGBT-Apr-2011.pdf.

Kinsey, A. C., Pomeroy, W. B., Martin, C. E. (1948). *Sexual behavior in the human male.* Philadelphia: Saunders.

Kinsey, A. C., Pomeroy, W. B., Martin, C. E., Gebhard, P. H. (1953). *Sexual behavior in the human female.* Philadelphia: Saunders.

Laumann, E. O., Gagnon, J. H., Michael, R. T., Michaels, S. (1994). *The social organization of sexuality: Sexual practices in the United States.* Chicago: University of Chicago Press.

Mosher, W. D. (2010). Use of contraception in the United States: 1982–2008. National Center for Health Statistics. *Vital and Health Statistics, 23*(29), 1–54.

Saewyc, E. M., Bauer, G. R., Skay, C. L., Resnick, M. D., Reis, E., Murphy, A. (2004). Measuring sexual orientation in adolescent health surveys: Evaluation of eight school-based surveys. *Journal of Adolescent Health, 35,* 345 e1–345 e15.

Seidman, S. (1996). Introduction. In S. Steven (Ed.), *Queer theory/sociology,* pp. 1–29. Cambridge: Blackwell.

Smith, T. W. (1991). Adult sexual behavior in 1989: Number of partners, frequency of intercourse and risk of AIDS.. *Family Planning Perspectives, 23,* 102–107.

StataCorp. (2011). *Stata survey data reference manual, release 12.* College Station: StataCorp.

Treiman, D. J. (2009). *Quantitative data analysis: Doing social research to test ideas.* San Francisco, : Jossey-Bass.

Chapter 23
Demographic Attributes of Mississippi Nursing Students and Family Influences

Ronald E. Cossman, Jeralynn S. Cossman and Philip B. Mason

Introduction

Recruitment of nurses is a challenge in any environment. In Mississippi there are additional challenges in recruiting to rural areas, as well as recruiting to poor communities (e.g., the Mississippi Delta). In 2009 the hospital registered nurse (RN) vacancy rate for the state of Mississippi stood at 5.0 %, with sub-county health district RN vacancy rates ranging from 1 to 11 % (Mississippi Office of Nursing Workforce 2009). While much work is done annually on measuring the overall supply of nurses (Mississippi Office of Nursing Workforce 2013) in terms of projected workforce available, very little research is conducted on the geographic concentration or mismatch of nurses to healthcare demand, and no research is done on the issue of recruitment of nurses to rural, poor, and otherwise underserved areas. Yet nursing students' affinity for rural places and the determinants of post-graduation relocation are critical to successful recruitment to rural places. If the supply of nurses is not flowing to where the demand for nurses is located, rural recruiters need to explore those determinants.

The purpose of this study was to augment traditional nursing student demographic profile data with students' perceived priorities and external (e.g., family, friends, and relationships) demographic factors, in order to identify factors that influence post-graduation employment decision making, especially as it relates to human capital retention within Mississippi. We quantified the roles that family and friends have on the initial decision to join the health care profession and on nurses'

R. E. Cossman (✉)
Social Science Research Center, Mississippi State University, Mississippi State, MS, USA
e-mail: Ronald.Cossman@ssrc.msstate.edu

J. S. Cossman
Department of Sociology, Mississippi State University, Mississippi State, MS, USA

P. B. Mason
Department of Sociology, University of South Carolina, Aiken, SC, USA

M. N. Hoque, L. B. Potter (eds.), *Emerging Techniques in Applied Demography,* Applied Demography Series 4, DOI 10.1007/978-94-017-8990-5_23,

post-graduation relocation decisions. We find that immediate family is a major factor in relocation decisions and must be taken into consideration in terms of nurse recruitment to rural places.

Literature Review

Much of the nursing recruitment literature is from the perspective of the hospital as the recruiter (Baggot et al. 2005; Wall 1988) or specifically focuses on the hospital's recruitment interactions with prospective nurses (Curran 2003; Kalisch 2003; Upenieks 2003). Less research has been done specifically on the recruitment of nurses and especially the recruitment of nurses to rural and underserved places. One study surveyed third year family practitioners and found that approximately half of the respondents desired to return and establish their practice in a small town (less than 10,000 residents), small city (10,000–50,000 residents), or moderate city (50,000–500,000 residents) (Costa et al. 1996). Interestingly, the factor that ranked the highest was "significant other's wishes," while "initial income guarantee" ranked 8th behind such factors as "recreation/culture" and "schools for children."

Another study surveyed a wide range of health care training graduates (ranging from nurse practitioner and nurse midwife to physician) and found that a rural background, participation in a rural-based training program, desire to serve community health needs, return to hometown, and financial incentives (e.g., education loan repayment) were significantly associated with a desire to establish a rural-based practice (Zina et al. 2007). However comparisons of this research to Mississippi are limited because the researchers defined "rural" as less than 50,000 residents and not part of an urban area and only 13 of Mississippi's 82 counties (16%) meet that criterion.

A factor that adds to the complexity of nurse recruitment and retention is that it is an expensive proposition. One study estimated the total cost to replace an RN (in a hospital setting) to be between $ 62,100 and $ 67,100 (2002 calculation) (Jones 2005). It is reasonable to assume that recruitment to a rural or underserved location is even higher, given the difficulty of identifying and then marketing to an individual who is willing to relocate to a rural or underserved area. There is some evidence of this rural recruitment penalty. By virtue of their location, it takes 60% longer to fill nursing vacancies in rural locations compared to counterpart facilities in urban locations (Tone 1999).

Survey Methodology

The Social Science Research Center obtained Mississippi State University human subjects protection approval and conducted a pilot on-line survey of Mississippi nursing students during the spring semester of 2010 ($n=101$). After analyzing the data and respondents' comments, the survey was modified and re-administered at the beginning of the fall semester of 2010 as a web based survey. An open-access URL (web address) was provided to deans of all 22 public and private nursing programs in Mississippi. Students from sixteen nursing programs participated in the survey. The total participating population was 4,527 (fall 2010 nursing student enrollment); total responses to the survey were 1,008, making the response rate 22 %. Response rates at participating schools ranged from 2 % to 100 %.

The higher second wave response rates were due—at least in part—to a cash response incentive program aimed at the individual nursing programs. The total number of respondents for the fall 2010 wave was 1,008. The cooperation rate (completed surveys versus incomplete surveys, partially completed surveys, and refusals) was 86 %. Individuals in various nursing school programs were not randomly sampled for participation; consequently, these findings are based on a convenience sample and margin of error statistics are not applicable. All questions in the survey, unless otherwise noted, provided for only one response/choice, usually in the context of most important factor. Most questions also included an option for "Not sure" and "No comment." Finally, some questions included an option for "Other" in which case the respondent was asked to explain in a pop-up text box. In all cases we examined the "other" responses, coded them, and added them to the existing response categories when appropriate.

Survey Responses

We begin with a review of student demographics. The vast majority of nursing students in the fall of 2010 were female, 88 %. Likewise, the majority of nursing students were white (75 %), with 21 % black and the remainder Asian, Native American, or had No Comment. More than half (61 %) were enrolled in two-year associate degrees in nursing (ADN), 30 % were enrolled in four-year Bachelor of Science degree programs in nursing (BSN), and 7 % were enrolled in a Master of Science degree program in nursing (MSN). The remainder of students were enrolled in doctoral or other programs or had no comment.

The age of nursing students was clustered around 20–23 years old; however, the tail was much longer than expected, with the oldest student claiming to be 64 years old. In terms of recruitment, this suggests that students can be recruited to nursing programs at virtually any age (Fig. 23.1).

To assess how students were influenced to enter the health care profession, with an eye toward recruitment, we asked, "Did a family member or a close personal friend influence you to enter the profession?" More than a third (38 %) said yes, 61 % said no, and 1 % were not sure or did not comment. Of the 38 % who said that someone did influence them, more than half (53 %) cited their mother, step-mother or mother-in-law as an influence on entering the nursing profession. Another 30 % cited an aunt, 26 % cited a close family friend, 23 % identified a father, step-father or father-in-law, slightly ahead of grandmother at 21 %. In short, if you want to recruit nursing students, market to mothers (Fig. 23.2).

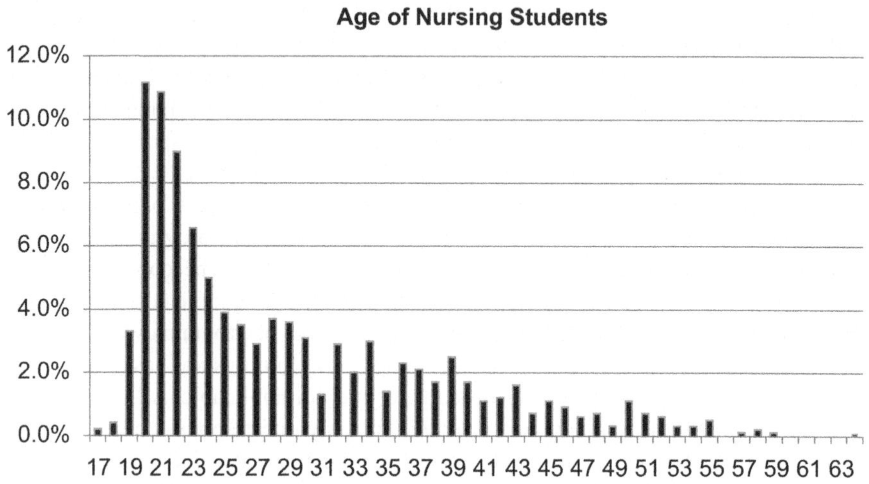

Fig. 23.1 Age of nursing students

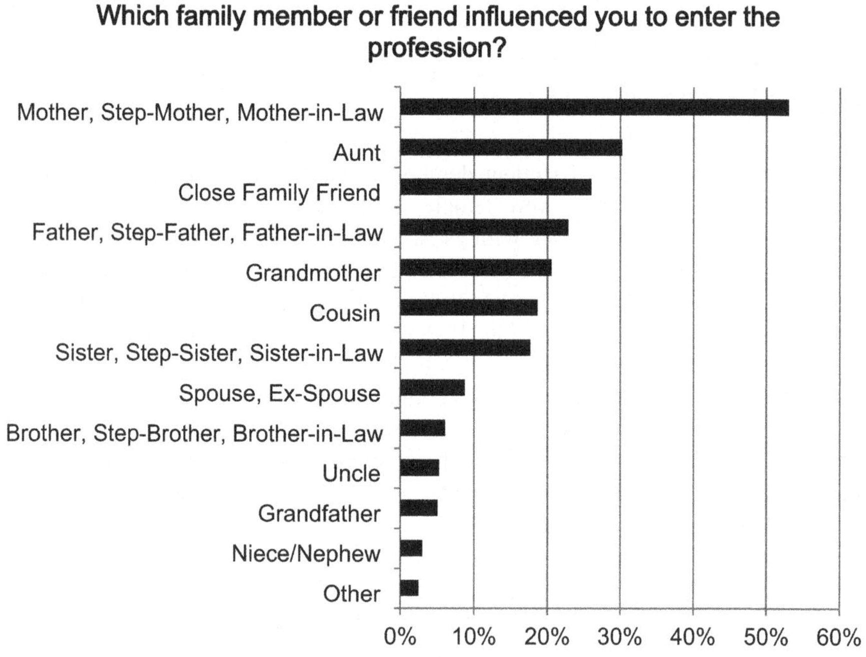

Fig. 23.2 Which family member or friend influenced you to enter the profession?

We asked "What was the single most important reason/factor for choosing their nursing program or school?" More than a third (39 %) said that the school was

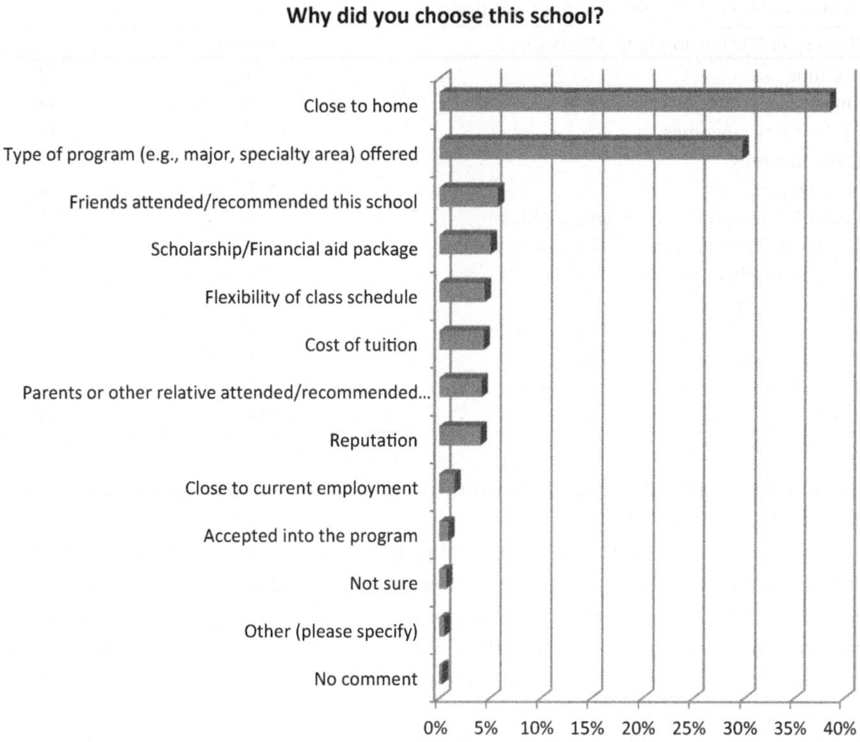

Fig. 23.3 Why did you choose this school?

close to home. Nearly another third (30 %) based their decision on the type of program (e.g., major, specialty area) offered. Once these two choices were selected, the percentage for other reasons fell off quickly. The next most important reason was friends attended or recommended this school, at 6 %. However, adding together all those categories that speak to the school's reputation and offerings (type of program, friends attended, parents attended, and reputation), this category accounts for 44 % of the responses. After examining the other response comments and recoding, the other category was reduced from 75 responses (7 %) to 5 responses (0.5 %). Most were added to existing categories, although two new categories were created," reputation" (4 %) and "accepted into the program" (1 %) (Fig. 23.3).

We asked: "Assuming that a suitable job opportunity (for example, salary, specialty area, etc.) was available, would you want to work in Mississippi when you graduate?" Overwhelmingly (90 %), nursing students responded "Yes, I would work in Mississippi after graduation." Obviously, the desire or at least the openness to remaining in state for a job opportunity is high among nursing students. A critical factor to recruitment is ensuring that nursing students are aware of available job opportunities within the state of Mississippi. Of the 10 % who would not work in Mississippi, the majority cited location, total salary package, lack of area amenities,

Table 23.1 Reason for NOT working in Mississippi

Reason for NOT working in Mississippi	Percent	*N*
Location	21	14
Total salary package	19	13
Lack of area amenities	19	13
Close to family	12	8
No comment	9	6
Lack of future professional opportunities	7	5
I do not believe that I can work in my specialty	4	3
The public school system	4	3
Climate (i.e., weather)	3	2
Few job opportunities for my spouse/partner	1	1
Working environment/conditions	0	0
Lack of additional training opportunities	0	0
Totals	100	68

and not being close to family as reasons for not considering post-graduation job offers in Mississippi (Table 23.1).

We then assessed external demographic factors in making a job-related relocation decision. We investigated the question, if the respondent was married or in a relationship, was the respondent a leading or trailing spouse? More than a third (36 %) were married and almost a third (30 %) were not married but in a relationship. The remaining respondents were single and not in a relationship, divorced, separated, or had no comment (Fig. 23.4).

We asked those who were either married or in a relationship ($n=669$), what would be the most important factors in terms of where they decided to move after graduation. More than half (56 %) said that it was an equally important decision for both them and their spouse. Another third (33 %) said that where they found a job was the most important factor. Trailing (literally) at 6 % was where their partner or spouse could find a job. Finally, 3 % were unsure, and 1 % had no comment. These findings suggest that successful nurse recruitment could use a family unit approach in which the position and location/community are marketed to the couple, rather than the individual prospective employee, to attract this segment of the nursing student community.

Another segment of nursing students is the choice leader, the individual who makes the decision on post-graduation job relocation. One third of married/partnered, graduating nurses claim that they are in a position to lead the choice about relocation upon graduation. Add to that group the number of nursing students who are single, never married and not in a relationship, separated, divorced or widowed, and the total is more than half (54 %) of all nursing respondents are in a position to decide independently or are in a position to lead in the decision making about post-graduation job relocation. Thus, recruitment would be to the individual or the leading spouse. This finding highlights that nursing graduates cannot be assumed to always be the trailing spouse (Fig. 23.5).

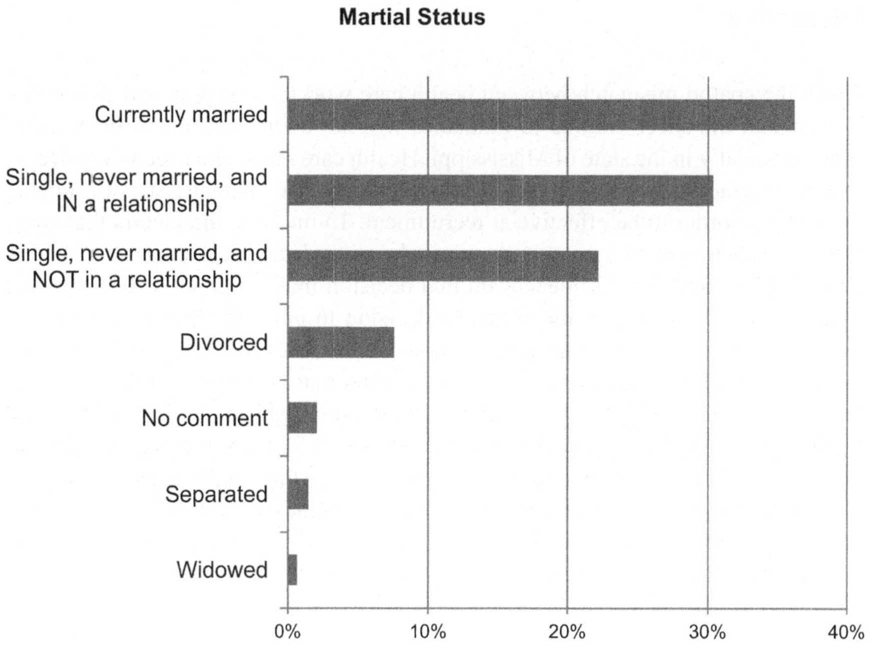

Fig. 23.4 Martial status

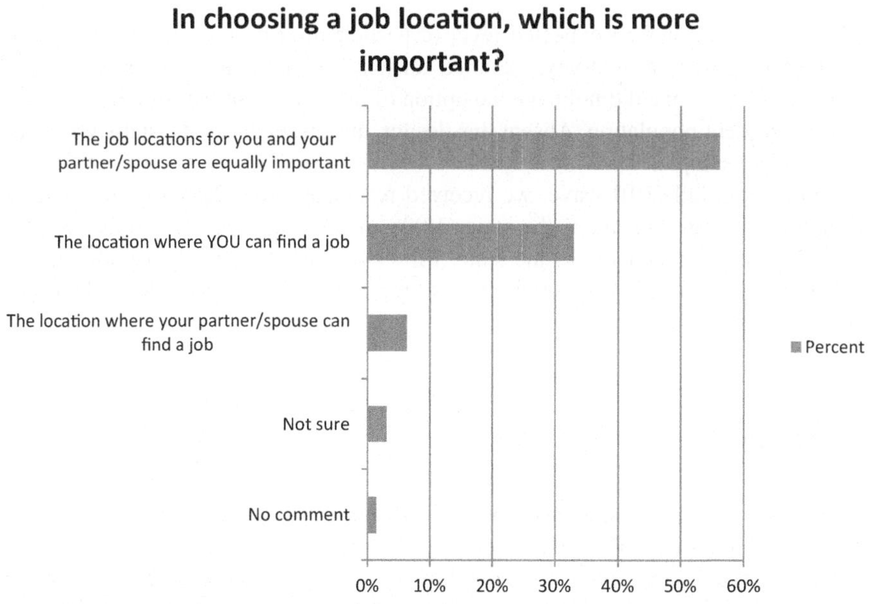

Fig. 23.5 Most important job location factors

Discussion

Given the spatial mismatch between health care workforce supply and demand, it is clear that the sheer volume of graduates will not address all underserved locations, especially in the state of Mississippi. Health care recruiters need to dig deeper than the surface of supply projections and demographic characteristics of nursing graduates in order to be effective at recruitment. To measure the factors that come into play when making a post-graduation relocation decision, we measured family demographics and their influences on that decision making process. The role that family and friends play in the student's decision to enter the health care profession cannot be understated and suggests potential avenues for marketing by nursing programs. For health care employment recruiters, marital status and the degree of mutual decision making is an important consideration, above and beyond the total numbers of graduates produced each year. Given that females dominate the field of nursing, and that more than half of surveyed nursing students are either married or in a relationship, the recruitment and marketing emphasis must shift from a focus on a single nursing graduate to a couple considering a relocation. This is a clear case where family demographics will trump individual characteristics in terms of employment relocation.

Study Limitations

There was a lower than expected level of participation by nursing programs and nursing students in this survey. As noted earlier, this survey is based on a "sample of convenience." We did not have the option of drawing a random sample from the nursing student population. Absent this design, the survey lacks the statistical rigor of a random sample.

During the fall 2010 wave, we received responses from 22 % of participating program nursing students in the state (1,008 of 4,527), which was only 18 % of all 5,546 nursing students in the state. Moreover, response rates at participating schools ranged from 2 % to 100 % and six programs (with 1,019 students) had zero participation.

Conclusion

This survey of nursing students provided some insights into external demographic factors and decision making on the part of the nursing student – to enter the profession, to attend a particular school, and how to choose a post-graduation relocation decision. Family and friends were influential for more than a third of nursing students in making the choice to enter the profession. This is useful information for those organizations that maintain the health care workforce pipeline, such as Area Health Education Centers (AHECs), around the nation. Nursing school recruiters should also consider this connection in marketing their program to prospective students. Not surprisingly, since the majority of students were enrolled in two-year programs, the most important factor in choosing a school was proximity to home. This priority is partially a function of Mississippi's extensive community college system. By design, no one lives more than an hour from a community college in Mississippi. Given the priority of convenience among would-be nursing students, a local geography basis for marketing would appear to be the most effective for nursing school recruiters. Finally we looked at the external demographic characteristic of marital status and its possible role in making post-graduate relocation decisions. More than half of those married or in a relationship would make a mutual relocation decision, suggesting that employers and communities might be wise to market to the family unit. Conversely, more than half of all nursing student respondents were either the lead decision maker or solo decision makers, suggesting another segment to which employers could market. Nursing graduation volume tells part of the story; it suggests how large the market could be. However, to effectively recruit to rural, poor, or underserved areas, the family demographics of the prospect must also be taken into consideration.

Funding Acknowledgement This research was funded by the Dreyfus Health Foundation, as part of a grant awarded to Dreyfus by the Kellogg Foundation. The findings, conclusions, and recommendations expressed in this publication are those of the author(s) and do not necessarily reflect the views of the Dreyfus Health Foundation or the Kellogg Foundation.

References

Baggot, D. M., Dawson, C., Valdes, M. S., & Zaim, S. (2005). Rethinking nurse recruitment: A return-on-investment approach. *Journal of Nursing Administration, 35*(10), 424–427.

Costa, A. J., Schrop, S. L., McCord, G., & Gillanders, W. R. (1996). To stay or not to stay: Factors influencing family practice residents' choice of initial practice location. *Family Medicine, 28*(3), 214–219.

Curran, C. R. (2003). Nurse recruitment: A waste of postage, paper and people. *Nursing Economics, 21*(1), 32.

Jones, C. B. (2005). The costs of nurse turnover, Part 2. *Journal of Nursing Administration, 35*(1), 41–49.

Kalisch, B. J. (2003). Recruiting nurses. *Journal of Nursing Administration, 33*(9), 468–477.

Mississippi Office of Nursing Workforce. (2009) Hospital RN vacancy rates (%) by public health district. Available at: http://www.monw.org/research/hospital/2009/2009%20Hospital%20RN%20Vacancy%20by%20PHD.pdf. Accessed 6 June 2013.

Mississippi Office of Nursing Workforce. (2013). Main website. Available at: http://www.monw.org/. Accessed 6 June 2013.

Tone, B. (1999) Looking for a job? Think about moving to the country. *NurseWeek* [serial online].

Upenieks, V. (2003). Recruitment and retention strategies: A magnet hospital prevention model. *Nursing Economics*, *21*(1), 7–13, 23.

Wall, L. L. (1988). Plan development for a nurse recruitment-retention program. *Journal of Nursing Administration, 18*(2), 20–26.

Zina, M. D., VanLeit, B. J., Skipper, B. J., Sanders, M. L., & Rhyne, R. L. (2007). Factors in recruiting and retaining health professionals for rural practice. *The Journal of Rural Health,* 23(1), 62–71.

Index

M. N. Hoque, L. B. Potter (eds.), *Emerging Techniques in Applied Demography*,
Applied Demography Series 4, DOI 10.1007/978-94-017-8990-5,

The manufacturer's authorised representative in the EU is Springer Nature Customer Service Centre GmbH, Europaplatz 3, 69115 Heidelberg, Germany. If you have any concerns regarding our products, please contact ProductSafety@springernature.com

Printed and bound by CPI Group (UK) Ltd, Croydon, CR0 4YY

30/09/2026

02225447-0014